FORTRAN
for Scientists
and Engineers

David G. Weinman

Hollins College

PWS-KENT Publishing Company
Boston

PWS-KENT
Publishing Company

20 Park Plaza
Boston, Massachusetts 02116

Library of Congress Cataloging-in-Publication Data

Weinman, David G.
    FORTRAN for scientists and engineers / David G. Weinman.
        p.   cm.
    Includes index.
    ISBN 0-87835-337-2
    1. FORTRAN (Computer program language)   I. Title.
QH76.73.F25W45 1989   88-19462
005.13′3 – dc19   CIP

Printed in the United States of America.
89 90 91 92 93 — 10 9 8 7 6 5 4 3 2 1

PREFACE

Fortran is one of the oldest, but still one of the most widely used computer programming languages, with many dialects or versions. This text deals with the national standard version of Fortran, called Fortran 77. Most Fortran versions adhere to the standards of Fortran 77 but contain extensions of this standard.

ABOUT THIS BOOK

Scientific Emphasis

This book, *Fortran for Scientists and Engineers*, is designed for a one-semester introductory programming course in Fortran. While other texts have similar titles, their emphasis on scientific material varies greatly. Many contain material that relates only to upper-level college science and engineering courses. This book is not one of those. Many of the examples here are rooted in math and statistics, mostly at the beginning college level. Mathematics, after all, is the language of science. This book also assumes no prior knowledge of computers or programming, and the scientific problems and examples will be easily understood by anyone with a solid high school science background.

Emphasis on Structured Programming

Many programming texts have titles containing the term *structured,* and spend a good deal of time discussing good and bad program structure. At the risk of oversimplifying, let me just say that a program has good structure if one can easily follow the logic in it. The concept of structure is, of course, much more complex than that.

I believe that practice is the best way to reinforce good program structure. This book provides more than 100 well-structured example programs, and several chapters, as listed below, cover specific major program structures:

Chapter 4 — Count-controlled loops or DO loops
Chapter 5 — IF statements and blocks
Chapter 6 — Condition-controlled loops or while loops
Chapter 9 — Functions
Chapter 10 — Subroutines

Comprehensive Coverage of Data Structures

There is another kind of structure in programming: data structure. The important data structures in Fortran are arrays and files. Chapter 8 introduces one-dimensional arrays, while Chapter 11 exclusively covers two-dimensional arrays. Chapter 4 introduces simple file techniques, while Chapter 12 is devoted entirely to files. Character data are introduced in Chapter 3 and used thereafter, but their unique structure is not fully discussed until Chapter 13.

Inclusion of Rarely Used Fortran Statements

There are a few statements used in this book which I urge programmers not to use. Appendix A contains most of them, but a few appear throughout the text. I have included these statements for two reasons. First, some programmers may prefer to use them. Second, although I do *not* recommend some of these statements and practices, students should be aware that they exist, as they may encounter them in revising and updating existing programs.

Wide Variety of Examples

While this text emphasizes a scientific and engineering approach, there are several examples included here which are not directly related to science or engineering. There are three reasons for this. First, scientists and engineers are human beings, too, with interests outside their specialized fields of knowledge. Second, sometimes nonscientific examples are better suited to illustrate programming concepts. In several chapters, for instance, I have used a payroll example to introduce new Fortran constructs. Third, I hope that at least a few nonscientists will find this book useful.

■
TO THE STUDENT

This book includes the major topics found in any programming text. However, my background is in mathematics and statistics, not computer science. My approach to programming is a practical one; I write programs because it is the best way to solve certain problems I encounter. (I also write some just for fun.) This book is designed to teach you to use Fortran to solve problems. I sincerely hope it does that.

Practice Writing Programs

Programming is not a spectator sport. I hope you will read and profit from this book, but keep in mind that even memorizing the entire book will not make you a good programmer. Programming is a skill that requires practice. This book provides plenty of programming exercises, and you should do as many as you can. Sometimes, however, the best exercises are the ones you make up yourself. You are bound to do a better programming job on a problem that really has your interest.

Be Precise

If you are a complete novice to programming, a few words of advice may help. Because a computer is a machine, and totally without intelligence, you must be very precise when giving instructions to it. Just one missing comma in an otherwise valid Fortran statement makes that statement completely unintelligible to the computer. You are certain to make a few such mistakes, and maybe even more than a few at first. It happens to everybody. The rules of a programming language are strict, but they are really easy to learn with a little practice. And learning to be precise will help you in many areas besides programming.

Experiment

After you learn to be accurate enough to make the computer carry out your instructions, be creative. Experiment. Neither this book nor any instructor can tell you everything about Fortran. You can always ask an instructor if something is not clear, but try writing some tiny programs to see if you can resolve the problem yourself. I have made quite a few discoveries about Fortran by writing programs with three or four lines.

If you are told one way to do a problem, and you think of another way that might work, try it. Break some of the rules and see what happens. You can learn much from this kind of experimenting, and what you learn this way will stay with you longer than anything you might read.

You will be more heavily involved in what you are doing. Better yet, you will have more fun.

TO EVERYONE

I would appreciate hearing your reactions to this book. If you have any comments or suggestions, please write to me at the address below. Questions are welcome, too, and I will try to respond to them quickly.

David Weinman
Department of Mathematics and Statistics
Box 9582
Hollins College, VA 24020

CONTENTS

CHAPTER SIX
Condition-Controlled Loops

185

CHAPTER SEVEN
Formats

217

CHAPTER TWELVE
Sequential and Direct-Access Files 405

FORTRAN
for Scientists
and Engineers

chapter 1
INTRODUCTION TO COMPUTERS AND PROGRAMMING LANGUAGES

The purpose of this book is to help you learn to write programs in Fortran, but we begin with a short general discussion of computers, programming languages, and data storage. This chapter also introduces the binary number system, because digital computers store all data as binary numbers. The chapter concludes with a simplified version of the methods computers use to store data.

1.1 COMPUTERS

A **computer** is an electronic device that stores data and instructions, and uses the instructions to manipulate the data. A set of instructions for a computer is a **computer program**, or simply a program. People often think of data as numbers, but data can also consist of characters such as letters and punctuation marks.

If properly instructed, a computer can store thousands of numbers and calculate their sum, or store vast arrays of names and sort them into alphabetical order. Tasks like these are ideal for the computer because it can store huge amounts of data and operate with incredible speed; one modern measurement unit for the speed of a computer is MIPS, an acronym for Millions of Instructions Per Second.

With all their awesome speed and storage capacity, computers are not intelligent machines. They can do nothing without programs. In no sense do they think. In fact, a list of the basic operations a computer can perform is very small:

1. Arithmetic – add, subtract, multiply, and divide
2. Input/Output – copy data from one place to another

3. Store – hold both data and programs
4. Comparison – compare two numbers, and use the result to decide what to do next

Any calculator can do operations 1 and 2, and most can store small amounts of data. Storing programs and the comparison operation are what make the computer so versatile. If the computer could not store programs, then every time a program was needed, some human operator would have to enter the entire program. The comparison operation allows one program to deal with a variety of situations. Still, some human being must write a program to tell the computer which numbers to compare, and what options exist for what to do next.

The IBM 9370 Model 90 computer

Computers come in all sizes. The smallest are **microcomputers** and the largest are **mainframes**. In between is a class called **minicomputers**. Many companies manufacture computers. The names Apple, Commodore, DEC, Hewlett Packard, Honeywell, IBM, NCR, and Radio Shack are widely recognized, and they are just a fraction of the total number of computer makers.

All these different brands and sizes of computers have a lot in common. Each computer has a **central processing unit** or **CPU**, and a **memory unit**. The CPU does arithmetic, makes comparisons, and generally controls the processing of data. The memory unit stores data and instructions. The CPU and memory unit together *are* the computer. Many other devices, called **peripheral devices**, attach to the computer to make it useful. The computer, together with these peripheral devices, is called a **computing system**.

The computer would be worthless if we had no way to get information in and out. A peripheral device for putting information *into* the computer memory is an **input device**, and one for getting information *out* of the memory is an **output device**. The input and output operations are often referred to as **I/O**.

The memory unit in the computer itself is often called **main memory** to distinguish it from **auxiliary memory**, or peripheral devices for extra storage. The most commonly used auxiliary storage devices are **disks** and **magnetic tapes**.

Figure 1.1 contains a diagram of the five basic components of a computing system.

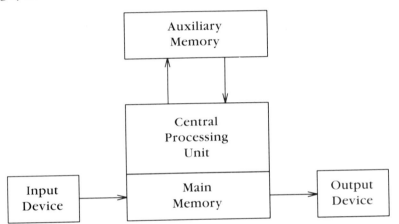

FIGURE 1.1
The elements of a computing system

You will probably work at a **terminal** with a **cathode ray tube (CRT) screen** and a **keyboard**. The keyboard is an input device; information you type at the keyboard will be stored in the computer. The CRT screen is an output device; the computer will print results on the CRT screen. Since the terminal performs both functions, we call it an input/output, or I/O, device.

There are many other input and output devices. At one time, nearly all computer systems used punched cards for input and output. A few still do. A **card reader** reads input from cards and stores the information in the computer. A **card punch** transfers information out of the computer by punching holes in cards.

Magnetic tape drives and **disk drives** are I/O devices. Through the drives, the computer can read information from tapes and disks into its memory, or write information from memory to tapes and disks.

A computer can print results on a CRT screen, but the word **printer** is reserved for an output device that prints on paper. A terminal that prints on paper is a **hardcopy terminal**, and the printed material is **hardcopy**.

The adjective *hard* generally refers to things that can be touched. Thus, all the computer devices discussed above, including the computer itself, are computer **hardware**. In contrast, **software** refers to sets of instructions for computers: utility programs, such as editors, word processors, and spread sheets; language translators or compilers; and user-written programs. The term **firmware** is now commonly used to refer to programmable hardware.

The IBM PERSONAL SYSTEM/2 Model 80 computer

■
1.2 PROGRAMMING LANGUAGES
AND FORTRAN

All the computers we have been discussing are **digital computers**; they store information as binary digits, or **bits**. We call the binary digits 0 and 1, but in the computer, bits are represented by current flowing in one of two possible directions.

Each computer has its own special **machine language** of zeroes and ones. This is the only language a computer can understand. However, you do not have to know machine language to use a computer. You can use a language closer to English, a **high-level programming language**, to write a **source program**. Each high-level language has a compiler, a program that translates your source program into a machine language program. (Some languages use **interpreters** that translate and execute one line at a time.)

There are many high-level languages in use today. Fortran, BASIC, COBOL, and Pascal are the most widely used, but there are many more. Fortran is an abbreviation for Formula Translator. It is the oldest high-level language, developed in 1954 for scientists and engineers. Since then, Fortran has undergone many changes. It is still the most popular scientific language, but it has become more flexible and easier to learn, so its popularity now extends far beyond the scientific community.

The development of a language involves **syntax** and **semantics**. Syntax is the set of formal rules for using the language, while semantics is concerned with the meaning of language statements. In English, a statement can violate the rules of syntax and still have meaning. The statement

Me and Bill went to the store.

violates the rules of English syntax, but its meaning is clear. In contrast, anything that violates the syntax rules of Fortran cannot be a Fortran statement, *therefore* it has no meaning in the Fortran language.

A syntactically incorrect English statement can convey meaning because people can make inferences about what is meant. A compiler, however, can recognize only language elements that were built into it. Anything else is meaningless. The statement

```
PRINT *, 'Hello'
```

has legal Fortran syntax, and its meaning is "Print the word Hello." However,

```
PRINT * 'Hello'
```

violates the syntax rules of Fortran because the comma is missing. The Fortran compiler cannot make sense of the latter statement, and therefore cannot translate it into machine language.

We have been saying *the* compiler, but there is actually a family of Fortran compilers and versions of Fortran. The American National Standards Institute (ANSI) sets standards for programming languages. In 1978, ANSI promulgated Fortran 77, which is now the official standard version of Fortran. Nearly every computer manufacturer has its own version of Fortran that includes virtually everything in Fortran 77, and a little more.

The Fortran language contains about 200 **keywords**, or words with special meaning to a Fortran compiler. However, you can start writing programs after learning only four or five keywords, and you can write large, meaningful programs with fewer than 20 keywords.

■

1.3 DATA STORAGE

As we have said, digital computers store binary representations of numbers and other things. The computer stores several different types of data. The most often used types are:

1. Integers, or whole numbers
2. Real numbers, or numbers with a decimal point
3. Characters

We give an overview of storage of these types of data here. A fuller discussion, including binary representations of integers and real numbers, appears in the next section. You can specify numbers and characters as you usually do, without knowing their binary representations, because the Fortran compiler deals with representations for you.

The smallest unit of storage is a bit, which can hold a 0 or a 1. Because a single bit holds so little information, we consider a **byte**, or several contiguous bits to be the basic unit of storage. Many computers consider a byte to be eight bits. Even an eight-bit byte cannot contain much information. With 8 bits, each of which can hold a 0 or 1, there are 2^8, or 256, different patterns of bits that can be stored in a byte.

Storing Integers

If integers were stored in one byte, then the computer could store only 256 different integers, and the same is true for real numbers. Some computers use four bytes to store integers and real numbers. These four bytes, or 32 bits, allow those computers to store 2^{32} (about 4.3 billion) different integers. Integers may be positive or negative, so the largest integer in size would be a little over 2 billion. You should find out how large an integer your computer can store.

Storing Real Numbers

A computer can store exactly as many different real numbers as integers in four bytes. However, the storage situation is quite different. The largest real number, in absolute value, that can be stored in four bytes is approximately

170,000,000,000,000,000,000,000,000,000,000,000,000 (37 zeroes)

and the smallest is about

0.00000000000000000000000000000000000029 (38 zeroes)

The real numbers that can be stored have a much greater range than the integers, but most of the real numbers between these two extremes cannot be precisely stored. Generally, real numbers that are sums of powers of 2 can be stored exactly. In 32 bits, a computer can exactly store the real number

2,147,483,648.0

because it is 2^{31}, and it can store the number

0.000000059604644775390625

exactly because it is 2^{-24}. Here again, you should find out roughly the largest and smallest real numbers your computer can store.

In contrast, numbers as simple-looking as 1.3 and 0.2 cannot be exactly stored; they can only be approximated. You often hear that the computer literally does what you tell it to do, but this is not true when telling the computer to store a real number. You can generally count on a real number being stored correctly to seven digits, and that is enough for most small programs with few calculations. However, when a program involves millions of calculations, the imprecise representation of real numbers can lead to serious problems. After thousands of multiplications with numbers that were correct to seven decimal places, the results may be correct to only two places. After millions of multiplications, they may not be correct to any places. This proliferation of imprecision is usually called **round-off error**.

Do not be unduly alarmed by the possibility of round-off error. Later we will mention some measures to keep the problem within reasonable bounds. Be aware of it so that, if the computer prints a number like 1.999999 when you were expecting 2.0, you will know what is happening.

Storing Characters

Little needs to be said now about character data, just that there are fewer than 256 characters available in Fortran, so one byte is sufficient to represent a character. Most computers store characters according to one of two collating sequences, **ASCII** or **EBCDIC**. ASCII stands for American Standard Code for Information Interchange, while EBCDIC means Extended Binary-Coded Decimal Interchange Code. Either collating sequence associates each character with a number from 0 to 127, called the ASCII or EBCDIC code for that character. Appendix B gives the ASCII and EBCDIC codes for printing characters.

Symbolic Names

The bit pattern in four contiguous bytes of storage could look like

10110011 00010110 11101001 01010001

This pattern could represent an integer, a real number, four characters, or any one of several other things. Fortunately, we do not have to know which it is, since Fortran keeps track of such things.

The storage locations in a computer are numbered by bytes, from byte 0 to some large number, depending on the amount of main memory. The number of a storage location is its **absolute address** in the machine. The term address is used because it tells *where* something is stored. We do not have to know the absolute address of a particular item of data, because Fortran keeps track of that too.

We do, however, need some way to refer to items of data that we store in the computer. Every high-level programming language provides **symbolic names** or **symbolic addresses**, which a programmer can use to refer to stored data. If, for example, we have a real number 17.52 that represents the width of a board in inches, we can use the name WIDTH to refer to this number when storing it. The computer will place a representation of the number in some storage location, and will associate the name WIDTH with the absolute address of that location. That is, WIDTH is a symbol that stands for the address. Later on, we can use the name WIDTH to cause the computer to find the number stored in that location. This symbolic addressing is sometimes called **indirect addressing**. We indicate the relationship between WIDTH and 17.52 as

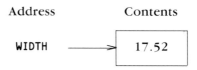

The term *address* seems more appropriate than *name* here, but computer scientists consistently use the word name. In fact, these symbolic addresses are usually called *variable names*, because they bear some resemblance to the variable names used in mathematics. We will also call them variable names, but in later chapters we will point out several places where they do not follow the rules of variable names in mathematics.

1.4 BINARY REPRESENTATION OF NUMERIC DATA

This section introduces the binary number system and storage of numeric data, integers and real numbers. The last part of the section deals with a hypothetical computer which stores integer and real data in eight bits or one byte. This small amount of storage makes the numbers easy to read and calculate, while illustrating the important fact that many real numbers cannot be represented exactly in a computer.

The number system we commonly use is the decimal number system. When we write something like 285, we often say we are writing the number 285. In fact, 285 is the *representation* of some number in the decimal system. We have used the decimal system so exclusively that we confuse the representation of a number with the number itself. Many other number systems exist. Because a computer stores numbers as binary digits, we introduce the binary number system. It is important to be familiar with the way numbers are stored in a computer, because the mode of storage determines which numbers the computer can represent exactly, and affects the results of calculations.

In the following discussion, we adhere to common usage by referring to 285, for example, as a decimal number, primarily to avoid lengthy phrases such as "the number represented by 285 in the decimal numbering system." (If this terminology is new to you, remember that the term decimal number does not mean a numeral that contains a decimal point, but rather refers to a numeral that contains decimal digits, 0 through 9.)

The Binary Number System

Any number system represents an integer (whole number) as a sequence of digits. In the decimal system we use, the digits are

$$0 \ 1 \ 2 \ 3 \ 4 \ 5 \ 6 \ 7 \ 8 \ 9$$

The *base* of the decimal number system is 10 because a number such as 285 means

$$2 \times 100 + 8 \times 10 + 5 \times 1$$

or

$$2 \times 10^2 + 8 \times 10^1 + 5 \times 10^0$$

where $10^0 = 1$. Digits in a number have **positional significance**; that is,

An IBM 9332 8-inch magnetic diskette (foreground) holds 25 million bits of information per square inch

the position of the digit in a number determines the power of 10 by which the digit is to be multiplied. For example, the 2 in 285 stands for 200, because of its position as the third digit from the right. In grade school, teachers say the 2 is in the hundreds place.

The binary system has base two, and the allowable digits are 0 and 1. Just as the number ten cannot be represented as a single digit in the decimal system, the number two cannot be represented as a single digit in the binary system.

To express a decimal number in binary notation, write the number as a sum of powers of two. For example, the decimal number 14 can be written as

$$1 \times 8 + 1 \times 4 + 1 \times 2 + 0 \times 1$$

or

$$1 \times 2^3 + 1 \times 2^2 + 1 \times 2^1 + 0 \times 2^0$$

Therefore, the binary representation of the decimal number 14 is 1110. The zero is important as a place holder; without it, we would have 111, which is the binary representation of the decimal number 7. Figure 1.2 shows the binary representations of the first ten positive integers.

Figure 1.3 gives binary representations of powers of two. The general rule is: The binary representation for two to the n power is a one followed by n zeroes.

Decimal	1	2	3	4	5	6	7	8	9	10
Binary	1	10	11	100	101	110	111	1000	1001	1010

FIGURE 1.2
Decimal and binary representations of the first ten positive integers

Power	0	1	2	3	4	5	6	7
Decimal	1	2	4	8	16	32	64	128
Binary	1	10	100	1000	100C0	100000	1000000	10000000

FIGURE 1.3
Decimal and binary representations of powers of two

We can find the binary expression for any decimal integer by expressing the integer as a sum of powers of two, and adding the binary representations of those powers. Try the decimal number 89, which is $64 + 16 + 8 + 1$. The sums in the two systems are done similarly:

Decimal	Binary
64	1000000
16	10000
8	1000
1	1
89	1011001

Thus, the decimal number 89 is the same as the binary number 1011001.

The same process in reverse makes it easy to express a binary number in decimal notation. Try it with the binary number 10101101:

Binary	Decimal
10000000	128
100000	32
1000	8
100	4
1	1
10101101	173

Thus, 10101101 in binary corresponds to 173 in decimal.

To avoid confusion when we are talking about two number systems at the same time, we will write the base of the number system as a subscript on the number. For example:

$$7_{10} = 111_2$$

or

$$1011001_2 = 89_{10}$$

Also, because binary numbers with many digits are hard to read, we will place a space between groups of four digits, starting from the right. The number 1011001 should be easier to read as

$$101\ 1001$$

Numbers with decimal points are expressed in any number system by using negative powers of the base. A negative power on a number gives the same result as that positive power on the reciprocal of the number; 10^{-3} is the same as $(1/10)^3$ or $1/1000$. The decimal number 0.5 means the same as

$$5 \times \frac{1}{10}$$

or

$$5 \times 10^{-1}$$

Similarly, the decimal number 0.7324 means

$$7 \times \frac{1}{10} + 3 \times \frac{1}{100} + 2 \times \frac{1}{1000} + 4 \times \frac{1}{10000}$$

or

$$7 \times 10^{-1} + 3 \times 10^{-2} + 2 \times 10^{-3} + 4 \times 10^{-4}$$

The binary system works the same way, with two as a base instead of ten. In binary, the . in a number is called the **binary point**. A negative power of two means the same as that positive power of one-half. The binary number 0.1011 means the same as

$$1 \times 2^{-1} + 0 \times 2^{-2} + 1 \times 2^{-3} + 1 \times 2^{-4}$$

or

$$1 \times \frac{1}{2} + 1 \times \frac{1}{8} + 1 \times \frac{1}{16}$$

In the decimal system this is

$$0.5 + 0.125 + 0.0625 = 0.6875$$

Therefore, $0.1011_2 = 0.6875_{10}$.

Figure 1.4 contains binary and decimal representations of some negative powers of two.

Power	−1	−2	−3	−4	−5	−6	−7
Decimal	.5	.25	.125	.0625	.03125	.015625	.0078125
Binary	.1	.01	.001	.0001	.00001	.000001	.0000001

FIGURE 1.4
Decimal and binary representations of some negative powers of two

The decimal number 0.375 is obviously 0.25 + 0.125, so the corresponding binary number is

$$0.01 + 0.001 = 0.011$$

Several methods facilitate conversion from decimal representations to binary. Here are two simple methods, one for whole numbers and one for numbers with only a fractional part.

The method for whole numbers involves successive divisions by two, keeping track of remainders. For example, consider the decimal number 19:

$$19 / 2 = 9 \text{ with remainder } 1$$
$$9 / 2 = 4 \text{ with remainder } 1$$
$$4 / 2 = 2 \text{ with remainder } 0$$
$$2 / 2 = 1 \text{ with remainder } 0$$
$$1 / 2 = 0 \text{ with remainder } 1$$

The binary representation for 19 is the sequence of remainders, read from the bottom up, or 10011. A shorthand version of the method deletes "/ 2 =" and "with remainder" from each line. Try it with the decimal number 11:

```
11
 5   1 ↑
 2   1 |
 1   0 |
 0   1 |
```

Reading the remainders from bottom to top, we see that the binary representation of the decimal number 11 is 1011.

For decimal numbers with only a fractional part, repeatedly multiply the number by two. At each step, if the product is greater than or equal to 1.0, write a binary digit 1 and at the next step, multiply only the fractional part of this number by two. If the product is less than 1.0, write a binary 0. Try this with the decimal number 0.8125:

$$2 \times 0.8125 = 1.6250 \text{ giving binary digit 1}$$
$$2 \times 0.6250 = 1.2500 \text{ giving binary digit 1}$$
$$2 \times 0.2500 = 0.5000 \text{ giving binary digit 0}$$
$$2 \times 0.5000 = 1.0000 \text{ giving binary digit 1}$$

(The fractional part of 1.0000 is zero, so we are finished.) In this case, read the binary digits from top to bottom. The binary representation of 0.8125 decimal is then 0.1101.

This method too has a shorthand version:

0.8125   (original decimal number)
_____

1.6250
1.2500
0.5000
1.0000

Read the digits, 1101, before each decimal point as the binary representation.

A word of caution concerning the second method: the process might not terminate. Consider the binary representation of the decimal number 0.4:

0.4   (original decimal number)
____

0.8
1.6
1.2
0.4
0.8
1.6

The binary representation to six places is 0.011001. The digits 1100 will repeat because the 1.6 at the sixth step is the same as the 1.6 at the second step. Therefore, the decimal number 0.4 cannot be precisely represented with a finite number of binary digits. This situation is analogous to the problem of representing one-third in decimal notation. We often write $1/3 = 0.3333$, recognizing that, no matter how many digits we write after the decimal point, the representation will never be exactly equal to $1/3$.

To represent 0.4 in binary, we must first decide how many binary places to use, then decide how to round. To round a binary number up at the nth place, look at the digit in the next place. If that digit is 0, just take the first n places. If that digit is 1, add 1 to the nth place. The best approximation to three places is 0.011, because the fourth place contains a 0. If you round to five places, notice that the sixth place contains a 1, so add

$$0.01100$$
$$+\ 0.00001$$

to get 0.01101.

The IBM System/36 computer

Simplified Storage

Many computers store numbers in four contiguous bytes, or thirty-two bits. That is just too many bits to look at, so we consider a hypothetical computer that uses only one byte of storage for numbers.

Half a byte is a **nibble**. We will write a byte of storage as two nibbles separated by a space, as in

1001 0101

The nibble on the left is the **high-order nibble**, and the nibble on the right is the **low-order nibble**. Similarly, the rightmost bit in a sequence of contiguous bits is the **low-order bit**, and the leftmost bit is the **high-order bit**.

Numbers with fractional parts are **real numbers**. Computers store real numbers and integers differently for several reasons. Integers are stored exactly, but some real numbers cannot be represented precisely. Integers are simpler and easier to deal with because they have no decimal points, so we begin with integer storage.

Integer Storage

The first question is: What integers can be stored in one byte? If we consider only non-negative integers, we can store every integer from 0 to

$$1111\ 1111_2$$

which is the same as $2^8 - 1$ or 255_{10}. However, we often want to use negative integers, so we choose the high-order bit in the byte to represent the sign. A 1 in the high-order bit indicates a negative number, and a 0 indicates a positive number. Only seven bits remain for the digits, so the largest positive number that can be stored is

$$0111\ 1111$$

which is $2^7 - 1$ or 127_{10}. The byte 0000 0110 represents the number 6_{10}, while 1000 0110 represents -6_{10}. This method of storing integers is called **sign-magnitude representation**, because the sign and the magnitude are stored separately. It allows us to store all the integers from -255 to 255. Notice that zero has two representations, 10000000 for minus zero and 00000000 for plus zero.

Most modern computers store integers in **twos-complement form**, which gives positive integers the same representation as in sign-magnitude form, but which stores negative integers quite differently. The twos complement form makes integer arithmetic simpler for the computer. We will stay with the sign-magnitude form, because it makes arithmetic simpler for human beings.

Adding binary numbers is quite simple. Since $1_2 + 1_2 = 10_2$, write down 0 and carry a 1 every time you add 1 and 1. Then to add, for example, the binary numbers 1010 and 111, we have

$$1010$$
$$+ \ 111$$
$$\overline{}$$
$$10001$$

The first (rightmost) addition has no carry, but the next three additions each require a carry of 1.

When we calculate a sum on paper, we can use as many places as we want. However, when numbers are stored in one byte, we can easily run out of places. For example, consider adding the two positive numbers below, each of which could be stored in one byte:

$$0110 \ 1010$$
$$+ \ 0101 \ 0101$$
$$\overline{}$$
$$1011 \ 1111$$

The sum has a 1 in the sign (leftmost) bit, so it represents a negative number! In decimal terms, we have calculated the sum of 106 and 85 to be −63. Technically, this situation is called **integer overflow**. Some compilers will print an error message when an integer addition or multiplication overflows, but some will simply calculate a negative result when adding two large positive numbers.

Real Number Storage

We can store real numbers in roughly the same way we store integers, and arbitrarily decide where to place the binary point. Suppose, for example, we agree to put the binary point after the fifth bit, so there are three binary places in each real number. Then the largest positive real number we can store in a byte would be stored as 0111 1111, representing $1111.111_2 = 15.875_{10}$. That is not a very big number. Also, the smallest positive binary number this storage can hold is 0.001_2, which is equivalent to 0.125_{10}. We often want to work with numbers much larger than 15.875 or smaller than 0.125, so we need a better way to store real numbers.

Exponential Notation

A decimal number in **exponential notation** is a number written as a decimal part times a power of ten. For example, the number

$$3.258 \times 10^4$$

is written in exponential notation or exponential form. The decimal part is 3.258 and the exponent, or power of ten, is 4. To write the number in standard decimal form, notice that each multiplication by ten simply moves the decimal point one place to the right. Multiplying by 10^4 moves the decimal point four places to the right, so the number 3.258×10^4 is equivalent to 32580.

In exponential form, the decimal point can come anywhere in the number. The decimal number 32580 is also equivalent to 0.3258×10^5 and to 325.8×10^2. Exponential form is often called **floating point** because different exponents make the decimal point move or float.

Similarly, 0.125×10^{-2} is an exponential form for 0.00125, because the decimal point in 0.125 must be moved two places to the *left* to get 0.00125. Moving a decimal point two places to the left is equivalent to multiplying by 10^{-2}, or dividing by 10^2.

A computer stores real numbers in two parts, a **fractional part** and an **exponent**. The computer first converts the real number to its binary equivalent in a standard notation similar to the exponential form used for real numbers. This **standard binary exponential notation** requires that the binary point be placed immediately before the first nonzero binary digit in the number. For example, the number 0.125_{10} is equivalent to 0.001_2, which is 0.1×2^{-2} in standard binary form. Every nonzero number has a standard binary exponential form. However, this form may be infinitely long. Even if the form is finite, it might be too long to fit in its allocated space.

To store a real number in one byte, we must decide which bits will represent the exponent, and which will represent the fractional part. For simplicity, we will store the exponent in the high-order nibble and the fractional part in the low-order nibble. See Figure 1.5.

FIGURE 1.5
Storage of a real number in one byte

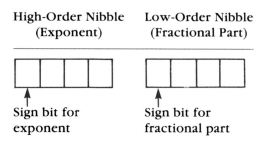

High-Order Nibble   Low-Order Nibble
(Exponent)   (Fractional Part)

Sign bit for   Sign bit for
exponent   fractional part

In each nibble, the high-order bit is the sign bit. The exponent is an integer in sign-magnitude form. As before, a sign bit of 1 signifies a negative number.

To store a decimal number such as 5.0, we first write it in binary form as 101, then in standard binary form as 0.101×2^3. The high-order nibble is then 0011, representing the exponent 3_{10}. The fractional part is 0.101, which is stored in the low-order nibble as 0101, since the first 0 represents the (positive) sign. The decimal number 5.0 then appears as 0011 0101 in one byte.

With this method of representation, only *four* different magnitudes for the fractional parts can be stored in the low-order nibble. The first bit gives the sign, and the second bit is always 1 because of the standard form, so only the two lower order bits can vary. These fractional parts are given in Figure 1.6, with sign bit 0 for positive numbers.

Low-Order Nibble	Fractional Part (Binary)	Fractional Part (Decimal)
0100	0.100	0.5
0101	0.101	0.625
0110	0.110	0.75
0111	0.111	0.875

FIGURE 1.6
The four positive fractional parts that can be stored in one nibble

Once we have a representation for a particular fractional part, say 0.625, we can easily find a representation for 0.625 times a power of 2. For example, the representation for 1.25 is 0001 0101; the exponent is 1, but the fractional part is the same as for 0.625. Similarly, 5.0 is 0.625×2^3, so the one-byte representation for 5.0 is 0011 0101, as we saw above. The nonzero multiples of 0.625 with their one-byte representations are given in Figure 1.7.

We have not used the high-order nibble 1000 in the table because it stands for exponent minus zero, which is the same thing as exponent plus zero, represented by 0000 in the high-order nibble. Notice that, by forcing a standard binary form to start with a 1 immediately after the binary point, we cannot have a zero fractional part. That is, we seem to have no way to represent the important real number zero. We can use the representation 1000 0000 for the real number zero because we do not need 1000 for any exponent. That is the only time we allow the low-order nibble to have a zero in the second position.

The representations for the four largest positive numbers are shown in Figure 1.8. That leaves some rather large gaps! A number such as 100.0 can only be approximated as 96.0, and 105.0 would have to be stored as 112.0.

To indicate just one problem that arises from these gaps, consider the problem of adding 8.0_{10} to 50.0_{10}. The sum is obviously 58.0, but our one-byte computer cannot store 58.0. The closest it can come is to store 58.0 as 50.0. Therefore, 50.0 + 8.0 = 50.0, according to our one-byte storage scheme!

Decimal	One-Byte Binary Representation
0.0048828125	1111 0101
0.009765625	1110 0101
0.01953125	1101 0101
0.0390625	1100 0101
0.078125	1011 0101
0.15625	1010 0101
0.3125	1001 0101
0.625	0000 0101
1.25	0001 0101
2.5	0010 0101
5.0	0011 0101
10.0	0100 0101
20.0	0101 0101
40.0	0110 0101
80.0	0111 0101

One-Byte Representation	Decimal Number
0111 0111	112.0
0111 0110	96.0
0111 0101	80.0
0111 0100	50.0

The smallest positive number has the largest possible negative exponent, so the high-order nibble is 1111, representing an exponent of −7. The smallest positive fractional part is 0.100_2, equivalent to 0.5_{10}, so the smallest positive decimal number that can be stored is

$$0.5 \times 2^{-7} = 0.00390625$$

The large real numbers with only zeroes after the decimal point have finite binary representations. For example, 105.0_{10} is the same as $110\ 1001_2$ or 0.1101001×2^7 in standard binary form. However, three binary bits cannot precisely represent the fractional part 0.1101001. The closest we can come is to use 0.111×2^7, so we can store the number as 0111 0111, which actually represents 112_{10}.

In contrast, the decimal number 0.2, for example, cannot be exactly represented with any finite number of binary bits. The best we can do is try to come close. From the table of negative powers of two in Figure 1.4, we find

$$0.2_{10} = 0.125_{10} + 0.0625_{10} + \cdots = 0.001_2 + 0.0001_2 + \cdots$$

or

$$0.2_{10} = 0.1875_{10} + \cdots = 0.0011_2 + \cdots$$

where the dots indicate that more terms are needed. We can get a closer approximation by adding the -6 power of 2 or 0.015625_{10}, which yields the binary approximation 0.001101_2 for the number 0.2_{10}. This approximation has the decimal value

$$0.1875 + 0.015625 = 0.202625$$

However, when 0.001101_2 is written in standard binary form and stored, the last 1 cannot be retained. Thus 0.2_{10} is best represented in binary by 0.00110_2 or 0.00111_2, which represent 0.1875_{10} and 0.21875_{10} respectively. The first representation is closer, so we would store 0.2_{10} as 1010 0110, which actually represents 0.1875_{10}.

We have illustrated two related problems caused by the inexact representation of real numbers. First, a number the user wants to store might not have an exact representation in the computer. Second, even if the computer stores the user's numbers precisely, calculations with these numbers can lead to results that are imprecise.

Since the first bit of a fractional part in standard binary form is always 1, most computers *assume* this bit and do not explicitly store it. We could have made this refinement in our storage system to gain one more bit of precision, but the point remains the same. No finite number of bits can precisely represent every real number.

Most computers store real numbers in at least four bytes instead of one, as we have done here. For example, some computers use one byte for the exponent, and three bytes for the fractional part. In each part, one bit designates the sign. Therefore, seven bits store the magnitude of the exponent, and twenty-three bits store the magnitude of the fractional part. (But be aware that different computers might use different amounts of storage for storing real numbers, and even computers that use four bytes might allocate different amounts of storage for the exponent and fractional part.)

With so many bits, the problem of imprecise representation is not as serious as it was with just eight bits of storage. Keep in mind, though, that the problem is still there. A computer cannot store exactly the decimal number 0.2 and many others. Similarly, a number added to a relatively much larger number can result in a sum equal to the larger number.

■

1.5 SUMMARY OF CHAPTER 1

■ Terms Introduced in This Chapter

ANSI, American National Standards Institute
ASCII, American Standard Code for
    Information Interchange
Bit
Byte
Compiler
Computer
    Parts: CPU, main memory
    Sizes: mainframe, microcomputer,
        minicomputer
EBCDIC, Extended Binary-Coded Decimal
    Interchange Code
Exponential notation
Firmware
Fortran
Fortran 77
Hardcopy
Hardware
High-level programming language

Indirect addressing
Integer
Machine language
Nibble
Peripheral Devices
    Input: card reader, keyboard
    Output: card punch, CRT screen, printer
    Input and output: disk drive, tape drive,
        terminal
    Storage: disk, magnetic tape
Program: machine-language program,
    source program
Real number
Semantics
Software
Symbolic address
Symbolic name
Syntax

■ What You Should Know

1. A computer is an electronic device that stores data and instructions, and uses the instructions to manipulate the data.
2. A program is a set of instructions that can be stored in a computer.
3. A computer can do arithmetic, copy data from one place to another, store data and programs, and compare two numbers.
4. A computer consists of a central processing unit (CPU) and a main memory unit.
5. Peripheral devices attach to a computer to enhance its usefulness.
6. A computer receives information from an input device such as a keyboard, tape or disk drive, or card reader.
7. A computer writes information to an output device such as a CRT screen, printer, tape or disk drive, or card punch.
8. Many computers have auxiliary memory for storage.
9. A bit is a binary digit, either 0 or 1. Bit also refers to a unit of storage which can hold a binary digit.

10. Each computer has its own machine language, composed of sequences of bits.
11. Fortran is a family of high-level programming languages, closer to English than to machine language.
12. Most modern versions of Fortran contain everything in Fortran 77 plus some extensions.
13. A Fortran compiler translates a Fortran source program into machine language.
14. The syntax of a language is the set of formal rules for constructing statements in that language.
15. The semantics of a language deal with the meaning of statements in the language.
16. Although a computer represents everything with bits, it can store representations of many different things, such as integers, real numbers, and characters.
17. A byte of storage in a computer is commonly eight contiguous bits, but some computers may use another number of bits.
18. Most computers store characters according to ASCII or EBCDIC code. Each character occupies one byte of storage.
19. A computer normally stores real numbers in two parts, a decimal part and an exponent.
20. A computer stores integers precisely, but can represent many real numbers only approximately.
21. Storage locations have absolute addresses that programmers do not need to know.
22. Programmers can refer to storage locations by means of variable names used as symbolic addresses.

■

1.6 EXERCISES

■ *Self-Test*

True/False

1. Computers are more intelligent than people.
2. A computer consists of a CPU and an input device.
3. All computers have a main memory unit.
4. All computers have auxiliary storage units.
5. The largest computers are microcomputers.
6. ANSI sets standards for the Fortran programming language.
7. Fortran is the machine language of scientific computers.
8. A byte is a binary digit.

9. Any statement that is syntactically correct in some version of Fortran is also correct in Fortran 77.
10. A computer can store more real numbers than integers in four bytes of storage.
11. Semantics is the set of formal rules of a language.

Fill in the Blanks

1. A set of instructions for a computer is a _____.
2. A device used to put information into a computer is an _____ device.
3. Devices that attach to computers are _____ devices.
4. The physical equipment contained in a computer and related devices is _____.
5. A number without a decimal point is an _____.
6. A byte is several contiguous _____.
7. Most computers store a character in _____ of storage.

Binary Exercises

1. Express the following decimal numbers in binary notation.

   a.   12
   b.   137
   c.   1234
   d.   0.75
   e.   0.55
   f.   123.45

   Express both e. and f. to six places after the binary point.

2. Express the following binary numbers in decimal form.

   a.   10101
   b.   1001011
   c.   0.101
   d.   1010.0101

3. Using one byte of storage and sign-magnitude form, find binary representations of the following decimal integers. If the number is too large to store in one byte, say so.

   a.   18
   b.   −43
   c.   −61
   d.   295

4. Using one byte of storage and sign-magnitude form, find the decimal integer equivalents of the following binary representations.

    a.   0000 1111
    b.   1010 0110
    c.   1011 0100
    d.   0011 1101

5. Using one byte of storage for a real number, the high-order nibble contains the exponent of the number in sign-magnitude form, and the low-order nibble contains a sign bit and three binary bits representing the fractional part of the number. What real decimal numbers have the following representations?

    a.   0000 1111
    b.   1010 0110
    c.   1011 0100
    d.   0011 1101

6. How would the following decimal numbers be represented in one byte of storage in the form specified in the previous problem?

    a.   2.5
    b.   −3.0
    c.   96.0
    d.   0.21

chapter 2 FORTRAN PROGRAMS

A Fortran program consists of several Fortran **statements**. Usually, each statement occupies one separate line. In this chapter, we present some simple Fortran programs using the fundamental Fortran statements:

- PROGRAM statement
- Type declarations
- PARAMETER statement
- READ statement
- Assignment statement
- PRINT statement
- DATA statement
- END statement

These statements will allow you to get data into programs, do calculations, and print results.

2.1 A SIMPLE PROGRAM

Consider the problem of calculating the area of a rectangular room. You probably recall that area is calculated according to the formula

$$Area = Length \times Width$$

Therefore, to solve the problem, we must first find values for the length and width of the room, and then multiply these values to find the area.

We shall arbitrarily decide to use a value of 18.0 for the length and 12.5 for the width. This is hardly a problem that calls for a computer, but we will use it to illustrate several statements in the Fortran language.

The purpose of most programs is to solve problems. Before writing a program, you should be sure you have a firm grasp of the problem. In particular, you should know what data will be supplied, or the **input**, and what information the program is to print, or the **output**. In our problem, the length and width will be input, and the area will be output. We will use the symbolic names `LENGTH`, `WIDTH`, and `AREA` for these three quantities.

Symbolic Names

Fortran 77 supports a uniform naming convention for symbolic names used in programs. Many entities can have symbolic names. In this chapter we mention three: *programs*, *variables*, and *constants*. No two entities can have the same name in a program. In Fortran 77, names can contain up to six letters and/or digits, of which the first must be a letter. (Many versions allow longer names, but some of these versions use only the first six characters and hence would consider `VELOCI` and `VELOCITY` to be the same name.) Here are some legal and illegal symbolic names in Fortran 77.

Symbolic Names in Fortran 77

Legal	Illegal	Reason
SUM	1SUM	First character must be letter.
SIDE12	SIDE%	Contains illegal character (%).
A1B2C3	VELOCITY	Too long.

A word of advice on symbolic names: use names long enough to tell a reader of the program what the names represent. Names such as `X`, `A`, or `Q` are not long enough to give a clue to what they represent.

All Fortran statements are placed in columns 7 through 72 of a line or punch card. Most Fortran programmers write programs in an editor, so we will generally use the term line instead of card. A statement can begin in or after column 7, but not before.

The program is shown as Program 2.1. Even if you are not familiar with programming, you should be able to understand many of the program statements since Fortran is a language similar to English. We next explain each line in the program.

PROGRAM 2.1

```
      PROGRAM FIRST
*-----------------------------------------------------------*
*              Calculate the floor area of a room.          *
*-----------------------------------------------------------*
      REAL  LENGTH, WIDTH, AREA

      LENGTH = 18.0
      WIDTH  = 12.5
      AREA   = LENGTH * WIDTH

      PRINT *, 'Area is', AREA

      END
```

The PROGRAM Statement

The first line in the program,

```
      PROGRAM FIRST
```

contains the PROGRAM statement. The general form of this statement is the word PROGRAM followed by the program name. This statement is optional, but when it appears, it must be the first statement in the program. We will name all programs in this text.

Comments

The next three lines in the program

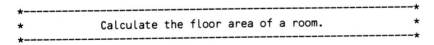

```
*-----------------------------------------------------------*
*              Calculate the floor area of a room.          *
*-----------------------------------------------------------*
```

contain **comments**, designated by the asterisk (*) in the first column. A comment is not a Fortran statement, so the Fortran compiler will not translate a line with * in the first column. Programmers write comments for people who read the programs; computers do not require them. Liberal use of comments is good programming practice. Long programs should have several, with each comment describing what a small section of the program is doing. The letter C in the first column also signals a comment line.

Finally, the Fortran compiler considers blank lines as comments. They make the program easier to read. There are three blank comment lines in the program.

Type Declaration Statements

The fourth line in the program,

```
REAL  LENGTH, WIDTH, AREA
```

contains a **type declaration statement**. Values for LENGTH, WIDTH, and AREA could be numbers with fractional parts, so we want to declare these variables to be REAL, not INTEGER. Notice the statement syntax: first the data type, then a list of variables to be given this data type. There must be a comma between each two variables, but no comma immediately after the data type. The type declaration statement belongs at the beginning of the program, because it specifies conditions for storage of data used by the program.

The type declaration statement is a **specification statement**, which provides information to the compiler. The statement directs the computer to set aside three storage locations for real numbers, and to label these locations LENGTH, WIDTH, and AREA. We usually say that LENGTH, WIDTH, and AREA are *variable names*, but they are more properly called *addresses*. When the computer stores information, each piece of data requires an address so the computer knows where to find it later. While the computer executes this program, the variable names LENGTH, WIDTH, and AREA will refer to three specific storage locations in the computer.

The type declaration statement sets up the following situation.

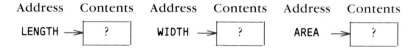

We have placed a question mark in each of the contents to stress the fact that these contents are not yet defined. Many versions of Fortran place a zero in the contents of each variable, but many do not, so wise programmers do not rely on the presence of a zero.

The Assignment Statement

The three statements

```
LENGTH = 18.0
WIDTH  = 12.5
AREA   = LENGTH * WIDTH
```

are **assignment statements**. The general form of the assignment statement is

< Variable name> = <Expression>

The computer must be able to calculate a value for the expression on the right side of the equal sign. It will then assign this value to the variable name on the left. Therefore, the expression should have the same type as the variable name. Expressions will be discussed more completely in the next chapter.

The first two assignment statements contain constants on the right of the equal signs. Constants are the simplest of expressions. After the computer executes these two statements, the stored values are:

Address	Contents	Address	Contents	Address	Contents
LENGTH →	18.0	WIDTH →	12.5	AREA →	?

The third assignment statement directs the computer to calculate the value of the expression LENGTH * WIDTH, and assign the calculated value to the variable AREA. The asterisk between LENGTH and WIDTH is a multiplication symbol. The other arithmetic symbols are the familiar ones: / for division, + for addition, and – for subtraction. To calculate the value of

LENGTH * WIDTH

the computer first finds the values 18.0 and 12.5 stored in LENGTH and WIDTH, then multiplies 18.0 * 12.5 to obtain 225.0. After the computer assigns 225.0 to AREA, the computer has three numbers stored:

Address	Contents	Address	Contents	Address	Contents
LENGTH →	18.0	WIDTH →	12.5	AREA →	225.0

We said previously that the computer must be able to calculate a value for the expression in an assignment statement. This implies that the computer must be able to find a value for each variable in the expression (and must be able to make sense of the expression). This leads to the following rule for Fortran programming:

> *Do not use a variable name on the right*
> *side of an assignment statement without*
> *first assigning a value to that name.*

In the example program, values *are* stored in LENGTH and WIDTH by two assignment statements before these values are used as expressions in another assignment statement. Thus, the computer finds meaningful values for the variables in the expression. When writing expressions in assignment statements, you should make sure that each variable in the expression has already been given a value by a previous statement.

Although the equal sign in the assignment statement looks like the mathematical equal sign you know so well, you should see that it behaves very differently. Mathematically, there is no distinction between

```
AREA = LENGTH * WIDTH
```

and

```
LENGTH * WIDTH = AREA
```

In Fortran, however, only the first is a legal assignment statement. The compiler considers the second statement to be a syntax error and simply does not know how to translate it. Remember, only a single variable name is allowed on the left of the equal sign. The computer calculates the value of the expression on the right and assigns this value to the variable on the left.

The PRINT Statement

The statement

```
PRINT *, 'Area is', AREA
```

is an example of a simple **output statement** in Fortran. Every program should contain at least one output statement to write out the results calculated by the program.

An output statement copies information from inside the computer to somewhere outside the computer. The statement must tell the computer not only what information to copy, but also where to place it and specifically how to write it.

The information to be copied is the **print list**, the list of items following

```
PRINT *,
```

Distinct items in the list are separated by commas. The computer copies characters between apostrophes exactly as they appear. The PRINT statement directs the computer to print two items: the words

```
Area is
```

and the number in the location called AREA. Items enclosed in apostrophes are character strings, character constants, or string literals. Always include some words in a PRINT statement to tell what results are being printed.

The variable name AREA is not enclosed in apostrophes, so the computer prints the value of the variable AREA, or the value stored at the address AREA, not the word AREA.

The computer can write output in many different places: your terminal, a line printer, a disk data file, and so on. The PRINT * statement directs the computer to type results at your terminal, or other standard output device.

Fortran also gives you the capability to specify exactly how output should be spaced, including, for example, the number of digits after the decimal point in real numbers. This specification is called **formatting**, and is the subject of Chapter 7. The * in the PRINT statement, however, lets the computer use its default options for typing results. Statements beginning with PRINT * are called **list-directed** output statements, because the list of items to be printed dictates the format for the printing.

When the computer executes this line, it will print

```
Area is        225.0000
```

The spacing and the extra zeroes come from the list-directed formatting, and will vary from one computer to another. For now, experiment to find out how your computer prints integers, reals, and quoted characters. In particular, determine how many columns your computer uses to print a real number and how many to print an integer. (Generally, the number of columns does not depend on the size of the number.) Also, see whether your computer places one or more spaces before and after a printed quantity.

The print list can include expressions as well as constants and variables. The two program statements

```
AREA = LENGTH * WIDTH
PRINT *, 'Area is', AREA
```

can be replaced by

```
PRINT *, 'Area is', LENGTH * WIDTH
```

The END Statement

The END statement is an easy one. Every Fortran program requires it to signal the compiler that there are no more statements to be translated. END must be the last statement in each program. If a program contains lines after the END statement, the compiler considers these lines to be the beginning of a new program unit.

Spaces in Statements

The Fortran compiler generally ignores spaces in statements, except for spaces inside apostrophes. The assignment statement, for example, could appear in one of the following four ways:

```
AREA=LENGTH*WIDTH
AREA = LENGTH * WIDTH
AREA     =      LENGTH   *      WIDTH
AR  EA=LE  NGTH*WIDT       H
```

The second of these seems the easiest to read. Make use of blank spaces in a line as well as blank lines to make your programs easier to read.

The READ Statement

Program 2.2 is a modest revision of Program 2.1, using a READ statement to get values of LENGTH and WIDTH into the program.

■
PROGRAM 2.2

```
      PROGRAM FIRST2
*------------------------------------------------------------------*
*  Calculate the floor area of a room, using READ for input.  *
*------------------------------------------------------------------*
      REAL LENGTH, WIDTH, AREA

      PRINT *, 'Length of the room?'
      READ  *, LENGTH
      PRINT *, 'Width of the room?'
      READ  *, WIDTH

      AREA = LENGTH * WIDTH
      PRINT *, 'Area is  ', AREA

      END
```

Instead of two assignment statements to obtain values for the variables LENGTH and WIDTH, we have used two READ statements:

```
READ *, LENGTH
READ *, WIDTH
```

The READ * statement is a simple **input statement**; it takes data values from some location and stores them in the computer. Just as with an output statement, an input statement must tell the computer what to copy, from where to copy it, and what form the information has.

The first READ statement, READ *, LENGTH, directs the computer to read a value for a variable called LENGTH. The computer will read a real number (LENGTH has been declared REAL), and store the number in the place labelled LENGTH. The READ * statement tells the computer to read the number from your terminal, or some standard input device. The * again denotes list-directed formatting; the computer simply reads whatever the user types, starting with the first nonblank character and continuing until the first blank, comma, or carriage return.

When you run this program, the first thing you will see is

```
Length of the room?
```

Then the program will seem to stop running. The computer is waiting for a number to be typed in response to the READ *, LENGTH statement. This READ statement makes the program **interactive**; you can interact with the program while it is running. Now, type a number for the length, ending with the carriage return as follows,

```
18.0<Return>
```

where <Return> means *press the carriage return*. The computer ignores extra blank spaces before and after the number, so you could also type

```
18.0   <Return>
```

A comma can terminate an input number, so the response could also be

```
18.0, Hi there<Return>
```

The computer ignores everything typed after the comma.

You can respond with the integer value

```
18<Return>
```

and the computer will still store the value 18.0 because LENGTH is declared REAL. Integer constants can be used almost anywhere a real constant is called for. The computer simply adds a decimal point to the integer. However, if the computer is attempting to read an integer value and finds a number with a decimal point, an error occurs and the program comes to a premature stop.

In any of the cases described above, the computer reads the number 18.0 and assigns it to the variable LENGTH. The computer then has

LENGTH $\longrightarrow$ | 18.0 |

Similarly, if you respond 12.5 to the question

Width of room?

the computer assigns 12.5 to the variable WIDTH, or stores 12.5 in the place with symbolic address WIDTH.

One READ statement can obtain values for several variables. We could have obtained values for LENGTH and WIDTH with the statement

        READ *, LENGTH, WIDTH

The set of items following

        READ *,

is the **read list**. *Only* symbolic addresses can appear in read lists. Proper responses to this READ statement are

18.0, 12.5 < Return >

or

18.0 12.5 < Return >

A comma, one or more spaces, or both, can separate the values typed in response to the READ statement. You can also place each value on a separate line, as in

18.0 < Return >
12.5 < Return >

With two separate READ statements, as in Program FIRST2, you must place the values on separate lines because each READ statement begins reading input from a new line.

If you write a program such as this and you are the one using it, you might think the PRINT statements preceding each READ statement are unnecessary. From the computer's standpoint, this is true; the computer will not be confused by the lack of such statements. Those PRINT statements are there for the benefit of the human user of the program. When your program asks for information from the user, always use a PRINT statement before the READ to let the user know what information the computer is expecting. Such PRINT statements are called **prompts**. A prompt should tell at least how many numbers to type. If the numbers must be integers, the prompt should say so.

Program FIRST2 has a big advantage over FIRST; it will calculate floor areas for rooms with *any* length and width. FIRST works for only the values 18.0 and 12.5. If you have a room with length 12.6 feet and width 8.4 feet, you would have to change the assignment statements to LENGTH = 12.6 and WIDTH = 8.4. FIRST2 is obviously more general; it applies to more situations.

■

2.2 ERRORS

Syntax Errors

You should now be ready to write a program with whatever medium you are using, and run it. You can simply copy one of the programs FIRST or FIRST2, or make one up. Unless your computer requires programs written on punch cards, you will probably use an **editor** utility program to help create your program. This book does not deal with the mechanics of editors or card punches, so you should seek help from a knowledgeable person at your installation.

If your source program contains statements that the Fortran compiler cannot translate, you have committed errors called **syntax errors**. These are **compile-time errors**, so called because the computer detects them during an attempted compilation. Suppose, for example, that line 9 in the program AREA is

```
AREA = LENGTH  WIDTH
```

When you attempt to compile this program, the computer might print a message like:

```
Missing operator or delimiter symbol
[LENGTH  WIDTH] in module MAIN at line 7
```

The syntax will vary, but most compilers print a brief description of the error, called a **diagnostic message**, and the line number of the statement that it could not translate. This lets you know where the error is and should give you a hint as to what went wrong. In our case, it should be easy to see that the * (an operator) is missing between LENGTH and WIDTH.

The first few times you compile programs, many syntax errors may occur, but you should find the number decreasing as you develop programming skills. Error messages are disturbing, but you can learn something from your mistakes.

Syntax errors are the easiest errors to correct. Look at the diagnostic messages for help. Often an error will be obvious to you once you know where it is. Learn to read the messages even though they will not always be meaningful to you. They are written to help you, and in most cases they do.

Run-Time Errors

Even if your program compiles and links properly, errors can occur when the program is running. These errors are called **run-time errors** or **execution errors**. The statement

```
DENSTY = WEIGHT / VOLUME
```

is a legitimate assignment statement and would compile properly. However, when the program is running, the value of VOLUME could be zero. An attempt to divide by 0 is a run-time error.

Similarly, a READ statement might be attempting to read an integer value, and you might mistakenly enter a number with a decimal point. This causes an *input conversion error*, a fatal error with most compilers. The program does not necessarily need fixing; simply run the program again, and type in an integer. (You should have a PRINT statement before READ that tells the user an integer is expected.) Or perhaps the number is not meant to be an integer. Then you must change the type declaration statement for the variable involved.

When a division-by-zero error occurs, you need to inspect the program to find out why the divisor variable value was zero. It is likely that the variable never received a meaningful value, and Fortran used the zero value that many compilers initially give numeric variables. Check to see that the offending variable is being given a nonzero value in a READ or assignment statement.

Logic Errors

The most insidious errors are logic errors. A program can compile and run without producing error messages, but give incorrect results. This means there were flaws in the programmer's logic, so such errors are called **logic errors**. The computer understands and does as it was instructed; it was just not instructed correctly. Simple examples are forgetting to include an output statement in the program or writing a minus sign in place of a plus sign.

It is painfully obvious when you forget a PRINT statement; some result you wanted does not get printed. A minus sign in place of a plus sign, however, may not be obvious. The program will still print some results. It is crucial that you do not blindly accept results the computer prints, but get in the habit of checking all results from your programs. If you can do the exact calculations, do them, at least for small data sets. If you wrote the program because you could not do the same calculations by hand, you should still check the results to see that they are reasonable. Think about the results you can expect, and check the printed results against your expectations. If you get a printed result of 12.6347 when you expected a number in the millions, something is wrong. Check your logic.

Debugging Programs

Errors in programs are called **bugs**, and the process of getting rid of them is called **debugging**. This terminology presumably arose when a programmer found a dead bug causing electrical problems inside an early computer. Surely there is a psychological basis for the continued use of this terminology; programmers would like to assume that something crawled into the program while no one was looking. This attitude puts the blame for mistakes on something outside the programmer. However, if there are errors in a program, rest assured that a programmer put them in. The best way to keep bugs out of a program is not to put them in.

Typing mistakes cause many syntax errors. Aim to be a careful typist rather than a speedy one. Some other causes of syntax errors are:

1. Confusion between zero (0) and uppercase O
2. Confusion between the digit one (1), lowercase l, and uppercase I
3. A missing comma or parenthesis in a complicated expression
4. Extending a statement past column 72
5. Misspelling a Fortran keyword

Execution errors usually turn out to be logic errors. The best advice here is, plan ahead. First be sure you understand the problem. Know what inputs will be given to the program and what outputs are required. Work out an **algorithm**, a plan for solving the problem without reference to a computer or computer language. When you are quite sure you know how to solve the problem, then tell the computer what to do (write the program).

It is an unfortunate fact that even well thought out programs usually do not run smoothly the first time. One standard debugging practice is to play the role of the computer. At the top of a sheet of paper, write down the names of all variables in the program. Then pretend you are the computer; follow the program, one statement at a time, performing the indicated operation. Whenever a variable value changes, write the new value under the variable name. With this method, you can usually find an error in a short time.

You can also build the previous method into the program by placing a PRINT statement immediately after each assignment statement, to print the variable name and the value assigned to it. These **debugging print statements** can be deleted when the program is running properly.

There are several variations on this theme. You could try to explain your program, step by step, to a friend, who is not necessarily a programmer. There is also a variation called a structured walk-through, in which the programmer walks through the program with an audience of critics who comment on the program. The main point, in any case, is critically examining each step of the program. We will say more about debugging later.

■

2.3   TWO PROGRAM EXAMPLES

An Example with INTEGER Variables

Here is another small example, primarily to illustrate the INTEGER data type and integer division. The program asks the user for a number of inches, and tells the user the equivalent number of feet and inches. For example, 27 inches is 2 feet and 3 inches.

The INTEGER Type Declaration

This program requires one input variable, which we will call INCHIN, to stand for the input number of inches. The problem specifies two output variables for the number of feet and the number of inches. We will call these FEET and INCHES. All variables will be declared INTEGER.

The INTEGER type declaration statement follows the rules for the REAL type declaration, with the word INTEGER in place of the word REAL. The type declaration statement for this program is

```
INTEGER  INCHIN, INCHES, FEET
```

Integer Division

The division symbol in Fortran is the slash (/), regardless of the type of the values involved. When the real number 7.0 is divided by 2.0, the result is 3.5, as you would expect. When one integer is divided by another, as in 7/2, the result of the calculation is an integer indicating how many times the denominator is contained in the numerator. Thus, 7/2 is 3 because 2 goes into 7 three times.

To calculate a value for FEET, use INCHIN/12. The number of inches remaining is INCHIN − FEET ∗ 12. See Program 2.3 for the complete program.

■
PROGRAM 2.3

```
      PROGRAM INCH
*-----------------------------------------------------------*
*         Convert a number of inches to feet and inches.    *
*-----------------------------------------------------------*
      INTEGER  INCHIN, INCHES, FEET

      PRINT *, 'How many inches (a whole number)?'
      READ  *, INCHIN
      FEET   = INCHIN / 12
      INCHES = INCHIN - FEET * 12

      PRINT *, INCHIN, ' inches is equivalent to'
      PRINT *, FEET, ' feet and', INCHES, ' inches'

      END
```

When the program runs, suppose you enter 35 in response to the question. FEET will receive the value 35/12, or 2. INCH will be assigned $35 - 2 \times 12$, or 11. Then the computer will print

```
35 inches is equivalent to
 2 feet and     11 inches
```

Notice the space after each initial apostrophe in the quoted strings

```
' inches is equivalent to'
' feet and'
' inches'
```

When a string follows a number in a print list, a space at the beginning of the string will prevent the first character of the string from starting immediately after the number, as in

```
35inches is equivalent to
 2feet and      11inches
```

Integer division is handy in problems like this. However, you are almost certain to have an integer division occur when you do not want it. Be clear about the distinction between REAL and INTEGER values. To be certain the computer interprets a value as REAL, write it with a decimal point.

Before starting a program, you must decide whether to declare each numeric program variable to be REAL or INTEGER. A variable whose values can have fractional parts must be REAL. Use INTEGER type for a variable whose values occur naturally as whole numbers. A specific example is a **counting variable** that counts the number of times something occurs: number of columns in a line, number of characters in a word, number of seconds in a week, and so on.

The PARAMETER **Statement**

The PARAMETER statement assigns a symbolic name to a **constant**. Often a program requires a constant such as π, which is approximately equal to 3.141593. We could declare a real variable PI and assign it the value 3.141593. However, the very word *variable* suggests something that can vary or change, and this value for PI should not change.

We can tell the computer that PI always stands for 3.141593 with a PARAMETER statement

```
PARAMETER (PI = 3.141593)
```

The general form of the PARAMETER statement is

```
PARAMETER (SN = C, SN = C, ...)
```

where SN stands for a symbolic name and C stands for a constant, the symbolic name of a predefined constant, or an expression involving constants and symbolic names of constants. We could, for instance, have

```
PARAMETER (PI = 3.141593, HALFPI = PI / 2.0)
```

Symbolic names of constants can be any legal symbolic names. After we define PI to be 3.141593 in the PARAMETER statement, the computer treats any reference to PI as a reference to 3.141593.

Notice that PI looks like a variable in the program, but it is a *constant*. Once we assign PI a value in a PARAMETER statement, a compile-time error will occur if we assign a value to PI later in the program. You might think that PI could as well be a variable name in the program, but the point is that variable values can change, *constant values cannot*. It *would* be a logical error to try to reassign a value to PI. It is far better to find such things out at compilation time than have some strange result occur at run time.

The PARAMETER statement is a nonexecutable statement that belongs after the type declaration statements, but before any executable statements in the program.

Defining PI in a PARAMETER statement has some obvious benefits. If the program requires the value of PI several times, PI is much easier to write than 3.141593. The PARAMETER statement also protects the programmer from typographical errors such as writing 3.141593 one time and 3.144593 another.

The most powerful reason for using a PARAMETER statement, however, involves defining as constants some things that are not really constants in the usual sense. Consider, for example, a payroll problem that involves such things as the Social Security tax rate. This rate is now approximately 7.15 percent, or 0.0715, but it surely will change in the future. Still, the rate must remain constant *during each execution of a payroll program*, so it is wise to define something like

```
PARAMETER (SSRATE = 0.0715)
```

in the payroll program. When the rate does change, the program requires only a new number in the PARAMETER statement. Without the PARAMETER statement, the programmer would have to hunt for each occurrence of the value of 0.0715 in the program, and change it.

The PARAMETER statement defines symbolic names to be constants just for the duration of a program's execution, so use it for entities that you want to remain constant during one run of the program.

A Payroll Program

Payroll programs are good programming examples because they range from very simple to extremely complex. The simplest payroll problem takes an employee's hourly rate and hours worked, and multiplies them to find the pay. Here we present a slightly more complicated example. You will see a few more versions of payroll programs throughout this book. Here is a statement of the problem.

Write a program to calculate a pay statement for an employee. The program should ask for:

> Hours worked
> Hourly rate of pay

Then the program should calculate:

> Gross pay = Hours worked × Hourly rate
> Federal income tax = 14 percent of Gross pay
> Social security tax = 7.15 percent of Gross pay
> Net pay = Gross pay − Federal tax − Social Security

The program should print values of all variables in a neat layout.

The statement of the problem points out all the necessary variables. We use some variable names whose meanings should be obvious.

Input Variable	Meaning	Output Variable	Meaning
HOURS	Hours worked	GROSS	Gross pay
RATE	Hourly rate of pay	FEDTAX	Federal income tax
		SOCSEC	Social Security tax
		NETPAY	Net pay

The values 0.14 and 0.0715 for the tax rates are constants for the duration of the program, so we assign them the names FDRATE and SSRATE in a PARAMETER statement.

This program, as every program, begins with a section declaring the names of the program, variables, and constants. We call this the **declaration** section of the program. The remainder of the program is the program **body**. Here is an outline of the program body:

1. Read the input data.
2. Do the calculations.
3. Write the results.

Many simple programs, and some very complicated ones, have the same outline. The outline is a standard programming technique that breaks a problem into smaller subproblems. An outline also helps make a program easier to read and understand. The headings in the outline usually serve as comments in the program.

Each step in the outline turns into several program statements. The statements to read input data and do calculations follow almost directly from the problem statement. The general output statements are fairly obvious too, but the problem statement does not specify the exact form of the printed output, so there are many ways to print the output in a neat layout. See Program 2.4.

■

PROGRAM 2.4

```
      PROGRAM PAYROL
*-------------------------------------------------------------*
*         Calculate a payroll statement for an employee.    *
*-------------------------------------------------------------*
      REAL  HOURS, RATE, GROSS, FEDTAX, SOCSEC, NETPAY
      REAL  FDRATE, SSRATE
      PARAMETER (FDRATE = 0.14, SSRATE = 0.0715)
*-------------------------------------------------------------*
*         Get input data, hours and hourly rate.           *
*-------------------------------------------------------------*
      PRINT *, 'How many hours worked?'
      READ  *, HOURS
      PRINT *, 'Hourly rate?'
      READ  *, RATE
*-------------------------------------------------------------*
* Calculate gross pay, federal tax, social security, net pay. *
*-------------------------------------------------------------*
      GROSS  = HOURS * RATE
      FEDTAX = FDRATE * GROSS
      SOCSEC = SSRATE * GROSS
      NETPAY = GROSS - FEDTAX - SOCSEC
*-------------------------------------------------------------*
*                    Print results.                        *
*-------------------------------------------------------------*
      PRINT *
      PRINT *, 'Hours worked        :', HOURS
      PRINT *, 'Hourly rate of pay :', RATE
      PRINT *
```

```
PRINT *, 'Gross pay         :', GROSS
PRINT *, 'Federal tax       : ', FEDTAX
PRINT *, 'Social Security tax:  ', SOCSEC
PRINT *, 'Net pay           :', NETPAY

END
```

Suppose you run the program and enter 40.0 for HOURS and 9.50 for RATE. Then the output looks like this:

```
Hours worked        :    40.00000
Hourly rate of pay  :    9.500000
Gross pay           :    380.0000
Federal tax         :      53.20000
Social Security tax:       27.17000
Net pay             :    299.6300
```

Carefully check the PRINT statements that produced this output. There are two **blank print** statements

```
    PRINT *
```

each of which prints a blank line. Also, the colons (:) in the PRINT statements line up, and the deductions are indented to make them stand out.

It is easy to slack off when it comes to writing output. The hard part of the problem is done, and you are bound to have "more important" things to do. Output *is* important, though. People will judge your work by your output, and many people believe that sloppy output is an indicator of sloppiness in other areas. It often is. Take some time to make the output look good.

2.4   MORE ON DATA DECLARATION

The DATA **Statement**

A DATA statement assigns initial values to variables. To assign 18.0 to LENGTH and 12.5 to WIDTH, but no initial value to AREA, use the statements

```
    REAL   LENGTH, WIDTH, AREA
    DATA   LENGTH /18.0/, WIDTH /12.5/
```

The initial value, enclosed in slashes (/) immediately follows the variable name. The separating commas come after the closing slash.

An alternative DATA statement is

```
DATA   LENGTH, WIDTH /18.0, 12.5/
```

That is, it is legal to write all the variable names first, followed by all the values enclosed in one pair of slashes.

We have been calling some statements *executable* and some *nonexecutable*, depending on *when* the statement takes effect. A nonexecutable statement takes effect at compile time; it is a directive to the compiler. The compiler does not translate nonexecutable statements into machine language. The nonexecutable statements we have discussed so far are the PROGRAM statement, the type declaration statements, and the PARAMETER statement.

Thus, the statement

```
DATA   LENGTH/18.0/, WIDTH/12.5/
```

takes effect at compile time, not at run time. The variables LENGTH and WIDTH already contain the values 18.0 and 12.5 when the computer begins to execute the program. Similarly, constants in PARAMETER statements receive their values at compile time.

The PRINT, READ, and assignment statements are executable, which means the compiler translates them into machine language. The executable statements actually take effect at *run time*, when the computer executes the translated program.

A DATA statement can contain variables of different types. We could have, for instance:

```
INTEGER  AGE, SIDES
REAL     HEIGHT, WEIGHT, VOLUME
DATA     AGE/37/, SIDES/3/, HEIGHT/35.62/, WEIGHT/18.64/
```

The DATA statement can also list all the variables first, followed by all the values to be assigned to them, as in

```
DATA     AGE, SIDES, HEIGHT, WEIGHT /37, 3, 35.62, 18.64/
```

The DATA statement can include a **repeat count** to assign several variables the same value. The statement

```
DATA     HEIGHT, WEIGHT, LENGTH/3*10.0/
```

assigns three values of 10.0 to the variables HEIGHT, WEIGHT, and LENGTH. The repeat factor and an asterisk precede the value to be repeated.

Implicit Typing

Fortran does not *require* variables to be declared REAL or INTEGER. In the absence of type declarations, an implicit typing takes place. A variable name beginning with the letters I, J, K, L, M, or N is given an INTEGER type. All other variable names are given type REAL. However, you should declare all variables used in a program, mainly because this forces you to think about what variables a program requires before you start to write the program. This is an important part of solving a problem.

In particular, a symbolic name in a PARAMETER statement should be given a data type in a type declaration statement preceding the PARAMETER statement. Failure to do so can cause errors. The PARAMETER statement

```
PARAMETER (M = 4.6235)
```

assigns the constant 4 to the symbolic name M unless M is declared REAL.

The IMPLICIT Statement

Fortran contains an IMPLICIT statement which declares variables to be REAL or INTEGER according to the first letter in the variable name. The statement

```
IMPLICIT REAL  (A, E, I, O, U)
```

declares that every variable whose name begins with a vowel has type REAL. Similarly,

```
IMPLICIT INTEGER  (C - F)
```

indicates that a variable name beginning with C, D, E, or F has type INTEGER.

We urge you *not* to use this statement, but to use type declarations for all variables in your programs.

In addition to REAL and INTEGER, Fortran allows several other data types which will be discussed later. All these other data types must be declared.

You should begin writing programs as soon as possible to test your mastery of this chapter. You can copy the example programs if you want practice in the mechanics of writing, compiling, and linking. You can devise simple problems for yourself or do some of the programming exercises below. There is no substitute for studying, but running programs will tell you what you don't know and give you confidence in the things you do know.

2.5   SUMMARY OF CHAPTER 2

■ *Terms Introduced in This Chapter*

Body of a program	Fortran statements	Implicit typing
Bug	Assignment statement	Integer division
Comment	DATA statement	Interactive
Debug	END statement	List-directed I/O statement
Declarations	IMPLICIT statement	PRINT
Error	PARAMETER statement	READ
Logic error	PRINT statement	Nonexecutable statement
Run-time error	PROGRAM statement	Outline
Syntax error	READ statement	Print list
Executable statement	Type declaration statements	Program
	INTEGER	Read list
	REAL	Source program

■ *What You Should Know*

1. A Fortran program contains several Fortran statements. Each statement must begin on a new line.
2. A comment is not a Fortran statement, but is used to make a program or part of a program more understandable.
3. The PROGRAM statement is optional, but when it is used, must be the first statement in a program.
4. Every Fortran program must have an END statement as the last statement of the program.
5. Every program should contain an output statement such as the PRINT statement.
6. Every variable in a Fortran program has a data type.
7. If a variable is not given a type in a type declaration statement, the type of the variable is INTEGER if the variable name begins with I through N, and is REAL if the name starts with any other letter.
8. The PRINT statement causes the computer to copy exactly any characters enclosed in apostrophes.
9. A variable is a symbolic address; the value of a variable is the value stored at that address.
10. When a print list contains an expression that is not enclosed in apostrophes, the computer prints the value of that expression.
11. A print list can contain expressions as well as variable names and constants.
12. The only items allowed in a read list are variable names.

13. Each READ * statement should be preceded by a PRINT statement telling the user what input is expected.
14. If a READ statement is reading a real value, it is permissible to enter an integer.
15. If a READ statement is reading an integer value, an error occurs when a real value is entered.
16. Only a single symbolic address can occur on the left of the equal sign in an assignment statement, but a constant, variable, or expression may appear on the right of the equal sign.
17. Division of one integer by another gives an integer result.
18. The PARAMETER statement assigns a symbolic name to a constant value.
19. A program outline breaks a large problem into smaller subproblems.
20. A numeric variable whose values might contain fractional parts should be declared REAL.
21. A symbolic name should describe what the name represents.

■
2.6 EXERCISES

■ *Self-Test*

True/False

1. A legal program name is a legal variable name.
2. A program name can be the same as the name of a variable in the program.
3. Every variable in a Fortran program has a type.
4. Nonexecutable statements are statements that do not cause the computer to do anything.
5. READ *, A * B is a legal Fortran statement.
6. A * B = C is a legal Fortran statement.

Short Answer

1. In what columns of a line are Fortran statements written?
2. Which of the following are valid variable names in Fortran? For those that are invalid, explain why.

    a.   Q5
    b.   LEGAL.SIZ
    c.   SIZE
    d.   SIZE*

e. 5Q
f. SUMOFSQUARES

3. What statement must appear in every Fortran program?
4. What three statements in Fortran can be used to assign values to variables?
5. Write a Fortran statement to indicate that NUMBER and AGE are INTEGER type variables.

■ *Programming Exercises*

1. Write a program that asks for a number, multiplies the number by itself, and prints:

   ```
   Your number is   xx
   Its square is    xxxx
   ```

   where xx stands for the number given and xxxx is its square. Let both numbers have INTEGER type.
2. Write a program that asks for a number of days and prints the number of seconds in that many days. Use INTEGER variables.
3. Write a program that asks for two sides of a rectangle and prints the circumference and area of the rectangle.
4. Write a program that asks for the costs of three items, calculates the sum of the costs, and adds 4 percent sales tax to get the final bill. Use a PARAMETER statement. Have the program print the values of all variables in a neat layout.
5. A rectangular box has sides of length a, b, and c. Write a program that asks for the three lengths, then calculates and prints the surface area and volume of the box.
6. When three resistors with resistances R_1, R_2, and R_3 (ohms) are hooked up in parallel, the equivalent resistance R is given by

$$\frac{1}{R} = \frac{1}{R_1} + \frac{1}{R_2} + \frac{1}{R_3}$$

   Write a program that asks for the three resistances, then calculates and prints the equivalent resistance.
7. Write a program that asks for the radius of a circle, then calculates and prints its circumference and area.
8. The gravitational acceleration constant g, for bodies falling near the earth's surface, is 9.80665 meters/sec^2. Write a program to find the value of g in feet/sec^2. Define two constants. (1 meter = 3.28084 feet.)
9. Write a program to find the number of seconds in a year. Find this result as an integer if you can, but if you can't, try something else.

3 THE FORTRAN LANGUAGE

This chapter gives a more formal introduction to the entire Fortran language, with particular emphasis on the data types REAL, INTEGER, and CHARACTER. The chapter also introduces twenty of the numeric functions contained in Fortran. These intrinsic functions are very useful. Most of the programs you write will contain one or more of them. The final section of the chapter deals with statement functions, which are functions defined by the programmer in one Fortran statement.

3.1 THE FORTRAN CHARACTER SET

Fortran utilizes forty-nine characters; the uppercase letters of the alphabet, the digits 0 through 9, space, and the twelve special characters listed in Figure 3.1.

Generally, Fortran makes no distinction between uppercase and lowercase letters. We can write PRINT as print, Print, or even pRiNt. We can also write variable names in uppercase or lowercase letters; the names LENGTH, length, and Length, all refer to the same storage location. Fortran differentiates the upper and lower cases only for CHARACTER constants, such as 'Length of Room?'. Following the usual Fortran convention, we shall use uppercase letters for everything except character constants.

FIGURE 3.1
Special Characters
Used In Fortran

Character	Name
=	Equal sign
+	Plus sign
−	Minus sign
⋆	Asterisk
/	Slash
,	Comma
.	Decimal point or Period
:	Colon
(	Left parenthesis
)	Right parenthesis
'	Apostrophe
$	Dollar sign

3.2 FORTRAN LINES

We have said that Fortran statements must begin in or after column 7, and that column 1 can be used to specify that the rest of the line holds only a comment. Here are the remaining details about the format of a Fortran line. A line in a Fortran program consists of 80 columns. Each noncomment line contains the following four fields:

1. Statement label field: columns 1 through 5
2. Continuation indicator field: column 6
3. Statement field: columns 7 through 72
4. Sequence number field: columns 73 through 80

Line Continuation

The Fortran compiler assumes a statement ends at the end of a line, unless there is a nonzero character in column 6 of the *next* line. Column 6 is generally left blank. Either a blank or a zero (0) in column 6 signifies the beginning of a statement on this line. Any other symbol in column 6 indicates that the statement on this line is a continuation of the statement on the previous line. The Fortran compiler considers characters after the continuation character as following immediately after the last character of the statement on the previous line. The following example uses a label, 12345, merely to show the spacing of the columns.

```
12345 PRINT *, 'The square of the height is ',
    1 HEIGHT * HEIGHT
```

as if it were

```
12345 PRINT *, 'The square of the height is ', HEIGHT * HEIGHT
```

You are not likely to have more than two lines containing a single statement, but lines can be continued nineteen times. Many programmers use a 1 in column 6 for the first continuation, a 2 for the second continuation, and so on. For example:

```
  PRINT *, 'A line with three continuation lines',
1 HEIGHT,
2 WEIGHT,
3 WEIGHT / HEIGHT
```

Comment lines cannot be continued this way, but they can appear between other continued lines.

Sequencing

The Fortran compiler ignores characters in columns 73 through 80, so be sure that statements do not run past column 72. These columns may contain *sequencing* information or comments. Programs written with editors rarely use the sequencing columns. When programs were punched on cards, it was important to number the cards so that they could be easily put in order if they ever got mixed up. In fact, today, the entire layout of Fortran lines follows from the layout of those 80-column cards.

■
3.3 SPECIAL WORDS IN FORTRAN

Keywords

Certain words, called **keywords**, have special meaning in Fortran. Some of the keywords we have already used are REAL, INTEGER, PRINT, END, and READ. We will discuss many others in the remainder of this text.

Fortran does not **reserve** keywords. That is, Fortran allows you to use a keyword as a variable name or program name. The program segment

```
PRINT = 3.1416
PRINT *, PRINT
```

is perfectly legal in Fortran. The compiler can determine from context whether PRINT is a variable name or the keyword PRINT. In the first statement, PRINT must be a variable name because it is followed by the equal sign. The first PRINT in the second statement must be the keyword because it is followed by an asterisk and comma. The last PRINT must be a variable name because it occurs in a print list.

Even though it is legal to use keywords such as PRINT and END as variable names, it is not wise to do it since it can be confusing to readers of the program.

Function Names

The Fortran language also contains special words called **function names**. A function named SQRT takes square roots, and a function named MAX finds the largest number in a set of numbers. We will discuss these and many other functions later in this chapter.

Fortran ignores spaces imbedded in keywords, function names, and variables. It is legal, but not advisable, to write

```
PR  INT *, 'Hi'
```

■

3.4   DATA TYPES

Fortran contains six data types: INTEGER, REAL, CHARACTER, LOGICAL, DOUBLE PRECISION, and COMPLEX. For now, we will concentrate on the data types REAL, INTEGER, and CHARACTER. We introduce the LOGICAL type in Chapter 5. Chapter 14 discusses the DOUBLE PRECISION and COMPLEX data types.

Each of the data types can be applied to constants, variables, and expressions. Constants are the simplest, so we start with them.

Integer Constants

INTEGER constants are whole numbers such as 12, –6429, 0 and 10000. INTEGER constants can contain only digits and a plus or minus sign. In particular, an INTEGER constant must not contain a decimal point, and commas must not be used as place markers in large numbers. The range of INTEGER constants in Fortran depends on the computer.

Here are examples of some valid INTEGER constants and some things Fortran would not recognize as INTEGER constants.

Valid	Invalid	Reason
12345	12,345	Comma not allowed
-23	-23.0	Decimal point not allowed
0	12E6	E not allowed

Real Constants

We can write REAL constants in two different forms. In our usual decimal form, or **fixed form**, the constant contains a decimal point, as in

$$10.987 \quad -325.1 \quad +2. \quad -12.5 \quad 0.00123$$

This fixed form can contain only digits, a single decimal point, and a leading plus or minus sign. The plus sign is not required in positive numbers. Although Fortran allows the decimal point to be the first or last character, as in .25 and 38., we recommend writing these numbers as 0.25 and 38.0 to make the decimal point easier to see.

We often call real numbers **floating-point numbers** because the decimal point can move, or float, in the number, as real numbers written in exponential notation. For example, we can write the real number 1234.56 as 1.23456E+3. The exponent is E+3, which indicates that the preceding number is to be multiplied by 10^3 or 1,000. This multiplication corresponds to moving the decimal point three places to the right.

We can also use negative exponents as in 1.23E-2, with the E-2 telling us to move the decimal point two places to the *left*, or to divide the preceding number 1.23 by 100. Thus, 1.23E-2 in decimal form is 0.0123.

Fortran considers a number expressed in exponential form to be real even if the number does not contain a decimal point; 12E5 is a REAL constant, equal to 1200000.0. The plus sign (+) is optional in positive exponents, but a number must precede the exponent; E-2 alone is not a valid REAL constant, but 1E-2 is valid.

The precision of a REAL constant is typically about seven **significant digits**, but some real numbers are stored with much greater precision. In determining significant digits, count every digit except leading zeroes. That is, the constant 0120.0 has four significant digits (all but the leading 0). Similarly, 0.000246853 has six significant digits.

The PRINT * statement will print some real numbers in exponential form, with a zero before the decimal point and a nonzero digit immediately after the decimal point. The number 26,345,000 appears as 0.263450E+08, and 0.00045 looks like 0.450000E-03. If you use the exponential form for input, you do not have to follow these rules. You can write 2.6345E7 and 45E-5 for the same numbers.

Here are some examples of valid and invalid **REAL** constants.

Valid	Invalid	Reason
12345678.0	12,345,678.0	Commas not allowed
1066.0	1066	Decimal point missing
−1.0123	$599.99	Dollar sign not allowed
123.63E4	5.793E398	Exponent too large
165E−27	4E−12.34	Decimal not allowed in exponent
−32.14E12	E+10	Number required before E

Arithmetic Expressions

An **expression** is a combination of constants, variables, and operators, which can be reduced to a single value. The reduction of an expression to a single value is termed **evaluating** the expression. Fortran has five arithmetic operators, most of which you already know:

+	addition
−	subtraction
/	division
*	multiplication
**	exponentiation or raising to a power

The exponentiation operator is the only one you might not have used before. To raise the number 2 to the fifth power, we usually write

$$2^5$$

but in Fortran this must be expressed as

$$2 ** 5$$

The simplest expressions are single constants or variables. An expression by itself is not a statement, just as a lone noun is not an English sentence. Expressions occur as *parts* of statements; recall that the form of an assignment statement is

$$< Variable\ name > = < Expression >$$

An expression will always have one of the Fortran data types. Here we will discuss arithmetic expressions, including the data types **INTEGER** and **REAL**. Much of this arithmetic will be familiar to you, but you may have to make a few adjustments.

We have already seen that division is a major difference in real and integer arithmetic. Most of the other operations on real numbers and integers give comparable results. In integers, 3 + 4 = 7, and 5 * 6 = 30. For reals, 3.0 + 4.0 = 7.0, and 5.0 * 6.0 = 30.0. Except for the decimal point required on real numbers, everything looks the same. Results for subtraction would be the same as well. We will discuss some differences involving exponentiation later.

Many of the expressions used in programs will have quite obvious meanings. Here are some examples.

Expression	Meaning
BASE * HEIGHT	Multiply values of BASE and HEIGHT.
MASS / VOLUME	Divide value of MASS by value of VOLUME.
RADIUS ** 2	Square the value of RADIUS.
VALUE + GAIN	Add the values of VALUE and GAIN.
WEIGHT − LOSS	Subtract the value of LOSS from the value of WEIGHT.

Even a fairly simple expression such as 12 / 6 * 2 can cause problems, however. If the division is performed first, the expression is equivalent to 2 * 2, or 4. If the multiplication is performed first, the expression reduces to 12 / 12, or 1. Fortran has a built-in set of rules called **precedence rules** that resolve such ambiguities.

Precedence

Each arithmetic operator has an associated **precedence order**, from first to third. When an expression contains more than one operator, the computer will first perform all operations of first precedence, then all operations of second precedence, and finally all operations of third precedence.

When two or more exponentiation operators appear, they are evaluated from right to left. That is, 2 ** 2 ** 3 means the same as 2 ** 8, or 256. Otherwise, when two or more operators of equal precedence appear, the computer evaluates them from left to right. The operators with precedence orders and directions are shown here.

Precedence of the Arithmetic Operators

Operator	Precedence	Direction
**	First	Right to left
* and /	Second	Left to right
+ and −	Third	Left to right

Since * and / have equal precedence, and are evaluated from left to right, the computer evaluates 12 / 6 * 2 as 2 * 2, or 4. Similarly, 5 – 3 + 4 is treated as 2 + 4, or 6. Figure 3.2 has three more complicated examples showing the order in which the computer performs operations.

FIGURE 3.2
Evaluation order for some arithmetic expressions

Expression	Step	Expression reduces to
a. 6 + 5 * 2 – 8 / 4	1	6 + 10 – 8 / 4
	2	6 + 10 – 2
	3	16 – 2
3 1 4 2	4	14
b. 4 ** 3 / 8 * 3 – 9 / 3	1	64 / 8 * 3 – 9 / 3
	2	8 * 3 – 9 / 3
	3	24 – 9 / 3
1 2 3 5 4	4	24 – 3
	5	21
c. 3 – 5 / 4 + 2 ** 2 ** 3	1	3 – 5 / 4 + 2 ** 8
	2	3 – 5 / 4 + 256
	3	3 – 1 + 256
	4	2 + 256
4 3 5 2 1	5	258

All operators in the examples in this section have been **binary operators.** That is, each operator operated on two numbers, the numbers before and after the operator. The plus and minus operators can also be **unary operators**, operating on just one number. For example, the minus sign in the expression −3 + 2 is a unary operator. Rather than indicating subtraction of 3 from a number, this minus sign applies only to the number 3, yielding the number which is the negative of 3. Unary plus signs are rarely used because we prefer the simpler 6 to +6. In either case, the unary operators take third precedence. The expression −4 ** 2 yields −16 because the exponentiation is performed first.

Parentheses

You can use **parentheses** in expressions to force a particular desired order of evaluation. If parentheses enclose part of an expression, the computer evaluates that part first. Thus, the computer evaluates

$$12 / (6 * 2)$$

as 12 / 12, or 1. Also,

$$(-4) ** 2$$

will be 16. In other words, parentheses take first precedence before the arithmetic operators.

Parentheses are often necessary to indicate multiplication or division of several operands by one operand, as in

$$(6.5 + 3.2 - 4.8) / 2.5$$

Without parentheses, as in

$$6.5 + 3.2 - 4.8 / 2.5$$

only the third operand, 4.8, is divided by 2.5.

The computer evaluates expressions *within* parentheses according to the usual precedence order.

When you **nest** parentheses (place parentheses inside other parentheses), the computer evaluates the expression inside the innermost parentheses first. For example, in the expression

$$((4.8 + 6.4) ** 5.6) / 8.4$$

the innermost parentheses are those enclosing 4.8 + 6.4, so the computer performs that addition first. If more than one set of parentheses is innermost, the computer evaluates them from left to right. In the expression

$$((4.8 + 6.4) ** (5.6 - 2.8)) / 8.4$$

the computer evaluates (4.8 + 6.4) before (5.6 - 2.8).

You should be able to tell how the computer will evaluate complicated Fortran expressions; however, when writing expressions, try to keep them as simple as possible. Use parentheses to make expressions clearer. Nonessential parentheses will not affect the way the computer evaluates an expression. Finally, be sure that parentheses pair up. Unpaired parentheses in an expression cause a very common syntax error.

Overflow and Underflow

A numeric value too large to be stored causes an **overflow error**. The precise meaning of too large depends on the computer involved. For example, an IBM 370 can store real numbers up to about 10^{76}, while a VAX can store real numbers up to roughly 10^{38}. Most computers cannot store the integer 10 ** 20 or the real number 1.0E100. Attempts to calculate such large numbers in a program can cause errors fatal to your program. Some compilers do not report integer overflows. It would be better if they did, because an error message is easier to deal with than an erroneous result.

A similar situation, **underflow**, occurs with a number too small to be stored. The real value 10.0 ** (-100) in a program would cause an error with most versions of Fortran. However, many versions simply evaluate the expression 10.0 ** (-100) as zero. This may not be a serious problem because 10.0 ** (-100) *is* very close to zero, but at times it will do serious harm.

Mode Mixing

In arithmetic expressions, the safest practice is to use only numbers and variables of the same type; use all REALs or all INTEGERs. When an arithmetic operation is performed on two numbers of the same type, the result is a number of that type.

Mixing different data types in an expression is called **mixing modes**, and the resulting expression is a **mixed-mode expression**. For now, we consider only mixed-mode operations involving a real number and an integer. The Fortran rule for handling a mixed-mode operation is to convert the integer to a real number, then perform real arithmetic. In an expression such as 8.4 / 2, the integer 2 is first converted to the real number 2.0; then real division yields 8.4 / 2.0 = 4.2.

The one exception to this rule is raising a real number to an integer power. We do not call 7.9 ** 3 a mixed-mode expression because Fortran treats this expression as if it were 7.9 * 7.9 * 7.9.

Suppose you have a real value for the diameter (DIAM) of a circle, and you want to calculate the radius (RADIUS). If you try

```
RADIUS = (1 / 2) * DIAM
```

the value of radius will be zero no matter what the value of DIAM, because integer arithmetic assigns 1 / 2 the value zero. One way to assign the correct value to RADIUS is

```
RADIUS = (1.0 / 2.0) * DIAM
```

but a simpler correct assignment is

```
RADIUS = DIAM / 2.0
```

If you forgetfully write 2 instead of 2.0 in this last statement, you have a mixed-mode expression, but the result will still be correct. Rewrite formulas to simplify the Fortran code when necessary. Be sure the Fortran code means the same as the formula.

Here are two additional examples involving mixed-mode expressions.

Expression	Result
6.2 + 10 / 4	10 / 4 is evaluated first. It is an integer division, yielding 2 (integer). The expression 6.2 + 2 is mixed-mode, so 2 is converted to 2.0, and the result is 8.4.
6.3 * 10 / 4	6.3 * 10 is evaluated first. It is a mixed-mode multiplication, so 10 is converted to 10.0 and the result is 63.0. Then 63.0 / 4 is mixed-mode so 4 is converted to 4.0, and 63.0/4.0 is 15.75.

Notice that the presence of one real number in the example expressions makes the type of the entire expression REAL. However, in evaluating the expressions, one must check operations one at a time to see when conversions occur. The operation 10 / 4 yields the integer 2 in the first expression, because it is the first operation performed. The operation 10 / 4 seems to be in the second expression too, but it is not; the computer evaluates 6.3 * 10 first.

We noted above that a real number raised to an integer power, such as 8.0 ** 3, is not a mixed-mode expression; it really means to multiply three values of 8.0: 8.0 * 8.0 * 8.0. In contrast, Fortran evaluates 8.0 ** 3.0 by using logarithms. When you have such a choice, use the integer power because it can give a more precise result.

We can raise any real number or integer to any *integer* power, with one exception: zero cannot be raised to a negative power because that would be equivalent to division by zero. A number with a *real* exponent must be positive because Fortran evaluates expressions such as X ** 3.5 using the logarithm of X, and logarithms are defined only for positive numbers. Here are some examples involving exponentiation. Results are from a VAX computer, and may differ from the results on your computer.

Expression	Result	Comment
8.2 ** 3	551.3680	Not mixed-mode. Same as 8.2 * 8.2 * 8.2.
8.2 ** 3.0	551.3679	Differs from result above because logs are used instead of multiplication.
3 ** (-2.0)	0.1111111	Mixed-mode: 3 is converted to 3.0.
4 ** 0.5	2.000000	Mixed-mode: 4 is converted to 4.0.
(-4) ** 2.5	ERROR	Negative number raised to real power.
0.0 ** (-2)	ERROR	Zero raised to negative power.

Assignment statements, too, will be mixed-mode statements when the data type of the variable on the left is not the same as the data type of the expression on the right. If TOTAL is a REAL variable, then TOTAL = 12 is a mixed-mode statement. In such cases, the computer converts the number on the right to the same data type as the variable on the left; 12 is converted to 12.0 and stored in TOTAL.

If LARGE is an INTEGER variable, then LARGE = 12.9 / 6.7 is a mixed-mode statement. Fortran uses real arithmetic to determine the quotient 12.9 / 6.7, which is roughly 1.92537, then converts this number to an integer. The conversion truncates digits after the decimal point and stores the integer 1 in LARGE.

Mixing modes is obviously not illegal, but it can be dangerous. Avoid mixed modes when you can reasonably do so. If you do mix modes, be aware of what can happen, and write comments to let readers of the program know why mixed modes occur.

CHARACTER **Constants and Variables**

A CHARACTER **constant** is a sequence of characters enclosed in apostrophes. The apostrophes themselves serve to delimit the constant and are not part of the constant. We used several CHARACTER constants in the last chapter, including 'Length of Room?', 'Width of Room?', and 'Area is'. We often call CHARACTER constants and variables **string** constants and variables, or just strings.

You *must* declare CHARACTER variables; Fortran assumes that undeclared variables in a program have type REAL or INTEGER. Each CHARACTER variable must have a declared **length**. Length of a CHARACTER variable actually means the length of the constants which that variable can hold. Each character requires one byte of storage, so we can consider the length of a CHARACTER constant to be either the number of characters in the constant or the number of bytes needed to store the constant. Remember that the enclosing apostrophes are not part of the constant; 'Area is' has length seven, including the space between the words.

To declare NAME to be a CHARACTER variable with length 20, use either of the following type declaration statements.

```
CHARACTER*20  NAME
CHARACTER  NAME*20
```

That is, you can append the length of the variable to the variable name or to the word CHARACTER.

When several CHARACTER variables with the same length appear in a type declaration statement, it is easiest to write, for example,

```
CHARACTER*20   NAME, CLASS, ADDRESS
```

although

```
CHARACTER  NAME*20, CLASS*20, ADDRESS*20
```

is also valid. Either type declaration sets aside 20 bytes of storage for each of the `CHARACTER` variables `NAME`, `CLASS`, and `ADDRESS`.

If both the word `CHARACTER` and a variable name have appended lengths, then the length on the variable name overrides the length on the word `CHARACTER`. Thus, the statement

```
CHARACTER*20   NAME, CLASS*9, ADDRESS
```

gives length 20 to `NAME` and `ADDRESS`, but length 9 to `CLASS`.

Finally, if a `CHARACTER` type declaration statement does not specify a length, the length is assumed to be 1. That is,

```
CHARACTER   STATE
```

assigns a length of one to the variable `STATE`.

We can assign values to `CHARACTER` variables in the same way we give values to `REAL` or `INTEGER` variables, with assignment, `READ`, and type declaration statements, among others. For example, a `CHARACTER` variable named `QUERY` with a declared length of 15 could be given the constant value `'Length of room?'` by an assignment statement such as

```
QUERY = 'Length of room?'
```

which Fortran stores as

```
QUERY  ─────────▸ Length of room?
```

We do not always know beforehand how long an answer to a question will be. A variable such as `NAME` often stores one or more names given by the user of the program. The length declared for `NAME` should be long enough to hold the longest name expected. Suppose `NAME` has length 20. If `NAME` takes the constant value `'JANE JONES'`, then Fortran actually stores

where the □ denotes a blank, or space. On the other hand, if the constant 'Arnold Schwarzenegger' is assigned to NAME, then it will be stored as

NAME ⟶ | Arnold Schwarzennegge |

Arnold's name is one character too long, so Fortran drops the last character. In either case, the length of NAME is 20; the length of a CHARACTER variable always remains as it was declared. The rules for these two cases are the following:

1. If the length of a string constant assigned to a CHARACTER variable is *less* than the declared length of the variable, Fortran adds blanks to the right of the constant until the declared length is reached. The string constant is said to be stored **left-justified**; 'JANE JONES' (above) is stored, left-justified, in a field of 20 characters.
2. If the length of the string constant is *more* than the length of the variable, Fortran deletes characters from the right end of the constant until the declared length is reached. This process is called **right-truncation**. The string constant 'Arnold Schwarzenegger' is right-truncated; it loses one character from the right end of the constant.

If an apostrophe is intended to be part of a CHARACTER constant, it must appear as two adjacent apostrophes (not to be confused with a double quote mark). Thus, if DEMAND is a CHARACTER variable with length 14, the assignment statement

```
DEMAND = 'Don''t do that!'
```

stores the contents of DEMAND as

DEMAND ⟶ | Don't do that! |

When responding to the list-directed READ statement, be sure to enclose your answer in apostrophes. If a program segment is

```
PRINT *, 'What is your name?'
READ  *, NAME
```

then in response to the question

```
What is your name?
```

type your name in apostrophes, as

`'MARY CONTRARY'`<Return>

If you forget to type the apostrophes, the program will crash (come to a halt because of a run-time error).

Program 3.1 illustrates the use of CHARACTER constants and variables. It asks for the user's name and prints a message.

■

PROGRAM 3.1

```
      PROGRAM CHAR1
*----------------------------------------------------------*
*     Illustrate use of CHARACTER constant and variables.  *
*----------------------------------------------------------*
      CHARACTER*20  NAME

      PRINT *, 'What''s your name (inside apostrophes)?'
      READ  *,  NAME

      PRINT *, 'Hi there, ', NAME
      PRINT *, 'Hope you like Fortran'

      END
```

When the program runs, the computer types

`What's your name (inside apostrophes)?`

If you then respond

`'Mary'`

the computer will type

```
Hi there, Mary
Hope you like Fortran
```

Be sure to use the apostrophes, or an error message will appear and your program will crash.

A Simple Formatted READ Statement

When responding to a list-directed READ statement, you might be annoyed by those apostrophes required around character constants. Every time you forget them, the program crashes. **A formatted** READ **statement** does away with this requirement.

The simplest formatted READ statement has the form

READ <*Label*>, <*Variable Name*>

where Label is an integer from 1 to 99999 placed in the first 5 columns of a FORMAT statement. The FORMAT statement itself looks like

<*Label*> FORMAT (<*Descriptor(s)*>)

The **format specification** consists of everything following the word FORMAT. In particular, the specification must have a **data descriptor**, which specifies how the value of the variable is to be read. Each data type in Fortran has one or more data descriptors. For now, we discuss only the **A data descriptor** for character values.

The A (for alphanumeric) descriptor tells Fortran to interpret and store the values being read as CHARACTER data, not as any other data type (such as INTEGER or REAL).

Suppose the variable NAME has been declared as CHARACTER*15, and the following lines occur later in the program.

```
      READ 10, NAME
10    FORMAT ( A )
```

If the user responds to the READ statement with

Andrew Johnson< Return >

the information is stored as

NAME ⟶

The main point is that apostrophes are *not* used in character constants given in response to formatted READ statements. Notice also that the response 'Andrew Johnson' contains only 14 characters, so it is left-justified and padded with a blank at the right end before storage.

Be careful to begin a character constant in column 1. If the response is

□□Andrew Johnson< Return >

the information is stored as

NAME ⟶

It can also happen that the name given in response to the READ statement is too long to be stored in NAME. Then, as before, NAME holds only the first 15 characters. Suppose, for example, the response to the READ statement is

Engelbert Humperdinck< Return >

This response is stored, right-truncated, as

NAME ⟶

3.5 SOME NUMERIC FUNCTIONS

Up to now we have used only the five arithmetic operators to build expressions. Fortran supplies many other operations in a library of **intrinsic functions**, also called **library functions** or **built-in functions**. Each of these functions is actually a program, permanently stored and available to all users of Fortran. Furthermore, you can define your own function with a statement in a program or a separate program unit called a function subprogram. In this section we will discuss some numeric library functions. Section 3.6 deals with numeric statement functions. Function subprograms are covered in Chapter 10.

Mathematically, a function is a rule, or procedure, for calculating a result from one or more input items called **arguments**. Note the singular in *a result*; a function always calculates *one* value. In mathematics, we usually designate a function by a single letter followed by an argument list in parentheses: $f(x)$ refers to a function called f which takes one argument; $g(x, y, z)$ refers to a function named g which takes three arguments.

Mathematical functions are usually defined with an equal sign followed by an expression, or formula, such as

$$f(x) = 6x - 5$$

or

$$g(x, y, z) = xy + z$$

The arguments given inside parentheses are known as *dummy arguments*. They are place holders for *actual arguments*, which are any legitimate values the function can operate on. To find the value of $f(2)$, replace the dummy argument x in the function definition by the actual argument 2:

$$f(2) = 6(2) - 5 = 7$$

Similarly,

$$g(1, 2, 3) = 1(2) + 3 = 5$$

Fortran function names obey the rules for variable names. Most intrinsic functions have 3-character names, such as ABS, INT, and MAX. These function names are always followed by an argument list in parentheses. Many functions take a single argument, but some can have several arguments.

To use a library function, you do not need to know how it does its calculations, but you must know some specific information about it:

1. The name of the function
2. The number of arguments and their data types
3. The type of value the function calculates or returns
4. What the function does

One intrinsic function named INT takes one real argument and returns the integer part of that argument, so INT(7.9), for example, returns the integer 7. Thus, we know:

1. The name of the function is INT.
2. The function INT takes one real argument.
3. The function INT returns an integer value.
4. The function calculates the integer part of its argument, or chops off the decimal part.

We call using an intrinsic Fortran function **invoking** the function. You invoke functions by using them in expressions as you would use a constant or variable. You can invoke the function named INT in many ways, among them:

```
COST = INT(X)
YEAR = 6 + INT( X**2 - Y**2 ) / 3
PRINT *, 'Rounded answer is', INT(ANSWER)
```

The second example is the most complicated, so let us study it to see what the computer does. Assume that YEAR is INTEGER and X and Y are REAL.

Operation	Effect on the Statement YEAR = 6 + INT(X**2 - Y**2)/3
Value A1 is calculated for X**2 - Y**2.	YEAR = 6 + INT(A1) / 3
Function INT is called with argument A1, and returns a value A2.	YEAR = 6 + A2 / 3
A2 is divided by 3 to obtain A3.	YEAR = 6 + A3
A3 is added to 6 to obtain the value A4 assigned to YEAR.	YEAR = A4

Specifically, if X is 4.5 and Y is 3.1, the computer calculates

$$X**2 - Y**2 = 20.25 - 9.61 = 10.64$$

Then it evaluates the expression

$$YEAR = 6 + INT(X**2 - Y**2)/3$$

as

$$YEAR = 6 + INT(10.64)/3 = 6 + 10 / 3 = 6 + 3 = 9$$

> **Warning!** Do not try to assign a value to a built-in function. Statements such as INT(X) = (*anything*) have no meaning and will cause an error.

Functions in Fortran have both generic names applicable to any type of argument and type of result, and specific names used for one specific combination of argument type and result type. We discuss here only the generic names.

The ABS **Function**

The ABS function calculates the absolute value of a number. It takes a single argument. If the argument is REAL or INTEGER, the function value has the same type as the argument.

Absolute value of a number x is usually defined as:

x, if x is greater than or equal to 0

$-x$, if x is less than 0

Thus, ABS(2.7) is 2.7, while ABS(-42) is -(-42) = 42. A simpler way to put it: take away the minus sign, if there is one; otherwise leave the argument as it is.

We often use absolute values when a distance between numbers is calculated; the distance is usually given as a positive number. To calculate the distance between two values, in variables X and Y, we can use the statement, DISTXY = ABS(X - Y). If the value of X happens to be less than the value of Y, DISTXY will still be positive. Program 3.2 illustrates the use of the ABS function.

■
PROGRAM 3.2

```
      PROGRAM ABSFUN
*------------------------------------------------------------------*
*                Illustration of ABS function.                     *
*------------------------------------------------------------------*
      REAL    X, Y
      INTEGER I, J
*------------------------------------------------------------------*
*                ABS of a real argument is real.                   *
*------------------------------------------------------------------*
      X =  2.7
      Y = -4.2
      PRINT *, 'Absolute value of', X, ' is', ABS(X)
      PRINT *, 'Absolute value of', Y, ' is', ABS(Y)
      PRINT *, 'Distance from    ', X, ' to', Y, ' is', ABS(X-Y)

      PRINT *
*------------------------------------------------------------------*
*                ABS of an integer argument is integer.            *
*------------------------------------------------------------------*
      I = -7
      J = 12
```

```
PRINT *, 'Absolute value of', I, ' is', ABS(I)
PRINT *, 'Absolute value of', J, ' is', ABS(J)
PRINT *, 'Distance from   ', I, ' to', J, ' is', ABS(I-J)

END
```

When this program is run, the output will be:

```
Absolute value of   2.700000   is   2.700000
Absolute value of  -4.200000   is   4.200000
Distance from       2.700000   to -4.200000      is   6.900000

Absolute value of            -7 is           7
Absolute value of            12 is          12
Distance from                -7 to          12 is          19
```

Notice the spaces after the word "from" in 'Distance from   '. These spaces line up the output. Also note the blank PRINT statement, which causes the computer to insert a blank line in the output.

The SQRT **Function**

The square root function, SQRT, takes a single real argument and returns a real number whose square is the given argument. Therefore, the argument must not be negative. The square root of X is designated by SQRT(X). Theoretically, X ** 0.5 gives the same result, but the algorithms Fortran uses to calculate SQRT(X) and X ** 0.5 are usually different; when their results differ, SQRT should be more precise.

We have said that Fortran allows an integer almost anywhere it would permit a real value. Here is an exception. An integer argument for the SQRT function causes a fatal error.

Program 3.3 is a simple program that uses the SQRT function to calculate the hypotenuse of a right triangle. Using BASE, HEIGHT, and HYPOT for the three sides, the Pythagorean theorem states

$$HYPOT^2 = BASE^2 + HEIGHT^2$$

so the value of the hypotenuse is the square root of $BASE^2 + HEIGHT^2$.

■

PROGRAM 3.3
_____

```
      PROGRAM SQRTFN
*-------------------------------------------------------*
*          Calculate the hypotenuse of a right triangle.      *
*-------------------------------------------------------*
      REAL  BASE, HEIGHT, HYPOT

      BASE   = 5.0
      HEIGHT = 12.0
      HYPOT  = SQRT(BASE ** 2 + HEIGHT ** 2)

      PRINT *, 'Base is      ', BASE
      PRINT *, 'Height is    ', HEIGHT
      PRINT *, 'Hypotenuse is', HYPOT

      END
```
_____

The output from this program is:

```
Base is        5.000000
Height is      12.00000
Hypotenuse is  13.00000
```

Again, notice that the extra spaces in two of the last three PRINT statements make the ouput line up nicely.

The MAX and MIN Functions

The MAX and MIN functions can take any number of arguments from two up to 256. If all the arguments are integers, each function returns an integer. If some or all of the arguments are real, MAX or MIN will return a real number. As the names imply, MAX gives the maximum value, and MIN gives the minimum value, of the arguments. That is,

```
MAX(2, 7, 4, 3, 5)      is 7
MAX(2.7, -9.2, 3.4)     is 3.4
MIN(3, -5, 2, 1000)     is -5
MIN(2.7, 2.69)          is 2.69
```

Program 3.4 uses MAX and MIN to calculate the largest and smallest of three input values.

■
PROGRAM 3.4

```
      PROGRAM MAXMIN
*---------------------------------------------------------*
*     Calculate the largest and smallest of three numbers.  *
*---------------------------------------------------------*
      REAL  A, B, C

      PRINT *, 'Enter three numbers in any order.'
      PRINT *, 'The largest and smallest will be calculated.'
      READ *, A, B, C

      PRINT *, 'The largest is ', MAX(A, B, C)
      PRINT *, 'The smallest is', MIN(A, B, C)

      END
```

The MOD Function

The MOD function takes two integer arguments and returns the (integer) remainder when the first argument is divided by the second. For instance, MOD(17, 5) is 2 because the remainder in division of 17 by 5 is 2.

See Program 3.5 for an illustration of the MOD function.

■
PROGRAM 3.5

```
      PROGRAM MODFUN
*---------------------------------------------------------*
*         Finding a remainder with the MOD function.        *
*---------------------------------------------------------*
      INTEGER  FIRST, SECOND

      PRINT *, 'Enter two integers, separated by a comma.'
      READ *, FIRST, SECOND
      PRINT *, 'The remainder when', FIRST, ' is divided by'
      PRINT *, SECOND, ' is', MOD(FIRST, SECOND)

      END
```

The INT, NINT, and IFIX Functions

The functions INT, NINT, and IFIX all convert real numbers to integers, usually to avoid mixed-mode expressions. Each takes one real argument and returns an integer. INT and IFIX give identical results for positive arguments, but might differ for negative arguments. We will use the more modern INT in this text.

INT truncates the decimal part of a real number. Thus, INT(6.9) is 6 and INT(-7.1) is -7.

The NINT function is called the **nearest integer function**. Like INT, it takes a real argument and returns an integer, the nearest integer to the argument. Thus, NINT(8.9) is 9, while INT(8.9) is 8. When the fractional part of the argument is exactly .5, the NINT function gives the value farther away from zero: NINT(6.5) is 7, and NINT(-2.5) is -3. Think of NINT as rounding *up* the absolute value of the number when the fractional part is exactly .5.

Program 3.6 illustrates the INT, NINT, and IFIX functions.

■
PROGRAM 3.6

```
      PROGRAM INIFUN
*-------------------------------------------------------------------*
*                 Illustrate INT, NINT, and IFIX.                   *
*-------------------------------------------------------------------*
      REAL  X

      PRINT *, '  X Value            INT(X)    NINT(X)    IFIX(X)'

      X = 2.99
      PRINT *, X, INT(X), NINT(X), IFIX(X)

      X = -3.02
      PRINT *, X, INT(X), NINT(X), IFIX(X)

      X = 1.5
      PRINT *, X, INT(X), NINT(X), IFIX(X)

      X = -1.5
      PRINT *, X, INT(X), NINT(X), IFIX(X)

      END
```

The output from this program is:

X Value	INT(X)	NINT(X)	IFIX(X)
2.990000	2	3	2
-3.020000	-3	-3	-3
1.500000	1	2	1
-1.500000	-1	-2	-1

The REAL and FLOAT Functions

REAL and FLOAT convert integers to real numbers. Each takes a single integer argument and returns a real number. These two functions give identical results. REAL is the more modern of the two, so we will use it in the remainder of the text. For an integer variable I, REAL(I) *gives* I *a decimal point*. For instance, REAL(6) is 6.0.

We usually use the REAL function to avoid mixed-mode expressions. For example, if SUM is a REAL variable and NUMBER is an INTEGER, then we write

        MEAN = SUM / REAL(NUMBER)

to avoid a mixed-mode division.

The rest of the intrinsic functions in this chapter are the logarithmic, exponential, trigonometric, and inverse trigonometric functions. The reader should be familiar with these functions before continuing. Readers who already know these functions will find the following presentations quite simple.

The LOG and LOG10 Functions

The LOG and LOG10 functions each take a single real argument and return a real number. LOG gives the *natural logarithm* of the argument, or the logarithm of the argument to the base *e*. The constant *e* is a very special number in mathematics, approximately equal to 2.71828. The LOG10 function gives the *common logarithm* of the argument, or the logarithm to the base 10.0. Thus, the value of LOG10(1000.0) is 3.0, because 10.0 ** 3.0 is 1000.0. Arguments for LOG and LOG10 must be *positive*.

While *e* and 10 are the most common bases for logarithms, any positive number other than 1.0 can be a base for a logarithm. To calculate the logarithm of 12 to the base 2, use

        LOG(12.0) / LOG(2.0)

For any positive base B not equal to 1.0, the logarithm of the number X to the base B is given by

        LOG(X) / LOG(B)

The EXP **Function**

EXP(X) stands for e^X, or the number e raised to the X power. The argument should be real, but an integer argument will be converted to its real equivalent; EXP(3) is treated as EXP(3.0). The value returned is real. If the value of e itself is needed, use EXP(1.0). The argument for EXP can be positive, negative, or zero.

An argument too large for EXP (approximately 88.0 on a VAX and 176.0 on an IBM 370) will cause an overflow error. Also, with too small an argument (about −88.0 on a VAX and −176.0 on an IBM 370), EXP will return a value of zero. This underflow is usually not an error condition in the computer, but may be considered an error by the user of the program.

The SIN, COS, **and** TAN **Functions**

The functions SIN, COS, and TAN represent the *trigonometric functions* sine, cosine, and tangent respectively. Each of these functions takes a single real argument and returns a real result. There are no intrinsic functions for cotangent, secant, and cosecant, but these functions are easily calculated from SIN, COS, and TAN:

Function	Fortran Equivalent
Cotangent(X)	1.0 / TAN(X)
Secant(X)	1.0 / COS(X)
Cosecant(X)	1.0 / SIN(X)

Argument values for the trigonometric functions are given in radians, with π radians equal to 180 degrees. Thus, to calculate the sine of X degrees, use SIN(X * PI / 180.0), where PI = 3.141593.

Program 3.7 calculates the six trigonometric functions for a given input angle.

■

PROGRAM 3.7

```
      PROGRAM TRIGFN
*-------------------------------------------------------------------*
*  Calculate the trigonometric functions of an angle in degrees.  *
*-------------------------------------------------------------------*
      REAL RADIAN, DEGREE, PI
      PARAMETER  (PI = 3.141593)
```

```
PRINT *, 'Enter an angle in degrees.  The computer prints'
PRINT *, 'the values of the trig functions of that angle.'
READ  *, DEGREE

RADIAN = DEGREE * PI / 180.0
PRINT *, 'Angle', DEGREE, ' degrees is', RADIAN, ' radians.'
PRINT *

PRINT *, 'SINE:       ', SIN(RADIAN)
PRINT *, 'COSINE:     ', COS(RADIAN)
PRINT *, 'TANGENT:    ', TAN(RADIAN)
PRINT *, 'COTANGENT: ', 1.0 / TAN(RADIAN)
PRINT *, 'SECANT:     ', 1.0 / COS(RADIAN)
PRINT *, 'COSECANT:  ', 1.0 / SIN(RADIAN)

END
```

If you enter 90.0 when the computer prompts for an angle in degrees, the output of the program (on a VAX) will be:

```
Angle   90.00000     degrees is   1.570796     radians.

SINE:          1.000000
COSINE:       -1.6292068E-07
TANGENT:      -6137956.
COTANGENT:    -1.6292068E-07
SECANT:       -6137956.
COSECANT:      1.000000
```

Notice that the computer has some problems calculating the values. Only sine and cosecant are correct! Cosine and cotangent should be zero, and tangent and secant should be undefined.

For the cosine and cotangent, the problem here is simply that we cannot specify an exact value for PI. Thus, the value for RADIAN will be slightly imprecise, making the value for COS(RADIAN) also off a little. (−1.6292068E-07 *is* fairly close to 0.) These problems occur for any multiple of 90 degrees. If your angle is not close to a such a multiple, the computer's calculations should agree with results given in tables.

Even if we could define PI precisely, however, you should not ask the computer to calculate the tangent or cotangent of 90 degrees, because that calculation is equivalent to calculating a division by zero.

The ASIN, ACOS, ATAN, and ATAN2 **Functions**

The functions ASIN, ACOS, and ATAN represent the *inverse trigonometric functions* Arcsine, Arccosine, and Arctangent respectively. Each takes a single real argument and returns a real result. ASIN(X) gives the value in radians of the angle between $-\dfrac{\pi}{2}$ and $\dfrac{\pi}{2}$ that has sine value X. ASIN(1.0) would be $\dfrac{\pi}{2}$, equivalent to 90 degrees.

ACOS(X) gives the value of the angle between zero and π that has cosine value X. ATAN(X) gives the value of the angle between $-\dfrac{\pi}{2}$ and $\dfrac{\pi}{2}$ that has tangent value X.

Although all values returned by the inverse trigonometric functions are in radians, these values are easily converted to degrees with multiplication by 180.0 / π. That is, Arccosine(X) in degrees is given by ACOS(X) * 180.0 / PI.

Unlike the three previous functions, ATAN2 takes *two* real arguments. ATAN2 generally returns the arctangent of the first argument divided by the second argument. When the second argument is zero, ATAN2 returns the value 0.0. ATAN2 makes use of the sign of both its arguments and returns an angle between $-\pi$ and π. See the following table for the difference between ATAN and ATAN2.

Y	X	ATAN(Y/X)	ATAN2(Y, X)
1.0	1.0	0.7853982	0.7853982
1.0	-1.0	0.7853982	-2.356194
-1.0	1.0	-0.7853982	2.356194
-1.0	-1.0	-0.7853982	-0.7853982

The other inverse trigonometric functions (Arccotangent, Arcsecant, and Arccosecant) are not in the function library but can be calculated as follows.

Function	Fortran Equivalent
Arccotangent(X)	ATAN(1.0 / X)
Arcsecant(X)	ACOS(1.0 / X)
Arccosecant(X)	ASIN(1.0 / X)

■
3.6 STATEMENT FUNCTIONS

The Fortran intrinsic functions are very useful in a wide variety of situations, but there always comes a time when a programmer needs a function that is not provided in the Fortran library. Fortran allows the user to define two types of functions, **statement functions** and **function subprograms**. This section deals with the simpler statement functions, whose purpose is to remove complicated calculations from the body of a program. Statement functions are defined by a single statement in a program and are invoked the same way intrinsic functions are invoked.

It frequently seems necessary to use a rather complicated expression several times in a program. Consider a program to calculate the value of the polynomial

$$7x^4 + 5x^3 - 3x^2 + 4x - 6$$

for four separate values of x: two input values and the sum and product of these values. The program could look like this:

```
PROGRAM BADPOL
REAL  X1, X2

PRINT *, 'Enter two real numbers to be '
PRINT *, 'substituted for x in the polynomial'
PRINT *, ' 4     3     2'
PRINT *, '7x  + 5x  - 3x  + 4x - 6'
PRINT *, 'The sum and difference of those values'
PRINT *, 'will also be substituted in the polynomial.'

READ  *, X1, X2

PRINT *, '   X VALUE     POLYNOMIAL VALUE'
PRINT *, X1, 7.0 * X1**4 + 5.0 * X1**3 - 3.0 * X1**2
1                + 4.0 * X1 - 6.0
PRINT *, X2, 7.0 * X2**4 + 5.0 * X2**3 - 3.0 * X2**2
1                + 4.0 * X2 - 6.0
PRINT *, X1 + X2, 7.0 * (X1 + X2)**4 + 5.0 * (X1 + X2)**3
1              - 3.0 * (X1 + X2)**2 + 4.0 * (X1 + X2) - 6.0
PRINT *, X1 - X2, 7.0 * (X1 - X2)**4 + 5.0 * (X1 - X2)**3
1              - 3.0 * (X1 - X2)**2 + 4.0 * (X1 - X2) - 6.0

END
```

There is not much to the program except the long and repetitious PRINT statements at the end of the program. A statement function will allow us to write the complicated expression only once instead of repeating it four times as we did here.

At the same time, we show a more efficient way to code the calculation of a polynomial. Instead of

$$7.0 * X**4 + 5.0 * X**3 - 3.0 * X**2 + 4.0 * X - 6.0$$

we can write

$$(((7.0 * X + 5.0) * X - 3.0) * X + 4.0) * X - 6.0$$

as you can easily verify by multiplying out the latter expression. The two expressions contain the same number of additions and multiplications, but the second expression contains no exponentiations. If the program must evaluate the function many times, the latter form will take considerably less time.

The Statement Function Definition

A **statement function definition** begins with the name of the function followed by an argument list in parentheses. The general form is

$$<name>(<argument\ list>) = <expression>$$

The function name conforms to the same rules as variable names, and should not be the same as the name of any other entity (variable, function, and so on) in the program. Let us call the function POLY. Fortran implicitly considers POLY to be real, but in accordance with our policy of declaring variables, we declare all function names too, so we will declare POLY to be REAL.

The function POLY takes one real argument, which we denote by X. Then the statement function definition is

$$POLY(X) = (((7.0 * X + 5.0) * X - 3.0) * X + 4.0) * X - 6.0$$

This is a nonexecutable statement, placed after the type declarations and before the executable part of a program. The compiler stores this formula to be used when an executable statement refers to POLY.

Dummy and Actual Arguments

We call X a *dummy argument* because it holds a place for the actual argument which occurs in references to the function. We will declare X to be REAL, because it is a placeholder for a real value.

In our program, the actual arguments will be values of X1, X2, X1 + X2, and X1 − X2. One function invocation, with actual argument X1, will be

```
PRINT *, X1, POLY(X1)
```

At this point in the program, the computer treats POLY just as it would an intrinsic function like SQRT. The computer refers to the definition of POLY and substitutes the value of X1 at each point where the dummy argument X occurred. The result of the calculation is stored in a location named POLY.

The program with a statement function appears in Program 3.8.

■
PROGRAM 3.8

```
      PROGRAM POLYFN
*--------------------------------------------------------------*
*           Use a statement function to calculate values        *
*           of a polynomial for four values of x.               *
*--------------------------------------------------------------*
      REAL X, X1, X2, POLY
*--------------------------------------------------------------*
*                This statement defines the function POLY.      *
*--------------------------------------------------------------*
      POLY(X) = (((7.0 * X + 5.0) * X - 3.0) * X + 4.0) * X - 6.0

      PRINT *, 'Enter two real numbers to be '
      PRINT *, 'substituted for x in the polynomial'
      PRINT *, ' 4     3     2'
      PRINT *, '7x  + 5x  - 3x  + 4x - 6'
      PRINT *, 'The sum and difference of those values'
      PRINT *, 'will also be substituted in the polynomial.'

      READ *, X1, X2

      PRINT *, '   X VALUE     POLYNOMIAL VALUE'
*--------------------------------------------------------------*
*   These four statements invoke the statement function POLY.   *
*--------------------------------------------------------------*
      PRINT *, X1, POLY(X1)
      PRINT *, X2, POLY(X2)
      PRINT *, X1 + X2, POLY(X1 + X2)
      PRINT *, X1 - X2, POLY(X1 - X2)

      END
```

Notice how much cleaner the body of the program looks with the complicated expression removed. Also, we had to write the polynomial expression only once.

Dummy argument names must be legal variable names, not constants or expressions (or array names or array elements, to be discussed in Chapter 9). In contrast, actual arguments *can* be constants, expressions, or array elements. If a program contains the declarations

```
REAL  X, Y, Z
```

and the definition of POLY above, it is legal to invoke POLY with any of the following statements.

```
Y = 4.5 + 6.2 * POLY(2.3)          |  Constant
PRINT *, POLY(Y ** 2 + Z ** 2)     |  Expression
R = POLY( POLY(6.6) )              |  Function reference
```

A statement function can have several arguments. When a program invokes a function, a correspondence is set up between the actual and dummy arguments according to their positions in the argument lists. For example, if a function definition is

```
POWER(X, N) = X ** N
```

and the function is invoked with the statement

```
Z = POWER(Y ** 2, 3)
```

then the actual argument Y ** 2 corresponds to dummy argument X and the actual argument 3 corresponds to dummy argument N. Thus the function value is the value of (Y ** 2) ** 3.

This correspondence dictates the following rules:

1. There must be exactly as many actual arguments in an invoking statement as there are dummy arguments in the function definition.

2. The type of each actual argument must agree with the type of the corresponding dummy argument.

Programmers violate rule 2 much more often than rule 1. Here is a simple example.

```
    PROGRAM BADAVG
*-----------------------------------------------------*
*  Type incompatibility in a statement function.  *
*-----------------------------------------------------*
    REAL X, Y, Z, MEAN
    MEAN(M, N) = (M + N) / 2.0

    READ *, X, Y
    Z = MEAN(X, Y)
    PRINT *, Z

    END
```

If you try to compile this program, most Fortran compilers will print an error message concerning an inconsistent statement function reference and point to line 6:

```
    Z = MEAN(X, Y)
```

The dummy arguments M and N are not declared, so they have type INTEGER by the implicit typing rules. But X and Y are declared REAL, so the types of the actual arguments do not match the types of the dummy arguments.

Be sure to declare *function names* too. Fortran will assume a type for undeclared function names just as it does for undeclared variable names. The function defined by

```
    NUMBER(X, Y, Z) = X * Y / Z
```

will return an integer value unless NUMBER is declared REAL.

Some Possible Name Confusions

Fortran will not allow two entities (programs, variables, functions) to have the same names in a program. The one exception to this rule is that dummy arguments *may* have the same names as other entities. To avoid confusion, give dummy arguments names that are not used for anything else.

For example, it is legal to call a dummy variable by a function name, as in

```
    COST(X, COST) = X * COST
```

The computer is not confused by two different entities having the same name, COST, because one of these is a dummy variable. A reader of the program could well be puzzled. However, a later statement such as

```
COST = 2.98
```

will cause an error because the compiler has catalogued COST as a function name.

A dummy argument name can also be the name of a variable in the program. That is, the first two lines of the program could have been

```
REAL  X, Y, Z, POLY
POLY(X) = (((7.0 * X + 5.0) * X - 3.0) * X  + 4.0) * X - 6.0
```

Later on, the program could contain the lines

```
READ *, Z
X = POLY(Z)
```

The computer considers this variable name X to be entirely distinct from the dummy argument X in the function definition. However, the human programmer or reader *could* be confused, so avoid using the same names for dummy arguments and program variables.

Fortran also allows the name of a statement function to be the same as the name of a library function, but this is also bad practice. The polynomial function above could have been defined as

```
SIN(X) =  (((7.0 * X + 5.0) * X - 3.0) * X  + 4.0) * X - 6.0
```

The compiler treats a later reference to SIN as a reference to this function, not the library SIN function. It could confuse readers of the program to see SIN used this way, so avoid doing it.

Program Variables in Statement Functions

Program variables can be used in the expression in the function definition. Program 3.9 contains a variable EXPONT used as part of a function definition.

■
PROGRAM 3.9

```
      PROGRAM POWER2
*----------------------------------------------------------------*
*         Illustrate program variable in statement function.     *
*----------------------------------------------------------------*
      INTEGER  NUMBER, EXPONT, POWER
      POWER(NUMBER) = NUMBER ** EXPONT

      PRINT *, 'What positive integer power of 2 would you like?'
      READ  *, EXPONT

      PRINT *, '2 to the', EXPONT, ' power is', POWER(2)

      END
```

We reiterate that a constant can be used as an *actual* argument for a function, but *not* as a *dummy* argument in the definition.

Using Function Names in Statement Functions

Function definitions can contain library functions. For example, the midrange of a set of numbers is defined to be the mean of the largest and smallest numbers, so a function to compute the midrange of three numbers can be defined as

```
      MIDRAN(X, Y, Z) = ( MAX(X, Y, Z) + MIN(X, Y, Z) ) / 2.0
```

One statement function definition can refer to another, as long as the other function was previously defined, as in the following statements.

```
      F(X, Y) = X ** Y + Y ** X
      G(X, Y, Z) =  F(X, Y) ** Z
```

Figure 3.3 shows some examples of valid and invalid function definitions.

We mentioned earlier that statement functions can remove complicated expressions from the body of a program, making the program easier to read. Another reason for using statement functions is ease of replacement. If you want to replace a function in a program with another function, it is easy to find the statement function definition which occurs just once, at the top of a program.

	Definition	Comment
FIGURE 3.3 Valid and invalid statement function definitions	A(X) = 3.1416 * X**2	Valid. A(X) calculates the area of a circle of radius X.
	ZERO(X) = X − X	Valid, but useless. Always returns 0.
	F(X, 2) = 2 * X ** 2	Invalid. Constant dummy argument (2).
	F(X, X) = 3.0 * X ** X	Invalid. Two dummy arguments with the same name (X).
	COST(X) = X * COST	Invalid. The second COST is not a dummy argument, so it must be the name of a variable in the program. A variable and a function cannot have the same name.

■

3.7 SUMMARY OF CHAPTER 3

■ *Terms Introduced in This Chapter*

Actual argument	Functions	NINT
Argument	Built-in, intrinsic,	REAL
Actual	or library functions	SIN
Dummy	ABS	TAN
CHARACTER	ACOS	Invoke
Data type	ASIN	Keywords
Type declaration statement	ATAN	Label
Constants	ATAN2	Label field
CHARACTER	COS	Line continuation
INTEGER	EXP	Mode mixing
REAL	FLOAT	Overflow
Data descriptor	IFIX	Nesting of parentheses
Dummy argument	INT	in arithmetic expressions
Exponential format	LOG	Parentheses in arithmetic expressions
Exponentiation	LOG10	Precedence of arithmetic operators
Expression	MAX	Sequencing
Fixed format	MIN	Statement function
FORMAT statement	MOD	Underflow

■ *What You Should Know*

1. A Fortran line contains a label field, a continuation field (or column), and a statement field.
2. The statement field contains columns 7 through 72.
3. Any character other than 0 (zero) or space in column 6 signifies line continuation.
4. CHARACTER constants in a program must have delimiting apostrophes.
5. The Fortran compiler ignores spaces in the statement field, except for characters enclosed in apostrophes.
6. Commas must not appear in REAL or INTEGER constants.
7. Overflow usually causes a fatal error, either at compile time or at run time.
8. Many versions of Fortran assign a zero value to an expression that underflows at run time.
9. Every variable, constant, and expression in a Fortran program has a data type.
10. A numeric expression contains numeric operands and the numeric operators +, −, *, /, and **.
11. Exponentiation has highest precedence among the arithmetic operators, followed by multiplication and division, then addition and subtraction.
12. Several exponentiations in an expression are evaluated from right to left. Otherwise, operators with equal precedence are evaluated from left to right.
13. Parentheses can cause the computer to change the normal order of evaluation in expressions.
14. Parentheses also can make an expression easier to read.
15. Fortran stores integers precisely but cannot represent many real numbers exactly.
16. Mode mixing is the use of both real numbers and integers in an operation, except for raising a real number to an integer power.
17. When evaluating a mixed-mode operation, Fortran converts the integer operand to a real number.
18. If the declared length of a CHARACTER variable is longer than the length of a constant assigned to it, the computer pads the constant with blanks on the right.
19. If the declared length of a CHARACTER variable is shorter than the length of a constant assigned to it, the computer drops characters from the right end of the constant.
20. A list-directed READ statement requires apostrophes on an input CHARACTER string.
21. A formatted READ statement reads character data without requiring delimiting apostrophes.
22. The names intrinsic function, built-in function, and library function all refer to functions included as part of the Fortran language.
23. Functions can be operands in expressions.
24. Except for MAX and MIN, each function takes a specified number of arguments.

25. The SQRT function will not accept an integer argument.

26. A statement function has one of the Fortran data types.

27. The type of a statement function and the types of its arguments should be declared.

28. A statement function can reference a user-defined function as well as an intrinsic function.

■

3.8 EXERCISES

■ *Self-Test*

1. Express the following numbers in decimal notation.

    a.   0.2645E+3
    b.   612.423E–5
    c.   .000654E+6

2. Express the decimal number 123.456 in exponential notation three different ways, with exponents

    a.   E+3
    b.   E–3
    c.   E+5

3. Specify the data type for each legal constant below, and tell which items are not legitimate constants in a Fortran program.

    a.   12.6
    b.   '12.6'
    c.   "12.6"
    d.   5E12
    e.   Hello
    f.   'Why, no'
    g.   0
    h.   '12'
    i.   'Don''t'
    j.   4,300
    k.   12345

4. Which of the expressions below are mixed-mode expressions?

    a.   6 * 5 / 4
    b.   6.0 * 5.0 / 4.0
    c.   11.0 * 5 / 3

     d.   5 ** 2 – 3 / 4 + 6 * 5

     e.   8 / 4 * 2

     f.   –3 * (8 + 4 – 5 / 2) / 3.0

     g.   3 * 5E2

     h.   (6 / 4 * 2.0) ** 3 – 12.8

5. Evaluate the expressions in Problem 4. Clearly distinguish between integer and real results.

6. Assume that `LARGE`, `NUMBER`, and `I` are integer variables, `TOTAL`, `RESULT`, and `X` are real variables, and `WORD` is a character variable of length 10. In which of the assignment statements below is the expression on the right a different data type from the variable on the left?

     a.   `NUMBER = 5.0 / 4.0`

     b.   `TOTAL = 5 / 4`

     c.   `LARGE = 2.5`

     d.   `WORD = 'Isn''t that funny?'`

     e.   `I = 6 * 5 ** 2`

     f.   `RESULT = 6 / 5 * 4 – 3`

     g.   `WORD = 'Orthodox'`

     h.   `X = (13.0 + 12.0 – 5.0) / 3`

     i.   `NUMBER = 24 / 3 / 2`

     j.   `NUMBER = 24 / 3 * 2`

7. Specify the value assigned to each variable in the assignment statements in Problem 6. Differentiate between reals and integers and show spaces in character constants, but do not enclose them in apostrophes.

8. Which of the following are valid statements to invoke intrinsic functions? For those that are invalid, explain why. Assume that all variables have type `REAL`.

     a.   `Y = SIN(X * Z)`

     b.   `D = REAL(INT(7.5))`

     c.   `R = SQRT(6)`

     d.   `EXP(X ** 5)`

     e.   `REM = MOD(5, 3, 2)`

     f.   `Z = ASIN(6.4)`

     g.   `NEW = MAX(OLD)`

     h.   `PRINT *, D * EXP(D)`

9. What are the following function values? Be sure to distinguish between `REAL` and `INTEGER` types.

     a.   `ABS(–32.4)`

     b.   `MAX(3, 6.5, 8, 4)`

     c.   `SQRT(64.0)`

    d.   `MOD(19, 7)`
    e.   `INT(19.9)`
    f.   `NINT(-6.5)`
    g.   `REAL(8)`
    h.   `LOG(1)`

10. True or false

    a.   When a statement function is invoked, the actual arguments must have the same names as their corresponding dummy arguments.
    b.   Statement functions must return real or integer values.
    c.   A dummy argument for a statement function can be a constant.
    d.   A statement function and a program variable can have the same name.

11. Which of the following are valid statement function definitions? For those that are invalid, explain why.

    a.   `F(X, Y) = X ** 4 - Y ** 4`
    b.   `F(X, 2.5) = X ** 4 + 2.5 ** 4`
    c.   `DIST(RATE, TIME) = DIST`
    d.   `AVG(X, Y, Z) = (X + Y) / 2.0`

12. Explain what is wrong in each of the following program segments.

    a.
```
REAL  A, B, C, D, E
D(A, B) = A ** B
  .
  .
  .
E = D(A, B, C)
```

    b.
```
REAL     X, Y, Z
INTEGER  M, N
Z(X, M) = X ** M
  .
  .
  .
PRINT *, Z(N, Y)
```

■ *Programming Exercises*

1. Write a program that asks for a Fahrenheit temperature and converts it to a Celsius temperature. The formula for the conversion is

$$\text{Degrees Celsius} = (5/9)(\text{Degrees Fahrenheit} - 32)$$

Let all variables be REAL. Check the program with the Fahrenheit temperatures 0.0, 32.0, 72.0, 100.0, 212.0.

2. The *arithmetic mean* of four real numbers x, y, z, w is

$$\frac{x + y + z + w}{4}$$

Write a program that asks for four (real) numbers and prints their arithmetic mean.

3. The *harmonic mean* of three numbers x, y, and z is

$$\frac{3}{\dfrac{1}{x} + \dfrac{1}{y} + \dfrac{1}{z}}$$

Write a program that asks for three (real) numbers and prints their harmonic mean.

4. The distance between a point (x, y) in the plane and the line whose equation is $ax + by = c$ is given by

$$\frac{|ax + by - c|}{\sqrt{a^2 + b^2}}$$

Write a program that asks for values of x, y, a, b, and c, and calculates the distance from the point to the line.

5. A *quadratic equation* is an equation of the form

$$ax^2 + bx + c = 0$$

Generally, there are two solutions to a quadratic equation with real coefficients a, b, and c. The solutions are given by the formulas

$$\frac{-b + \sqrt{b^2 - 4ac}}{2a} \quad \text{and} \quad \frac{-b - \sqrt{b^2 - 4ac}}{2a}$$

The graph of a quadratic equation, with coefficient a not equal to 0, is a parabola. The solutions are the places where the parabola crosses the x-axis.

Write a program to ask for the coefficients a, b, and c, and calculate the two solutions. This program cannot take care of all possibilities, given what you know

now. The expression under the square root sign above might be negative; then there are no solutions to the equation. The expression might be zero, in which case there is only one repeated solution. Don't worry about these cases. We will see how to take care of them later. Just write the program and assume that

$$b^2 - 4ac > 0$$

The first three sets of values for a, b, and c below will give two different solutions. The last one will give one. Try at least these and check your answers.

a	b	c
1.0	3.0	2.0
2.0	−7.0	6.0
3.5	−9.8	−20.0
4.0	−12.0	9.0

6. Write a program that rounds a real number to the second decimal place. The number 6.247 rounds to 6.25, and 6.244 rounds to 6.24. *Hint:* move the decimal point two places to the right, use the NINT function, and move the decimal point back.

7. Write a program that asks for a positive real number and prints the logarithm of that number to the base 2.

8. Write a program to find Arcsine(x) and Arccosine(x) for a given value of x. Give answers in both degrees and radians. A prompt should tell the user what input values are legal.

9. A triangle has sides a, b, c and angles A, B, C, where side a is opposite angle A, and so on. The *law of cosines* states:

$$c^2 = a^2 + b^2 - 2ab \cos(C)$$

Write a program that asks for the values of a, b, and the included angle C, and gives the values for side c and angles A and B. Write the angles in degrees.

10. Workers at a factory are paid at an hourly rate for hours worked up to 40 hours per week. For any hours over 40 in a week, they are paid time and a half, or 1.5 times their regular rate. A worker's gross pay is the sum of pay at the regular hourly rate and overtime pay, if any.

    a. Write an expression using the MIN function to calculate a worker's regular pay.

    b. Write an expression using the MAX function to calculate a worker's overtime pay.

    c. Rewrite the payroll program in Program 2.4, incorporating the statements in a. and b. to account for the possibility of overtime. Also, ask for and print the worker's name.

11. A taxi company charges $1.00 plus 40 cents per mile or fraction of a mile. Write a program with a statement function to calculate the charge for a given distance. Use at least the distances 3.9, 8.2, and 6.0 miles. You may assume that all mileages will be given to the nearest tenth of a mile.

12. When an odd number of values is arranged in order, the middle value is the *median* of the scores. The median of the numbers 5, 12, and 8 is 8 because 8 is the middle number when the numbers are arranged in increasing order: 5, 8, 12. Write a program to ask for three real values and invoke a statement function that calculates the median of the three values. *Hint:* after MAX and MIN, what is left must be the median.

13. Write a program with a statement function that rounds a real number X to the Nth decimal place, where N is an integer. If X is 6.247 and N is 2, the function should calculate 6.25. If X is 9321.4 and N is -1, the function should return 9320.0. That is, a negative N means that X should be rounded N places before the decimal point.

14. The formula for the frequency f (swings per second) of a pendulum near the earth's surface is

$$f = \frac{1}{2\pi} \sqrt{\frac{g}{L}}$$

where $g = 9.80665$ meters/sec^2 and L is the length of the pendulum in meters. Write a program that asks for the length of a pendulum, then calculates and prints the frequency and period (length of time for one swing). Use a PARAMETER statement to define two constants and a statement function to calculate f.

DO LOOPS

Up to now, we have written all our programs in a strictly *sequential* order; the computer simply executed one line of code after another until it reached an END statement. We can write much more powerful programs by making use of the computer's capacity to:

1. *Loop* – repeat a line or sequence of lines several times
2. *Branch* – choose which statement to execute next

Fortran implements loops with DO statements and IF statements. In this chapter we discuss the DO statement, which causes the computer to repeat lines of code several times. Chapter 5 discusses branching or selection with IF statements, and Chapter 6 introduces loops constructed with IF statements.

4.1 THE DO STATEMENT

Consider Program 4.1 below, which will cause the computer to type the word HELLO five times on five separate lines.

PROGRAM 4.1

```
PROGRAM HELLO
INTEGER I
```

```
      DO 11 I = 1, 5
         PRINT *, 'HELLO'
11    CONTINUE

      END
```

The Simple Form of the DO Statement

The first line in the body of the program contains the DO statement, whose simplest form is:

DO *<label>* *<variable name>* = *<initial value>*, *<limit>*

The second line

```
      PRINT *, 'HELLO'
```

is the loop **body**. The body of a loop is the line, or sequence of lines, to be repeated. The third line

```
11    CONTINUE
```

actually defines the body of the loop; the body contains all statements between the DO statement and the statement labelled 11 (the CONTINUE statement). Notice that we indent the body of the loop to make the program easier to read.

The CONTINUE statement is executable, but it is a "do nothing" statement, used as the target of some other statement. The CONTINUE statement is not necessary, since we can write the loop as

```
      DO 11 I = 1, 5
11       PRINT *, 'HELLO'
```

We will always use a CONTINUE statement to define the end of a DO loop because it makes a program easier to read.

Example 4.2 Evaluating a Function at Five Points

Usually, you will want to do something slightly different each time the body of the loop is executed. Suppose you want to evaluate the function

$$e^{-x^2} \times \sin(x)$$

for five different values of x. Program 4.2 shows how to do this.

■
PROGRAM 4.2
_____

```
      PROGRAM FUNC5
*----------------------------------------------------------*
*           Evaluate a function at five different points.   *
*----------------------------------------------------------*
      REAL    X, FUNC
      INTEGER I

      PRINT *, 'This program evaluates the function'
      PRINT *, 'EXP( -(X**2) ) * SIN(X)'
      PRINT *, 'at five different points.'
      PRINT *

      DO 11 I = 1, 5
         PRINT *, 'x-value?'
         READ *, X
         FUNC = EXP( -(X**2) ) * SIN(X)
         PRINT *, 'At x =', X, ' the function value is', FUNC
11    CONTINUE

      END
```

The Loop Counter

The variable after DO is called the **loop counter** or **loop index**. We have used I as a loop counter in both programs 4.1 and 4.2, but any other integer variable name would do as well. Also, in both cases the loop body contains no reference to the value of I. In such cases, the statement

```
      DO 11 I = 1, 5
```

simply means *repeat the body of the loop five times*. Let us look more closely at what happens to the loop counter as the loop is performed. Consider the loop

```
      DO 11 J = 1, 4
         PRINT *, J
11    CONTINUE
```

This program causes the computer to type

```
1
2
3
4
```

so the loop counter J actually takes on the values 1, 2, 3, and 4 in succession. However, if the DO statement were

```
DO 11 J = 4, 1
```

the computer would not type anything.

When the computer encounters a loop, it first determines the **trip count**, which is the number of times to execute the body of the loop. The trip count for this simple form of the DO loop is

$$\text{MAX } (limit - initial\ value + 1, 0)$$

In a loop beginning

```
DO 11 J = 1, 4
```

the trip count is

$$\text{MAX}(4 - 1 + 1, 0) = \text{MAX}(4, 0) = 4$$

However, if the loop begins with

```
DO 11 J = 4, 1
```

the trip count is

$$\text{MAX}(1 - 4 + 1, 0) = \text{MAX}(-2, 0) = 0$$

so the computer will not execute the loop body even once.

> **Warning!** Some versions of Fortran implement DO loops differently. After the computer executes the loop beginning
>
> ```
> DO 11 J = 1, 4
> ```
>
> the value of J is 4 in some versions, 5 in other versions, and undefined (having no predictable value) in still other versions. For this reason, it is bad programming practice

to use the value of the loop counter after the end of the loop.

The General Form of the DO Statement

In step three, the computer assumes the **increment**, or **step**, is one. We say one is the **default** step value because the computer uses this value if you do not specify something else. You can specify another step value, say two, by writing

DO 11 I = 1, 10, 2

That is, after the limit value, enter a comma and the desired step size. This is an example of the general form of the DO statement:

DO $<label>$ $<name>$ = $<initial>$, $<limit>$, $<step>$

The initial, limit, and step values are the **loop parameters**.

The limit value does not have to be a value that the loop counter can assume. The trip count for a general DO loop is

$$\text{MAX}\left[\text{INT}\left[\frac{limit - initial + step}{step}\right], 0\right]$$

In the loop beginning

DO 11 I = 1, 10, 2

the trip count is

$$\text{MAX}\left[\text{INT}\left[\frac{10 - 1 + 2}{2}\right], 0\right] = \text{MAX}(\text{INT}(5,0) = \text{MAX}(5, 0) = 5$$

Thus the computer executes the loop body five times, with I assuming the values 1, 3, 5, 7, and 9.

Fortran even allows *negative* steps, assuming that the initial value is larger than the limit value. You might, for example, begin a loop

DO 11 J = 10, 0, -3

specifying that J starts at 10 and decreases by 3, but the loop is not to be performed when J goes *below* 0. The trip count is

$$\text{MAX}\left[\text{INT}\left[\frac{0-10+(-3)}{-3}\right],\ 0\right] = \text{MAX(INT}(4.3),\ 0) = \text{MAX}(4,\ 0) = 4$$

The loop will be performed four times with corresponding J values 10, 7, 4, and 1.

Example 4.3 Table of Squares and Square Roots

Often you will want to use the loop counter to generate data within a program. Inside a loop, the loop counter variable can be used as any other variable. If you want a table of squares and square roots for the whole numbers from 10 to 200 in steps of 10, it is far easier to use a loop counter to generate these numbers than to input them from the keyboard. Program 4.3 demonstrates the point.

■
PROGRAM 4.3

```
      PROGRAM TABLE
*-------------------------------------------------------*
*        Calculate a table of squares and square roots.  *
*-------------------------------------------------------*
      INTEGER I

      PRINT *, '       NUMBER       SQUARE SQUARE ROOT'

      DO 11 I = 10, 200, 10
         PRINT *, I, I * I, SQRT( REAL(I) )
11    CONTINUE

      END
```

REAL(I) is necessary in the PRINT statement because the SQRT of an integer would cause an error message.

The output from the program will be

NUMBER	SQUARE	SQUARE ROOT
10	100	3.162278
20	400	4.472136
30	900	5.477226
40	1600	6.324555
50	2500	7.071068

60	3600	7.745967
70	4900	8.366600
80	6400	8.944272
90	8100	9.486833
100	10000	10.00000
110	12100	10.48809
120	14400	10.95445
130	16900	11.40175
140	19600	11.83216
150	22500	12.24745
160	25600	12.64911
170	28900	13.03840
180	32400	13.41641
190	36100	13.78405
200	40000	14.14214

Example 4.4 Summing Odd Integers

Program 4.4 adds all the odd integers from 1 to 200:

$$1 + 3 + 5 + \cdots + 199$$

The sum of the first n odd integers is n^2, so we do not need a program to tell us the answer is 10,000. However, the program illustrates a standard programming technique dealing with sums.

■
PROGRAM 4.4

```
      PROGRAM ADD
*--------------------------------------------------------*
*            Add the odd integers from 1 to 200.         *
*--------------------------------------------------------*
      INTEGER I, SUM

      SUM = 0

      DO 11 I = 1, 200, 2
         SUM = SUM + I
11    CONTINUE

      PRINT *, 'The sum of the odd integers from 1 to 200 is', SUM

      END
```

The DO statement causes I to begin at 1, then increase by 2 each iteration, but remain below 200. The body of the loop,

```
SUM = SUM + I
```

illustrates the use of the variable SUM as an **accumulator**. Before the loop, SUM is set to 0, and each time through the loop, the new value of SUM is calculated as the old value of SUM plus the current value of I. Thus, SUM accumulates all the values assumed by I.

Depending on your compiler, it may not be strictly necessary to give SUM the initial zero value, because many Fortran compilers do that automatically. Initializing accumulator variables is good programming practice, though, since many programming languages do not initialize variables. Also, in a larger program that calculates many sums, it is important to set SUM to zero just before the computer calculates each new sum.

Notice that certain statements must come before the loop: the variable declarations and the initialization statement, SUM = 0. Fortran requires the declarations to come first, and SUM must be set to 0 just once, before numbers are added to it. The statement

```
SUM = SUM + I
```

belongs *inside* the loop, because each value of I must be added to SUM. Finally, the PRINT statement belongs *after* the loop; it is to be executed only once, and the results are not complete until the loop is finished.

A run of the program produces the output

```
The sum of the odd integers from 1 to 200 is    10000
```

Expressions for Initial, Limit, and Step Values

A program that uses specific constant initial and limit values for loops is rarely useful. A program for adding five numbers will not help anyone who needs to add more or fewer than five numbers. Fortran allows *expressions* for initial, limit, and step values in a DO statement. If the loop variable is an integer, these expressions also should be integer expressions. Fortran will convert them to integer if they are real, but you should avoid this kind of mode mixing.

Example 4.5 Summing Input Data

You will frequently want to start a loop index at 1 and increase in steps of 1, but let the user decide on the limit value. Suppose you want a program to add as many real numbers as the user wants to input. Simply ask the user how many numbers are to be added, call the answer N, and use a loop with N as the limit value to input and add the numbers to an accumulator variable TOTAL. Program 4.5 shows how this is done.

■
PROGRAM 4.5
_____

```
      PROGRAM ADDINP
*-----------------------------------------------*
*                 Find the sum of input values.          *
*-----------------------------------------------*
      INTEGER I, N
      REAL    NUMBER, TOTAL

      TOTAL = 0.0

      PRINT *, 'This program adds numbers.'
      PRINT *, 'How many numbers do you have?'
      READ *, N

      DO 11 I = 1, N
         PRINT *, 'Number?'
         READ *, NUMBER
         TOTAL = TOTAL + NUMBER
11    CONTINUE

      PRINT *, 'The total of your numbers is', TOTAL

      END
```

REAL **Loop Counters**

Older versions of Fortran allowed only INTEGER variables as loop-index variables. You *can* use REAL variables as loop counters, but be warned: they can give unexpected results if the step size is not a number that Fortran can represent exactly. Consider the loop

```
      DO 11 R = 0.0, 2.0, 0.1
         PRINT *, R
11    CONTINUE
```

It seems obvious that the loop will cause the computer to print twenty-one values, beginning with 0.0 and ending with 2.0. However, what one computer (a VAX) actually prints is

```
0.0000000E+00
0.1000000
0.2000000
0.3000000
0.4000000
0.5000000
0.6000000
0.7000000
0.8000001
0.9000001
1.000000
1.100000
1.200000
1.300000
1.400000
1.500000
1.600000
1.700000
1.800000
1.900000
```

The last value of R inside the loop is not 2.0, but 1.9. The two printed numbers 0.8000001 and 0.9000001 give a hint as to what went wrong. The computer cannot represent the exact step size 0.1. The representation must be for a number slightly larger than 0.1, because after eight steps the value of the loop counter is 0.8000001.

Reasonable step sizes are numbers the computer can represent precisely. Briefly, whole numbers are represented precisely, and so are reciprocals of powers of 2 (1/2, 1/4, 1/8, and so on) and sums of such reciprocals. The real number 1/2, or 0.5, is a reasonable step size, and so is 0.15625 = 5/32 = 1/8 + 1/32.

Example 4.6 Simple Interest

The program presented here calculates the interest cost for one year at varying interest rates. We use simple interest, which means that interest is not compounded during the year. The user states the principal (PRINC) and the lowest (LOW) and highest (HIGH) interest rates. The computer calculates interest for rates between the lowest and highest rates given, in steps of 0.5. The loop begins with the DO statement

```
DO 11 RATE = LOW, HIGH, 0.5
```

Inside the loop, the computer calculates and prints the interest (INTRST).

People customarily specify interest as a percentage, so the computer will ask for the low and high rates as percentages, then divide the value of RATE by 100.0. INTRST is then calculated as

```
INTRST = PRINC * RATE / 100.0
```

The loop itself is a rather small, but very important, part of the program. Several statements must come before the loop:

1. The usual type declarations
2. Asking for the loop limits
3. Printing headers

In any program involving loops, you should ask yourself what is required before the loop, inside the loop, and after the loop. It should be obvious that the three steps listed above must be completed before the loop begins. For example, the headers should be printed only once, at the top of the columns, so the statement to print headers must come before the loop. The calculation and printing of interest obviously must be performed for each interest rate, so these statements should be inside the loop. In this case, nothing remains to be done after the loop. The program is shown in Program 4.6.

■

PROGRAM 4.6

```
      PROGRAM INTABL
*----------------------------------------------------------------*
*  Calculate interest cost for year at varying interest rates. *
*----------------------------------------------------------------*
      REAL PRINC, LOW, HIGH, RATE, INTRST

      PRINT *, 'What is the principal?'
      READ *, PRINC

      PRINT *, 'What are the lowest and highest interest rates?'
      PRINT *, 'Please enter rates as whole numbers.'
      READ  *, LOW, HIGH
      PRINT *

      PRINT *, 'SIMPLE INTEREST FOR ONE YEAR ON', PRINC
      PRINT *
```

```
      PRINT *, ' INTEREST RATE   INTEREST'
      DO 11 RATE = LOW, HIGH, 0.5
         INTRST = PRINC * RATE / 100.0
         PRINT *, RATE, INTRST
11    CONTINUE

      END
```

A run of the program might go as follows, with the user's responses underlined.

```
What is the principal?
8500
What are the lowest and highest interest rates?
Please enter rates as whole numbers.
10, 12

SIMPLE INTEREST FOR ONE YEAR ON    8500.000

   INTEREST RATE    INTEREST
      10.00000      850.0000
      10.50000      892.5000
      11.00000      935.0000
      11.50000      977.5000
      12.00000     1020.000
```

This program works well if the user enters two whole numbers such as 10 and 12. If, however, the user enters 10 and 11.9, the computer will not calculate interest for 11.9 percent.

Example 4.7 Payroll Problem with Several Employees

Recall the payroll example from Chapter 2, which calculated gross pay, tax, Social Security, and net pay, for a single employee. If calculations must be done for several employees, we can enclose the calculations and PRINT statements for a single employee in a loop. We cannot just put a loop around the entire previous program; programming is not quite that simple.

We have variable declarations at the beginning of the program as before. The program requires two new variables: N represents the total number of employees, and I is a loop counter. The program will ask for the number of employees. Finally, we place a loop around the calculations and PRINT statements for a single employee. See Program 4.7.

■

PROGRAM 4.7

```
      PROGRAM PAYROL
*-----------------------------------------------------------*
*  Program to calculate gross pay, tax, social security, and  *
*  and net pay for several employees.                         *
*-----------------------------------------------------------*
      INTEGER I, N
      REAL    HOURS, PARATE, GROSSP, FEDTAX, SOCSEC
      REAL    NETPAY, FTRATE, SSRATE
      PARAMETER (FTRATE = 0.14, SSRATE = 0.0715)

      PRINT *, 'How many employees?'
      READ  *, N

      DO 11 I = 1, N
         PRINT *, 'Hours worked and pay rate?'
         READ  *, HOURS, PARATE

         GROSSP = HOURS * PARATE
         FEDTAX = FTRATE * GROSSP
         SOCSEC = SSRATE * GROSSP
         NETPAY = GROSSP - FEDTAX - SOCSEC

         PRINT *
         PRINT *, 'Hours worked   :', HOURS
         PRINT *, 'Hourly rate    :', PARATE
         PRINT *, 'Gross pay      :', GROSSP
         PRINT *, 'Income tax     :', FEDTAX
         PRINT *, 'Social security:', SOCSEC
         PRINT *, 'Net pay        :', NETPAY
         PRINT *

11    CONTINUE

      END
```

Data Files

When a program requires a large amount of input data, reading input from the keyboard is not efficient. Most people would make at least one mistake when entering as few as twenty numbers. After the computer reads a wrong number, there is no way to correct it (yet), so the only recourse is to start the program running again and reenter the data. This recopying of data can be especially annoying when the program is in the debugging stage. What we need is a place outside of the program to store input data so we won't have to rewrite it several times. A **data file** is such a place.

You can prepare an input data file in an editor. Suppose we want a program to read a file with twelve scores. Then we can put in the file the number 12 followed by twelve scores as follows:

```
12
38.5
12.6
19.7
92.4
86.4
18.2
12.5
24.8
30.1
28.9
14.2
15.0
```

Reading from a Data File

A program that reads a data file must first prepare the file with an OPEN **statement**. If the data file is named INPUT.DAT, a program that reads the file should contain the OPEN statement

```
OPEN (11, FILE = 'INPUT.DAT', STATUS = 'OLD')
```

This statement contains three OPEN **statement specifiers**:

1. The number 11 is the **unit specifier**, or **logical unit number**. It will be used in the remainder of the program to refer to the file INPUT.DAT. The unit number can be any integer from 1 to 99.
2. The clause, FILE = 'INPUT.DAT', is the **file specifier**. The file name appears in apostrophes after the equal sign. This specifier could be simply FILE = 'INPUT'; Fortran assumes a file type of .DAT if the file specifier does not include a file type.
3. The third clause, STATUS = 'OLD', is the **status specifier**. 'OLD' means that the file already exists.

The OPEN statement connects the program to the file named in the file specifier.

The list-directed READ statement to read from a file has the form

```
READ (<unit number>, *) <read list>
```

where the unit number must be the same as in the OPEN statement. Suppose our program uses the variable N to represent the number of scores. Then the READ statement to obtain a value for N can be

```
READ (11, *) N
```

A program that reads a file should contain a CLOSE **statement** of the form

```
CLOSE (<unit number>)
```

The CLOSE statement breaks the connection between the program and the file. We use a CLOSE statement for any files used in a program.

Example 4.8 Finding the Smallest Score in a File

The following program finds the smallest score in a set of real scores. The program reads from the data file INPUT.DAT, which contains the number of scores on the first line, and one score on each succeeding line.

We will use the variable name X for the scores, and SMALL for the smallest score. The intrinsic function MIN will be used to find SMALL. Each time the computer reads a score X, the value of SMALL should change if the new value of X is less than SMALL. We can accomplish this with the statement

```
SMALL = MIN(X, SMALL)
```

The only question left is how to get an initial value for SMALL. If you know you are going to use the data file INPUT.DAT given above, you might be tempted to start with SMALL = 100.0, or some other number you know is larger than the smallest score in the file. However, this will not work for a file with all scores above 100.0. We can simply let SMALL start with the value of the first score, then compare it to the rest of the scores in a loop running from 2 to N. The program is shown in Program 4.8.

■

PROGRAM 4.8

```
        PROGRAM LEAST
*------------------------------------------------------------*
*       Read scores from file INPUT.DAT and calculate smallest.  *
*       First data element is the number of scores.              *
*------------------------------------------------------------*
```

```
      INTEGER N, I
      REAL    X, SMALL

      OPEN (1, FILE = 'INPUT', STATUS = 'OLD')

      READ (1, *) N
      READ (1, *) X
      SMALL = X

      DO 11 I = 2, N
         READ (1, *) X
         SMALL = MIN(X, SMALL)
11    CONTINUE

      CLOSE (1)

      PRINT *, 'The smallest number in the file is', SMALL

      END
```

The output from the program is

```
The smallest number in the file is   12.50000
```

Writing to a Data File

You can use data files to store output too. When a program sends output to a file, it must first create the file. The OPEN statement, with STATUS = 'NEW', creates a file. Our next program calculates some factorials and puts them in a file, so we will call the file FACTRL.DAT. The appropriate OPEN statement is

```
OPEN (12, FILE = 'FACTRL', STATUS = 'NEW')
```

A new output statement, a WRITE **statement**, writes output to a file. The form of the list-directed WRITE statement is

WRITE (*<unit number>*, *) *<write list>*

where the unit number is the number used in the OPEN statement that created the file. We plan to put values of two variables, I and FACTRL, into the file, so an appropriate WRITE statement is

```
      WRITE (12, *) I, FACTRL
```

Example 4.9 Calculating Factorials

For a positive integer *n*, we usually designate *n*-factorial as *n*!, and define it with the formula:

$$n! = n(n - 1)(n - 2) \cdots (1)$$

For example, 4! = 4(3)(2)(1) = 24. A program to calculate factorials is almost identical to a program to sum the numbers 1, 2, 3, . . ., *N*. The factorial accumulates a product instead of a sum, so multiplication replaces addition. Also, where the variable for the sum would be initialized to 0, the variable representing the factorial will be initialized to 1.

We will have the program calculate the factorials of the integers from 1 to 12 and store them in a file FACTRL.DAT. The program is quite simple, as shown in Program 4.9.

■
PROGRAM 4.9
_____

```
      PROGRAM FACT12
*--------------------------------------------------------------*
*  Calculate the factorials of the first 12 positive integers.  *
*  Store them in the file FACTRL.DAT.                            *
*--------------------------------------------------------------*
      INTEGER  FACTRL, I

      OPEN (12, FILE = 'FACTRL', STATUS = 'NEW')

      WRITE (12, *) '       NUMBER      FACTORIAL'
      FACTRL = 1

      DO 11 I = 1, 12
         FACTRL = FACTRL * I
         WRITE (12, *) I, FACTRL
11    CONTINUE

      CLOSE (12)

      END
```
_____

When you run this program, you will see no output. One way to see the file is to write a Fortran program that reads the file and prints its contents. Most systems have other means by which you can see the contents of a file. Check with your instructor.

Example 4.10 Calculating Numbers of Combinations

The number of ways that k items can be chosen from a set of n items is often designated by $C(n, k)$. It can be shown that

$$C(n, k) = \frac{n!}{k!(n - k)!}$$

As an example, the number of ways that three items can be chosen from a set of five items is

$$C(5, 3) = \frac{5!}{3!2!} = \frac{5(4)(3)(2)(1)}{3(2)(1)(2)(1)} = \frac{5(4)}{2(1)} = 10$$

$C(n, k)$ is also called a *binomial coefficient* because it is the coefficient of x^k in the expansion of $(1+x)^n$. To calculate $C(n,k)$ generally, we could calculate three factorials, $n!$, $k!$, and $(n - k)!$, then divide $n!$ by the product of the other two factorials.

Aside from making the computer do many needless calculations, this method would not allow certain calculations because the factorials involved would be too large for the computer to store. For example, 100! is too large for the computer to store (as an integer), but

$$C(100, 2) = \frac{100!}{(2!98!)}$$

is easily calculated as $100(99)/2$, or 4950, because a large part of the numerator is cancelled by a factorial in the denominator.

It is instructive to look closer at how $C(n, k)$ can be calculated by hand. Consider the calculation of $C(11, 5)$.

$$C(11, 5) = \frac{11!}{(5!)(6!)} = \frac{11(10)(9)(8)(7)(6)(5)(4)(3)(2)(1)}{5(4)(3)(2)(1)(6)(5)(4)(3)(2)(1)}$$

To keep the arithmetic as simple as possible, we should cancel the larger factorial in the denominator with the same terms in the numerator. Cancelling 6! from both numerator and denominator leaves

$$C(11, 5) = \frac{11(10)(9)(8)(7)}{5(4)(3)(2)(1)} = \frac{7(8)(9)(10)(11)}{1(2)(3)(4)(5)}$$

We have reversed the order of the numbers in both the numerator and denominator to make some calculations more obvious. The terms in the denominator go from 1 to 5, and for each term in the denominator, there is a corresponding term in the numerator. If we were to finish the calculations by hand, we would make all possible cancellations: for instance, divide the 5 in the denominator into the 10 in the numerator. However, it is difficult to tell the computer how to do this in a general way.

The simplest way to proceed is to calculate the numerator and the denominator and divide the former by the latter. This is left as an exercise. We finish the calculations in the following way:

1. $1 \times 7 / 1 = 7$
2. $7 \times 8 / 2 = 28$
3. $28 \times 9 / 3 = 84$
4. $84 \times 10/ 4 = 210$
5. $210 \times 11/ 5 = 462$

In following this pattern, all integer divisions will be exact: the 1 in the denominator can never cause trouble; when the divisor is 2, the numerator value will be even; when the divisor is 3, the numerator will be divisible by 3; and so on.

Let COMBIN stand for the desired number of combinations. The general rule for calculating COMBIN is to start with COMBIN = 1, and at each step let

```
COMBIN = COMBIN * NUM / DEN
```

where DEN stands for a term in the denominator, and NUM a term in the numerator. In this case each term in the numerator is 9 more than the term below it in the denominator, so we can replace NUM with (DEN + 9). In general, the 9 can be replaced by MAX(K, N−K). Also, the number of terms in the denominator, as well as the numerator, is MIN(K, N−K). Thus, if we let

```
MAXI = MAX(K, N-K)
```

and

```
MINI = MIN(K, N-K)
```

we can calculate COMBIN with the statement

```
COMBIN = COMBIN * (DEN + MAXI) / DEN
```

We place this statement inside a DO loop with DEN going from 1 to MINI. The program is shown in Program 4.10.

■
PROGRAM 4.10

```
      PROGRAM COMBINATION
*-----------------------------------------------------------*
*               Calculate binomial coefficient C(n, k).      *
*-----------------------------------------------------------*
      INTEGER  N, K, COMBIN, DEN, MAXI, MINI

      PRINT *, 'This program calculates the number of ways k'
      PRINT *, 'objects can be chosen from a set of n objects.'
      PRINT *, 'What are the values of n and k?'
      READ  *, N, K
*-----------------------------------------------------------*
*     Cancel the larger of k! and (n-k)! from the numerator. *
*-----------------------------------------------------------*
      MAXI = MAX(K, N-K)
      MINI = MIN(K, N-K)

      COMBIN = 1
      DO 11 DEN = 1, MINI
         COMBIN = COMBIN * (DEN + MAXI) / DEN
11    CONTINUE

      PRINT *, K, ' objects can be selected from a set of', N
      PRINT *, 'objects in', COMBIN, ' ways.'

      END
```

Example 4.11 Finding the Area Under a Curve

A standard calculus problem is finding the area under a curve between two points a and b, or taking the definite integral from a to b of the function defining the curve. For many functions, the only way to find such an area is by **numerical integration**, which roughly means any approximate method for finding the area under a curve.

One of the simplest methods for numerical integration is approximation by rectangles. Consider the curve shown in Figure 4.1, which is the graph of the function

$$f(x) = \sqrt{x^4 - 3x^2 + 4}$$

for values of x between 0 and 3.

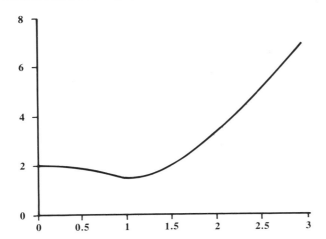

FIGURE 4.1
Graph of $y = \sqrt{x^4 - 3x^2 + 4}$

We can approximate the area under $f(x)$ between a and b by the sum of the areas of the four rectangles shown in Figure 4.2.

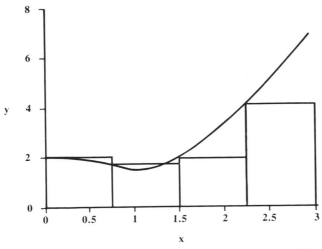

FIGURE 4.2
Approximating area
with four rectangles

You can see that this sum of four areas will not be exactly equal to the desired area. However, we can use more rectangles, eight for example, to get a better approximation to the area under the curve. See Figure 4.3. And if eight rectangles is not enough, try sixteen, and so on.

First, let us see how to calculate the sum of the areas of several rectangles, say N of them. Then we will use a DO loop beginning

FIGURE 4.3
Approximating area
with eight rectangles

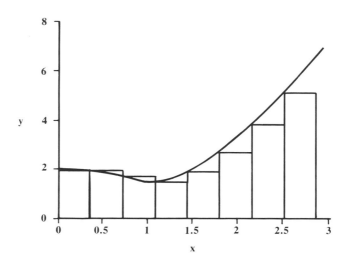

```
DO 22 I = 1, N
```

and inside the loop we will calculate the area of one rectangle and add it to an accumulator SUM. Since SUM is an accumulator, we set it to zero before the loop.

The area of a rectangle is its base times its height. Using BASE for the base, we must have

```
BASE = (B - A) / REAL(N)
```

because the interval from A to B is being split into N parts. We can place this assignment statement before the loop, because each rectangle has the same base.

The height of any rectangle is the function value at the appropriate *x* value. If we let X be the midpoint of an interval, the height at X is

```
SQRT(X ** 4 - 3.0 * X ** 2 + 4.0)
```

We will use a statement function F defined by

```
F(X) = SQRT(X ** 4 - 3.0 * X ** 2 + 4.0)
```

Then in the program body we can refer to the height as F(X).

The only remaining question is how to get X to be the midpoints of the intervals. The first interval runs from A to A + BASE, so its midpoint is A + BASE / 2.0. Each succeeding midpoint is the preceding midpoint plus BASE. Therefore, we can start X at A - BASE / 2.0 outside the loop, and increment X with X = X + BASE inside the loop. Assuming N has some positive value, we can calculate the sum of N rectangles with the following code.

```
      SUM  = 0.0
      BASE = (B - A) / REAL(N)
      X    = A - BASE / 2.0
      DO 22 I = 1, N
         X = X + BASE
         SUM = SUM + BASE * F(X)
22    CONTINUE
```

The rest of the program is relatively simple. Program 4.11 shows the complete program.

■
PROGRAM 4.11

```
      PROGRAM AREA
*----------------------------------------------------------*
*  Approximate the area under a curve by the sum of the areas *
*  of N rectangles.  Let the user specify a value for N.      *
*----------------------------------------------------------*
      INTEGER N, I
      REAL    A, B, X, BASE, SUM, F
      F(X) = SQRT(X ** 4 - 3.0 * X ** 2 + 4.0)

      PRINT *, 'Approximating the area under a curve.'
      PRINT *, 'How many rectangles?'
      READ  *, N

      SUM  = 0.0
      BASE = (B - A) / REAL(N)
      X    = A - BASE / 2.0
      DO 22 I = 1, N
         X = X + BASE
         SUM = SUM + BASE * F(X)
22    CONTINUE

      PRINT *, 'The approximate area is', SUM

      END
```

In using this program, try small values for N as well as large values (say 100 and 200). Notice how close the approximate values are for various values of N. We will return to this problem in Chapter 6. Also, Exercises 16 and 17 ask you to program different methods for finding area under a curve.

Changing Values of the Loop Variable and Loop Parameters

Many versions of Fortran allow you to change the loop variable value within the loop, but most will print a warning message if you do so. That is, the following program might compile and run, but the compiler might print a warning message concerning an assignment to a DO variable within a loop.

```
      DO 11 I = 1, 8
         PRINT *, I
         I = I + 1
11    CONTINUE
      END
```

The warning message is printed because this is a dangerous practice; when beginning programmers change the value of a loop counter, errors usually occur. At best, the program becomes harder to read. If all you want is to print the numbers 1, 3, 5, and 7, then the DO statement should be

```
      DO 11 I = 1, 8, 2
```

and the statement I = I + 1 can be deleted.

The initial, limit, and step values for a loop are evaluated *once*, when the DO statement is first executed, and are not changed during execution of the loop. The following program segment will print numbers from 1 to 5 even though the value of the variable TERM is changed to 2 inside the loop.

```
      TERM = 5
      DO 11 I = 1, TERM
         PRINT *, I
         TERM = 2
11    CONTINUE
```

Fortran actually sets up a temporary variable for the limit value of the loop; although TERM is changed inside the loop, this temporary variable is not. The same would be true of a variable used to specify the step size. Do not try to change these values inside the loop. It will not work, and will only make the program harder to understand.

Program Structure

The **structure** of a program means the logical organization of the program statements. Our first programs had a simple sequential organization, with one statement following another. Still, we can see structure in those programs. Consider again the payroll program of Chapter 2, stripped of comments.

```
PROGRAM PAYROL
REAL  HOURS, RATE, GROSSP, FEDTAX, SOCSEC, NETPAY
REAL  FTRATE, SSRATE
PARAMETER (FTRATE = 0.14, SSRATE = 0.07)

PRINT *, 'How many hours worked?'
READ  *, HOURS
PRINT *, 'Hourly rate?'
READ  *, RATE

GROSSP = HOURS * RATE
FEDTAX = FTRATE * GROSSP
SOCSEC = SSRATE * GROSSP
NETPAY = GROSSP - FEDTAX - SOCSEC

PRINT *
PRINT *, 'Hours worked        :', HOURS
PRINT *, 'Hourly rate of pay :', RATE
PRINT *
PRINT *, 'Gross pay           :', GROSSP
PRINT *, 'Federal tax         :   ', FEDTAX
PRINT *, 'Social Security tax:   ', SOCSEC
PRINT *, 'Net pay             :', NETPAY

END
```

We often call a sequence of statements that logically belong together a **block**. The program above consists of the four blocks:

1. Specification statements
2. Statements to obtain input
3. Calculations
4. Statements to write output

Simply listing the blocks in a program does not specify the structure of the program, any more than listing 40,000 bricks specifies the structure of a building. We complete the description of the program structure by saying that the computer executes blocks 2, 3, and 4 of the program in sequential order: first block 2, then 3, then 4.

Each part of a structure can have a structure of its own. The calculation block in the payroll program consists of the statements

```
GROSSP = HOURS * RATE
FEDTAX = FTRATE * GROSSP
SOCSEC = SSRATE * GROSSP
NETPAY = GROSSP - FEDTAX - SOCSEC
```

Inside the calculation block, parts of statements execute sequentially. Sequential structure is truly the simplest possible organization, and we strive to attain it because it is so easy to understand.

A **control structure** is any structure in which the computer does not simply execute the parts sequentially. The DO loop is the first control structure we have discussed. The DO statement and its partner CONTINUE control the execution of the loop body. The structure of a DO loop is no longer purely sequential because, after executing the last statement in the loop body, the computer often returns to the first statement.

The DO loop is a **repeat structure**; it repeats a block of statements a specified number of times. After sequential structure, the DO loop is one of the simplest structures, and it is used in nearly all large Fortran programs. If you master DO loops, you will have an important building block to use in creating complex but well-structured programs.

A **well-structured program** is just a program whose structure is easy to describe or easy to discern. Structure is inherent in the program; the statements either logically belong together or they don't. The blank lines and spacing in the program can help to make the structure more visible, but they do not *make* the structure.

■

4.2 NESTED LOOPS

Nesting loops is the process of placing one loop inside another loop. For example, in

```
      DO 22 I = 1, 3
         DO 11 J = 1, 2
            PRINT *, I, J
11       CONTINUE
22    CONTINUE
```

the J loop is nested inside the I loop. The indentation should help you see the nesting. This program segment causes the computer to print

1	1
1	2
2	1
2	2
3	1
3	2

The value of I is set to 1; then J assumes values 1 and 2. At this point, the J loop terminates at the first CONTINUE, so control passes to the second CONTINUE, and I is increased by 1 to become 2. Then the J loop begins again, with J set first to 1, then to 2. Again, the J loop terminates, I increases to 3, and J takes on the values 1 and 2. Each time the value of the outer loop variable changes, the entire inner loop is executed.

The body of nested loops is executed once for every possible combination of values of the loop counters. Therefore, nested loops appear in programs that require a calculation to be performed for every combination of values of two or more variables. We may, for example, wish to calculate interest on a deposit at various interest rates for various terms of years. We would then use nested loops, with one loop counter representing interest rates, and the other representing various terms of years.

With nested loops, the outer loop contains the entire inner loop. We indented to make clear which CONTINUE is paired with each DO. The computer pays no attention to such indenting; it pairs a CONTINUE statement to the DO statement with the same label.

Example 4.12 Compounding Interest with Varying Rates and Terms

Suppose you have $5,000 to invest in a money market certificate, and you can get certificates with interest rates varying from 8 to 12 percent in steps of 1 percent, and terms from one to five years in steps of one year. The formula for the value of your investment at the end of a term, assuming compounding at the end of each year, is

$$Value = Principal \times \left[1 + \frac{Rate}{100} \right]^{Term}$$

A program to calculate final values of the investment under all possible conditions consists mainly of a TERM loop nested inside a RATE loop. An assignment statement and PRINT statement inside the TERM loop do most of the work. See Program 4.12.

■
PROGRAM 4.12

```
      PROGRAM FINVAL
*-------------------------------------------------------------*
*  Calculate value of $5,000 invested at various rates and terms. *
*-------------------------------------------------------------*
      REAL    PRINC, RATE, VALUE
      INTEGER TERM
      DATA    PRINC /5000.0/

      PRINT *, '$5,000 is invested for varying rates and terms'
      PRINT *
      PRINT *, 'INTEREST RATE        TERM  FINAL VALUE'

      DO 22 RATE = 8.0, 12.0
         DO 11 TERM = 1, 5
            VALUE = PRINC * (1.0 + RATE/100.0) ** TERM
            PRINT *, RATE, TERM, VALUE
11       CONTINUE

         PRINT *

22    CONTINUE

      END
```

The output from this program is

```
$5,000 is invested for varying rates and terms

INTEREST RATE        TERM  FINAL VALUE
    8.000000          1    5400.000
    8.000000          2    5832.000
    8.000000          3    6298.561
    8.000000          4    6802.446
    8.000000          5    7346.642

    9.000000          1    5450.000
    9.000000          2    5940.500
    9.000000          3    6475.146
    9.000000          4    7057.909
    9.000000          5    7693.122
```

10.00000	1	5500.000
10.00000	2	6050.000
10.00000	3	6655.000
10.00000	4	7320.500
10.00000	5	8052.551
11.00000	1	5550.000
11.00000	2	6160.500
11.00000	3	6838.155
11.00000	4	7590.353
11.00000	5	8425.291
12.00000	1	5600.000
12.00000	2	6272.000
12.00000	3	7024.640
12.00000	4	7867.597
12.00000	5	8811.709

Later we will learn better ways to print such tables.

Example 4.13 Means for Several Tests

Suppose a certain course requires several tests, and the instructor wishes to calculate the mean score on each test. If NRSTUD denotes the number of students in the course, we can easily calculate the mean of one test with the following program segment.

```
      SUM = 0.0

      DO 11 STUDNT = 1, NRSTUD
         PRINT *, 'Grade?'
         READ *, GRADE
         SUM = SUM + GRADE
11    CONTINUE
      PRINT *, 'Mean grade is', SUM / REAL(NRSTUD)
```

To calculate mean grades for the four tests, enclose this program segment in a loop beginning

```
      DO 22 TEST = 1, 4
```

We should also ask for the number of students; we assume this number is the same for each test, so we ask before the first loop. Variable declarations and a descriptive statement could complete the program, but we include a PRINT statement giving the test number. This statement must come after the DO 22 TEST statement so that TEST has a value; it belongs before `DO 11 STUDNT` because the test number remains the same while the `STUDNT` loop is being executed. See Program 4.13.

■
PROGRAM 4.13

```
      PROGRAM TESTAV
*-----------------------------------------------------------------*
*        Calculate the mean grade on each of four tests.          *
*-----------------------------------------------------------------*
      INTEGER TEST, STUDNT, NRSTUD, NTEST
      REAL     GRADE, SUM
      DATA     NTEST /4/

      PRINT *, 'Calculate mean grade on each of 4 tests.'
      PRINT *
      PRINT *, 'How many students in the class?'
      READ  *, NRSTUD

      DO 22 TEST = 1, NTEST

         SUM = 0.0
         PRINT *, 'Test number', TEST

         DO 11 STUDNT = 1, NRSTUD
            PRINT *, 'Grade?'
            READ *, GRADE
            SUM = SUM + GRADE
11       CONTINUE

         PRINT *, 'Mean grade is', SUM / NRSTUD
         PRINT *

22    CONTINUE

      END
```

The structure of this program is more complicated than many of our previous programs. However, it is mainly just a `DO` loop within a `DO` loop. When writing such programs, you should consider the five parts:

1. Before the first `DO` statement: Always put variable declarations and descriptive comments here. Consider things that should happen only once, such as asking for input, printing headers, and initializing variables.

2. Between the DO statements: Consider things which should be done once for each repetition of the outer loop, such as asking for input, printing headers, and initializing. The statement SUM = 0.0 belongs here because SUM must start at zero each time the inner loop is executed.

3. Inside the inner loop: Whatever is here, at the heart of the program, will be executed once for every possible combination of values of the loop variables. Most of the calculations are here. Results might be printed here if a table is being printed as in the previous example.

4. Between the CONTINUE statements: Print results here if the desired results are based on outcomes from the inner loop, as they are in this example. As with part 2, anything done here is repeated once for each repetition of the outer loop.

5. After both CONTINUE statements: Print here those results that are summarized from both loops. In a more complex program, there might be much more work to do here.

Remember that any PRINT statement outside both loops (parts 1 and 5) is executed only once, while statements inside the outer loop, but outside the inner loop (parts 2 and 4), are executed once for each value of the outer loop variable.

Often the number of iterations for the inner loop depends on the value of the outer loop variable. A trivial example is:

```
      DO 22 OUTER = 1, 3
          DO 11 INNER = 1, OUTER
              PRINT *, OUTER, INNER
11        CONTINUE
22    CONTINUE

      END
```

The program causes the computer to type

```
1       1
2       1
2       2
3       1
3       2
3       3
```

The inner loop always starts at INNER = 1, and continues until the value of INNER is equal to the value of OUTER. The next example extends this idea.

Example 4.14 Many Levels of Nesting: Making Change for a Dollar

Fortran allows as many as twenty DO loops, each one nested inside the one before. You are not likely to need that many, but here is a program with four loops.

We want to find the number of ways to make a dollar from change: half-dollars, quarters, dimes, nickels, and pennies. We will use variable names HALF, QUARTR, DIME, and NICKEL to stand for the values of the coins used, in cents. That is, the possible values for HALF will be 0, 50, and 100 cents, representing 0, 1, or 2 half-dollars. Similarly: the possible values of QUARTR are 0, 25, 50, and 100; DIME can be 0, 10, 20, ..., 100; and NICKEL can be 0, 5, 10, ..., 100. We don't need to worry about pennies, because after determining the numbers of all the other coins, there will be only one possible number of pennies.

If you think about doing this problem by hand, you would probably come up with a scheme similar to the following:

1. Choose one of the possible values for HALF.

2. Choose a possible value for QUARTR, remembering that the value of HALF + QUARTR must be less than or equal to 100. That is, the maximum value of QUARTR is 100 − HALF.

3. Choose a value for DIME. In this case, HALF + QUARTR + DIME cannot exceed 100, so the maximum value of DIME is 100 − HALF − QUARTR.

4. Choose a value for NICKEL. The maximum value for NICKEL is 100 − HALF − QUARTR − DIME.

5. Count the preceding combination of choices as one way to make one dollar. (You might think that the value of the pennies should be chosen here. Actually, there is no choice left. If you have taken exactly one of each other coin, for instance, then you have a total of 90 cents, so you need exactly 10 pennies.)

6. Repeat steps 1 through 5 until all possibilities are exhausted. Presumably, you would make the choices in an orderly fashion, so that no choices would be repeated and you would know when you were finished.

It should seem reasonable to have a loop for each of our variables. The HALF loop can obviously be

```
DO 44 HALF = 0, 100, 50
```

because the value of the half-dollars can be anything from 0 to 100 in steps of 50. From our reasoning in step 2, the QUARTR loop should be

```
      DO 33 QUARTR = 0, 100 - HALF, 25
```

Similarly, for dimes the loop is

```
      DO 22 DIME = 0, 100 - HALF - QUARTR, 10
```

This DO statement should give you pause. If the value of HALF is 50 and the value of QUARTR is 25, then the value of 100 − HALF − QUARTR is 25. Does it seem reasonable to have the following DO statement?

```
      DO 22 DIME = 0, 25, 10
```

In this case, DIME would take on values 0, 10, and 20, so the DO statement for DIME is correct. Finally, for NICKEL we have

```
      DO 11 NICKEL = 0, 100 - HALF - QUARTR - DIME, 5
```

All that must be done inside these loops is to count how many times the computer gets to the inside of them. Thus, a single statement

```
      NUMBER = NUMBER + 1
```

will suffice. The counter NUMBER is just a special accumulator; it accumulates ones. See Program 4.14.

■
PROGRAM 4.14

```
      PROGRAM CHANGE
*------------------------------------------------------------*
*        Count the number of ways to make change for a dollar.    *
*------------------------------------------------------------*
      INTEGER HALF, QUARTR, DIME, NICKEL, NUMBER

      NUMBER = 0

      DO 44 HALF = 0, 100, 50
         DO 33 QUARTR = 0, 100 - HALF, 25
            DO 22 DIME = 0, 100 - HALF - QUARTR, 10
               DO 11 NICKEL = 0, 100 - HALF - QUARTR - DIME, 5
                  NUMBER = NUMBER + 1
11             CONTINUE
22          CONTINUE
33       CONTINUE
44    CONTINUE
```

```
PRINT *, 'The number of ways to make $1.00 is', NUMBER

END
```

With a program such as this, suppose the number 276 is printed as the final answer. Do you have any idea whether it is correct? It would be a good idea to put two more statements inside the program, right after NUMBER = NUMBER + 1:

```
PENNY = 100 - HALF - QUARTR - DIME - NICKEL
PRINT *, HALF, QUARTR, DIME, NICKEL, PENNY
```

The value of the pennies is obviously 100 minus the value of all the other coins, but the main point is that the printing will let you see whether the program is running correctly. PRINT statements can often be used in this way to aid in debugging programs.

Many other counting problems can be solved by writing a program that is essentially a collection of nested loops with a counter inside. Programming Exercises 12 and 13 are examples. The key to such problems is setting proper limits on the loops.

4.3 SUMMARY OF CHAPTER 4

■ *Terms Introduced In This Chapter*

Accumulator
Binomial coefficient
Block
CLOSE statement
Combination
CONTINUE statement
Control structure
Default file names
DO statement
Factorial
FILE specifier, in OPEN statement
Increment
Initial value

Limit value
Loop
Loop counter
Loop parameters
Nested loops
OPEN statement
Repeat structure
STATUS specifier, in OPEN statement
Structure
Trip count
Unit number
Unit specifier
WRITE statement

■ *What You Should Know*

1. A DO loop is a structure that causes the computer to repeat execution of a block of statements a specified number of times.
2. A DO statement requires a label, a loop variable, and initial and limit values.
3. A DO statement may contain a step value, or increment.
4. If a DO statement does not contain a step value, the default step value is 1.
5. The loop counter takes on the initial value in a DO statement, but it does not necessarily take on the limit value.
6. The DO loop parameters are the initial, final, and step values in the DO statement.
7. Changing the values of the loop variable and loop parameters inside a DO loop is legal in Fortran, but is poor programming practice.
8. A variable used to find the total of values of another variable is an accumulator variable. For example, if the statement TOTAL = TOTAL + X occurs in a loop, the variable TOTAL is accumulating the values of variable X.
9. An accumulator variable should be initialized to zero.
10. A variable that accumulates products instead of sums should be initialized to one.
11. A counter variable is a special kind of accumulator variable that accumulates ones to count the number of times something occurs in a program.
12. REAL loop counters are dangerous because REAL arithmetic is not exact.
13. One loop can be nested inside another. The computer executes the entire inner loop for each value of the outer loop variable.
14. Programs that require large amounts of data should read the data from a file.
15. Fortran can read data from existing data files, and can create data files for output.
16. A program that uses a file should contain an OPEN statement that connects the file to the program.
17. The OPEN statements we have used contain three specifiers: a unit specifier, a file specifier, and a status specifier.
18. After the OPEN statement, the program uses the unit number to refer to the file in READ, WRITE, or CLOSE statements.
19. The list-directed statement to place output in a file uses the word WRITE instead of PRINT.

■ 4.4   EXERCISES

■ *Self Test*

1. How many times will the computer execute the body of each loop below? What will be printed in each case?

a.
```
        DO 11 I = 2, 6
           PRINT *, I
    11  CONTINUE
```

b.
```
        DO 22 K = 12, 0, -3
           PRINT *, K
    22  CONTINUE
```

c.
```
        DO 33 NUM = 20, 1
           PRINT *, NUM
    33  CONTINUE
```

d.
```
        DO 44 Z = 0.25, 2.0, 0.5
           PRINT *, Z
    44  CONTINUE
```

2. What will the computer print after the following loops? Assume all variables have INTEGER type.

a.
```
        SUM = 0
        DO 11 I = 3, 5
           SUM = SUM + I
    11  CONTINUE
        PRINT *, SUM
```

b.
```
        PROD = 1
        DO 11 J = 1, 8, 2
           PROD = PROD * J
    11  CONTINUE
        PRINT *, PROD
```

c.
```
        SUM = 0
        DO 11 I = 1, 5
           SUM = SUM + 1 / I
    11  CONTINUE
        PRINT *, SUM
```

d.
```
        SUM = 0
        DO 11 I = 1, 10
           SUM = SUM + MOD(I, 2)
    11  CONTINUE
        PRINT *, SUM
```

3. a. Write a DO statement that initializes the index variable ITEM at 5, increments by 4, and stops execution of the loop body when ITEM becomes greater than 100.

b. Write a DO statement that initializes the index variable NUMBER at 100, increments by −7, and stops execution of the loop body when NUMBER becomes
less than 0.

4. How many times does the computer execute the body of the nested loops below?
What is printed in each case?

a.
```
        DO 22 I = 1, 2
          DO 11 J = 1, 2
            PRINT I, J
  11      CONTINUE
  22    CONTINUE
```

b.
```
        DO 22 I = 1, 3
          DO 11 J = I, 3
            PRINT J - I
  11      CONTINUE
  22    CONTINUE
```

■ Programming Exercises

1. Write a program to sum the even integers from 2 through 100 and print the result.

2. Write a program to add the squares of the first 100 positive integers and print the result.

3. Suppose you borrow $5,000 at 12% simple interest per year. At the end of each year, you repay $1,000 of the loan. Write a program to print the balance on the loan at the end of each year for six years.

4. Write a program that asks the user for positive integers n and k, then calculates the value of $C(n, k)$. Calculate the numerator and denominator separately, after cancelling the larger factorial in the denominator; then divide the numerator by the denominator. This program is probably easier to understand than the program in Example 4.10. What is the advantage to the latter program?

5. For a set of N real numbers, let SUM stand for the sum of the numbers and $SUMSQ$ for the sum of the squares of the numbers. Then the **mean** of the set of numbers is defined to be SUM/N and the **standard deviation** of the numbers is the square root of

$$\frac{SUMSQ - \dfrac{SUM^2}{N}}{N - 1}$$

Write a program that reads the value of N and the N real numbers from a data file, and calculates the mean and standard deviation of the set of numbers.

6. Given the present population level (Present), birth rate (Birth), and death rate (Death), the predicted population level (Future) at a time *n* years from now is given by the equation

$$Future = Present\,(1\,+\,Birth\,-\,Death\,)^n$$

This assumes that the birth and death rates remain constant over the *n* years. Write a program to predict future population levels of the earth through the year 2,000. On July 1, 1987, the population of the earth was estimated to be about 5 billion, the birth rate about 2.4 percent, and the death rate 0.9 percent. The rates in the equation are expressed in decimals, not percents.

7. Make the necessary changes to the payroll program in Example 4.7 so the program reads the input data from a file and writes the output to a file. The input data should include a five-digit identification number, as well as hours worked and pay rate for each employee. Include the possibility of overtime, as in Programming Exercise 10 in Chapter 3.

8. In a course with NRSTUD students, NRTEST tests are given. Write a program to calculate the mean grade on the tests for each student. Also calculate the mean grade on all NRSTUD * NRTEST tests. Read input data from a file.

9. Three (small) classes are given the same test. Write a program to calculate the mean grade for each class, and the mean for the combined classes. Allow the classes to have different numbers of students. Read input data from a file.

10. When interest is compounded *n* times per year, the formula in the text for the final value becomes

$$Value = Principal \times \left[1 + \frac{Rate}{100n} \right]^{n \times Term}$$

Write a program to print a table showing accumulated value on an initial investment of $1,000 for 1 year with interest rates from 9 to 10 percent in steps of 1/4 percent, and compounding one, two, three, or four times per year.

11. The volume of a right circular cylinder is its height times the area of its base. The base is a circle whose area is π times the square of its radius. The value of π is about 3.141593. Calculate the volumes of right circular cylinders for all values of height from 3 to 5 inches in steps of 1/2 inch, and all values of radius from 1 to 2 inches in steps of 1/4 inch.

12. Write a program to count the number of ways to make 3 gallons using containers that will hold gallons, quarts, pints, and cups. (Recall that 2 cups = 1 pint, 2 pints = 1 quart, and 4 quarts = 1 gallon.)

13. Write a program to list and count the number of ways three different digits can be chosen from the digits 0 through 9, without regard to order. That is, if (0 1 2) is one way, do not count (2 0 1) or (1 2 0).

14. Given a set of *n* pairs of scores (*x*, *y*), the **correlation coefficient** *r* measures the strength of the linear relationship between *x* and *y*. If *r* = 1 or *r* = −1, the graph (*x*, *y*) pairs falls on a straight line. If *r* = 0, the pairs have no linear relationship. (With *r* = 0, the pairs might have a strong *nonlinear* relationship. For example, the graph of the pairs might fall on a circle.) Let *xmean* and *ymean* be the means of the *x* and *y* values. Let *sumxx* be the sum of the squares of the *x* values. Similarly, let *sumyy* be the sum of the *y* values, and let *sumxy* be the sum of the products *xy*. We define some intermediate values, *ssx*, *ssy*, and *sp*, to aid in calculating *r*.

$$ssx = sumxx - n(xmean)^2$$

$$ssy = sumyy - n(ymean)^2$$

$$sp = sumxy - n(xmean)(ymean)$$

Then the correlation coefficient *r* is

$$r = \frac{sp}{\sqrt{(ssx)(ssy)}}$$

Write a program that reads pairs of (*x*, *y*) values and calculates the correlation coefficient *r*.

15. Paired data, as in Exercise 14, always have a **least squares** line, which minimizes the sum of squares of the vertical deviations of the points from the line. Using the standard slope-intercept equation of the line as

$$y = a + bx$$

and the notation of Exercise 14, we can calculate the slope *b* and *y*-intercept as

$$b = \frac{sp}{ssx}$$

$$a = ymean - b(xmean)$$

Write a program that reads pairs of (*x*, *y*) values and calculates the slope and intercept of the least squares line.

16. Example 4.11 approximated the area under a curve with a sum of rectangles. We can often get a better approximation by using *trapezoids* in place of rectangles. See Figure 4.4. You may recall that the area of a trapezoid is equal to the base times the average height, or

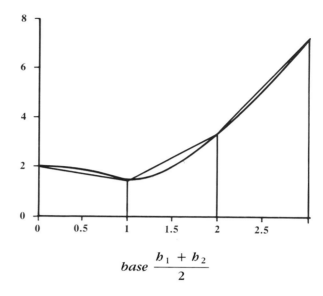

FIGURE 4.4
Approximating area
with three trapezoids

$$base \ \frac{h_1 + h_2}{2}$$

Then, the sum of the areas of the three trapezoids in Figure 4.4 is

$$SUM = base \ \frac{h_1 + h_2}{2} + base \ \frac{h_2 + h_3}{2} + base \ \frac{h_3 + h_4}{2}$$

$$= base \ \frac{h_1 + 2h_2 + 2h_3 + h_4}{2}$$

$$= base \ \left[\frac{h_1}{2} + h_2 + h_3 + \frac{h_4}{2} \right]$$

With any number of trapezoids, inside the parentheses the first and last heights have coefficient 1/2, while all intermediate heights have coefficient 1.

If the function $f(x)$ defining the curve is monotone (either increases or decreases, but not both) on the given interval, then a fairly simple formula gives the number of trapezoids required to approximate the area to within a specified error. Let a and b be the endpoints of the interval, E the specified error, and n the number of trapezoids. Then

$$n = \left| \frac{(b - a)[f(b) - f(a)]}{2E} \right|$$

Write a program using trapezoids to approximate the area under a curve between two points a and b. Print the number of rectangles used as well as the approximate area. (Remember, the formula for the number of trapezoids is valid only for *monotone* functions.) If you know calculus, try your program on some functions you can integrate by hand and some you cannot. Here are two functions you probably do not know how to integrate.

$$\text{a.} \ \sqrt{x^4 + 3x^2 + 5} \qquad \text{b.} \ \frac{e^{-x^2}}{\sqrt{2\pi}}$$

17. **Simpson's rule** for the approximate area under a curve is a formula that generally gives a better approximation than rectangles or trapezoids. Here is one version of Simpson's rule, which uses an even number n of equal subdivisions of the interval (a, b). The endpoints of these subdivisions are given by

$$a = x_0 \ x_1 \ x_2 \ x_3 \ \cdots \ x_{n-1} \ x_n = b$$

Simpson's rule approximates the area under the curve $f(x)$ by multiplying one-third the subdivision width times the sum

$$f(a) + 4f(x_1) + 2f(x_2) + 4f(x_3) + 2f(x_4) + \cdots +$$

$$4f(x_{n-1}) + f(b)$$

Write a program to find the area under some curve. Let the user enter the endpoints of the interval and the number of subdivisions to use.

Hint: Calculate the sum in three parts:

    a.   The odd terms with subscripts from 1 to $n-1$
    b.   The even terms with subscripts from 2 to $n-2$
    c.   The endpoints

5 IF STATEMENTS

Aside from DO loops, the major control statements in Fortran are IF statements. The primary purpose of IF statements is **selection**; if a certain condition is true, select certain statements to execute. IF statements can also control loops, a use which we discuss in the next chapter.

Fortran contains three different IF statements: the logical IF, a block IF construct, and the arithmetic IF. Most of this chapter is devoted to the block IF construction, but we start with the simpler logical IF statement. The obsolete arithmetic IF statement is given in Appendix A.

■ 5.1   THE LOGICAL IF STATEMENT

The **logical** IF statement has the form

> IF < condition >   < statement >

where < condition > stands for any logical expression. When the condition is true, the statement is executed; when the condition is false, the statement is not executed.

Relational Expressions

The technical term for a condition is a **logical expression**. The data type of a logical expression is LOGICAL. The LOGICAL type contains only the two constant values

> .TRUE.   .FALSE.

The periods before and after the words must be present.

Since IF statements require logical expressions, we introduce here a simple form of logical expression called a **relational expression**. We give a more detailed discussion of logical expressions at the end of this chapter.

A relational expression consists of two numeric or two character expressions and a **relational operator**. There are six relational operators in Fortran, corresponding to the six relations given in Figure 5.1.

FIGURE 5.1
The relational operators in Fortran

Relation	Fortran Relational Operator
Equals	.EQ.
Less than	.LT.
Greater than	.GT.
Less than or equal	.LE.
Greater than or equal	.GE.
Not equal	.NE.

Some simple relational expressions are:

```
I .NE. 2              (I is an integer variable.)
AREA .GE. 1.5 * HEIGHT   (AREA and HEIGHT are real.)
NAME .LT. 'N'         (NAME is CHARACTER.)
```

Several important rules govern the use of relational expressions.

1. The relational operator must begin and end with periods.
2. The relational operator stands between two expressions.
3. The two expressions must have the same type: INTEGER, REAL, or CHARACTER.
4. A relational expression is also a logical expression, so its type is LOGICAL, and the only values it can assume are .TRUE. and .FALSE..

Numeric Operands

Usually it is easy to determine the value of a relational expression when the operands are numeric expressions. For instance, 3 is less than 4, so if I has value 3 and J has value 4, then the relational expression

$$I .LT. J$$

is true, or its value is .TRUE.. If AREA has value 16.2, SIDE has value 7.5, and HEIGHT has value 5.1, then the expression

```
        AREA .GE. SIDE * HEIGHT
```

has the value .FALSE..

Most Fortrans will accept a relational expression with one REAL operand and one INTEGER, but you should avoid such mixed-mode expressions. The computer converts the INTEGER operand to REAL before evaluating the relational expression.

String Operands

For character strings consisting of a single uppercase letter, the operator .LT. means *prior to, in alphabetical order*. Thus, if NAME has the value 'D', then the expression

```
        NAME .LT. 'B'
```

has the value .FALSE.. The .EQ. operator means *identical to, except possibly for trailing blanks*. For instance, the value of

```
        'A' .EQ. 'A  '
```

is .TRUE.. The meanings of the other relational operators with string expressions follow from these two: .GT. means *follows in alphabetical order*; .LE. means *is prior to, or equal, in alphabetical order*; and so on.

Similarly, strings containing only lowercase letters can be alphabetized the same as strings of uppercase letters.

Strings can contain any printable characters, not just capital letters, so there must be a precedence order for all characters. The VAX and many other computers use the ASCII collating sequence, while IBM and many other computers use the EBCDIC sequence. These sequences appear in Appendix B. The following information, true for either collating sequence, is adequate for now.

1. The uppercase letters are in alphabetical order.
2. The lowercase letters are in alphabetical order.
3. The digits, '0' through '9', are in standard numerical order.
4. The space, or blank, is prior to all digits and letters. Here are some examples that follow from these rules.

.TRUE.	.FALSE.
'A' .LT. 'C'	' ' .GE. 'x'
'z' .GT. 'a'	'2' .LT. '1'
'B' .NE. 'b'	'J' .EQ. 'j'

Comparing string operands with more than one character is exactly like alphabetizing words for a dictionary. Start with the leftmost characters, and continue comparing corresponding characters until the outcome is obvious. For instance, 'C' is less than 'P', so we can tell 'ACT' is less than 'APPLE' by simply looking at the second characters in each string. To compare 'A3x27' with 'A3x25', we have to compare the fifth characters, '7' and '5', before we know that 'A3x25' is less than 'A3x27'.

When comparing two CHARACTER expressions of different lengths, the computer adds blanks to the right side of the shorter one, until the two lengths are equal. Thus, 'ABC' is less than 'ABC2'. Watch out for strings of digits with different lengths; '123' is less than '20' because '1' is less than '2'. Also note that the comparison of '123' with '20' is a *character* comparison, not a comparison of numeric quantities.

Here are several more examples of relational expressions with string operands.

.TRUE.	.FALSE.
'BC' .LT. 'ACB12'	'abc' .GE. 'abcx'
'abc' .GT. 'ab'	'123' .LT. '1 23'
'BOY' .NE. 'Boy'	'Ab3' .LE. 'Ab25'

The logical IF statement is a **compound** statement because it contains another complete statement after its condition. The statement in a logical IF statement can be almost any executable statement. The most commonly used are assignment and PRINT statements. The only executable statements which *cannot* follow the condition in a logical IF statement are those beginning with DO, END, or IF. Some examples of logical IF statements are:

```
IF (A .LT. B) A = B

IF (GRADE .GE. 90) ACOUNT = ACOUNT + 1

IF (X - Y .GT. U - V) PRINT *, 'First difference is greater'
```

In the first case, if the value stored in A is less than the value stored in B, then the value in B is placed in A. In the second case, if the value in GRADE is 90 or above, the variable ACOUNT increases by 1. In the third case, the values X - Y and U - V are calculated and compared; if the first value is greater than the second, the computer executes the PRINT statement. In each case, if the condition in parentheses is not true, the computer ignores the statement after the condition.

Example 5.1 Counting with the Logical IF Statement

Counting is a standard use of the logical IF statement. We have already seen counting statements such as N = N + 1, used to count *all* occurrences of some other statement. With the logical IF, the computer can count occurrences of a special condition. Suppose we have a list of grades (numbers from 1 to 100) and want to count the number of A grades (grades of 90 or above). A statement that counts those grades is

```
IF (GRADE .GE. 90) ACOUNT = ACOUNT + 1
```

Program 5.1 is a program to count A grades.

■

PROGRAM 5.1
_____

```
      PROGRAM COUNTA
*-------------------------------------------------------*
*                Count all grades 90 or above.          *
*-------------------------------------------------------*
      INTEGER GRADE, ACOUNT, NUMBER, I

      PRINT *, 'How many grades?'
      READ  *, NUMBER

      PRINT *, 'Enter the grades, one at a time.'

      ACOUNT = 0
      DO 11 I = 1, NUMBER
         PRINT *, 'Grade?'
         READ  *, GRADE
         IF (GRADE .GE. 90) ACOUNT = ACOUNT + 1
11    CONTINUE

      PRINT *, ACOUNT, ' grades were 90 or above.'

      END
```

_____

Example 5.2 Finding the Largest Number in a List

Consider the problem of finding the largest number in a list of numbers input by the user of a program. In Chapter 4 we wrote a similar program to find the smallest number in the list. We could write an almost identical program with MAX in place of MIN, but instead we will use a logical IF statement to help find the largest number.

The program should read the numbers one at a time, and after reading a number, the program should decide if it is the largest number read *up to now*. Let NUMBER represent any one of the numbers in the list, and let LARGE represent the largest number read before NUMBER was read. Then, to determine whether NUMBER *is* the largest number read up to now, we can use an IF statement beginning

        IF (NUMBER .GT. LARGE)

The next question is what should be done if NUMBER *is* greater than LARGE. Then the value of NUMBER should be stored in LARGE, and the computer should go on to read the next number in the list. The statement that stores the value of NUMBER in LARGE is

        LARGE = NUMBER

so the complete IF statement is

        IF (NUMBER .GT. LARGE) LARGE = NUMBER

If NUMBER is not greater than LARGE, then some previous number in the list must have been greater than NUMBER, so we simply ignore this value of NUMBER and read the next number in the list.

The only remaining question is how to get the first value for LARGE. When the first number in the list is read, it *is* the largest value read up to now, so LARGE can be set to the first value of NUMBER without using an IF statement. That is, after the first

        READ *, NUMBER

statement, we can simply assign the value of NUMBER to LARGE with the statement

        LARGE = NUMBER

We will let the user specify how many numbers are to be entered, and we will store this value in HOWMNY. The program will read one value for NUMBER and store this number in LARGE. Then the program will read the rest of the numbers in a DO loop with loop counter I beginning at 2. Program 5.2 shows the complete program.

■
PROGRAM 5.2

```
      PROGRAM LARGST
*-------------------------------------------------------*
*              Find the largest number in a list.        *
*-------------------------------------------------------*
      REAL     NUMBER, LARGE
      INTEGER  I, HOWMNY

      PRINT *, 'This program finds the largest number in a list.'
      PRINT *, 'How many numbers do you wish to enter?'
      READ  *, HOWMNY

      PRINT *, 'Enter the numbers one at a time.'
      PRINT *, 'Number?'
      READ  *, NUMBER
      LARGE = NUMBER

      DO 11 I = 2, HOWMNY
         PRINT *, 'Number?'
         READ  *, NUMBER
         IF (NUMBER .GT. LARGE) LARGE = NUMBER
11    CONTINUE

      PRINT *, 'The largest number in your list is', LARGE

      END
```

■
5.2 IF **BLOCKS**

The logical IF statement is a valuable tool, but it is restrictive because only one statement can follow the condition in the IF statement. The **block** IF **statement**, or IF **block**, allows several statements to be performed when a condition is true.

The IF...THEN **Block**

The simplest form of block IF is the IF...THEN **block**. It works like this:

```
IF (I .EQ. J) THEN
    PRINT *, 'Values are equal.'
    I = I + 1
    J = J - 1
END IF
```

If the value of I is equal to the value of J, then the computer will execute the three statements after THEN: it prints 'Values are equal', increments the value of I by 1, and decrements the value of J by 1. If the values of I and J are not equal, the computer ignores these three statements and proceeds to the first statement after END IF.

The general form of the IF...THEN block is:

```
IF (<Logical expression>) THEN
        .  .  .    (Block
        .  .  .       of
        .  .  .    statements)
END IF
```

The block IF, like the logical IF, begins with IF <condition>, but there are three major differences.

1. The keyword THEN appears immediately after <condition> and must be the last word on the line.

2. There is a block of one or more statements to be performed whenever <condition> is true. Each statement appears on a separate line following THEN. Indenting these statement lines is not required, but makes the program easier to read.

3. The END IF statement terminates the IF block. When the condition after IF is true, the computer will execute all statements between THEN and END IF. When the condition is false, the com-.puter ignores these statements and proceeds to the first executable statement after END IF.

Example 5.3 Finding the Largest Number and its Position

Consider the problem of Example 5.2, finding the largest number in a list. Suppose we also want to find the position (first, second, third, or whatever) of this number in the list. A program to do this is an easy extension of the program in Example 5.2, with an IF...THEN block replacing the logical IF statement.

A new variable POSIT takes an initial value of 1 when the first number is read. Then, whenever the value of LARGE changes, the value of POSIT must change too. Since the numbers are being read inside a DO loop with index I, the position of a number being read inside the loop is the current value of I. Therefore, whenever the computer executes

```
LARGE = NUMBER
```

in the loop, it must also execute

```
POSIT = I
```

See Program 5.3. Note the similarity of this program to the previous one.

■
PROGRAM 5.3

```
      PROGRAM LARGEP
*------------------------------------------------------------*
*        Find the largest number and its position in a list.  *
*------------------------------------------------------------*
      REAL      NUMBER, LARGE
      INTEGER   I, HOWMNY, POSIT

      PRINT *, 'This program finds the largest number in a list.'
      PRINT *, 'How many numbers do you wish to enter?'
      READ  *, HOWMNY

      PRINT *, 'Enter the numbers one at a time.'
      PRINT *, 'Number?'
      READ  *, NUMBER

      LARGE = NUMBER
      POSIT = 1

      DO 11 I = 2, HOWMNY

         PRINT *, 'Number?'
         READ  *, NUMBER

         IF (NUMBER .GT. LARGE) THEN
             LARGE = NUMBER
             POSIT = I
         END IF

11    CONTINUE
```

```
PRINT *, 'The largest number in your list is', LARGE
PRINT *, LARGE, ' first occurred in position', POSIT

END
```

The last PRINT statement tells where the largest number *first* occurred. If two or more numbers have the same largest value, the final value of POSIT will be the position of the first one, because the logical operator in the IF condition is .GT.. If the operator had been .GE., then the final value of POSIT would be the position of the *last* of the largest values. If there were only one largest value, then it would not matter whether .GT. or .GE. were used. Be aware that the difference between .GE. and .GT. is often important.

Beginning programmers sometimes get confused between IF...THEN blocks and loops. There are some similarities, but the major distinction is that IF...THEN blocks do not automatically repeat. When the computer comes to END IF, it passes on to the next statement. You can force the block to repeat by placing it inside a DO loop.

Example 5.4 Swapping Values of Variables

A standard programming device involves swapping values of two variables, A and B. By *swapping* we mean putting the value of B into A and the value of A into B. This device is useful in programs that sort lists of numbers or strings. It is tempting to write

```
A = B
B = A
```

but you should see that this will *not* swap values of A and B. Suppose, for concreteness, that A has value 6 and B has value 3. Then the statement A = B will give A the value 3 but leave B unchanged (with value 3). The value of 6 has been lost. To save the value 6, a temporary storage place is needed. Let T stand for the name of this temporary place. First, put the value of A into T to save it (T = A). Next, put the value of B into A (A = B). Finally, give B the original value of A, which is now the value of T (B = T). Pictorially, we have originally:

Then, each statement below causes the result following it.

Statement	Result

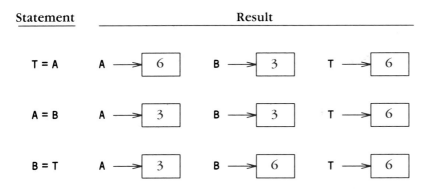

	A → [6]	B → [3]	T → [6]
T = A	A → [6]	B → [3]	T → [6]
A = B	A → [3]	B → [3]	T → [6]
B = T	A → [3]	B → [6]	T → [6]

A simple program using this technique is given in Program 5.4.

■
PROGRAM 5.4

```
PROGRAM ORDER
*-----------------------------------------------------------------*
*       Put values of two variables in increasing order.         *
*-----------------------------------------------------------------*
      INTEGER  A, B, T

      PRINT *, 'Enter two different integers.'
      PRINT *, 'The computer will print them in increasing order.'
      READ  *, A, B
*-----------------------------------------------------------------*
*   If A > B then swap values.  Otherwise leave them as they are.  *
*-----------------------------------------------------------------*
      IF (A .GT. B) THEN
         T = A
         A = B
         B = T
      END IF

      PRINT *, 'The values in increasing order are', A, B

      END
```

If the user enters values of A and B in increasing order, then the computer will not execute the IF block, so it will print A and B in their given order. When the values are not in the proper order, the statements in the IF block will swap them.

The IF...THEN...ELSE **Block**

The IF...THEN block is most useful when the programmer has one set of statements that must be executed in some circumstances and not executed in others. In Program 5.4, the statements

```
T = A
A = B
B = T
```

were sometimes executed and sometimes not. When they were not executed, nothing in particular needed to be done but to continue with the flow of the program. Sometimes the programmer will have one set of statements to be performed when a condition is true, and another set of statements to be performed when the condition is false. This situation requires an extension of the IF...THEN block called the IF...THEN...ELSE **block**. The form of this block is:

```
IF <condition> THEN
      . . .          (Block of statements
      . . .           to be performed when
      . . .           condition is true)
ELSE
      . . .          (Block of statements
      . . .           to be performed when
      . . .           condition is false)
END IF
```

This construct, from the beginning IF to the ending END IF, is *one* Fortran statement. We refer to the word ELSE and its associated block as an ELSE *clause*, to stress that these elements are only *part* of a statement. ELSE cannot stand alone but must occur as part of a block IF statement.

The next two examples illustrate the use of IF...THEN...ELSE blocks.

Example 5.5 An IF...THEN...ELSE **Block to Count Odd and Even Numbers**

Program 5.5 reads a list of integers from the file ODDEV.DAT and counts the numbers of odd and even numbers. After reading an integer, the program will print the integer and Odd or Even, as appropriate.

We assume the first number in the data file is an integer representing the remaining number of integers. We will read that number into NINTEG, then read the integers inside a loop beginning

```
DO 11 I = 1, NINTEG
```

We need two accumulators; NODD and NEVEN will denote the numbers of odd and even integers. When the computer reads an odd integer, we want the computer to print Odd and count the integer as odd. Thus we will have

```
IF (MOD(INTEG, 2) .EQ. 1) THEN
    PRINT *, INTEG, ' Odd'
    NODD = NODD + 1
```

When the integer is even, or not odd, the computer must print Even and count the integer as even, so the ELSE clause is

```
    PRINT *, INTEG, ' Even'
    NEVEN = NEVEN + 1
```

The heart of this program is this IF...THEN...ELSE block within a loop. Program 5.5 contains the complete program.

■

PROGRAM 5.5

```
    PROGRAM ODDEVN
*----------------------------------------------------------------*
*    Count odd and even integers with an IF...THEN...ELSE block   *
*    Integers are in a file named ODDEV.DAT, one integer per line. *
*    The first number in the file is the number of integers.      *
*----------------------------------------------------------------*
    INTEGER  INTEG, NINTEG, I, NODD, NEVEN
    DATA     NODD, NEVEN /2*0/

    OPEN (20, FILE = 'ODDEV.DAT', STATUS = 'OLD')

    PRINT *, 'This program counts odd and even integers.'
    PRINT *
    READ (20, *) NINTEG
*----------------------------------------------------------------*
*                    Repeat for each integer.                     *
*----------------------------------------------------------------*
    Do 11 I = 1, NINTEG

        READ (20, *) INTEG
        IF (MOD(INTEG, 2) .EQ. 1) THEN
            PRINT *, INTEG, ' Odd'
            NODD = NODD + 1
```

```
        ELSE
            PRINT *, INTEG, '  Even'
            NEVEN = NEVEN + 1
        END IF

11      CONTINUE

     PRINT *
     PRINT *, 'Number of odd integers: ', NODD
     PRINT *, 'Number of even integers:', NEVEN

     END
```

Example 5.6 Finding a Root by Bisection

A common mathematical problem is finding a **root** of a function $f(x)$, or a value of x that makes $f(x) = 0$. We have formulas for finding the roots of many functions, including a quadratic function of the form

$$f(x) = ax^2 + bx + c$$

There are, however, many functions for which we do not know formulas, and in most cases all we can do is find an approximate root, a value of x that makes $f(x)$ very small. Nearly all methods for finding approximate roots involve iteration or repetition; start with an initial approximation (guess or estimate) of the root, and continue finding better approximations.

Bisection of an interval is one of the simplest methods for finding approximate roots of a function. For example, consider finding a root of the function

$$f(x) = x - e^{-x}$$

This problem is equivalent to finding a value x such that $x = e^{-x}$. Figure 5.2 shows a graph of the two functions $y = x$ and $y = e^{-x}$. The figure shows that $f(x)$ has a root somewhere between $x = 0$ and $x = 1$. Moreover,

$$f(0) = 0 - e^{-0} = 0 - 1 = -1$$

and

$$f(1) = 1 - e^{-1} = 1 - 1/e = 1 - 0.3679 = 0.6321$$

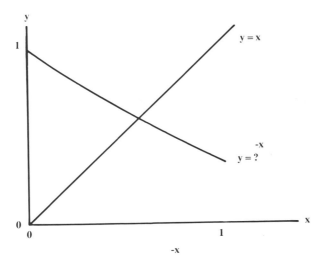

FIGURE 5.2
Graphs of $y = x$ and $y = e^{-x}$

Thus we have found two values, 0 and 1, with $f(0)$ negative and $f(1)$ positive. Since $f(x)$ is obviously continuous on the interval from 0 to 1, $f(x)$ must cross the x-axis somewhere between 0 and 1. That is, $f(x)$ must have a root between 0 and 1.

If we were doing this problem by hand, we would cut the interval from 0 to 1 in half with the value 0.5. Then

$$f(0.5) = 0.5 - e^{-0.5} = 0.5 - 0.6065 = -0.1065$$

Since $f(0.5)$ is negative and $f(1)$ is positive, we know that the root must lie between 0.5 and 1. We cut this interval in half with the value 0.75 and determine that

$$f(0.75) = 0.75 - e^{-0.75} = 0.75 - 0.4724 = 0.2776$$

Since $f(0.75)$ is positive and $f(0.5)$ is negative, we know the root is between 0.5 and 0.75.

We could continue this process with a hand calculator until our approximate root was sufficiently close to the real root, but we will write a program to do the calculations for us.

Some important points are:

1. The user must be able to specify two values A and B, with $A < B$, such that $f(A)$ and $f(B)$ have different signs.

2. The function must be continuous on the interval from A to B. (If $f(A)$ and $f(B)$ have different signs and f is continuous on the interval from A to B, then $f(x)$ must be zero at some point x between A and B.)

3. The user specifies a maximum desirable error, or discrepancy between the approximate root and the true root. The program calculates the number N of times the given interval must be halved

to make the length of the search interval less than the specified error. Then a DO loop with I ranging from 1 to N cuts the interval in half at each step. In theory, this will work, but the limited precision of the computer will often make the error greater than the maximum specified error.

Realizing that we seldom find the exact value of the root, we must now specify a maximum error that we can tolerate. Suppose we choose the value *ERROR*. Since we use the midpoint of an interval as an approximate root, the error cannot be more than half the length of the interval. Thus, an interval of length 2 *ERROR* guarantees the error is not more than *ERROR*.

Let N denote the number of times we bisect an interval. Since our original interval has length $B - A$, we must cut the interval in half N times, so we require

$$\frac{B - A}{2^N} \leq 2 \; ERROR$$

or

$$2^N \geq \frac{B - A}{2 \; ERROR}$$

Taking logarithms gives

$$N \log(2) \geq \frac{\log(B - A)}{2 \; ERROR}$$

or

$$N \geq \frac{\log\left(\dfrac{B - A}{2 \; ERROR}\right)}{\log(2)}$$

Since N must be an integer, we write the Fortran code as

```
N = 1 + INT( LOG( (B - A) / (2.0 * ERROR) ) / LOG(2.0) )
```

We begin by setting LOW to the value of A and HIGH to the value of B and calculating the function values FL and FH at the endpoints of the interval by

```
FL = F(LOW)
FH = F(HIGH)
```

Then, inside a loop beginning

```
DO 11 I = 1, N
```

we calculate the midpoint, ROOT, of the interval, and the value FROOT of the function at this midpoint, with the statements

```
ROOT  = (HIGH + LOW) / 2.0
FROOT = F(ROOT)
```

If FROOT has the same sign as FH, or if FROOT * FH is positive, then the root is in the lower half-interval, so we set HIGH to the value of ROOT and FH to the value of FROOT with

```
IF (FROOT * FH .GT. 0) THEN
    HIGH = ROOT
    FH   = FROOT
```

If FROOT does not have the same sign as FH, then the root is in the upper half-interval, so we complete the IF block with

```
ELSE
    LOW = ROOT
    FL  = FROOT
END IF
```

See Program 5.6 for the complete program.

■

PROGRAM 5.6

```
     PROGRAM BISECT
*-----------------------------------------------------------------*
*  Find root of a function by repeatedly bisecting an interval. *
*  Note: The function must be continuous in the given interval. *
*        The error bound specified might not be attainable      *
*        because of the limited precision of the computer.      *
*-----------------------------------------------------------------*
     REAL    ROOT, ERROR, F, FX, FH, FL, A, B, LOW, HIGH, X
     INTEGER N, I
     DATA    A, B, ERROR /0.0, 1.0, 1E-6/
     F(X) = X - EXP(-X)

     LOW  = A
     HIGH = B
```

```
      FL   = F(LOW)
      FH   = F(HIGH)
*-------------------------------------------------------------*
*  Calculate the number of iterations required to reduce the  *
*  search interval to a length less than the maximum error.   *
*-------------------------------------------------------------*
      N = 1 + INT( LOG((B - A) / ERROR) / LOG(2.0))
*-------------------------------------------------------------*
*                Perform a binary search for the root.        *
*-------------------------------------------------------------*
      DO 11 I = 1, N

         ROOT = (HIGH + LOW) / 2.0
         FX   = F(ROOT)

         IF (FX * FH .GT. 0) THEN
             HIGH = ROOT
             FH   = FX
         ELSE
             LOW = ROOT
             FL = FX
         END IF

11    CONTINUE

      PRINT *, 'Approximate root:', ROOT
      PRINT *, 'Function value:  ', FX
      PRINT *, N, ' Iterations used.'

      END
```

The IF **Block with** ELSE IF...THEN

IF...THEN...ELSE blocks cover situations involving two sets of statements. Several ELSE IF...THEN clauses can be added to deal with any number of sets of statements. Consider again a grading problem, in which numerical grades are converted to letter grades according to the following scheme.

Numerical Grade	Letter Grade
90 or above	A
80–89+	B
70–79+	C
60–69+	D
Below 60	F

where 89+ indicates that a grade of 89.999, for example, is a B. Let GRADE be a variable containing a numerical grade, and let LETTER be the string variable to contain the corresponding letter grade. Then the following IF block assigns the proper value to LETTER.

```
IF (GRADE .GE. 90) THEN
        LETTER = 'A'
ELSE IF (GRADE .GE. 80) THEN
        LETTER = 'B'
ELSE IF (GRADE .GE. 70) THEN
        LETTER = 'C'
ELSE IF (GRADE .GE. 60) THEN
        LETTER = 'D'
ELSE
        LETTER = 'F'
END IF
```

Look at the first ELSE IF...THEN:

```
ELSE IF (GRADE .GE. 80) THEN
        LETTER = 'B'
```

We do *not* need to check that GRADE is less than 90 here. The meaning of ELSE is *if the preceding statement is not true*. Therefore, if LETTER has already been assigned the value 'A' because GRADE is 90 or above, the computer will not even look at the following ELSE IF conditions. Similarly, for the second ELSE IF,

```
ELSE IF (GRADE .GE. 70) THEN
        LETTER = 'C'
```

the computer will not try to determine the value of (GRADE .GE. 70) if one of the previous conditions (GRADE .GE. 90) or (GRADE .GE. 80) were true. Thus the computer will never execute more than one block of statements in a block IF construction. The ELSE without a following IF guarantees that at least one block of statements will be performed. If LETTER was not assigned a value of 'A', 'B', 'C', or 'D', then it will be given the value 'F'.

This most general type of IF block has the form:

```
IF <condition 1> THEN
        block 1
ELSE IF <condition 2> THEN
        block 2
```

```
      ELSE IF <condition 3> THEN
              block 3
          .     .    .
          .     .    .
          .          .    .
      ELSE
              block n
      END IF
```

Each block stands for a set of one or more statements, to be executed when the condition immediately preceding it is the *first* true condition. There can be any number (including zero) of ELSE IF...THEN clauses. ELSE without a following IF is also optional, but when it appears, it must be the last ELSE.

Example 5.7 Assigning Letter Grades

The IF block above serves as the center of a program to assign letter grades to numerical grades. We shall also count the number of letter grades of each type. As before, we read from a file GRADE.DAT and assume the first number in the file is the number of grades. See Program 5.7.

■
PROGRAM 5.7
──

```
      PROGRAM LETGRD
*--------------------------------------------------------------------*
*  Assign letter grades to numerical grades.  Count letter grades.   *
*  Grades are in file GRADE.DAT; first number is number of grades.   *
*--------------------------------------------------------------------*
      REAL      GRADE
      INTEGER   I, NGRADE, ACOUNT, BCOUNT, CCOUNT, DCOUNT, FCOUNT
      CHARACTER LETTER
      DATA      ACOUNT, BCOUNT, CCOUNT, DCOUNT, FCOUNT /5 * 0/

      OPEN (12, FILE = 'GRADE', STATUS = 'OLD')

      PRINT *, 'Letter grades are assigned as follows:'
      PRINT *
      PRINT *, 'NUMBER GRADE    LETTER GRADE'
      PRINT *, '----------------------------'
      PRINT *, '90 or above        A'
      PRINT *, '80 - 89+           B'
      PRINT *, '70 - 79+           C'
      PRINT *, '60 - 69+           D'
      PRINT *, 'Below 60           F'
      PRINT *
```

```
      READ (12, *) NGRADE
      DO 11 I = 1, NGRADE

          READ (12, *) GRADE
          IF (GRADE .GE. 90) THEN
                LETTER = 'A'
                ACOUNT = ACOUNT + 1
          ELSE IF (GRADE .GE. 80) THEN
                LETTER = 'B'
                BCOUNT = BCOUNT + 1
          ELSE IF (GRADE .GE. 70) THEN
                LETTER = 'C'
                CCOUNT = CCOUNT + 1
          ELSE IF (GRADE .GE. 60) THEN
                LETTER = 'D'
                DCOUNT = DCOUNT + 1
          ELSE
                LETTER = 'F'
                FCOUNT = FCOUNT + 1
          END IF

          PRINT *, GRADE, ' is a ', LETTER

11    CONTINUE

      CLOSE (12)

      PRINT *
      PRINT *, 'GRADE      COUNT'
      PRINT *, '----------------'
      PRINT *, '  A', ACOUNT
      PRINT *, '  B', BCOUNT
      PRINT *, '  C', CCOUNT
      PRINT *, '  D', DCOUNT
      PRINT *, '  F', FCOUNT

      END
```

This relatively long program still has a simple structure:

1. Data declaration and initialization
2. Several PRINT statements explaining the program
3. A statement to read the first grade

4. A DO loop containing:

    a.   A statement to read the next grade

    b.   A block IF to assign and count grades

    c.   A PRINT statement to give the letter grade

5. Several PRINT statements to give counts of letter grades

IF blocks are often nested inside DO loops, as you have seen in several examples. As with any nesting, one structure must be completely inside the other. It would be illegal to have

```
       DO 10 ...                 | This
              IF (...) THEN       | is
                 .  .  .          | an
                 .  .  .          | example
                 .  .  .          | of
  10        CONTINUE              | illegal
              END IF              | nesting
```

Similarly, loops can be nested within IF blocks, but each loop must be entirely within one statement block. See Figure 5.3.

FIGURE 5.3
Legal and Illegal Nest-
ing of Loops within IF
Blocks

```
            LEGAL                          ILLEGAL

       IF (...) THEN                  IF (...) THEN          | Illegal
          DO 11 I = ...                  DO 11 I = ...       | because
             .                              .                | DO loop
             .                              .                | extends
             .                              .                | over two
  11        CONTINUE               ELSE IF (...) THEN         | statement
       ELSE IF (...) THEN       11     CONTINUE              | blocks
          DO 22 J = ...                     .
             .                              .
             .                              .
             .                     ELSE                       | Illegal
  22        CONTINUE                  DO 22 I = ...            | because
       ELSE                             .                     | DO loop
             .                          .                     | extends
             .                          .                     | outside
             .                     END IF                     | IF block
       END IF                   22     CONTINUE
```

You also can nest IF blocks within other IF blocks. Once again, the inner IF block must be entirely within one statement block of the outer IF block. Program 5.9 illustrates the nesting of IF blocks.

■
5.3 LOGICAL **OPERATIONS**

As we stated earlier, the condition in an IF statement can be any logical expression; the relational expressions are simple types of logical expressions. A **logical expression**, like any expression, is a valid combination of operators and operands. The **logical operands** are logical constants (.TRUE. and .FALSE.), logical variables, and relational expressions. We will start with logical variables, and then turn to the logical operators.

Logical Variables

Logical variables must be declared in type declaration statements such as

        LOGICAL FOUND, READY

If READY is a logical variable, an IF statement using READY is

        IF (READY) PRINT *, 'Here we go!'

If the variable READY contains the value .TRUE., the computer will execute the PRINT statement; otherwise it will not.

We can give values to logical variables in the same ways we give values to other types of variables:

1. With an assignment statement such as FOUND = .TRUE. (the periods are needed) or FOUND = X .EQ. Y. Some Fortran compilers require parentheses around logical expressions as in

        FOUND = (X .EQ. Y)

2. By initialization in a DATA statement, as in

        LOGICAL FOUND
        DATA   FOUND /.FALSE./

3. Through READ statements, as in READ *, FOUND. The computer considers a response beginning with .T or T to be .TRUE. and a response beginning with .F or F to be .FALSE.. Responses beginning with any letter other than T or F will cause a list-directed syntax error.

Example 5.8 Illustrating Logical Variables

When the computer prints values of logical expressions, it prints just a T or an F. Program 5.8 below gives examples of the use of logical variables in programs.

■
PROGRAM 5.8

```
      PROGRAM LOGICL
*-----------------------------------------------------*
*    Illustrate logical variables and expressions.    *
*-----------------------------------------------------*
      LOGICAL  A, B, C, D
      PRINT *, 'Please enter four logical values.'
      READ  *, A, B, C, D
      PRINT *, 'A is', A
      PRINT *, 'B is', B
      PRINT *, 'C is', C
      PRINT *, 'D is', D
      A = (2.6 .LT. 2.6)
      PRINT *, 'The expression (2.6 .LT. 2.6) is', A
      B = (2.6 .LE. 2.6)
      PRINT *, 'The expression (2.6 .LE. 2.6) is', B
      END
```

When this program runs and the computer asks for four logical values, suppose the user types

```
T, F, THANKS, FOLKS
```

Then the computer will type

```
A is T
B is F
C is T
D is F
The expression (2.6 .LT. 2.6) is F
The expression (2.6 .LE. 2.6) is T
```

Example 5.9 Scoring a Bowling Game

A program to score a bowling game provides a good illustration of logical variables as well as nested IF blocks. In tenpin bowling, each player bowls ten **frames**. In each frame, the bowler rolls one ball. If that ball knocks down all ten pins, the frame is over and the bowler scores a **strike**. If the first ball does not knock down all ten pins, the bowler rolls a second ball. If the first and second ball together knock down all ten pins, the bowler scores a **spare**.

Scoring of bowling is somewhat complicated because, whenever the bowler scores a strike or spare, the score for that frame cannot be determined until the next frame, or possibly the next two frames. Here are the scoring rules:

1. If the bowler scores a strike in one frame, the score for that frame is 10 plus the number of pins the bowler knocks down on the next two balls. (Bowlers refer to a roll as a **ball**.)

2. If the bowler scores a spare in one frame, the score for that frame is 10 plus the number of pins the bowler knocks down on the next ball.

3. If the bowler knocks down fewer than ten pins with two balls, the score for that frame is the total number of pins knocked down with the two balls.

The scorer in bowling records just the *cumulative* frame totals, or the game score. That is, he or she writes down the first frame score, then the total of the first two frames, then the total of the first three frames, and so on. Here is an example of scoring a game:

Frame	1	2	3	4	5	6	7	8	9	10	
First ball	9	10	10	10	8	9	10	9	10	10	8
Second ball	0				2	1		1			2
Game Score	9	39	67	87	106	126	146	164	184	203	

In the first frame, the bowler knocked down 9 pins on the first ball and no pins on the second ball, so the first frame score is 9 and the cumulative score is also 9.

In the second frame the bowler got a strike (all ten pins on the first ball), so the score could not be written until the bowler rolled two more balls. Those next two balls were also strikes, so the second frame score is 30, or 10 plus the total of the two strikes. The cumulative score is now $9 + 30 = 39$.

In the third frame, the bowler also got a strike, and the next two balls scored 10 and 8, so the third frame total is $10 + 10 + 8 = 28$. The game score is then $39 + 28 = 67$.

Another strike in the fourth frame! The next two balls get 8 and 2 pins, so the fourth frame score is $10 + 8 + 2 = 20$. The game score is $67 + 20 = 87$.

The bowler gets a spare (8 and 2) in the fifth frame, so the frame score is 10 plus the next ball score of 9, or 19. The game score is $87 + 19 = 106$.

That should be enough for now. If you have never kept a bowling score, you should check the rest of the frames. Notice that the bowler got a strike in the tenth frame, which necessitated throwing two extra balls to get a score for the tenth frame.

Several program variables practically suggest themselves. We will use the integer variables:

FRAME   for the frame number
SCORE   for the game score
FIRST   for the number of pins knocked down
            by the first ball
SECOND   for the number of pins knocked down
            by the second ball

In scoring the game, we were able to look *ahead* to see what happened on the next ball or two. However, in our program we will read one ball at a time, and will need to look *back* to see what happened in previous frames. Thus, we must keep track of what happened in previous frames. In particular, we need to know if the previous frame had a strike or a spare. We will use the logical variables STRIKE and SPARE for this purpose. STRIKE will be .TRUE. when the last frame had a strike, and .FALSE. otherwise (and similarly for SPARE).

Recall the strikes in frames 2 and 3 of the example game, which meant that we could not record the score for frame 2 until the first ball of frame 4. Whenever the bowler gets two strikes in a row (a **double**), we cannot write the score for the frame of the first strike until *two* frames later. Thus, we also need a logical variable to tell us whether the previous two frames had strikes. We will use TWOSTR for this purpose.

All these logical variables require updating. In a particular frame, STRIKE, SPARE, and TWOSTR tell us whether the previous frame had a strike or spare, and whether the previous two frames had strikes. After we have used this information to score the three frames involved (the current frame, the previous frame, and the one before that), we need to calculate new values for STRIKE, SPARE, and TWOSTR to get ready for the next frame.

There is always some initial work to do. We begin with the three logical variables having value .FALSE., and with SCORE having value 0. We assume that the separate ball scores are in a file BOWL.DAT which we will open as unit 9.

A bare-bones outline of the remainder of the program is as follows:

1. For frames 1 to 10 do the following:

   a. Read the first ball score.
       Write the scores which can now be calculated.

   b. Read the second ball if necessary.
       Write the scores which can now be calculated.

   c. Update the logical variables.

2. Deal with the tenth frame if necessary.

Part 1 is simple; use a DO loop beginning

```
DO 11 FRAME = 1, 10
```

For the first part of 1a, use

```
READ (9, *) FIRST
```

For the second part, we must decide which scores can be calculated after reading the first ball. If the previous frame had a spare, then we can write the score for that frame with the code

```
IF (SPARE) THEN
    SCORE = SCORE + 10 + FIRST
    PRINT *, FRAME - 1, ' Spare ', SCORE
```

The only other possibility we must deal with is two strikes previously, and we take care of that with

```
ELSE IF (TWOSTR) THEN
    SCORE = SCORE + 20 + FIRST
    PRINT *, FRAME - 2, ' Strike', SCORE
END IF
```

For part 1b, *Read the second ball if necessary* is coded as

```
IF (FIRST .LT. 10) THEN
    READ (9, *) SECOND
```

Inside this IF block, we can write a score for the previous frame, if it had a strike, with another IF block

```
              IF (STRIKE) THEN
                  SCORE = SCORE + 10 + FIRST + SECOND
                  PRINT *, FRAME - 1, ' Strike', SCORE
              END IF
```

We can also write a score for the current frame if the two balls have a total less than 10. This takes a second IF block

```
              IF (FIRST + SECOND .LT. 10) THEN
                  SCORE = SCORE + FIRST + SECOND
                  PRINT *, FRAME, '         ', SCORE
              END IF
```

Notice that these must be two separate IF blocks, not one IF...THEN...ELSE block, because we might be able to write both scores. Also, the order of the two blocks is crucial because we must write the previous frame score *before* the current frame score.

Part 1c, updating the logical variables, is not too tricky. The main point here is keeping the updating separate from the score calculations (and, of course, *after* them). We do not show the updating code here, but point out that the updating depends on what happened this frame: strike, spare, or neither. Thus, the updating takes place in an IF block with three statement sections corresponding to the current frame having a strike, spare, or neither.

Also, we do not discuss the Fortran code for part 2 dealing with the tenth frame. You should try writing that code before looking at Program 5.9.

■

PROGRAM 5.9

───

```
      PROGRAM BOWL
*-------------------------------------------------------*
*     Read scores from a file and score a bowling game.    *
*-------------------------------------------------------*
      INTEGER    FIRST, SECOND, FRAME, SCORE
      LOGICAL    STRIKE, TWOSTR, SPARE
      CHARACTER  BLANK*7
      DATA       STRIKE, TWOSTR, SPARE, SCORE /3 * .FALSE., 0/
      PARAMETER (BLANK = '       ')

      PRINT *, '        Frame            Score'

      OPEN (9, FILE = 'BOWL.DAT', STATUS = 'OLD')
```

```
        DO 11 FRAME = 1, 10

          READ (9, *) FIRST
*-----------------------------------------------------------*
*    Check for spare last frame or double two frames ago.   *
*-----------------------------------------------------------*
          IF (SPARE) THEN
              SCORE = SCORE + 10 + FIRST
              PRINT *, FRAME - 1, ' Spare ', SCORE
          ELSE IF (TWOSTR) THEN
              SCORE = SCORE + 20 + FIRST
              PRINT *, FRAME - 2, ' Strike', SCORE
          END IF
*-----------------------------------------------------------*
*     If first ball is not a strike, get second ball.       *
*-----------------------------------------------------------*
          IF (FIRST .LT. 10) THEN

              READ (9, *) SECOND

              IF (STRIKE) THEN
                  SCORE = SCORE + 10 + FIRST + SECOND
                  PRINT *, FRAME - 1, ' Strike', SCORE
              END IF

              IF (FIRST + SECOND .LT. 10) THEN
                  SCORE = SCORE + FIRST + SECOND
                  PRINT *, FRAME, BLANK, SCORE
              END IF

          END IF
*-----------------------------------------------------------*
*  Update logical variables for spare, strike, and double.  *
*-----------------------------------------------------------*
          IF (FIRST .EQ. 10) THEN

              IF (STRIKE) THEN
                  TWOSTR = .TRUE.
              ELSE
                  TWOSTR = .FALSE.
              END IF

              STRIKE = .TRUE.
              SPARE  = .FALSE.
```

```
          ELSE IF (FIRST + SECOND .EQ. 10) THEN

              SPARE  = .TRUE.
              STRIKE = .FALSE.
              TWOSTR = .FALSE.

          ELSE

              SPARE  = .FALSE.
              STRIKE = .FALSE.
              TWOSTR = .FALSE.

          END IF

11    CONTINUE
*-------------------------------------------------------------*
*       Check for mark in tenth frame and deal with it.       *
*-------------------------------------------------------------*
      IF (SPARE) THEN

          READ (9, *) FIRST
          SCORE = SCORE + 10 + FIRST
          PRINT *, 10, ' Spare ', SCORE

      ELSE IF (STRIKE) THEN

          READ (9, *) FIRST, SECOND

          IF (TWOSTR) THEN
              SCORE = SCORE + 20 + FIRST
              PRINT *, 9, ' Strike', SCORE
          END IF

          SCORE = SCORE + 10 + FIRST + SECOND
          PRINT *, 10, ' Strike', SCORE

      END IF

      CLOSE (9)

      END
```

If `BOWL.DAT` contains the ball scores from the game we scored above, the program output is

```
Frame              Score
  1                  9
  2 Strike          39
  3 Strike          67
  4 Strike          87
  5 Spare          106
  6 Spare          126
  7 Strike         146
  8 Spare          164
  9 Spare          184
 10 Strike         203
```

Logical Operators

We can also form logical expressions by combining two or more relational expressions with **logical operators**. Fortran contains five logical operators: `.AND.`, `.OR.`, `.NOT.`, `.EQV.`, and `.NEQV.`. The most frequently used are `.AND.`, `.OR.`, and `.NOT.`.

The table in Figure 5.4 lists the logical operators and their meanings. The letters p and q stand for logical expressions. For each operator, we tell when the example expression is true; in any other circumstance, the expression is false.

Operator	Example	Meaning
`.AND.`	p `.AND.` q	True if both p and q are true. (Logical conjunction)
`.OR.`	p `.OR.` q	True if either p or q is true, or both are true. (Inclusive or)
`.NOT.`	`.NOT.` p	True if p is false. (Negation)
`.EQV.`	p `.EQV.` q	True if p and q are both true or both false. (Equivalent)
`.NEQV.`	p `.NEQV.` q	True if one of p, q is true, the other false. (Not equivalent) Also called "exclusive OR."

FIGURE 5.4
The Logical Operators in Fortran

We often use **truth tables** to describe the effects of the logical operators. Each logical expression has two values, `.TRUE.` and `.FALSE.`, so there are four possible combinations of values for two expressions, p and q. A truth table simply lists the possible values for p and q together with the values for logical expressions containing p and q. Figure 5.5 contains a truth table for the Fortran logical operators.

FIGURE 5.5
Truth Table for the
Fortran Logical
Operators

p	q	p .AND. q	p .OR. q	.NOT. p	p .EQV. q	p .NEQV. q
true	true	true	true	false	true	false
true	false	false	true	false	false	true
false	true	false	true	true	false	true
false	false	false	false	true	true	false

The third column of the table shows that p .AND. q is true when p and q are both true, and is false in all other cases. The fourth column shows that p .OR. q is false when p and q are both false, and is true in all other cases. Similarly, the expression .NOT. p is true when p is false and is false when p is true.

Suppose we want to perform a block of statements only when the value of a variable A is smaller than the values of both variables B and C. Then we can write

```
IF (A .LT. B .AND. A .LT. C) THEN
```

and the block will execute only when both conditions, A .LT. B and A .LT. C, are true. Similarly, the statement

```
IF (A .LT. B .AND. A .LT. C .AND. B .LT. C) THEN
```

causes the computer to execute the block of statements only when all three conditions are true.

The .OR. operator causes the computer to execute the block of statements if either or both of two conditions are true. Suppose we want a block executed if X is less than or equal to 0.0, or Y is greater than 10.0, or both. The appropriate IF statement is

```
IF (X .LE. 0.0 .OR. Y .GT. 10.0) THEN
```

Let A, B, C, and D be logical variables. An expression with several .OR. operators, such as

```
A .OR. B .OR. C .OR. D
```

is true if *at least one* of the variables has the value .TRUE.. We use an expression like this in the following example program.

Example 5.10 Compound Logical Expressions

Program 5.10 reads, from a file EMP.DAT, an employee's identification number (IDNUM), hourly rate (RATE), and hours worked (HOURS). If the values for HOURS and RATE are valid, the program then calculates PAY simply as HOURS * RATE. The program serves mainly to illustrate an IF block that checks for valid data: HOURS must be greater than 0.0 and less than or equal to 80.0.; RATE must be at least 2.35 and not more than 18.00.

■
PROGRAM 5.10

```
      PROGRAM CHEKIN
*-------------------------------------------------------------*
*  Check for valid number of hours worked and rate of pay.    *
*  Data are in file EMP.DAT.  First record contains number of *
*  employee records.  Each other record has IDNUM, HOURS, and RATE. *
*-------------------------------------------------------------*
      INTEGER NREC, IDNUM, I
      REAL    RATE, HOURS, PAY

      OPEN (2, FILE = 'EMP.DAT', STATUS = 'OLD')
      READ (2, *) NREC

      PRINT *, '    ID number      PAY'

      DO 11 I = 1, NREC
         READ (2, *) IDNUM, RATE, HOURS

         IF (HOURS .LE. 0. .OR. HOURS .GT. 80. .OR.
     1       RATE .LE. 2.35 .OR. RATE .GT. 18.0) THEN
               PRINT *, IDNUM, ' Invalid data'
         ELSE
               PAY = HOURS * RATE
               PRINT *, IDNUM, PAY
         END IF
11    CONTINUE

      CLOSE (2)

      END
```

The logical operators .AND. and .OR. are *binary* operators; they operate on two expressions. The .NOT. operator negates only one logical value, just as the unary minus sign negates one numeric value. If you want to execute a block when two integer variables I and J do *not* have the same value, you could write

    IF (.NOT. I .EQ. J) THEN

However, you could also use

    IF (I .NE. J) THEN

which most people find easier to read. Avoid using .NOT. if you can easily do so.

The .NOT. operator also is unique because of the following rule: two logical operators cannot be adjacent unless the second one is .NOT.. That is, it is not legal to write

    IF (X .LT. Y .AND. .OR. Y .LT. Z) THEN

but it is permissible to have

    IF (X .LT. Y .AND. .NOT. Y .LT. Z) THEN

We will never use a logical expression more complicated than this throughout the remainder of the text. However, for those who want more detail about complex logical expressions, here it is.

Precedence in Logical Expressions

The table in Figure 5.6 gives the order of precedence for evaluating logical expressions, including the usual order for evaluating arithmetic expressions.

FIGURE 5.6
Precedence in Logical
Expressions

Precedence	Operators
1	**
2	* /
3	+ −
4	.EQ. .LT. .GT. .LE. .GE. .NE.
5	.NOT.
6	.AND.
7	.OR.
8	.EQV. .NEQV.

Glancing at the table, we can see that arithmetic calculations are performed first, then relational operations, and finally logical operations. When several operators in a statement have the same precedence number, they are evaluated from left to right, except for adjacent exponentiation operators.

Consider the following rather complicated logical expression. Bold-face numbers under the expression indicate the order of execution.

X * Y .LE. Z .AND. U − V .GT. R ** 2 .OR. I .EQ. J + 4

2   5   8   3   6   1   9   7   4

This is not as complicated as it looks, because there are only three groups of expressions.

1. All *numeric* expressions are evaluated in the usual order: first R ** 2, second X * Y, third U − V, fourth J + 4.
2. All *relational* expressions are evaluated left to right: first X * Y .LE. Z, then U − V .GT. R ** 2, finally I .EQ. J + 4.
3. The expression is now in the form: p .AND. q .OR. r. According to Figure 5.5, .AND. has higher precedence, so p .AND. q is evaluated first to give a value, say s. Finally, s .OR. r is evaluated.

Parentheses in logical expressions can change the usual order of evaluation, and can make the expression clearer. Step 3 says that an expression such as

$$p \text{ .AND. } q \text{ .OR. } r$$

will be evaluated as if it were

a. $(p$ .AND. $q)$ .OR. r

and not as if it were

b. p .AND. $(q$ .OR. $r)$

Does it matter whether the interpretation in a. or b. is chosen? Suppose the truth values of the logical expressions p, q, and r are:

Expression	Value
p	.FALSE.
q	.TRUE.
r	.TRUE.

Then a. will be evaluated as

$$(.FALSE. \; .AND. \; .TRUE.) \; .OR. \; .TRUE. \; = \; .FALSE. \; .OR. \; .TRUE. \; = \; .TRUE.$$

But b. turns out to be

$$.FALSE. \; .AND. \; (.TRUE. \; .OR. \; .TRUE.) \; = \; .FALSE. \; .AND. \; .TRUE. \; = \; .FALSE.$$

Thus, the order of precedence *is* crucial. If you do not want to remember the order, then use parentheses as in a. or b. to get the meaning you want.

Similarly, suppose we have the logical expression

$$.NOT. \; X \; .LT. \; Y \; .OR. \; Y \; .NE. \; Z$$

The operator .NOT. operates only on X .LT. Y, as if the expression were

$$(.NOT. \; X \; .LT. \; Y) \; .OR. \; Y \; .NE. \; Z$$

If you want the .NOT. to negate the entire expression following it, you should write

$$.NOT. \; (X \; .LT. \; Y \; .OR. \; Y \; .NE. \; Z)$$

However, the original expression is equivalent to the more readable

$$X \; .GE. \; Y \; .OR. \; Y \; .NE. \; Z$$

so it is wise to look for simpler forms of complicated logical expressions.

As a final example, consider the logical expression

$$p \; .OR. \; .NOT. \; q \; .AND. \; r$$

According to the precedence rules, .NOT. q is evaluated first, as if the expression were

$$p \; .OR. \; (.NOT. \; q) \; .AND. \; r$$

Next the .AND. in (.NOT. q) .AND. r is evaluated as if the expression were

$$p \; .OR. \; (\; (.NOT. \; q) \; .AND. \; r \;)$$

As with numerical expressions, use parentheses with logical expressions to make the meanings clear.

Example 5.11 Truth Tables for Compound Logical Expressions

We have written truth tables for the logical operators in Fortran. These tables can be constructed for complicated logical expressions. Using such tables, you can get the computer to do logical calculations for you. Suppose you do not know how to evaluate expressions such as

A = p .AND. q .OR. .NOT. (q .AND. r)
B = .NOT. p .OR. q .AND. (p .OR. .NOT. r)
C = p .OR. q .OR. .NOT. (r .OR. .NOT. p)

We can define A, B, C, P, Q, and R as LOGICAL variables and write a truth table for all possible truth values of P, Q, and R. The only tricky part is getting P, Q, and R to take on all possible values. We will use three nested DO loops, one for each variable P, Q, and R. Each loop ranges from 1 to 2 for the two values .TRUE. and .FALSE.. We initialize P, Q, and R to .TRUE., and at the end of each loop, we change the truth value of one of the variables with a statement like

P = .NOT. P

See Program 5.11.

■
PROGRAM 5.11
_____

```
      PROGRAM TRUTH
*-------------------------------------------------------------*
*        Truth table for complicated logical expressions      *
*-------------------------------------------------------------*
      LOGICAL  P, Q, R, A, B, C
      INTEGER  I, J, K
      DATA     P, Q, R /3 * .TRUE./

      PRINT *, 'A = p .AND. q .OR. .NOT.(q .AND. r)'
      PRINT *, 'B = .NOT. p .OR. q .AND. (p .OR. .NOT. r)'
      PRINT *, 'C = p .OR. q .OR. .NOT. (r .OR. .NOT. p)'
      PRINT *
      PRINT *, 'p q r A B C'
      PRINT *, '-----------'
```

```
      DO 33 I = 1, 2
         DO 22 J = 1, 2
            DO 11 K = 1, 2
*-----------------------------------------------------------*
*  Calculate truth values for A, B, C and print all values.  *
*-----------------------------------------------------------*
               A = P .AND. Q .OR. .NOT.(Q .AND. R)
               B = .NOT. P .OR. Q .AND. (P .OR. .NOT. R)
               C = P .OR. Q .OR. .NOT. (R .OR. .NOT. P)
               PRINT *, P, Q, R, A, B, C
*-----------------------------------------------------------*
*                  Change truth value of R.                  *
*-----------------------------------------------------------*
               R = .NOT. R
11             CONTINUE
*-----------------------------------------------------------*
*                  Change truth value of Q.                  *
*-----------------------------------------------------------*
            Q = .NOT. Q
22          CONTINUE
*-----------------------------------------------------------*
*                  Change truth value of P.                  *
*-----------------------------------------------------------*
         P = .NOT. P
33       CONTINUE

         END
```

The output from this program is

```
A = p .AND. q .OR. .NOT.(q .AND. r)
B = .NOT. p .OR. q .AND. (p .OR. .NOT. r)
C = p .OR. q .OR. .NOT. (r .OR. .NOT. p)

p q r A B C
-----------
T T T T T T
T T F T T T
T F T T F T
T F F T F T
F T T F T T
F T F T T T
F F T T T F
F F F T T F
```

First, look at the column labeled r. The printed truth values begin with T and then alternate, because the statement

```
R = .NOT. R
```

is contained *in* the innermost loop. In the q column, two Ts alternate with two Fs because the value of Q is changed *after* every completion of the innermost loop. Finally, the p column contains four Ts and then four Fs because the value of P is changed only in the *outermost* loop. You should look at the other columns to see whether your logic agrees with the computer's logic.

■

5.4 SUMMARY OF CHAPTER 5

■ *Terms Introduced in This Chapter*

Binary search	data type	Relational operator
ELSE clause	expression	.EQ.
ELSE IF clause	variable	.GE.
END IF statement	Logical operators	.GT.
.FALSE.	.AND.	.LE.
IF statement	.NOT.	.LT.
IF block	.OR.	.NE.
Logical IF statement	.EQV.	THEN
LOGICAL	.NEQV.	.TRUE.
constant	Relational expression	Truth table

■ *What You Should Know*

1. A condition is a logical expression.
2. The only logical values are .TRUE. and .FALSE..
3. The condition in an IF statement must be enclosed in parentheses.
4. IF statements instruct the computer to execute some other statement(s) if a given condition is true.
5. The logical IF instructs the computer to execute a single statement if a given condition is true, and to ignore the given statement if the condition is false.
6. The logical IF statement does *not* contain the word THEN.
7. Relational expressions are simple types of logical expressions.

8. Relational expressions use the relational operators:

    .EQ.   .GE.   .GT.   .LT.   .LE.   .NE.

9. The Fortran logical operators are:

    .AND.   .OR.   .NOT.   .EQV.   .NEQV.

10. The precedence order for logical expressions has the arithmetic operations first, then the relational operations, and finally the logical operations.

11. Parentheses can change the order of evaluation in a logical expression, just as they do in arithmetic expressions.

12. Parentheses also can make the order of evaluation clearer, whether or not they change that order.

13. The simplest block IF statement instructs the computer to execute a block of statements if a given condition is true, and to ignore the block if the condition is false.

14. The block IF with an ELSE clause contains two blocks of statements, one to be performed when a condition is true, the other to be performed when the condition is false.

15. Blocks with ELSE IF clauses can contain many blocks of statements, with each block to be performed if an associated condition is true.

16. In block IF statements with ELSE IF clauses, each IF is followed by a condition and the word THEN.

17. In IF blocks with ELSE IF clauses, only one block of statements can execute; the first one whose associated condition is true.

18. An ELSE clause in a block IF guarantees that one block of statements will execute.

19. Without an ELSE clause, it can happen that *no* block of statements in a block IF is executed.

20. The meaning of ELSE in a block IF is *if no condition above is true.*

21. The ELSE clause is optional in an IF block. If present, it must be the last clause.

22. END IF does not cause a block of statements within a block IF to repeat.

23. Aside from sequential structure, the two major structures we have covered so far are DO loops and IF blocks.

24. Either of the two structures can be nested inside another such structure.

25. The word *nesting* implies that one structure is entirely contained in another; with nested structures, the one that begins last must finish first.

■

5.5 EXERCISES

■ *Self-Test*

1. What is wrong with the following logical IF statements?

   a.   IF (A .GT. B) THEN PRINT *, 'First is bigger.'
   b.   IF (I .EQ. 0) I = I + 1, PRINT *, 'Increasing'
   c.   IF A - B .LT. C - D A = B + C - D
   d.   IF (X > SQRT(Z)) Z = X * X
   e.   IF (A .LT. B) IF (B .LT. C) PRINT *, 'A is smallest.'
   f.   IF (I .LT. J) I .EQ. J

2. What are the logical flaws in the following IF statements?

   a.   IF (I .NE. 0 .OR. I .NE. 1) PRINT *, 'Bad value'
   b.   IF (I .EQ. 0 .AND. I .GT. 1) I = I + 2

3. If p is true, q is false, and r is true, what is the value of each of the following logical expressions?

   a.   p .AND. q .AND. r
   b.   p .AND. q .OR. r .AND. q
   c.   .NOT. p .OR. r
   d.   p .AND..NOT. (q .OR. r)
   e.   p .OR. q .OR. r
   f.   p .OR. q .AND. q .OR. r

4. Let X = 2.5, Y = 10.4, Z = 100.9, I = 2, J = 6, and K = 12. Give the values of the following logical expressions.

   a.   X .LE. Y / 3.0 .AND. I .EQ. K / J
   b.   X ** 2 .GE. Y .OR. Y ** 2 .GE. Z - 7.9
   c.   X * Y .GT. Z / Y .AND. J - I .LE. K - J
   d.   .NOT. X .LT. Y .OR. Y. LT. Z .AND. J .LE. 2 * I
   e.   Y / X .LE. Z / Y .AND. J * I .EQ. K .OR. K .GT. I + J

5. Consider the following three statements:

   X is less than 0.0
   Y is greater than 100.0
   NAME is 'ZZZZ'

   Write five separate conditions for IF blocks that will cause the computer to execute a block of statements if:

    a.   At least one of the statements is true.
    b.   All three of the statements are true.
    c.   None of the statements is true.
    d.   The first two statements are false, but the last is true.
    e.   The first two statements have the same truth value.

■ *Programming Exercises*

1. Write a program that asks for an integer value and tells whether the given value is even or odd.

2. Write a program to find the smallest number and its position in a list. If there are several smallest values, give the last position.

3. Write a program that asks for three values and prints the largest and smallest values. Do not use the built-in functions MAX and MIN, but use an IF statement.

4. Write a program that reads numbers from a file, then prints the total of the positive numbers, the total of the negative numbers, how many positive, and how many negative numbers are in the file.

5. Furniture salespeople in a company earn a salary of $50 per week, plus a commission of 5 percent a week on the first $3,000 of sales and 10 percent on any sales over $3,000. Write a program that reads weekly sales from a file and calculates total pay for each sales value.

6. The sum of the interior angles of a triangle is 180 degrees. Write a program to ask for two angles in degrees, and then calculate the third angle. The program should tell the user if any of the angles is negative or zero. If all angles are positive, the computer should tell the user whether the triangle is *equilateral* (all angles equal), *isosceles* (exactly two angles equal), or *scalene* (no two angles equal).

7. A teacher calculates a numerical grade for each student at the end of a course. Before converting the numerical grade to a letter, he considers the student's attendance record. Depending on the number of days the student was absent, the letter grade assignments are made according to the table below.

	Days Absent		
Letter Grade	0 or 1	2, 3, or 4	5 or more
A	87 or above	90 or above	92 or above
B	76–86+	80–89+	83–91+
C	65–75+	70–79+	74–82+
D	54–64+	60–69+	65–73+
F	Below 54	Below 60	Below 65

Write a program to read ID numbers, numerical grades, and the numbers of days absent for each student in a class, then calculate the proper letter grade.

8. A *quadratic equation* is usually written in the form

$$ax^2 + bx + c = 0$$

The *discriminant* of the equation is $d = b^2 - 4ac$. The equation can have zero, one, or two solutions, depending on the value of d.

Value of d	Solution(s)
Negative	None
Zero	One: $x = \dfrac{-b}{2a}$
Positive	Two: $x = \dfrac{-b \pm \sqrt{d}}{2a}$

Write a program that asks for the coefficients a, b, and c of a quadratic equation, and gives the solution(s) or says there are no solutions. Try the program with at least the following data.

a	b	c
2.0	4.0	2.0
2.0	−7.0	6.0
4.0	3.0	2.0
9.0	7.0	1.25

9. Write a program that prints the coins required to make any amount of change, from 1 cent to 99 cents. Use the smallest number of coins possible, including half-dollars, quarters, dimes, nickels, and pennies.

10. Write a program to do one of three calculations for a user:

   a. area of a right triangle, given the side
   b. area of a trapezoid, given the base and two heights
   c. area of any triangle, given the three sides

For c., let s be half the sum of the sides a, b, and c of a triangle. *Heron's formula* for the area of the triangle is

$$Area = \sqrt{s(s - a)(s - b)(s - c)}$$

11. A classic problem deals with three bandits who robbed a stagecoach and took the strongbox containing a certain number of pieces of gold. That night, while his partners in crime slept, the first bandit got up and decided to make certain he got his share of the gold. He divided the gold pieces into three equal piles, and had one

piece left over. After hiding one pile and the one odd gold piece, he put the remaining two piles back in the box and went back to sleep.

Soon after, the second bandit awoke, and went through the same procedure. After dividing the gold pieces into three equal piles, there was one left over, so he secreted one pile plus the one odd piece, put the remainder back in the strongbox, and went back to bed.

The third bandit awoke just before morning and performed the same division into three piles plus one odd piece, cached away one pile plus the odd piece, and went back to sleep.

After breakfast, when the three bandits got together to divide up the gold pieces in the strongbox, they found three equal piles and one left over. All three died in the ensuing fight over the odd gold piece.

The question is: How many gold pieces were originally in the strongbox? There are many possible answers, but it might take you a long time to find one by trial and error. Write a computer program that checks all integers from 1 to 1000 and prints any possible solutions to this problem. (You might also benefit from trying this problem by hand.)

12. Purple Cross offers three health insurance plans: a high-benefit plan, including office visits for dental care and eye care; a regular plan; and a low-benefit plan that pays only for hospital confinements lasting more than 30 days. Costs also depend on the number of people covered under the plan, including single persons, married couples without children, and married couples with children. Monthly costs of these plans appear in the following table.

Monthly Cost of Health Insurance

Benefit Level	Single	Married	
		No Children	Children
Low	36.25	56.50	98.35
Regular	48.90	74.70	136.75
High	69.80	99.45	174.55

Write a program to ask for the level of the plan and the number of persons covered, and print the monthly payment for the plan. Do not concern yourself with improper input; we will see how to deal with it in the next chapter.

13. A small company plans to install a central computer with links to five departments. According to their floor plan, the peripheral devices for the five departments will be situated as shown by asterisks in the following diagram.

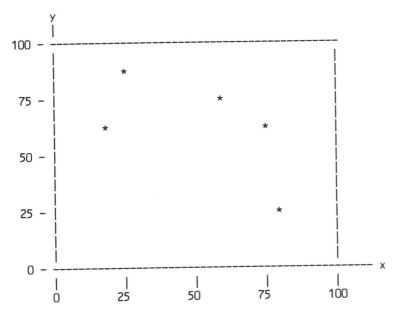

Each device will be wired directly to the main computer. The company wants to put the computer in the place that will minimize the total wiring. Write a program to calculate the coordinates of that place. Use nested DO loops and consider only integer coordinates. The coordinates of the points in the diagram above are:

$$15.0 \quad 60.0$$
$$25.0 \quad 90.0$$
$$60.0 \quad 75.0$$
$$75.0 \quad 60.0$$
$$80.0 \quad 25.0$$

chapter **6** CONDITION-CONTROLLED LOOPS

A DO loop is sometimes called a **count-controlled loop**, because a DO statement specifies a certain *number* of times to repeat a block of statements. In contrast, a **condition-controlled loop** executes *while* a given condition is true, and stops executing when the condition becomes false. Many programmers use the term **while loop** for a condition-controlled loop, partly for brevity and partly because most modern high-level programming languages use some type of WHILE statement to implement condition-controlled loops. In this chapter we discuss the construction of condition-controlled loops.

■
6.1 WHILE **LOOPS**

Fortran 77 does not contain a WHILE statement. Nevertheless, we can construct a condition-controlled loop from IF and GO TO statements, and we call such a loop a *while loop*.

The GO TO **Statement**

Recall that any statement in a Fortran program can have a label, which is an integer from one to five digits long, in the first 5 columns of the line on which the statement begins. We will left-justify line numbers in the first five columns. That is, we will write

```
11    READ *, X
```

A line number can make a statement the **target** of a GO TO statement. The GO TO statement (sometimes called an **unconditional transfer**) has a simple form

        GO TO xx

where xx is the label of a target line in the same program. For example, we can have:

11   READ *, NAME, AGE
            .
            .
            .
        GO TO 11

which causes a *branch* back to line 11. Thus, the statements from line 11 to the GO TO statement will be repeated a number of times. We also can have:

        GO TO 22
            .
            .
            .
22   PRINT *, A, B, C

which causes the computer to skip the statements between the GO TO statement and the PRINT statement.

GO TO statements are almost always used in conjunction with IF statements. In the first example, we would not *always* want to GO TO line 11; the program would be in an endless loop, forever repeating the statements between the READ and GO TO statements. In the second example, we would not *always* want to skip the statements between the GO TO and PRINT statements; otherwise it would be simpler to delete those lines (and the GO TO) from the program. Using GO TO statements in conjunction with IF statements means that *sometimes* we want to branch back in the program, and *sometimes* we want to skip ahead.

Example 6.1 Bad Programming with GO TO

Program 6.1 illustrates bad programming practices involving GO TO statements. If you read older Fortran programs, you will see many similar programs. The program asks for a number x and will give the square root of x if x is nonnegative. The program works, but it has bad form.

■
PROGRAM 6.1

```
      PROGRAM BADGO
*-------------------------------------------------------*
*                Bad usage of GO TO statements.          *
*-------------------------------------------------------*
      REAL X

      PRINT *, 'Enter a number whose square root you want.'
      READ  *, X

      IF (X .LT. 0.0) GO TO 11
      PRINT *, 'The square of your number is', SQRT(X)
      GO TO 22
11    PRINT *, 'Cannot take square root of a negative number.'

22    END
```

The first GO TO, in the IF statement,

```
      IF (X .LT. 0.0) GO TO 11
```

skips over the PRINT statement containing SQRT(X) to avoid attempting to take the square root of a negative number. Specifically, GO TO 11 directs the computer to a PRINT statement warning the user that negative numbers do not have square roots.

If X is *not* less than zero, the computer should execute the first PRINT statement but not the second. Therefore, after the first PRINT statement the program needs a GO TO statement that skips over the second PRINT statement.

You probably see the solution already; replace the four statements from IF through the second PRINT with an IF block:

```
      IF (X .LT. 0.0) THEN
          PRINT *, 'Cannot take square root of a negative number'.
      ELSE
          PRINT *, 'The square of your number is', SQRT(X)
      END IF
```

This block is much easier to read and contains no GO TO statement. As a general rule, avoid using GO TO statements to skip over certain other statements.

Overuse of GO TO statements leads to poor program structure and makes programs hard to read. Therefore, use GO TO statements sparingly in your programs and look for alternatives that do not use GO TO statements. In this chapter we present two specific ways to form loops with GO TO statements. In particular, we always use a GO TO statement to branch *back* in a program, never ahead.

Example 6.2 A While Loop to Check for Valid Input

The previous program calculates a square root for nonnegative input and prints a warning for negative input. The program would seem more friendly if it gave the user a chance to correct erroneous input. Program 6.2 gives the user several chances to do this by setting up a loop with an IF...GO TO statement.

■
PROGRAM 6.2

```
      PROGRAM IFLOOP
*------------------------------------------------------------*
*   Check for negative data with a logical IF statement.  *
*------------------------------------------------------------*
      REAL  X

      PRINT *, 'This program calculates a square root.'
*------------------------------------------------------------*
*                   Start of loop                          *
*------------------------------------------------------------*
11    PRINT *, 'Please enter a nonnegative number.'
         READ  *, X
      IF (X .LT. 0.0) GO TO 11
*------------------------------------------------------------*
*                    End of loop                           *
*------------------------------------------------------------*
      PRINT *, 'The square root of your number is', SQRT(X)

      END
```

If the user enters a negative number, the statement

```
      IF (X .LT. 0.0) GO TO 11
```

sends control back to line 11 to ask for a nonnegative number. If the user persists in entering negative numbers, the computer continues just as obstinately to ask for a nonnegative number. When the input number is not negative, the GO TO 11 statement is ignored, and the computer prints the square root of the number.

Stopping a Program

A loop that never terminates is an **endless** or **infinite loop**. If you create an infinite loop, your program will either print out pages of results you do not want, or it will appear to be doing nothing for a long time. In such cases, you need a way to interrupt the running of the program. On some computers, you can interrupt an interactive program by holding down the Control key while typing Y. We refer to this action as typing **Control/Y**, or **CTRL/Y**, because on many terminals the Control key has the letters CTRL. If nothing happens, repeat the CTRL/Y.

Before running interactive programs with GO TO statements, find out how to interrupt the execution of a program on your computer. (With batch jobs on a large computer, the operating system usually has a built-in limit to the amount of time a program can use.)

Example 6.3 Possible Repetition of a Program

Consider a program that performs simple calculations for the user, such as the following:

```
PROGRAM POWER4
REAL X

PRINT *, 'Please enter a number.'
READ *, X
PRINT *, 'The 4th power of that number is', X ** 4

END
```

If the user wishes to perform several such calculations, the program must be run several times. The program can handle several calculations if, inside a while loop, the computer asks if the user wants to enter more data. Assuming that the answer can be YES or NO, the IF statement is

```
IF (ANSWER .EQ. 'YES') GO TO 11
```

The program is a bit picky because the user must respond literally YES, not yes or Y, for the program to continue. See Program 6.3.

■
PROGRAM 6.3

```
     PROGRAM POWER4
*-------------------------------------------------------*
*  Calculate fourth power.  Ask if user wishes to repeat. *
*-------------------------------------------------------*
     CHARACTER*3  ANSWER
     REAL         X

11   PRINT *, 'Please enter a number.'
     READ *, X
     PRINT *, 'The 4th power of that number is', X ** 4

     PRINT *, 'Do you want to enter another number (YES/NO)?'
     READ 10, ANSWER
10       FORMAT (A)
     IF (ANSWER .EQ. 'YES') GO TO 11

     END
```

Example 6.4 Printing All Factorials Less Than 10,000

Suppose you want to print values of integers (NUMBER) and their factorials (FACTOR), up to and including the largest factorial less than 10,000. This problem should make you think of a while loop with an IF statement beginning

```
     IF (FACTOR .LT. 10000)
```

In fact, that is nearly all there is to the program.

Inside the loop, we will increase NUMBER and calculate FACTOR with

```
     NUMBER = NUMBER + 1
     FACTOR = FACTOR * NUMBER
```

We will also print the values of NUMBER and FACTOR.

The major question is whether the PRINT statement should come before or after the calculations in the loop. Since we will start both NUMBER and FACTOR with value 1, it should be clear that we want to print values *before* the statements that calculate a new value of FACTOR. (It also should be clear that the value of FACTOR must become *greater than* 10,000 in order

to stop looping, and we do not want to print such a value of FACTOR.) See
Program 6.4.

■

PROGRAM 6.4

```
      PROGRAM F10000
*------------------------------------------------------------*
*   Calculate and print all factorials less than 10,000.   *
*------------------------------------------------------------*
      INTEGER NUMBER, FACTOR

      PRINT *, '       NUMBER     FACTORIAL'
      PRINT *

      NUMBER = 1
      FACTOR = 1

11    PRINT *, NUMBER, FACTOR
         NUMBER = NUMBER + 1
         FACTOR = FACTOR * NUMBER
      IF (FACTOR .LT. 10000) GO TO 11

      END
```

The output from this program is

NUMBER	FACTORIAL
1	1
2	2
3	6
4	24
5	120
6	720
7	5040

The computer actually calculates until FACTOR becomes larger than
10,000. It does not print the final value of FACTOR because the PRINT statement in the loop comes before the statement to calculate the new NUMBER
and FACTOR. If the problem had required printing factorials up to and
including the first factorial greater than 10,000, we could simply add a
PRINT statement after the END IF statement.

Example 6.5 A Pre-test While Loop

All our previous examples of while loops are called **post-test loops** because the IF...GO TO statement came at the *end* of the loop. Since no checking occurs until the end of the loop, the computer always executes the body of a post-test loop at least once.

Sometimes we will want to test a condition *before* the loop begins, in which case we call the loop a **pre-test loop**. There are several ways to set up a pre-test loop in Fortran 77. Program 6.5 is rather trivial and serves mainly to illustrate one specific way to do it. We use an IF block to contain the loop body and place a GO TO statement right before the END IF statement.

■
PROGRAM 6.5

```
      PROGRAM PRTEST
*-------------------------------------------*
*     Illustrate a pre-test while loop.      *
*-------------------------------------------*
      INTEGER I, J
      I = 1
      J = 7

11    IF (I .LT. J) THEN
          I = I + 1
          J = J - 1
          PRINT *, I, J
          GO TO 11
      END IF

      END
```

One major distinction between DO and while loops is that while loops do not have a loop variable. Thus there are no starting, terminal, and step values built into the IF statement. The variables in this IF expression, I and J, must therefore be given values before the computer executes the IF statement. These values must make the expression I .LT. J true to cause the computer to execute the body of the loop. When the condition in the IF statement is false, the computer skips over the loop.

Although the IF statement is

```
      IF (I .LT. J) THEN
```

the expression I .LT. J must become *false* inside the loop so the loop can terminate. Therefore, at least one of the variables, I or J, must be changed in the body of the loop; if we deleted the statements I = I + 1 and J = J − 1, the loop would never cease. Since I is increasing by 1 and J is decreasing by 1 each time through the loop, the condition I .LT. J is sure to become false at some point.

The computer does not jump out of a while loop as soon as the condition becomes false. Once the computer starts executing the loop body, it will execute every statement in that body. The computer evaluates the condition when it first reaches the IF statement, but it does not evaluate the condition again until it reaches the IF statement again. If the condition is false when the computer reaches IF, the computer exits from the loop.

We can trace through the program to see what the computer will do.

1. First time through the loop: When the computer first reaches the IF statement, I is 1 and J is 7. The condition I .LT. J is true, so the computer executes the loop body. I increases to 2, J decreases to 6, and the computer prints the values 2 and 6. The GO TO statement sends the computer back to the IF statement, and the condition is still true, so the computer executes the loop body again.

2. Second time through the loop: Now I becomes 3, J becomes 5, and the computer prints these values. At IF for the third time, the condition is still true, so the computer executes the loop body a third time.

3. Third time through the loop: I increases to 4 and J decreases to 4. The condition I .LT. J is now false, but the computer is not continuously monitoring the condition, so it prints these values and reaches IF for the fourth time. Now the computer evaluates I .LT. J as .FALSE., and exits from the loop.

The output from the program is, as we have seen

```
2        6
3        5
4        4
```

Testing for Equality

Suppose the IF statement in the program had been

```
IF (I .NE. J) THEN
```

Then the program would have performed exactly the same way, although the .NE. relation can be dangerous. If the program had begun with I = 5 as before, but with J = 6, then I and J would never be equal at the IF statement, so the loop would never terminate. (Check this.)

Similarly, with real expressions, avoid IF statements with the .NE. relation. Round-off error can make supposedly equal quantities unequal, so the loop might never terminate. The following trivial program tries to start with X = 0.0 and increment X by 1/3 until X takes on the value 4.0.

```
      PROGRAM BADCON
*-----------------------------------------*
*         Nonending while loop.           *
*-----------------------------------------*
      REAL X
      X = 0.0

11    IF (X .NE. 4.0) THEN
         X = X + 1.0 / 3.0
         PRINT *, X
         GO TO 11
      END IF

      END
```

Most computers will print the value 4.000000, but will continue printing results until the user interrupts execution, or until a time limit is exceeded. Even though X does assume a value that is correct to six decimal places, the crucial value is never exactly the same as 4.0. The problem is that 1.0 / 3.0 cannot be represented exactly in the computer. The representation gives a value a little more or a little less than 1/3.

The remarks of the last chapter are appropriate here. Decimal values can be exactly represented if they are sums of powers of 1/2. Even in this case, a number that requires too many binary digits cannot be exactly stored.

Beginning and Ending a While Loop

The most common problems with while loops involve initialization and termination, or the beginning and the end. Consider the trivial problem of printing the integers from 1 to 5. The best way to do this is with a DO loop beginning DO 11 I = 1, 5. However, you will find many uses for a while loop with an associated counting variable, so be sure to understand the following examples.

First, here are four ways *not* to do it.

```
a.      N = 1
     11  IF (N .LE. 5) THEN
             N = N + 1
             PRINT *, N
             GO TO 11
         END IF


b.      N = 0
     11  IF (N .LE. 5) THEN
             N = N + 1
             PRINT *, N
             GO TO 11
             IF


c.      N = 0
     11  IF (N .LT. 5) THEN
             PRINT *, N
             N = N + 1
             GO TO 11
         END IF


d.      N = 1
     11  IF (N .LT. 5) THEN
             PRINT *, N
             N = N + 1
             GO TO 11
         END IF
```

In program segment a, the computer will not print the value of 1 because N begins at 1, and increases to 2 before the computer executes the PRINT statement for the first time. Also, the unwanted value of 6 appears because the computer starts executing the body of the loop when the value of N is already 5; then N increases to 6 before the PRINT statement.

In segment b, the unwanted 6 appears for the same reason as in a, but the first value printed is 1, as desired.

In segment c, the incorrect value 0 appears first, because the PRINT statement precedes N = N + 1 in the loop. Also, the last value printed is 4, again because N = N + 1 is the last statement in the loop and the loop condition is (N .LT. 5). When N increases to 5, the loop will terminate without printing this value.

Segment d does start printing with the correct value of 1. However, it still stops after printing 4.

Two points stand out here. First, if you initialize a variable to the first value you want to use, make sure you use it before you change it. In our example, if you start with N = 1, put the PRINT statement in the loop before the increment statement.

The second point involves the relational expression in the while statement. Often you are faced with a choice between .LT. and .LE.. Generally, if the increment comes at the *end* of the body of the loop, use the operator .LE. along with the last value you want to use in the loop, as shown in segment A below.

```
A.          N = 1
      11    IF (N .LE. 5) THEN
                PRINT *, N
                N = N + 1
                GO TO 11
            END IF

B.          N = 0
      11    IF (N .LT. 5) THEN
                N = N + 1
                PRINT *, N
                GO TO 11
            END IF
```

Segment B also works properly. Notice the differences. In B, N begins at 0, so N must be incremented before printing. Further, since N increases before the PRINT statement, the condition in the while statement should be (N .LT. 5). When N is incremented to 5 and printed, the loop should terminate.

Either A or B works, and there is not much to choose between them. We will use A as a model because it seems a bit more natural. Get in the habit of using one or the other as a model whenever the situation arises. The constructions you use most often will become familiar to you, and you will soon be able to use them without much effort. Nevertheless, always think about what the loop will do at its endpoints.

Example 6.6 Using an End-of-Data Flag

When the computer executes a DO statement, it must know the terminal value for the loop variable. While loops allow for more flexibility; data can be entered until the computer reads a special constant, signalling that there are no more data. This special constant is called an **end-of-data flag** or **sentinel value**. The exact constant to be used will depend on circumstances. It should be something that could not possibly be valid data. For instance, if you are entering names, a value of **'ZZZZ'** could be a good flag; it is highly unlikely that you really want to process such a name. The situation can be more difficult with numbers, but if all valid data must be positive, then zero or any negative number could serve as a flag.

We use −1 as a flag in the following program to calculate the mean grade on a test, assuming that all grades will be positive. Since the number of grades is not known at the beginning of the while loop, a counter variable called **NUMBER** is used to count the grades.

We put the data in a file **GRADE.DAT** as

```
87
96
79
68
76
84
55
93
82
71
-1
```

It is often safer to use a pre-test loop with an end-of-data flag because it is possible that there will be no data on which to operate (in this case only a −1 in the file). See Program 6.6.

■
PROGRAM 6.6
_____

```
      PROGRAM MNTEST
*----------------------------------------------------*
*    Calculate mean grade.  Data are in file GRADE.DAT.  *
*    with -1 as an end-of-data flag.                  *
*----------------------------------------------------*
      REAL    GRADE, SUM
      INTEGER NUMBER

      OPEN (9, FILE = 'GRADE.DAT', STATUS = 'OLD')

      NUMBER = 0
      SUM = 0.0

      PRINT *, 'Calculating mean grade in file GRADE.DAT.'
      PRINT *
      PRINT *, '   GRADES '

      READ (9, *) GRADE
```

```
11    IF (GRADE .NE. -1.0) THEN
         PRINT *, GRADE
         NUMBER = NUMBER + 1
         SUM = SUM + GRADE
         READ (9, *) GRADE
         GO TO 11
      END IF

      CLOSE (9)

      PRINT *
      PRINT *, NUMBER, ' grades read'
      IF (NUMBER .EQ. 0) THEN
         PRINT *, 'No calculations performed.'
      ELSE
         PRINT *, 'The mean grade is', SUM / REAL(NUMBER)
      END IF

      END
```

Again, the PRINT and READ statements just before the loop recur right before GO TO 11. The computer executes the body of the loop once for each grade entered. When GRADE is −1, the loop terminates, and the computer prints the mean grade.

When you use a counter, think of the increment statement

```
      NUMBER = NUMBER + 1
```

as counting the number of times the computer executes a certain statement. Then place the increment statement adjacent to that statement. In this program, you want to count the number of times GRADE is added to SUM, so the increment statement is placed next to SUM = SUM + GRADE. It does not matter which statement comes first.

Example 6.7 Comparing DO and While Loops

DO loops are special cases of while loops in the sense that any action performed with a DO loop also can be done with a while loop. To see that this is true, consider the most general form of the DO statement,

```
      DO <label> I = INITIAL, FINAL, STEP
```

where all the variables are assumed to be integers. It does not matter what is inside the loop, so let the loop body be just

```
    PRINT *, I
```

Then the following program segments are equivalent. (We assume that INI-TIAL, FINAL, and STEP have been given values.)

DO Loop	While Loop
``` DO 11 I = INITIAL, FINAL, STEP PRINT *, I 11 CONTINUE ```	``` I = INITIAL 11 IF (I .LE. FINAL) THEN PRINT *, I I = I + STEP GO TO 11 END IF ```

The DO loop is a simpler construction, and is safer because it cannot be an infinite loop, so use it when you can specify how many times to repeat the loop body.

Example 6.8 Constant Payments on a Loan

Mr. Brown borrows $10,000.00 from a friend at 8 percent simple interest. They agree that he will repay $1,000.00 on each yearly anniversary of the loan as long as the debt is at least $1,000.00. When the debt is below $1,000.00 on the anniversary, Mr. Brown will pay the full amount of the debt. We will write a short program indicating his progress at paying off the loan.

We need at least the following variables:

YEAR	The number of years since the making of the loan
RATE	The interest rate
OWED	The amount remaining to be paid on the loan
PAYMNT	The constant $1,000.00 repaid each year

YEAR is an INTEGER variable, and the rest are REAL.

Consider what happens for the first two years. The amount owed starts out at $10,000.00. At the end of the first year, 8 percent interest is added, so Mr. Brown owes $10,800.00. He makes a payment of $1,000.00, so the amount owed is now $9,800.00.

For the second year, interest is figured on $9,800.00. This interest comes to $784.00, so at the and of the year Mr. Brown owes $10,584.00. The $1,000.00 reduces the amount owed to $9,584.00. It will take a while to pay off this loan.

These calculations serve two purposes. They help us see what the program needs to do, and they provide a check on the output of the program.

We will print each YEAR, the amount OWED at the end of the year, the PAYMNT, and the amount OWED after the payment. We calculate OWED at the end of each year as

```
OWED = OWED * (1.0 + RATE /100.0)
```

After the payment, Mr. Brown owes the amount OWED - PAYMNT, so we print values for YEAR, OWED, PAYMNT, and OWED - PAYMNT. This amount OWED - PAYMNT is now the amount owed, so we need the statement

```
OWED = OWED - PAYMNT
```

to prepare for next year. We also must increment the value of YEAR.

Since Mr. Brown makes the $1,000.00 payments as long as that payment is less than or equal to what he owes, the while loop begins with

```
IF (PAYMNT .LE. OWED)
```

It seems natural to set up the loop as follows.

```
      YEAR = 1
11    IF (PAYMNT .LE. OWED) THEN
          OWED = OWED * (1.0 + RATE /100.0)      | Results  for
          PRINT *, YEAR, OWED, PAYMNT, OWED - PAYMNT   | this  year

          YEAR = YEAR + 1                        | Prepare  for
          OWED = OWED - PAYMNT                    | next  year
          GO TO 11
      END IF
```

The loop terminates before the final payment is made, so we need one final PRINT statement after END IF to print the last payment. This payment is equal to the amount OWED, since PAYMNT must now be greater than the amount owed. Program 6.8a contains the program.

■

PROGRAM 6.8a

```
      PROGRAM CONPAY
*---------------------------------------------------------------------*
*       Calculate progress of a loan with constant payments.          *
*---------------------------------------------------------------------*
      INTEGER    YEAR
      REAL       OWED, PAYMNT, RATE
      DATA       OWED /10000.0/
      PARAMETER  (PAYMNT = 1000.0, RATE = 8.0)
```

```
      PRINT *, '       YEAR   OWED BEFORE        PAYMENT     OWED AFTER'
      PRINT *, '               PAYMENT                        PAYMENT '
      PRINT *, '       _____'

      YEAR = 1
11    IF (PAYMNT .LE. OWED) THEN
          OWED = OWED * (1.0 + RATE /100.0)
          PRINT *, YEAR, OWED, PAYMNT, OWED - PAYMNT

          YEAR = YEAR + 1
          OWED = OWED - PAYMNT
          GO TO 11
      END IF
*-----------------------------------------------------------------------*
*                                                                       *
*             The second OWED below is the final payment.               *
*                                                                       *
*-----------------------------------------------------------------------*
      PRINT *, YEAR, OWED, OWED, 0.0

      END
```

The output from this program is

YEAR	OWED BEFORE PAYMENT	PAYMENT	OWED AFTER PAYMENT
1	10800.00	1000.000	9800.000
2	10584.00	1000.000	9584.000
3	10350.72	1000.000	9350.720
4	10098.78	1000.000	9098.777
5	9826.680	1000.000	8826.680
6	9532.814	1000.000	8532.814
7	9215.439	1000.000	8215.439
8	8872.675	1000.000	7872.675
9	8502.489	1000.000	7502.489
10	8102.688	1000.000	7102.688
11	7670.904	1000.000	6670.904
12	7204.576	1000.000	6204.576
13	6700.942	1000.000	5700.942
14	6157.018	1000.000	5157.018
15	5569.579	1000.000	4569.579
16	4935.146	1000.000	3935.146
17	4249.957	1000.000	3249.957
18	3509.954	1000.000	2509.954
19	2710.750	1000.000	1710.750
20	1847.610	1000.000	847.6100
21	847.6100	847.6100	0.0000000E+00

As always, the output is something less than desirable. We should have rounded the numbers to two decimal places. But the results for the first two years confirm our calculations. The numbers 9800.000 and 9584.000 are where they should be. Also, the last payment comes where it should, the first time the amount owed is less than $1000.00. Do you notice anything else?

The amount owed before payment in the 21st year is exactly the same as the amount owed at the end of the 20th year. We forgot to add an interest payment for the last year. That's easy to fix. The trick is to notice it in the first place. Learn to scrutinize your output, especially at the beginning and end.

We can fix the major problem by adding the statement

```
OWED = OWED * (1.0 + RATE /100.0)
```

just after END IF.

As long as we are fixing things, let us round off the values of OWED to two decimal places with the statement

```
OWED = REAL( NINT(100.0 * OWED) ) / 100.0
```

We place this statement just after the assignment statement

```
OWED = OWED * (1.0 + RATE /100.0)
```

The new program produces the output

YEAR	OWED BEFORE PAYMENT	PAYMENT	OWED AFTER PAYMENT
1	10800.00	1000.000	9800.000
2	10584.00	1000.000	9584.000
3	10350.72	1000.000	9350.720
4	10098.78	1000.000	9098.780
5	9826.680	1000.000	8826.680
6	9532.810	1000.000	8532.810
7	9215.430	1000.000	8215.430
8	8872.660	1000.000	7872.660
9	8502.470	1000.000	7502.470
10	8102.670	1000.000	7102.670
11	7670.880	1000.000	6670.880
12	7204.550	1000.000	6204.550
13	6700.910	1000.000	5700.910
14	6156.980	1000.000	5156.980
15	5569.540	1000.000	4569.540
16	4935.100	1000.000	3935.100

17	4249.910	1000.000	3249.910
18	3509.900	1000.000	2509.900
19	2710.690	1000.000	1710.690
20	1847.550	1000.000	847.5500
21	915.3500	915.3500	0.0000000E+00

The output looks much better. We will see in Chapter 7 how to cause the computer to print exactly two decimal places. Notice that the amount owed at the end of the 20th year is six cents less than the corresponding amount in the previous table, because of the rounding. Mr. Brown and his friend might not care about the difference, but banks would.

So, do you believe the program is correct? It works for the given data, but consider what would have happened if the amount owed after payment had been $980.00 at the end of a year. The computer would exit from the loop, but the amount owed at the end of the next year would be

$$980.00 \times 1.08 = 1058.40$$

which is more than the payment. It seems our IF statement is incorrect. We can fix it by *looking ahead* to see what amount will be owed at the end of the next year. That amount is

OWED * (1.0 + RATE /100.0)

so the IF statement should be

IF (PAYMNT .LE. OWED * (1.0 + RATE / 100.0)) THEN

Since the expression

OWED * (1.0 + RATE / 100.0)

occurs several times in the program, we will make a statement function NEXT of it, as follows:

NEXT(X) = X * (1.0 + RATE / 100.0)

Also, since we have two round-off statements in the program, we define a statement function

ROUND2(X) = REAL(NINT(X * 100.0)) / 100.0

Our final version (scout's honor) of the program is in Program 6.8b.

■

PROGRAM 6.8b

```
      PROGRAM CONPAY
*-------------------------------------------------------------*
*        Calculate progress of a loan with constant payments.  *
*-------------------------------------------------------------*
      INTEGER YEAR
      REAL    OWED, PAYMNT, RATE, X, ROUND2, NEXT
      DATA    OWED /10000.0/, PAYMNT /1000.0/, RATE /8.0/
      ROUND2(X) = REAL( NINT(X * 100.0) ) / 100.0
      NEXT(X)   = X * (1.0 + RATE / 100.0)

      PRINT *, '      YEAR  OWED BEFORE      PAYMENT     OWED AFTER'
      PRINT *, '                PAYMENT                     PAYMENT '
      PRINT *, '            ------------------------------------------'

      YEAR = 1
11    IF (PAYMNT .LE. NEXT(OWED)) THEN
         OWED = NEXT(OWED)
         OWED = ROUND2(OWED)
         PRINT *, YEAR, OWED, PAYMNT, OWED - PAYMNT

         YEAR = YEAR + 1
         OWED = OWED - PAYMNT
         GO TO 11
      END IF

      OWED = NEXT(OWED)
      OWED = ROUND2(OWED)
*-------------------------------------------------------------*
*            The second OWED below is the final payment.       *
*-------------------------------------------------------------*
      PRINT *, YEAR, OWED, OWED, 0.0

      END
```

We shall seldom beat a program to death as we did this one, but you should certainly learn to test your programs, and the ones in this book, in as many ways as you can. For example, you can even gain something by rewriting this program so that the PRINT statement is the first statement in the body of the while loop.

Example 6.9 Finding the Area Under a Curve

In Example 4.11 we discussed the approximation of areas under curves by sums of rectangles. We consider the same problem here, but now we will have the program automatically increase the number of rectangles until two succeeding sums are very close together.

First we should define what we mean by *two succeeding sums are very close together*. Suppose one sum is OLDSUM, and after increasing N we calculate a new sum called SUM. Then if OLDSUM and SUM have nearly the same value, we should stop and consider the value of SUM to be our final approximation to the area under the curve.

How close should we require OLDSUM and SUM to be? It is tempting to say we want SUM and OLDSUM to be within one one-millionth of each other and use a criterion such as

$$\text{ABS(SUM - OLDSUM) .GT. 1E-6}$$

to decide whether to continue. Consider, however, what would happen if the true area is about 9000. Then to get within 1E-6 of the correct area, the computer must calculate SUM precisely with four digits (9000) before the decimal place and six digits (1E-6) after the decimal place. Most computers cannot calculate real numbers correctly to ten digits. It would be better to base the decision on a relative error, the size of the error relative to the size of what is being calculated. Thus, we might use a condition such as

$$\text{ABS(SUM - OLDSUM) .GT. 1E-5 * SUM}$$

If this condition is true, we need to calculate a new value for SUM. We will have to increase the number N of rectangles, and we decide to double N with N = 2 * N. Also, we must save the value of SUM in OLDSUM (OLDSUM = SUM).

From Chapter 4 we already know how to calculate the sum of N rectangles and store that value in SUM. Now we must do the following:

1. Initialize OLDSUM and N.
2. Calculate SUM, the sum of the areas of N rectangles.
3. If SUM and OLDSUM are not close enough, then

    a.   Double the number of rectangles.

    b.   Set OLDSUM to the value of SUM.

    c.   Return to step 2 to get a new value for SUM.

See Program 6.9.

■

PROGRAM 6.9

```
      PROGRAM AREA
*-----------------------------------------------------------------*
*     Approximate area under a curve by sum of areas of rectangles.  *
*     Height of rectangle is value of function at interval midpoint.  *
*-----------------------------------------------------------------*
      REAL     A, B, OLDSUM, SUM, BASE, X, FRAC, F
      INTEGER N, I
      DATA     FRAC / 1E-5 /
      F(X) = SQRT(X ** 4 + 3.0 * X ** 2)

      PRINT *, 'Limits of integration?'
      READ  *, A, B
      N = 8
      OLDSUM = 0.0
*-----------------------------------------------------------------*
*          Start loop to calculate sum of areas of rectangles.     *
*-----------------------------------------------------------------*
11    SUM = 0.0
         BASE = (B - A) / N
         X = A - BASE / 2.0
         DO 22 I = 1, N
            X = X + BASE
            SUM = SUM + BASE * F(X)
22       CONTINUE
*-----------------------------------------------------------------*
* Check whether OLDSUM and SUM are too far apart.  If so, double N, *
* set the value of OLDSUM to the value of SUM, and recalculate SUM.  *
*-----------------------------------------------------------------*
         IF (ABS(SUM - OLDSUM) .GT. FRAC * SUM) THEN
            N = 2 * N
            OLDSUM = SUM
            GO TO 11
         END IF

      PRINT *, 'Area is', SUM
      PRINT *, N, ' rectangles used.'

      END
```

The exercises at the end of this chapter suggest two better, but slightly more complicated, ways to approximate the area under a curve.

Example 6.10 Using the END Specifier in the READ Statement

Consider a file, POWERS.DAT, containing the first four integer powers of the first five integers:

```
1    1    1     1
2    4    8    16
3    9   27    81
4   16   64   256
5   25  125   625
```

It is easy to read the file and print its contents with a DO loop:

```
        DO 11 I = 1, 5
            READ (7, *) ONE, TWO, THREE, FOUR
            PRINT *, ONE, TWO, THREE, FOUR
11      CONTINUE
```

We know this segment will read the entire file POWERS.DAT, because we know the file has exactly five records.

In many situations, we want to read an entire file without knowing in advance how many records are in the file. Fortran has a special device to handle this situation.

The END Specifier

The READ statement can contain an END **specifier**, whose form is

```
        END = <label>
```

When the computer tries to read a record and finds no more records, control passes to the statement with the label given after END =. The END specifier is placed in the parentheses after READ, as in

```
        READ (<unit>, *, END = <label>) <read list>
```

Then we can set up a loop with the READ statement as follows.

```
11      READ (7, *, END = 22) ONE, TWO, THREE, FOUR
            PRINT *, ONE, TWO, THREE, FOUR
        GO TO 11
```

The unconditional transfer GO TO 11 might make the loop appear endless, but the END specifier in the READ statement has the effect of a block IF statement:

```
            IF (the end of the file has been reached) THEN
                GO TO 22
            ELSE
                READ (7, *) ONE, TWO, THREE, FOUR
            END IF
```

Program 6.10 uses the END = specifier to read the file POWERS.DAT. Also we have the program count the number of records in the file.

■

PROGRAM 6.10

```
      PROGRAM REDEND
*----------------------------------------------------------*
*         Illustrate use of the END specifier.             *
*----------------------------------------------------------*
      INTEGER  ONE, TWO, THREE, FOUR, COUNT

      OPEN (7, FILE = 'POWERS', STATUS = 'OLD')

      PRINT *, 'CONTENTS OF FILE POWERS.DAT'

      COUNT = 0

11    READ (7, *, END = 22) ONE, TWO, THREE, FOUR
         COUNT = COUNT + 1
         PRINT *, ONE, TWO, THREE, FOUR
      GO TO 11
*----------------------------------------------------------*
*         The ONLY way to get here is to be sent           *
*         by END = 22 in the READ statement.               *
*----------------------------------------------------------*
22    CLOSE (7)

      PRINT *
      PRINT *, The file contains', COUNT, ' records.'

      END
```

■
6.2 OTHER CONTROL STATEMENTS

The STOP Statement

The STOP **statement** terminates execution of a program. At one time, all Fortran versions required a STOP statement immediately before the END statement, but now very few versions do. When the computer executes a STOP statement, it stops executing the program and prints FORTRAN STOP. The word STOP can be followed by a string in apostrophes. When such a STOP statement is executed, the computer will print the quoted string, as illustrated in the simple Program 6.11.

■
PROGRAM 6.11

```
      PROGRAM STOPPR
*-----------------------------------------------------------*
*  Illustrate the STOP statement with quoted strings.  *
*-----------------------------------------------------------*
      PRINT *, 'Please enter two numbers.'
      READ *, A, B

      IF (A .LT. B)  STOP 'First is less.'
      IF (A .EQ. B)  STOP 'Numbers are equal.'
      IF (A .GT. B)  STOP 'First is greater.'

      END
```

Here is what the computer will do when the user enters various values.

User Enters	Computer Prints
2 6	First is less.
8 8	Numbers are equal.
3 -2	First is greater.

We do not recommend this use of the STOP statement. An IF...THEN...ELSE block is more appropriate here. However, the STOP statement is often helpful in debugging a large program. Several STOP statements can be placed at critical points in the program, with each STOP followed by a different quoted string. When the program *does* stop, the quoted string tells you *which* STOP statement actually stopped the program.

Other Control Statements

Fortran 77 contains two other control statements, the **computed** GO TO **statement** and the **arithmetic** IF **statement**. We do not recommend the use of either statement, but Appendix A contains examples of them.

■

6.3 SUMMARY OF CHAPTER 6

■ *Terms Introduced in This Chapter*

Arithmetic IF statement
Computed GO TO statement
Condition-controlled loop
Endless loop

End-of-data flag
GO TO statement
Infinite loop
Post-test loop

Pre-test loop
STOP statement
While loop

■ *What You Should Know*

1. GO TO statements can lead to badly structured programs.
2. Use GO TO statements in a controlled manner, to keep your programs readable.
3. While loops test a condition to determine whether the computer should execute the loop body.
4. While loops can do everything DO loops can do, and more.
5. The IF condition in a while loop is not under continuous review. The computer checks the condition only when it encounters the IF statement.
6. Unlike DO loops, while loops almost always require some variable initialization before the loop.
7. The condition in the IF statement must become false for the computer to exit the while loop.
8. Use a DO loop when the computer can calculate the number of times to perform a loop body.
9. Use a while loop when the loop body must be performed while a condition is true, or until a condition is false.
10. Avoid testing for equality of real quantities.
11. Use a post-test loop if you are certain you want the loop body performed at least once.
12. Use a pre-test loop when it is possible to encounter situations in which the loop body should not be executed.

■

6.4 EXERCISES

■ *Self-Test*

1. What will the following loops cause the computer to print?

a.
```
          I = 0
    11    IF (I .LE. 10) THEN
             PRINT *, I
             I = I + 2
             GO TO 11
          END IF
```

b.
```
          I = 0
    22    IF (I .LT. 10) THEN
             I = I + 3
             PRINT *, I
             GO TO 22
          END IF
```

c.
```
          I = 64
          J = 27
    33    IF (I .GE. J) THEN
             PRINT *, I, J
             I = 3 * I / 4
             GO TO 33
          END IF
```

d.
```
          X = 0.0
          Y = 4.0
    44    IF (X .LT. Y) THEN
             X = X + 0.25
             Y = Y - 0.50
             PRINT *, X, Y
             GO TO 44
          END IF
```

2. What is wrong with each of the following while loops?

a.
```
          I = 0
    11    IF (I .LE. 10) THEN
             I = I - 2
             PRINT *, I
             GO TO 11
          END IF
```

b.
```
            I = 0
     22  IF (I .LT. 5) THEN
            PRINT *, I
            J = J + 2
            GO TO 22
         END IF
```

c.
```
            I = 0
     33  IF I .LT. 10 THEN
            PRINT *, I
            I = I + 1
            GO TO 33
         END IF
```

d.
```
            I = 0
     44  IF (I < 10) THEN
            PRINT *, I
            I = I + 2
            GO TO 44
         END IF
```

3. Set up a while loop to accomplish each of the following. Include initialization of variables.

   a. Print each of the integers from 1 to 10.
   b. Print the numbers 12, 9, 6, 3, and 0.
   c. Beginning with the second power, print all powers of 3 that are less than 10,000.
   d. Begin with X = 20.25, and repeatedly increase X by letting X = X + SQRT(X) until X is greater than 99.99. Print the starting value of X and all succeeding values up to, but not including, the first value greater than 99.99.
   e. Begin with X = 1000.0 and Y = 1.5. At each step, double Y and cut X in half. Print initial values of X and Y, and all succeeding values up to and including the first pair of values for which X is less than Y.

4. a. What value does C take on if the computer executes the following lines with A = 4.2, B = 8.1, D = 3.0?

```
         IF (A .LE. B) GO TO 11
         C = 8.4 * D
         GO TO 55
     11  IF (A .LE. B / 2.0) GO TO 22
         C = 4.2 * D
         GO TO 55
     22  IF (A .LE. B / 3.0) GO TO 33
         C = 2.1 * D
         GO TO 55
```

```
33  IF (A .LE. B / 4.0) GO TO 44
    C = 1.1 * D
    GO TO 55
44  C = D
55  CONTINUE
```

b.   Write a program segment, equivalent to these lines, that contains no GO TO statements or line numbers.

■ Programming Exercises

1. Write a program to find the smallest integer power that can be placed on 0.5 to yield a number less than 0.0001. Print the number as well as the power.

2. Write a program that adds reciprocals of the positive integers 1, 2, 3, ..., until the sum is greater than 10. The program should print the sum and the number of terms added to obtain the sum.

3. The **geometric mean** of n positive numbers is the nth root of the product of the numbers. For example, the geometric mean of 0.5, 4.0, and 13.5 is

$$(0.5 \times 4.0 \times 13.5)^{1/3} = 27.0^{1/3} = 3.0$$

   Write a program that asks for positive numbers and calculates their geometric mean. The program should read numbers and count them until the user types a negative number.

4. Write a program that asks the user for a number and prints the Arcsine (in degrees) of the number. Sine values can vary between -1.0 and 1.0; check for valid input.

5. The program of Example 4.10 calculates the number of combinations of n objects, taken k at a time. The value of n must be positive, and the value of k must be in the range from 0 to n inclusive. Insert a while loop in that program to check for proper input.

6. The value for e^x is given by a famous expression:

$$1 + x + \frac{x^2}{2!} + \frac{x^3}{3!} + \cdots + \frac{x^n}{n!} + \cdots$$

   Although this expression is an infinite sum, we can find a good approximation to its value by adding up a large but finite number of terms. Write a program that asks for a value of x and adds a finite number of terms in the expression, stopping when the last term added is less than 0.000001, or 1E-6. Check the output of the program for several values of x. What values of x might cause problems? *Suggestion:* Do not calculate each term from scratch, because the terms are very similar. For example, two succeeding terms are

$$\frac{x^3}{3!} \quad \text{and} \quad \frac{x^4}{4!}$$

The second term above is the first term times $\frac{x}{4}$.

7. Another famous expression for e^x is

$$\lim_{n \to \infty} \left(1 + \frac{x}{n}\right)^n$$

or *the limit as n approaches infinity of* $(1 + x/n)^n$. Here, as in Exercise 6, we can attain a good approximation to e^x by letting n become large. Consider the case $x = 2$. With $n = 2$, the approximation is $(1 + 2/2)^2 = 4$. With $n = 4$, $(1 + 2/4)^4 = 1.5 = 5.0625$. For $n = 8$, we have $(1 + 2/8)^8 = 5.9605$. As n increases, the value of the expression increases, but when n is very large, a large increase in n produces a very small increase in $(1 + x/n)^n$.

   Write a program that asks for a value of x and calculates an approximation to e^x by this method. Keep track of two successive approximations by referring to one as NEWVAL and the other as OLDVAL. Start with $n = 2$ and keep doubling n until the ratio NEWVAL / OLDVAL is less than 1.001.

8. Total known sources of a natural resource are 7.5 million units, and past experience indicates that new sources are found at a rate of 360,000 units per year. 480,000 units per year are being consumed now, but consumption is expected to grow at a rate of 6.5 percent per year. Print a table giving the year, yearly consumption, and remaining sources at the end of the year, for all years in which supply meets or exceeds demand. Print a summary statement indicating that the resource is exhausted and telling how long it lasted.

9. A 65-year-old woman with $200,000 wants to set up an annuity for herself. She can place the money in a bank at 8 percent interest per year, compounded quarterly, and have the bank send her a check at the end of each year, just after the interest is paid. If she needs $20,000 per year, how long will the annuity last? Each year, print the year, interest gained for the year, and the balance in the account both before her check is sent and after. When the balance before the check is sent drops below $20,000, send her the balance and close the account.

10. Write a program that asks the user for numbers, one at a time, and counts and adds the given numbers that are at least 1 but not more than 100. Use the number zero as an end-of-data flag. For example, if the given numbers are 17, −32, 12, 58, 120, 35, and 0, the computer should print something like:

```
The sum of  4 numbers in the range from 1 to 100 is    122
```

11. In two-dimensional space, the distance from a point (x, y) to a line, $ax + by = c$, is

$$distance = \frac{\mid ax + by - c \mid}{\sqrt{a^2 + b^2}}$$

Write a program that asks the user to enter the coordinates x, y of a point, and the coefficients a, b, c for a line, then calculates the distance from the point to the line. Put a while loop in the program to ask if the user wishes to run the program again.

12. Each record in a data file named DATA1.DAT was written with a list-directed WRITE statement and contains two integers and one real number. Write a program that will read the file, print its contents, and tell how many records are in the file.

13. An integer is **prime** if it is not divisible by any integers but itself and 1. Thus, 6 is not prime because 6 / 2 = 3. The number 1 is not considered prime, so the first six primes are 2, 3, 5, 7, 11, and 13.

    Write a program that asks for an integer and determines if that integer is prime. If it is not prime, the program should print the smallest divisor (factor) of the given integer. *Suggestion:* The integer D is a divisor of the integer N if D * (N / D) = N, or if MOD(N, D) is zero. Also, when trying to decide if N is prime, try dividing N by 2 first, then by 3, 5, 7, and so on. The largest divisor that must be checked is something like SQRT(N), but SQRT(N) would cause an error.

14. Binary Search for a Number. Here is a guessing game you can play with the computer. You pick a number from 1 to 100 and have the computer try to guess your number. After each guess, you will tell the computer whether its guess was high, low, or correct. If the guess was not correct, the computer must guess again. The point of the program is the computer's strategy for selecting numbers to guess.

    Put yourself in the computer's place, and try to program a strategy for selecting numbers to guess. Imagine that some other person is the user of the program. A possible strategy is to have the computer guess the numbers 1, 2, 3, 4, and so on, until it gets to the correct number. Besides being dull, this strategy will sometimes take very many guesses to get the right number. We are looking for a strategy that will keep the number of guesses to a minimum.

    A reasonable first guess is 50; even if it is not correct, it splits the range of numbers roughly in half. Then for the next guess, the search narrows down to half as many numbers as there were at the start. Suppose the computer guesses 50 first and the user responds that the guess is low. Then the number must be in the range from 51 to 100. Following the same strategy, a good second guess would be 75 or 76, to cut the range in half again.

    This binary search strategy is similar to the binary search for a root in the BISECT program of Example 5.6. Write a program to "guess" a number in the range from 1 to 100, using a binary search strategy.

15. A two-player game starts with 17 matches. Each player in turn must take 1, 2, or 3 matches. The loser is the one who must take the last match (or the winner is the one who leaves exactly one match). Write a program to play this match game with one player, letting the player go first. Include a while loop to check for proper input from the human player. *Hint:* The computer can always win. Figure out a strategy. If the player takes x matches, the computer should take . . . .

16. Write a program similar to PROGRAM AREA of Example 6.9, using *trapezoids* instead of rectangles to approximate the area under a curve. (See also Programming Exercise 16 in Chapter 4.)

    When the number of trapezoids doubles, you can calculate the sum of the function values at every *other* subinterval endpoint because the sum at the remaining endpoints was already calculated.

17. Write a program similar to PROGRAM AREA of Example 6.9, using *Simpson's rule* to approximate the area under the curve. (See also Programming Exercise 17 in Chapter 4.)

18. **Numerical differentiation**. Recall that the derivative of a function f at the value x is

$$\lim_{c \to 0} \frac{f(x + c) - f(c)}{c}$$

Therefore, even if you do not know how to differentiate a particular function, you can sometimes find an **approximate derivative** of f at c by calculating

$$\frac{f(x + c) - f(c)}{c}$$

for a suitably small value of c. Write a program to find the approximate derivative of a function. Use a statement function in the program and let the program user input x.

    Start with a relatively small value of c and calculate the approximate derivative. Then cut c in half and find a new value for the derivative. Continue until the new and old derivative values differ by less than one-millionth of the new value ($abs(new - old) < new/10^{-6}$), or until c has been cut in half 15 times.

    This program provides many opportunities for overflow, because the value of c quickly gets very small. The small values of c also increase the likelihood that the computer will calculate $f(x + c)$ and $f(c)$ as equal even when they are not, yielding a poor approximation for the derivative. Finally, if the true value of the derivative is near zero, the approximate values might underflow without satisfying the condition above. At first, do not worry about overflow and zero values. After your program runs in several cases, try to take care of at least some of these problems.

19. The **Newton-Raphson method** is a fairly powerful method for finding an approximate root of a function $f(x)$, or a value for x that makes $f(x)$ approximately zero. To use this method you must know how do take the derivative of the function. Start with an estimate x_0 of the root. Then generate successive approximations with the formula

$$x_{i+1} = x_i - \frac{f(x_i)}{f'(x_i)}$$

where f' is the derivative of f. As in the previous exercise, continue until the difference between the last two approximations is a small fraction of the last approximation, or until the computer calculates some preset number of approximations, whichever comes first.

7 FORMATS

The only output statements we have used up to now are the list-directed PRINT and WRITE statements. These statements are easy to use and work well for simple output. However, the programmer has very little control over the exact spacing of output and over the form of printed numbers. **Formatted** output allows the programmer to specify exactly where output should appear and the precise form of printed data. (Technically, list-directed output statements *are* formatted statements, but the format is built into the Fortran compiler and the programmer has no control over it.)

When output is printed on a printer or terminal screen, we will speak of *lines* of output. The printed lines are the component parts of the entire output. When output is sent to a file, or input read from a file, we normally call the components of the file *records*. Record is the more general term, and is often used to refer to a line of output or input.

■ 7.1 OUTPUT FORMATS

In this section we illustrate formatted output with PRINT statements, which write output at your terminal. Formatted WRITE statements are similar, but each WRITE statement also contains a unit number indicating the file to which output is written.

Planning ahead is always a good idea, and setting up the layout of output is no exception. Professional programmers always decide exactly how printed output will look before they write a program. In particular, specific columns are set aside for each item of data. Aids for planning the layout of data include Fortran coding sheets and graph paper with blocks large enough to hold letters and numbers. One simply prints, by hand, in the spaces or blocks, and counts the number of columns (spaces or blocks) used.

The device we use is well suited to terminals or typewriters. At the top of the desired output, type

```
         1         2         3         4         5         6
1234567890123456789012345678901234567890123456789012345678901234567890
```

Beneath these numbers, place the desired data. Do not be too specific about what is printed. For example, write XXXX.XX instead of 1432.56. We will always use X to stand for a single digit or a minus sign, so XXXX.XX represents a real number with two digits after the decimal point, and up to four characters (digits or a minus sign) before the decimal point. Similarly, XXX would represent an integer (because there is no decimal point) up to three digits long, or two digits and a minus sign. We do mention minus signs quite often; a very common mistake in planning output is forgetting to leave room for a possible minus sign. For character data, we use a string of As; AAAAAAA represents a string of seven characters.

Suppose one output line is to hold a character string, an integer, and a real number, in that order. These items might be values of variables NAME, AGE, and SALARY. One possible way to allot columns for these data is

```
         1         2         3         4
12345678901234567890123456789012345678901234567890
   AAAAAAAAAAAAAAAAAA    XX        XXX.XX
```

The numbers make it clear that

1. The string begins in column 4 and ends in column 21
2. The integer is in columns 25 and 26
3. The real number begins in column 34 and ends in column 39

The list-directed PRINT statement cannot print data exactly this way, but a **formatted** PRINT **statement** can. The only change in the PRINT statement itself is a label replacing the asterisk, such as

```
PRINT 10, NAME, AGE, SALARY
```

The FORMAT **Statement**

The label, 10 in this case, is placed on a FORMAT **statement** whose general form is

<label> FORMAT (*<list of descriptors, separated by commas>*)

The entire list of descriptors, including the parentheses, is called the FOR-MAT **specification**.

Data Descriptors

For each item in the print list, the FORMAT specification must contain a **field descriptor**, or **data descriptor**, specifying the **width** of the **field**, the data type, and the format of the item to be printed in that field. For our problem, we need the following data descriptors:

1. The A **data descriptor** for character data has the form Aw where w is an integer specifying the width of the field. In our example, the width of the field for NAME is 18 columns, so the appropriate descriptor is A18 (The A descriptor can also appear without a field width, as we used it in input formats in Chapter 3.)

2. The I **data descriptor** for integer data has the form Iw where w is again an integer specifying the width of the field. In our example, the width of the field for AGE is two columns, so the appropriate descriptor is I2

3. The F **data descriptor** for real data has the form F$w.d$ where w, as always, is an integer specifying the width of the field, and d is an integer specifying the number of digits to be printed after the decimal point. The printed number is rounded to d decimal places. In our example, the field width for SALARY is 6 (counting a space for the decimal point), and two digits are to be printed after the decimal point, so the appropriate descriptor is F6.2

In addition to the data descriptors, the FORMAT statement can contain **edit descriptors** specifying editing functions to be performed. We mention only one edit descriptor here, the X **descriptor**, which has the form

$$n\text{X}$$

where n is an integer. The X means *skip a column*, so nX means *skip n columns*. The X edit descriptor allows the desired precise spacing between columns.

Returning to our original specification,

```
          1         2         3         4
1234567890123456789012345678901234567890
   AAAAAAAAAAAAAAAAAA   XX      XXX.XX
```

notice that the computer should:

1. Skip three columns before the value of NAME is printed.

2. Skip three columns after NAME.

3. Skip seven columns after AGE.

Thus the descriptors, in order, for our problem are

3X, A18, 3X, I2, 7X, F6.2

These descriptors tell the computer to do the following:

Descriptor	Action
3X	Skip 3 columns.
A18	Print 18 characters, adding blanks at the left, if the string to be printed contains fewer than 18 characters.
3X	Skip 3 columns.
I2	Print an integer value in 2 columns, adding a blank at the left, if necessary.
7X	Skip 7 columns.
F6.2	Print a real number in 6 columns, rounded to 2 digits after the decimal point. Add blanks on the left, if necessary.

Carriage Control

There is one remaining item before the FORMAT specification is complete. The *first* character of every record transferred to a printer does not print, but is used as a **carriage control character**. The carriage control character specifies the spacing between *lines*. This spacing is carried out *before* the line is printed. Carriage control characters and their effects are listed in Figure 7.1.

FIGURE 7.1
Carriage control characters

Character	Effect (before printing)
X or 1X or ' '	Advance 1 line (single spacing). (Some compilers accept only 1X, not X alone.)
'0'	Advance 2 lines (double spacing).
'1'	Advance to top of next page.
'+'	Do not advance. (This line will be printed on top of the previous line.)

Assume that we want single spacing. Then the complete FORMAT specification is

(1X, 3X, A18, 3X, I2, 7X, F6.2)

so the complete PRINT and FORMAT statements are

PRINT 10, NAME, AGE, SALARY

10   FORMAT (1X, 3X, A18, 3X, I2, 7X, F6.2)

We have drawn lines between the statements to show that each item in the
PRINT list corresponds to one data descriptor in the FORMAT specification.
You should always make a mental correspondence between items in an
output list and data descriptors in the FORMAT statement.

The 1X and 3X in the FORMAT statement could be combined to give a FOR-
MAT specification

(4X, A18, 3X, I2, 7X, F6.3)

We suggest that you write the carriage control character separately, at least
while you are getting used to FORMAT specifications, to remind yourself
always to think about carriage control.

Fortran ignores spaces inside a FORMAT specification, except for spaces
inside a quoted string. Thus, the following specifications are equivalent.

(4X, A18, 3X, I2, 7X, F6.3)
(4X,A18,3X,I2,7X,F6.3)
(4X , A18 , 3X , I2 , 7X , F6.3)

This book will follow the form of the first specification, with one space
after a comma and no space before.

Any character not in the list of carriage control characters is treated as
a blank and deleted from the list of characters to be printed. Thus if the
PRINT and FORMAT statements are

PRINT 10, 'Hello'
10   FORMAT (A5)

the computer will use the H as a carriage control character, treat it as a blank, and print

```
ello
```

The FORMAT statement is nonexecutable and can be placed almost anywhere in a program. For now, we will write a FORMAT statement immediately after the first PRINT statement that uses it. Many programmers believe that FORMAT statements disrupt the flow of a program for a reader and prefer to put all FORMAT statements together right before the END statement, or just before the first executable statement in the program. Later we will put FORMAT statements at the bottom of programs that include many such statements.

With the list-directed PRINT statement, it is often difficult to line up the columns in a table underneath the appropriate words in the header (words at the top of the table). In our example, there might be many values of the variables NAME, AGE, and SALARY to be written in a table. These values should line up under some appropriate words such as Name, Age, and Salary. It is easy enough to take the original layout and insert a line with these words in proper places:

```
          1         2         3         4
1234567890123456789012345678901234567890
       Name          Age      Salary
   AAAAAAAAAAAAAAAAAA   XX      XXX.XX
```

We have approximately centered the words above the fields they describe. There are ten columns before Name, nine columns between Name and Age, and seven columns between Age and Salary, so the PRINT and FORMAT statements are

```
        PRINT 10, 'Name', 'Age', 'Salary'
10      FORMAT (1X, 10X, A4, 9X, A3, 7X, A6)
```

Similarly, if NAME, AGE, and SALARY are the variables whose values are to be printed, the PRINT/FORMAT pair of statements could be

```
        PRINT 20, NAME, AGE, SALARY
20      FORMAT (1X, 3X, A18, 3X, I2, 7X, F6.2)
```

Example 7.1 Illustrating A, I, F, and X Data Descriptors

To see how the formatted PRINT statement works, give some specific values to NAME, AGE, and SALARY. Program 7.1 reads three sets of values for NAME,

AGE, and SALARY from the file DATA1.DAT. The file contains the following three lines, or records.

```
'Alfred E. Newman'    7 123.46
'Hubert H. Humphrey' 65 125.00
'Englebert Jones'    42 12.62
```

■
PROGRAM 7.1

```
       PROGRAM FORM1
*-----------------------------------------------------------------*
*      Illustrate the A, I, and F data descriptors and the        *
*      X edit descriptor.  Data are in DATA1.DAT.                  *
*-----------------------------------------------------------------*
       CHARACTER*20 NAME
       INTEGER      AGE
       REAL         SALARY

       OPEN (26, FILE = 'DATA1', STATUS = 'OLD')

       PRINT *, '          1         2         3         4         5'
       PRINT *, '12345678901234567890123456789012345678901234567890'
       PRINT 10, 'Name', 'Age', 'Salary'
10     FORMAT (1X, 17X, A4, 9X, A3, 7X, A6)

       DO 11 I = 1, 3

           READ (26, *) NAME, AGE, SALARY

           PRINT 20, NAME, AGE, SALARY
20         FORMAT (1X, 3X, A25, 3X, I2, 7X, F6.2)

11     CONTINUE

       CLOSE (26)

       END
```

Here is the output

```
         1         2         3         4         5
12345678901234567890123456789012345678901234567890
              Name            Age       Salary
     □□□□□Alfred E. Newman□□□□  □7       123.46
     □□□□□Hubert H. Humphrey□□  65       125.00
     □□□□□Englebert Jones□□□□□  42       □12.62
```

When the program reads the names from the file, it stores them as

```
Alfred E. Newman□□□□
Hubert H. Humphrey□□
Englebert Jones□□□□□
```

The names have some added blanks at the right because **NAME** has length 20, and none of the names is that long. Five blanks appear before each name in the output because the data descriptor is A25.

In the output line after Alfred E. Newman, the value of AGE is 7 and the data descriptor is I2, so a blank also appears before the 7. The printed value of SALARY is rounded to two decimal places by the F6.2 descriptor.

On the Hubert H. Humphrey line, the value 65 fills the I2 field and 125.00 fills the F6.2 field.

For Englebert Jones, the I2 format exactly fits the value 42. The number 12.62 is shorter than the field width 6, so a blank precedes it.

From the printed data we can infer a rule for data descriptors:

> When the field width *w* is *larger* than needed to print an item, data items are *right-justified* in their fields. That is, the last printed character in a field is at the right end of the field. Blanks are placed at the left of the field.

Notice, however, that for character strings, some of the printed characters on the right end of the strings might be blanks.

You should make sure that data descriptors allow enough room to print the associated data items. The following example shows what happens when the field widths are too small.

Example 7.2 Short Field Widths on A, I, and F FORMAT Descriptors

In the previous program, let us change only the first and last **FORMAT** statements to

```
10    FORMAT (1X, 7X, A4, 9X, A3, 7X, A6)
30    FORMAT (1X, 3X, A15, 3X, I2, 7X, F6.2)
```

In the first FORMAT specification, the second descriptor is now 7X instead of 17X. The corresponding change in the second specification puts A15 in place of A25, and will show what happens when the field width (15) is shorter than the length (20) of a character string.

We also make two changes in the data file DATA1.DAT, to get values too large for the I2 and F6.2 data descriptors:

```
'Alfred E. Newman'   7 123.456
'Hubert H. Humphrey' 65 1250.0      <---- New salary value
'Englebert Jones'   102 12.62       <---- New age value
```

Then the printed output is

```
          1         2         3         4
1234567890123456789012345678901234567890
    Name         Age      Salary
    Alfred E. Newma    7    123.46
    Hubert H. Humph   65    ******
```

(possibly followed by "Output conversion error" message)

```
    Englebert Jones   **      12.62
```

(possibly followed by "Output conversion error" message).

With the A15 data descriptor, the computer prints the first 15 characters of each name. Although characters are lost, no error occurs, as you can see from the first line of output under the header.

In the next output line, the 1250.0 value of SALARY is too large to fit in a field of width 6 with two digits after the decimal point. The computer fills the field with six asterisks, and then might print an "Output conversion error" warning. However, the program continues to run.

In the last output line, the AGE value of 102 is too large for the I2 descriptor, so two asterisks are printed. The computer finishes printing the line, then prints the warning again.

The rule here is: When the field width w in a data descriptor is not large enough to contain a data item,

1. The computer prints only the first w characters of a character string. No warning is given.
2. The computer prints w asterisks for numeric data, when possibly a warning message and a program halt after executing the entire output statement.

Considering the problem of too small a field width, we note that the FORMAT specification

```
(1X, 3X, A18, 3X, I2, 7X, F6.2)
```

could be replaced by

$$(1X, A21, I5, F13.2)$$

Any data that the first specification can print without error will appear exactly the same way under the second specification. Any number of Xs in front of a data descriptor can be absorbed into the field width of the descriptor, so A21 can replace 3X, A18; I5 can replace 3X, I2; and F13.2 can replace 7X, F6.2. The latter FORMAT specification will obviously cause fewer of those unwanted asterisks.

As usual, there is a trade-off. The 3X and 7X in the first FORMAT specification guarantee three and seven blank columns, but the second specification will allow the data to run together if the value of the real number does require 13 columns.

When laying out a FORMAT specification for numeric data, be sure to make the field width w large enough to accommodate a possible minus sign, and count a column for the decimal point in real numbers. Use a FORMAT specification that will handle the largest possible numbers the program may encounter.

Example 7.3 Compound Interest: Example 4.11 with Formatted Output

We have already printed several tables with list-directed PRINT statements, and in most cases we mentioned that there are better ways to print such tables. An instance is Example 4.11, where we printed a heading with the statement

```
PRINT *, 'INTEREST RATE      TERM  FINAL VALUE'
```

The spacing seems strange, but it was forced on us by the list-directed PRINT statement inside the loops of the program:

```
PRINT *, RATE, TERM, VALUE
```

This PRINT statement also printed values for RATE with six decimal places and values for VALUE with three places. We can now do better.

A reasonable layout for this problem is

```
         1         2         3         4
12345678901234567890123456789012345678990
INTEREST RATE   TERM   FINAL VALUE
     XX.X         X      XXXXX.XX
```

which could use the PRINT/FORMAT pairs

```
      PRINT 10, 'INTEREST RATE', 'TERM', 'FINAL VALUE'
10    FORMAT(1X, A13, 3X, A4, 3X, A11)
```

and

```
      PRINT 20, RATE, TERM, VALUE
20    FORMAT (1X, 6X, F4.1, 8X, I1, 5X, F8.2)
```

Program 7.3 shows the complete program.

■
PROGRAM 7.3

```
      PROGRAM FINVAL
*-------------------------------------------------------------------*
*  Calculate value of $5,000 invested for various rates and terms. *
*-------------------------------------------------------------------*
      REAL    PRINC, RATE, VALUE
      INTEGER TERM

      PRINC = 5000.0
      PRINT *, '$5,000 is invested for varying rates and terms'
      PRINT *
      PRINT 10, 'INTEREST RATE', 'TERM', 'FINAL VALUE'
10    FORMAT(1X, A13, 3X, A4, 3X, A11)

      DO 22 RATE = 8.0, 12.0

         DO 11 TERM = 1, 5
            VALUE = PRINC * (1.0 + RATE/100.0) ** TERM
            PRINT 20, RATE, TERM, VALUE
20          FORMAT (1X, 6X, F4.1, 8X, I1, 5X, F8.2)
11       CONTINUE

         PRINT *

22    CONTINUE

      END
```

The output from this program is

$5,000 is invested for varying rates and terms

INTEREST RATE	TERM	FINAL VALUE
8.0	1	5400.00
8.0	2	5832.00
8.0	3	6298.56
8.0	4	6802.45
8.0	5	7346.64
9.0	1	5450.00
9.0	2	5940.50
9.0	3	6475.15
9.0	4	7057.91
9.0	5	7693.12
10.0	1	5500.00
10.0	2	6050.00
10.0	3	6655.00
10.0	4	7320.50
10.0	5	8052.55
11.0	1	5550.00
11.0	2	6160.50
11.0	3	6838.16
11.0	4	7590.35
11.0	5	8425.29
12.0	1	5600.00
12.0	2	6272.00
12.0	3	7024.64
12.0	4	7867.60
12.0	5	8811.71

More on Data Descriptors

Each data descriptor is known by a single letter, which stands for the type of output the descriptor produces. The A stands for *alphanumeric*, which means letters and digits, although characters can be other things too. I stands for *integer*, and F stands for *floating-point*.

The data descriptors A, I, and F are certainly some of the most frequently used data descriptors. In this section we will explain these descriptors more fully and introduce three more. Fortran also has the descriptors E (*exponential*) and G (*general*) for real numbers, and L for *logical* data.

Every data descriptor contains a *field width*, which we designate with the letter *w*. The field width is a positive integer constant; it specifies the number of columns in which to print an item of data. The field width must be large enough to hold any data item that might occur. For example, the real number −123456.78 requires a field width of ten or more, because it contains eight digits, a decimal point, and a minus sign.

COMMON DATA DESCRIPTORS

Data Type	Data Descriptor	Comments and Examples
INTEGER	I*w*	The integer is printed right-justified in a field of *w* columns. Thus, if the field is columns 5-9, an I5 descriptor prints the value 12 as 1234567890 □□□12
	I*w.d*	Same as above, but at least *d* digits will be printed, with leading zeroes if necessary. The I3.2 data descriptor prints the value 7 as □07
CHARACTER	A*w*	If *w* is not large enough to print the entire string, characters are truncated from the right side of the string. That is, if NAME is 'Rumplestiltskin' and the data descriptor is A10, then the computer prints only Rumplestil If *w* is larger than the number of characters in the string, the string is right-justified and padded with blanks on the left. That is, if NAME is 'Harvey' and the data descriptor is A10, then the computer prints □□□□Harvey
	A	With no field width specified, the width of the field is the length of the character expression to be printed.

REAL   F*w.d*   The letter *d* stands for the number of places after the decimal point. The value of *w* should be at least *d* + 3, to allow for a decimal point, a sign, and at least one digit before the decimal point. The printed value is rounded to *d* digits and right-justified in the field.

E*w.d*   *Exponential format.* The number will appear with a leading minus sign if necessary, a 0, a decimal point, *d* digits after the point, and an exponent in the form E+*xx*. Thus, *w* should be at least *d* + 7. The printed number is rounded to *d* digits and right-justified. The data descriptor E12.4 causes the number 62.358 to appear as

□□0.6236E+02

G*w.d*   The *d* denotes the number of significant digits to appear in the output number. The G data descriptor acts as an F or E descriptor, depending on the size of the corresponding data item *M*:

1. If $M < 0.1$ or $M \geq 10^d$, the computer uses the descriptor E*w.d*.
2. For other values of *M*, the computer prints d significant digits of *M*, with a decimal point at the proper place, followed by four spaces.

For example, the G12.4 descriptor prints the value 45678.9 as

□□0.4568E+05

so G12.4 acts as E12.4 on the number 45678.9. This same descriptor prints the number 32.853 as

□□□32.85□□□□

so G12.4 acts as (F8.4, 4X) on the number 32.853.

LOGICAL   L*w*   Fortran prints T or F for the logical val-
                      ues .TRUE. and .FALSE.. The descriptor
                      L*w* causes the T or F to appear right-
                      justified in a field of *w* columns. That
                      is, L4 causes a value of .TRUE. to appear
                      as

          □□□T

The F, E, and G descriptors for real data round *output values*, but they do not change the values *stored* in the computer. For example, if X has value 8.257, then an F5.2 descriptor prints the value 8.26, but the value stored in X is still 8.257.

Both the E and G descriptors are new, so we illustrate them with a simple program.

Example 7.4 Illustrating the E and G Real Data Descriptors

Program 7.4 illustrates the action of the E and G data descriptors. The program starts with an X value of 0.0013579 and repeatedly multiplies the value of X by 10, writing each value of X with an F16.4, an E16.4, and a G16.4 descriptor.

■
PROGRAM 7.4

```
      PROGRAM EFG
*-------------------------------------------------*
*       Illustrate the E and G data descriptors.    *
*-------------------------------------------------*
      REAL  X

      X = 0.0013579

      PRINT 10, 'F-FORMAT', 'E-FORMAT', 'G-FORMAT'
10    FORMAT (1X, 3A16)
      PRINT *
```

```
      DO 11 I = 1, 10

            PRINT 20, X, X, X
20          FORMAT (1X, F16.4, E16.4, G16.4)
            X = X * 10.0

11    CONTINUE

      END
```

The output from the program is

F-FORMAT	E-FORMAT	G-FORMAT
0.0014	0.1358E-02	0.1358E-02
0.0136	0.1358E-01	0.1358E-01
0.1358	0.1358E+00	0.1358
1.3579	0.1358E+01	1.358
13.5790	0.1358E+02	13.58
135.7900	0.1358E+03	135.8
1357.9001	0.1358E+04	1358.
13579.0020	0.1358E+05	0.1358E+05
135790.0156	0.1358E+06	0.1358E+06
1357900.1250	0.1358E+07	0.1358E+07

The E descriptor gives its data a uniform appearance. The items in the middle column are identical except for the final digit in the exponent.

The third column makes two things obvious. First, the $Gw.d$ descriptor always prints d significant digits, four in this case. Second, in a column of numbers printed with a G data descriptor, the decimal points will usually not line up.

For the numbers printed with the G16.4 descriptor, the computer prints the first two numbers, and the last three, as if the descriptor were E16.4. It prints the middle five as if the descriptor were an F12.d descriptor, with d varying from 4 down to 1, followed by 4X. The four trailing blanks, which you cannot see in the output, make the field width of the moderate values as long as the field width for values in E format.

Use the F or E descriptors for tables and any other output that must look good. Most people prefer the F; it produces very readable output as long as the output values are reasonably similar. The major drawback to the F descriptor is that unexpectedly large or small numbers can cause output errors.

Both the E and G descriptors can print, without causing an error, any real values the computer can hold. The E descriptor gives a better overall appearance. Some people do not like to read numbers in exponential format and so prefer the G descriptor, which will print many numbers in F format.

Repeat Counts

The *n* in an *n*X descriptor is a **repeat count**. Repeat counts can also appear in front of any *data* descriptor. The descriptor

3I5

means exactly the same as

I5, I5, I5

Thus, to print three integers with an I5 descriptor, use

```
      PRINT 10, N1, N2, N3
10    FORMAT (1X, 3I5)
```

To print three integers with an I6 descriptor, and then two real numbers with an F8.2 descriptor, use

```
      PRINT 20, N1, N2, N3, HEIGHT, WEIGHT
20    FORMAT (1X, 3I5, 2F8.2)
```

Repeat counts can also be placed before parenthesized subsets of FORMAT specifications. Suppose you want to print names (characters) and ages (integers) of two people with the same output statement. Each name takes an A20 descriptor, and each age an I4 descriptor. The appropriate PRINT and FORMAT statements are

```
      PRINT 20, NAME1, AGE1, NAME2, AGE2
20    FORMAT (1X, 2(A20, I4) )
```

The FORMAT statement is equivalent to

```
20    FORMAT (1X, A20, I4, A20, I4)
```

Edit Descriptors

The only edit descriptor mentioned so far is the X descriptor. We present several more in this section.

Character Constants as Edit Descriptors

Character constants can function as edit descriptors, as in

```
      PRINT 10, RESULT
10    FORMAT (1X, 'The result is ', F6.2)
```

If the value of RESULT is 132.5, the output is

```
The result is 132.50
```

We would get exactly the same output with

```
      PRINT 10, 'The result is ', RESULT
10    FORMAT (1X, A13, F6.2)
```

or with

```
      PRINT 10, 'The result is ', RESULT
10    FORMAT (1X, A, F6.2)
```

Thus, character constants can be placed in either the print list or in the FORMAT specification. If the constant is in the print list, the FORMAT specification must contain a matching A or A*w* data descriptor.

Some programmers prefer ' ' to 1X or X. This is really a question of taste. However, for several blank columns, it is certainly better to write 5X, say, than '   '. It is hard to see how many blank spaces are between those quotes.

With no print list, the comma after the label in the PRINT statement is omitted

```
      PRINT 10
10    FORMAT (1X, 'This is a test.')
```

Fortran also contains an H descriptor for character constants. (The H honors Herman Hollerith, who invented the Hollerith card, which many people today call an IBM card.) The general form of the H descriptor is *n*H, followed by *n* characters. For example:

```
                13HThe result is
```

Here the character constant is the 13 characters immediately following the H. The statements

```
      PRINT 10, RESULT
10    FORMAT (1X, 13HThe result is, F6.2)
```

produce the same output as the statements above. The H descriptor is out of style; most programmers prefer quoted character constants.

The Slash (/) Edit Descriptor

Up to now, every FORMAT specification described one line or record of output. The slash (/) descriptor causes an output statement to print more than one record. When the computer encounters a slash in a FORMAT specification, it begins a new line (performs a carriage return and line feed). Therefore, the slash is often called a carriage control character, but it does not have to be placed first in the FORMAT specification.

The slash is also unique in that it does not require commas around it to separate it from other descriptors, so it is a kind of separator, like the comma. A simple example of its use is

```
      PRINT 10, 54321, 12345
10    FORMAT ( 1X, I5 / 1X, I5)
```

The resultant output is

```
54321
12345
```

Notice the 1X immediately following the slash. If it were not there, the output would be

```
54321
```

(several blank lines)

```
2345
```

Because the leading 1 in 12345 acts as a carriage control character for the new line, a **page eject**, or an advance to the top of the next page, occurs. Whenever you use a slash that is not the *last* specifier in a FORMAT specification, be sure to include a carriage control character immediately after the slash.

The slash can occur *first* in a FORMAT specification, and will not be taken as *the* carriage control character. It simply causes a carriage return and line feed, so it will cause a blank line. The segment

```
      PRINT 10, 'Hello'
10    FORMAT (1X, A5)
      PRINT 20, 'there'
20    FORMAT (/ 1X, A5)
```

writes the output

Hello

there

The effect is the same as if line 20 were

```
20    FORMAT ('0', A5)
```

A slash at the *end* of a FORMAT specification does not affect the line being printed, but it will affect the *next* output statement. A blank line can be placed between Hello and there with the statements

```
      PRINT 10, 'Hello'
10    FORMAT (1X, A5 /)
      PRINT 20, 'there'
20    FORMAT (1X, A5)
```

Several adjacent slashes cause several blank lines. *n* slashes at the beginning or end of a FORMAT statement produce *n* blank lines. Since each slash starts a new line, *n* slashes in the middle of a FORMAT statement produce *n* − 1 blank lines. The statements

```
      PRINT 20, 12345, 54321
20    FORMAT (1X, I5 /// 1X, I5)
```

write the numbers with two blank lines between them

12345

54321

The slash descriptor and character constants cannot be preceded by a repeat count. However, both can be placed inside parentheses, with a repeat count in front of the left parenthesis. An illustration is

```
      PRINT 20, 'John', 'Mary', 'Dave'
20    FORMAT ( 3(1X, 'Name is ', A4 /) )
```

The output is

Name is John
Name is Mary
Name is Dave

The Tab Edit Descriptors

Three edit descriptors serve as column specifiers. The T **edit descriptor** has the form

$$Tn$$

which means *tab to column n*. On output, the first column is used for carriage control, so the tab is actually to column $n - 1$. For example,

```
      PRINT 10, 'Hello'
10    FORMAT (1X, T20, A)
```

causes the word Hello to be printed starting in column 19. It makes no difference if the 1X is deleted from the FORMAT specification.

The T descriptor can be used in any situation where the X descriptor is appropriate, but the T descriptor is more versatile because it can tab to the left as well as the right. If an item has just been printed ending in column 50, then a T11 causes the next printed item to begin in column 10. For example,

```
      PRINT 10, 'Goodbye', 'Hello'
10    FORMAT (1X, T21, A, T11, A)
```

causes the words to be written as

```
         1         2
12345678901234567890123456789
         Hello     Goodbye
```

with Goodbye starting in column 20, and Hello starting in column 10.

The T edit descriptor is an **absolute tab specifier**. In contrast, the TL and TR specifiers are used to tab left and right from the current position, so they are known as **relative tab specifiers**. An example with T and TL

```
      PRINT 20, 'Goodbye', 'Hello'
20    FORMAT (1X, T31, A, TL20, A)
```

causes the words to appear as

```
         1         2         3
123456789012345678901234567890123456789
         Hello     Goodbye
```

First the computer prints Goodbye beginning in column 30. After printing Goodbye, the current position is column 37. Then TL20 causes the computer to tab left 20 spaces from column 37, ending in column 17. The computer then prints Hello starting in column 17.

Some programmers routinely use TR*n* where we use *n*X. Skipping three columns is equivalent to tabbing three columns to the right of the current column.

Format Reversion

Earlier we said that each item in a print or read list should have one data descriptor in the FORMAT specification. However, Fortran does allow an imbalance between printed items and data descriptors. If there are more data items than data descriptors, all or part of the FORMAT specification is reused. This process is called FORMAT **reversion**. Consider the following PRINT and FORMAT statements, where all variables are real.

```
      PRINT 10, A, B, C, D
10    FORMAT (1X, F8.3, F7.2)
```

Values for A and B take the F8.3 and F7.2 formats respectively, then the right parenthesis in the FORMAT specification is encountered. Normally this right parenthesis signals the end of format control, but because there are still items in the PRINT list, format control reverts to the left parenthesis. The left parenthesis *causes an advance to the next line*, then values for C and D appear according to the specification

$$(1X, F8.3, F7.2)$$

If A is 123.456, B is 23.52, C is 182.3579, and D is −18.5, the output will be

```
         1
123456789012345
 123.456  23.52
 182.358 -18.50
```

The reversion process can occur several times. If three new variables, E, F, and G, with values −264.32, 14.761, and 351.245, are added to the print list, the output from

```
      PRINT 10, A, B, C, D, E, F, G
```

will be

```
        1
123456789012345
  123.456  23.52
  182.358 -18.50
-264.320  14.76
  351.245
```

The entire specification was not used in printing the fourth line; this causes no problem in Fortran.

Example 7.5 Format Reversion with Interior Parentheses

Again, assume that there are more items in the PRINT list than data descriptors in the FORMAT specification. If parentheses occur *within* the FORMAT specification, then when the final right parenthesis is encountered, format control reverts to the *left parenthesis* that matches the *last interior right parenthesis*. See the following FORMAT specification:

(last interior right parenthesis)

(1X, F8.3, (1X, I5, F8.3))

(matching left parenthesis)

Program 7.5 is a trivial program using the FORMAT specification above.

■
PROGRAM 7.5

```
      PROGRAM REVERS
*------------------------------------------*
*      Illustrate Format reversion.        *
*------------------------------------------*
      REAL     A, B, C, D
      INTEGER  I, J, K

      A = 123.456
      B = 23.524
      C = 185.2479
      D = 23.65
      I = 123
      J = -246
      K = 135
```

```
      PRINT 10, A, I, B, J, C, K, D
10    FORMAT (1X, F8.3, (1X, I5, F8.3) )

      END
```

The first printed line contains values of A, I, and B. Then the data descriptors in the FORMAT specification are exhausted, so control reverts to the interior left parenthesis. Values of J and C appear on the second output line according to the specification

$$(1X, I5, F8.3)$$

Again the final right parenthesis is encountered and control reverts to the interior left parenthesis, so values of K and D appear on the third output line according to the FORMAT specification

$$(1X, I5, F8.3)$$

The complete output is

```
        1
123456789012345 1234567
 123.456   123  23.524
-246 185.248
 135   23.650
```

When inner parentheses are present, and the rightmost parenthesized group is preceded by a repeat count, format reversion includes that repeat count. If we change the PRINT and FORMAT statements in the above program to

```
      PRINT 10, A, I, B, J, C, K, D, I, B
10    FORMAT (1X, F8.3, 2(1X, I5, F8.3) )
```

then the output would be

```
        1         2         3
1234567890123456789012345678901234567890123456
 123.456   123  23.524  -246 185.248
 135   23.650   123  23.524
```

The first output line contains values for A, I, B, J, and C. Then the data descriptors are exhausted and format control reverts to

$$2(1X, I5, F8.3)$$

to print values for K, D, I, and B.

Format reversion occurs when the number of items in the PRINT list exceeds the number of data descriptors in the FORMAT specification. The reverse situation can also hold. If there are *fewer* items in the PRINT list than data descriptors, then format control ends at the *first data descriptor without a corresponding item in the print list.* Consider the following two examples.

```
    PRINT 20, 'Herbert Hoover', 31
20  FORMAT (1X, A, 1X, 'was the', I3, 'st president.')
```

which gives as output

```
Herbert Hoover was the 31st president.
```

If the FORMAT specification contains an extra data descriptor, as in

```
20   FORMAT (1X, A, 1X, 'was the', I3, F6.2, 'st president.')
```

then the output is

```
Herbert Hoover was the 31
```

because format control ends when the F6.2 data descriptor is encountered. The F6.2 could have been any data descriptor.

■

7.2 INPUT FORMATS

If you understand output formats, this short section on input formats should be easy because no new descriptors are involved, and we strive to avoid complicated input formats.

The simplest **formatted input statement**, for reading data from the terminal, has the form

```
    READ <label>, <read list>
```

where label is a line number placed on a FORMAT statement. All the data descriptors used for input are the same as those used for output, but a few distinctions should be made.

Character Data

We have already used a simple formatted input statement to read character data, as in

```
     READ 10, NAME
10   FORMAT (A)
```

where `NAME` was declared to have type `CHARACTER`. If the declared length is 15 and the user responds to the `READ` statement with

Andrew Johnson<Return>

the information is stored as

NAME

Remember that the `FORMAT` specification for a `READ` statement requires no carriage control character.

When reading character data with a formatted `READ` statement, we have used a field descriptor `A` without a specific field width, just to keep things simple. Fortran assumes a field width equal to the declared length of the variable.

Alternatively, we can explicitly give a width. In the example above, the `FORMAT` statement could have been

```
10   FORMAT (A15)
```

Generally, the field width w can differ from the declared length L of the character variable. If $w < L$, you are not likely to get into trouble; the computer will store w characters followed by $(L - w)$ spaces. However, if $w > L$, the computer will store the L *rightmost* characters in the input field. If, for example, `NAME` is declared `CHARACTER*10` and `NAME` is read with an A15 data descriptor, the response

```
123456789012345
Richard Kennedy<Return>
```

will be stored as

NAME

When reading from a data file, the formatted READ statement takes the form

>   READ < *unit number*, *label*> *read list*

For example, to read two names from the file opened as logical unit 22, according to the FORMAT statement labelled 10, we can use

>   READ (22, 10) NAME1, NAME2

Numeric Data

Formatted input statements are not needed for reading strictly numeric data from a terminal or file, but they will be useful later for reading data files with both character and numeric data on the same line. For now, we practice writing short program segments which use formatted input statements to read all kinds of data from a terminal. We use the word *response* to denote a user's entry at a terminal, but the response could appear in a data file as well.

We use the descriptor I*w* to read integer data. If the integer constant read is not large enough to fill the field, it must be right-justified in the field. Thus, if the READ and FORMAT statements are

>   READ 10, NUMBER
> 10   FORMAT (I5)

the responses below will give NUMBER the values shown.

Response	Value of NUMBER
□□123	123
□123□	1230 *or* 123
123□□	12300 *or* 123
1□2□3	10203 *or* 123

With *list-directed* formatting, a blank can signal the end of an input number. However, with *formatted terminal input*, Fortran may consider trailing and imbedded blanks as zeroes *or* as null characters. The ANSI standard does not specify which; some versions use zeroes and other versions use nulls.

Fortran treats blanks in an OPEN*ed data file* as null characters, so it would read 123□□, □123□, and 1□2□3 as 123. You do not have to remember how Fortran treats imbedded and trailing blanks; just do not use them.

With the F*w.d* data descriptor, there are several ways to assign the same value to a real variable. The `READ` and `FORMAT` statements

```
      READ 20, AREA
20    FORMAT (F6.2)
```

can assign the value 7.25 to `AREA` with any of the following responses.

Response	Comment
□□7.25	These are the normal ways to write 7.25 in a
007.25	field of six columns.
725E-2	The input number can be in E-notation even though it is read with an F data descriptor.
□□□725	With no decimal point present, the F*w.d* descriptor causes a decimal point to be placed before the last *d* digits in the field.

As with integers, different versions of Fortran may treat imbedded and trailing blanks as zeroes or nulls when reading formatted real values from a terminal. Standard Fortran 77 treats blanks in `OPEN`ed files as nulls.

Since the `F` descriptor can handle real data in exponential form, we shall not discuss the `E` and `G` data descriptors, although they can also be used to read real data.

The `X` descriptor can be used for input as well as output, and it still means *skip a column*. Similarly, *n*X means *skip n columns*. Consider the following `READ`/`FORMAT` pair

```
      READ 10, I, J
10    FORMAT (I2, X, I2)
```

A typical response to this `READ` statement might be

```
13 42
```

which assigns the value 13 to I and 42 to J. Even if the response were 13942, I and J would still get values 13 and 42; the column containing the 9 is skipped.

Repeat counts apply also on input. The `READ`/`FORMAT` pair

```
      READ 20, I, J, K, L, M, N
20    FORMAT (6I2)
```

would read the response

987654321234

and assign the following values to the variables:

I	J	K	L	M	N
98	76	54	32	12	34

For input from a terminal, the formatted READ statement we have been discussing is not user-friendly. A pair of statements such as

```
      READ 10, NAME, AGE, SALARY
10    FORMAT ( A15, I3, F6.2 )
```

would require the user to type the various constants in specific columns. Thus, we suggest that you use formatted READ statements, for data input from a terminal, only for character data. Formatted input is more important when the computer reads data from data files, which we discuss in the next chapter.

■
7.3 SPECIFYING FORMATS AT RUN TIME

The FORMAT statement is nonexecutable, which means the Fortran compiler takes care of FORMAT specifications. We can create all or part of a FORMAT specification at run time with **run-time formats**.

A character variable can store a FORMAT specification, and its value can be specified when the program is running. Such a variable is called a **run-time format specification**.

Consider the PRINT and FORMAT statements

```
      PRINT 20, I, X
20    FORMAT (1X, I5, F8.2)
```

An alternative method to produce the same result is

```
      CHARACTER*15  FORM
      FORM = '(1X, I5, F8.2)'
              .
              .
              .
      PRINT FORM, I, X
```

The variable FORM acts directly in the PRINT statement, in place of a FORMAT statement label. Notice that the FORMAT specification must include the beginning and ending parentheses.

In place of the variable FORM, the string constant can appear in the PRINT statement, as in

```
PRINT '(1X, I5, F8.2)', I, X
```

We sometimes use this device with simple FORMAT specifications. If you use it, do not forget the apostrophes or the parentheses.

A useful application of run-time formats involves reading the desired FORMAT specification, as in the segment

```
      CHARACTER  FORM*80, NAME*20
      INTEGER    AGE
      REAL       HEIGHT, WEIGHT
                 .
                 .
                 .
      PRINT *, 'Please enter a FORMAT specification for printing'
      PRINT *, 'a string, an integer, and two real numbers.'
      READ 10, FORM
10    FORMAT (A)
      PRINT FORM, NAME, AGE, HEIGHT, WEIGHT
```

A possible response to the READ statement is

```
(A15, 3X, I4, 2X, 2F10.2)<Return>
```

■

7.4   SUMMARY OF CHAPTER 7

■ *Terms Introduced in This Chapter*

A data descriptor	FORMAT	Repeat count, in format specification
Carriage control	descriptor	Run-time FORMAT
Data descriptor	specification	Slash (/) edit descriptor
E data descriptor	statement	Tab edit descriptors
Edit descriptor	G data descriptor	Tab specifiers
F data descriptor	H data descriptor	T edit descriptor
Field descriptor	I data descriptor	TL edit descriptor
Field width	Input format	TR edit descriptor
	Output format	X edit descriptor

■ *What You Should Know*

1. Formatted output allows you to print data in precise form and in specific positions.
2. Each data type has at least one associated data descriptor.
3. The first character in a data descriptor is a letter; we often refer to the descriptor by that letter.
4. Each item in a formatted print or read list has an associated data descriptor in the FORMAT statement.
5. The A data descriptor applies to character data.
6. The A descriptor can appear with or without a field width.
7. The I data descriptor applies to integer data.
8. The L data descriptor applies to logical data.
9. The REAL data type has three data descriptors: F, E, and G.
10. Each data descriptor can contain an integer field width immediately after the first letter.
11. If numeric output data items require more columns than the field width allotted, the computer fills the field with asterisks and prints an error message.
12. The F descriptor is the most used real data descriptor for output, because it prints numbers of moderate size in the most readable form.
13. Unexpectedly large or small numbers can cause output errors with the F data descriptor.
14. The E and G data descriptors can print any number the computer can hold.
15. The F descriptor for input can accept real data either in decimal or exponential notation.
16. If an output character string length exceeds the field width w allotted by the A descriptor, no error occurs, but only the first w characters appear.
17. If an input character variable of length L is read from a field of width w, with $L < w$, the rightmost L characters are stored in the variable.
18. The X edit descriptor leaves a blank column on output and skips a column on input.
19. The slash edit descriptor causes the computer to begin a new line on both input and output.
20. The T edit descriptor tabs to a specific column.
21. The TR and TL edit descriptors tab right and left, respectively, from the current column.
22. All data descriptors, and the X edit descriptor, can be preceded by a repeat count, a positive integer specifying the number of times to repeat the descriptor.
23. A *run-time* FORMAT is a character variable used in place of an entire FORMAT specification.
24. The first character that would appear in an output line is the *carriage control character* for that line. The most common output error is forgetting about carriage control.

■

7.5 EXERCISES

■ *Self-Test*

1. What is wrong with the following FORMAT specifications?

   a.
   ```
          PRINT 10, 'Hello', 12
       10 FORMAT (1X, 'I am', I5, X, 'years old.')
   ```

   b.
   ```
          PRINT 10, 'Nothing', 12.65, 460
       10 FORMAT ('0', A10, I10, F8.2)
   ```

   c.
   ```
          CHARACTER NAME * 10
          INTEGER   MONEY
          REAL      WEIGHT
          DATA      NAME, MONEY, WEIGHT /'Jill', 435, 122.5/
          PRINT 20, MONEY, NAME, WEIGHT
       20 FORMAT (I3, A6, F10.1)
   ```

2. Show the exact output from the following program segments. Label the columns or use paper with vertical lines to show columns. Do not expect that all output will look good.

   a.
   ```
          PRINT 10, 12, 25.6
       10 FORMAT (1X, I5, ' is integer but', F6.3, ' is real.')
   ```

   b.
   ```
          PRINT 20, 'George Washington', 1
       20 FORMAT (1X, A, 1X, 'was the', I2, 'st president.')
   ```

   c.
   ```
          CHARACTER*15 NAME
          INTEGER      AGE
          REAL         HEIGHT
          DATA         NAME, AGE, HEIGHT /'Jack', 23, 67.5/
          PRINT 10, NAME, AGE, HEIGHT
       10 FORMAT (1X, 'Name', A5 / 'Age', I5 / 'Height', F8.3)
   ```

   d.
   ```
          REAL    X, Y
          INTEGER M, J
          DATA    X, Y, M, J /18.653, 123.456, 1234, 23/
          PRINT 30, X, M, Y, J
       30 FORMAT ( 2(1X, F8.2, I5) )
   ```

3. A program contains the following declarations.

```
CHARACTER*10 NAME
INTEGER      AGE, COUNT
REAL         LENGTH, WIDTH, AREA, SALARY
```

Write `PRINT` and `FORMAT` statements to produce exactly the following output. The words in the output tell which variables to use.

a.
```
          1         2
12345678901234567890
    Count is  XXX
```

b.
```
          1         2
1234567890123456789012345678
Name is AAAAAAAA  Age is XX
```

c.
```
          1         2
12345678901234567890
Length :  XXX.XX
Width  :  XXX.XX
Area   : XXXX.XX
```

d.
```
          1         2
1234567890123456789012345678
    Name      Age  Salary
    AAAAAAAAAA XXX  XXX.XX
```

4. Assume that variables I, J, and K are `INTEGER`; X, Y, and Z are `REAL`; and `NAME` and `STREET` are `CHARACTER*10`, with values

X	Y	Z	I	J	K	NAME	STREET
12.63	8.279	−4.026	17	8	123	CORIOLANUS	WILLOW RUN

Show the specific lines and columns in which the following `PRINT`/`FORMAT` pairs will print their output. Do not expect all output to look good.

a.
```
      PRINT 10, NAME, STREET, X, I, Y, J, Z, K
   10 FORMAT (1X, 2A12, 3(/ 1X, F6.2, I4) )
```

b.
```
      PRINT 20, X, Y, Z, I, NAME, J, STREET, K
   20 FORMAT (1X, 3F8.1, 3(1X, I3, A8 /) )
```

5. Specify exactly what is stored in the variables in the following READ statements when the given responses are made. Count very carefully!

    a.
```
      CHARACTER*12  TITLE
      READ 10, TITLE
   10 FORMAT (A)
```
        Column: 1234567890
        Response: ORTHODOXY

    b.
```
      REAL  X, Y
      READ 20, X, Y
   20 FORMAT (F6.2, 2X, F5.3)
```
        Column: 1234567890123
        Response: 1849 19.42

    c.
```
      CHARACTER*20  NAME
      INTEGER      AGE
      READ 40, NAME, AGE
   40 FORMAT (A12, I5)
```
        Column: 123456789012345
        Response: SAM SMITH 35

    d.
```
      REAL    X
      INTEGER N
      READ 30, X, N
   30 FORMAT (F8.4, I5)
```
        Column: 123456789012345
        Response: 12.7   6234

6.   a.   Expand the following FORMAT specification to get rid of the repeat count.

$$(1X, 3(F8.2, I5, A10))$$

    b.   Use repeat counts to simplify the following FORMAT specification.

$$(1X, I6, 3X, I6, 7X, F10.2, 4X, F10.2, 4X, F10.2)$$

■ Programming Exercises

1. Rewrite the program of Example 4.3, using formatted PRINT statements to write the numbers and squares to one decimal place and the square roots to five decimal places.
2. Rewrite the program of Example 4.6, using formatted PRINT statements to write the interest rate to one decimal place and the interest to two decimal places.
3. Rewrite the program of Example 4.12 to round dollar figures to two decimal places. Use formatted PRINT statements to line up columns under the appropriate headers.

4. Rewrite the program of Example 6.8 to round dollar figures to two decimal places. Use formatted PRINT statements to line up columns under the appropriate headers.

5. Write a program to print a department store receipt for several purchases. Allow purchases of the four items listed in the receipt below. Ask if the user wishes to buy a particular item; if so, then ask the price. Calculate a subtotal and sales tax (4% of the subtotal). The output should resemble the following, including the border around the receipt.

```
|----------------------------------------|
|            David's Department Store    |
|              1066 Oregon Street        |
|              Oshkosh, WI 54901         |
|                                        |
|----------------------------------------|
|ITEM              NUMBER         COST    |
|----------------------------------------|
|Blouse              1           12.95    |
|----------------------------------------|
|Skirt               1           24.95    |
|----------------------------------------|
|Pants               1           18.50    |
|----------------------------------------|
|Suit                1          139.95    |
|----------------------------------------|
|----------------------------------------|
|      Subtotal                  196.35   |
|----------------------------------------|
|      Sales Tax                   7.85   |
|----------------------------------------|
|----------------------------------------|
|      Total                     204.20   |
|----------------------------------------|
|      THANK YOU FOR SHOPPING AT DAVID'S  |
|----------------------------------------|
```

6. Banks often set up loan payment schedules so that payments are made once a month. Then, if an amount P is borrowed at a rate R per month, with payments for n months, the monthly payment is

$$P \; \frac{(1 + R)^n}{(1 + R)^{n-1}}$$

Write a program that asks the user for the amount borrowed, the yearly interest rate in percent, and the number of monthly payments. The program should print the monthly payment and ask if the user wishes to see the payment schedule. The payment schedule should show the payment number, the interest paid with that payment, and the loan balance after the payment.

7. Write a program to sketch the graph of a function $f(x)$ by printing asterisks in appropriate positions. That is, a sketch of half a period of $\sin(x)$ might look like

Notice that the usual horizontal axis becomes a vertical axis here.

First decide on an interval and a step size for x. Then determine the approximate minimum and maximum values of $f(x)$ on this interval. Call these $xlow$ and $xhigh$. The computer should print the minimum value $f(xlow)$ near the left margin, say in column 5. The maximum value $f(xhigh)$ should be near the right margin; about in column 75. To determine the appropriate column for any value $f(x)$, use the formula

$$\text{column} = 5 + 70 \times \frac{f(x) - f(xlow)}{f(xhigh) - f(xlow)}$$

Once you can get the computer to draw a sketch, get it to draw the horizontal and vertical axes.

8 ONE-DIMENSIONAL ARRAYS

At any given moment, a variable can have only one value, but we have often used a single variable to store many values in a program. The variable SQUARE in the following segment takes on ten values, one after the other.

```
      DO 11 I = 1, 10
         SQUARE = I * I
         PRINT *, SQUARE
11    CONTINUE
```

Each

```
      SQUARE = I * I
```

statement causes a new value to be placed in SQUARE, and therefore, the old value of SQUARE is lost (no longer available to the computer). This method is generally efficient because only one storage space is needed for several values, and only one variable name is necessary, instead of several names such as SQUAR1, SQUAR2, and so on.

However, sometimes it is more convenient, or even necessary, that the computer hold all the values of a variable at one time. In previous chapters, several values of certain variables were stored in data files. Here we consider another way to store, simultaneously, several values of a variable.

■

8.1 ARRAYS AND SUBSCRIPTS

Mathematicians often denote several values of a variable X by the letter x with different subscripts, such as

$$x_1, x_2, x_3, \ldots$$

The computer does not allow subscripts written on a separate line, but we can denote several values of the same variable by the name of the variable followed by a *subscript* in parentheses, as in

$$X(1), X(2), X(3), \ldots$$

We call a variable X used in this way an **array variable** or simply an **array**. The more explicit term **one-dimensional array** signifies that only one subscript is used. In this chapter we deal exclusively with one-dimensional arrays, and we refer to them simply as arrays. Chapter 11 discusses arrays with two subscripts, or two-dimensional arrays.

The variable name X refers to the entire array; it is called the **array name**. Every element in a particular array has the same data type. If SQUARE holds integer elements, we say SQUARE is an *integer array*; we also can have *real arrays*, *character arrays*, and so on.

A specific **array element** is referred to by the array name followed by the position of the element in the array. Thus, X(12) refers to the twelfth element in the array X, and X(K) refers to the Kth element (where K is an integer variable). Strictly speaking, array element names are not the same as variable names, but they can be used almost anywhere that (nonarray) variable names can be used.

Subscripts can be any integer expressions, as in the examples below.

Array Element	Subscript	Subscript Description
X(3)	3	Constant
A(K)	K	Variable
NAME(2*K + 1)	2*K + 1	Expression
INDEX(N(I))	N(I)	Element name

The subscript can in fact be a real expression, but we advise against it. Fortran will truncate the value of the expression to its integer part. That is, Fortran considers X(2.9) to be X(2).

If an array SQUARE has five values, 1, 4, 9, 16, and 25, the computer stores these values as

That is, the name SQUARE points to only *one* storage location. The computer stores the values for the elements of SQUARE in contiguous locations, beginning at the location pointed to by SQUARE. It then can find a particular element, say SQUARE(3), by finding the address of SQUARE and taking the

third number after this address. It is probably more convenient for you to think of the array being stored as

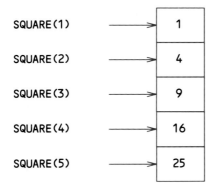

Declaring and Initializing Arrays

Arrays *must* be declared so the computer can reserve consecutive memory locations for the values of array elements. The simplest way to declare that SQUARE is an array with five integer elements is with a type declaration statement such as

```
INTEGER  SQUARE(5)
```

In this declaration statement, SQUARE(5) is an **array declarator**; it looks like the name of the fifth array element, but it is not. Here SQUARE(5) indicates that SQUARE is an array of integer values, and that allowable subscripts for the array elements are 1, 2, 3, 4, and 5. The 5 in parentheses is the largest subscript allowed in the program; it is known as the **subscript bound**, or **size** of the array.

The array SQUARE can be initialized in a DATA statement, as can any variable. Since SQUARE is an array with five elements, then five values should be given, as in

```
INTEGER  SQUARE(5)
DATA     SQUARE /1, 4, 9, 16, 25/
```

It is often desirable to initialize all elements in an array to the same value. The real array PRODCT with fifty elements can be initialized with the declarations

```
REAL  PRODCT(50)
DATA  PRODCT /50 * 1.0/
```

The number 50 before the * is a repetition factor; 50 * 1.0 means the same thing as 1.0, 1.0, ..., 1.0, with 1.0 appearing fifty times. The first twenty-five elements of PRODCT can be initialized to 1.0, and the last twenty-five values to 2.0, with the statement

```
REAL   PRODCT(50)
DATA   PRODUCT /25 * 1.0, 25 * 2.0/
```

Arrays can also have CHARACTER data type; every element in the array will hold a character constant of the same length. Appropriate declarations are

```
CHARACTER*20  NAME(100)
```

or

```
CHARACTER  NAME(100)*20
```

As before, the length can be placed after the word CHARACTER or the array name and size. Character arrays can be initialized too. The following declarations initialize a forty-element array PLACE with forty values of 'EMPTY'.

```
CHARACTER * 5  PLACE(40)
DATA           PLACE /40 * 'EMPTY'/
```

So far we have assumed, as Fortran does, that the first element in an array has subscript 1. In counting, 1 seems the natural place to begin. If a different starting value is desired, the minimum subscript value, as well as the maximum, can be specified in the type declaration statement as follows:

```
INTEGER  VALUE(2:10), TOTAL(-1:20)
```

VALUE is an array whose nine elements are

```
VALUE(2), VALUE(3), ..., VALUE(10)
```

and TOTAL is an array with twenty-two elements: TOTAL(-1) through TOTAL(20). (Do not forget TOTAL(0).) Such type declarations also guarantee that no subscript in the program will be smaller than the minimum in the declaration. Expressions involving VALUE(1) or TOTAL(-3) will cause errors.

Only integer *constants* can be used to declare subscript bounds in a Fortran program. Declarations such as INTEGER NUMBER(5*2) are illegal. Remember that items in a PARAMETER statement are considered to be constants in the remainder of the program, so it is legal to have

```
INTEGER   MAXNUM, LOW, HIGH
PARAMETER (MAXNUM = 100, LOW = -5, HIGH = 5)
REAL      X(MAXNUM), A(LOW : HIGH)
```

Fortran also contains a DIMENSION **statement** for declaring arrays. Instead of

```
REAL   SUM(100)
```

we could have

```
REAL      SUM
DIMENSION SUM(100)
```

We will not use the DIMENSION statement.

The programmer often does not know in advance exactly how many values will be stored in an array each time the program runs. In such cases, reserve storage for the largest number of values any user is likely to have. We will often use sizes of 100, even though an example program requires only a few values to be stored. In large commercial applications, sizes of 5,000 or more might be appropriate.

Reading and Writing Arrays

Array elements are typically given values inside loops. The following program segment declares the array SQUARE, and gives array elements the values 1, 4, 9, 16, and 25 using an assignment statement in a DO loop.

```
      INTEGER I, SQUARE(5)
      DO 11 I = 1, 5
         SQUARE(I) = I * I
11    CONTINUE
```

Other possibilities include reading values of the array elements, either from a file or from the user's terminal. This segment asks for six names and stores the names in NAME(1) through NAME(6).

```
      CHARACTER * 20  NAME(6)

      DO 11 K = 1, 6
         PRINT 'Name?'
         READ '(A)', NAME(K)
11    CONTINUE
```

The Short-List Technique

An I/O statement can use the array name alone to read or write the entire array. This is often called the **short-list** technique. For example, if A is a real array with 30 elements, the statement

```
PRINT 10, A
```

will print all 30 elements of A.

Example 8.1 Writing an Array with the Short-List Technique

Program 8.1 uses one short-list PRINT statement to print an entire array.

■
PROGRAM 8.1

```
      PROGRAM SHORTL
*----------------------------------------------------------------*
* Illustrate the short-list technique for writing an array.  *
* Initialize the array with six 1s, twelve 2s and twelve 3s. *
*----------------------------------------------------------------*
      REAL  A(30)
      DATA  A /6 * 1.0, 12 * 2.0, 12 * 3.0/
*----------------------------------------------------------------*
*            This is the short-list statement.              *
*----------------------------------------------------------------*
      PRINT 10, A
10    FORMAT (1X, 5F8.2)

      END
```

The FORMAT specification determines how many values will be printed on one line or in one record. In this case, there will be five values on a line because of the specification (1X, 5F8.2). The output from the program is

```
    1.00    1.00    1.00    1.00    1.00
    1.00    2.00    2.00    2.00    2.00
    2.00    2.00    2.00    2.00    2.00
    2.00    2.00    2.00    3.00    3.00
    3.00    3.00    3.00    3.00    3.00
    3.00    3.00    3.00    3.00    3.00
```

Similarly, a program can read an entire array with a short-list statement, as in the following segment:

```
INTEGER  NUMBER(6)

PRINT *, 'Enter six integers, separated by commas.'
READ  *, NUMBER
```

The short-list technique requires that the *entire* array be read or written. If the response to READ *, NUMBER has only four values, the computer will simply wait for two more to be entered because NUMBER was given size 6. If the program were reading from a data file with only four values, an end-of-file error would occur.

More than one array can be read with the same READ statement:

```
INTEGER  NUMBER(6), TOTAL(10)
READ *, NUMBER, TOTAL
```

The computer will read a total of sixteen integer values, with the first six values assigned to NUMBER and the last ten assigned to TOTAL.

We have already used the short-list technique in DATA statements as well as input and output statements. In later chapters we will use array names as arguments for subprograms. In assignment statements, however, the array name must always be followed by a subscript in parentheses. If TOTAL is an integer array, statements such as

```
TOTAL = 25
```

or

```
X = 12 * TOTAL
```

are syntax errors.

Example 8.2 Calculating Fibonacci Numbers

The *Fibonacci numbers* are usually defined in the following way:

$$F(1) = 1 \text{ and } F(2) = 1$$

$$F(N) = F(N - 1) + F(N - 2) \text{ for } N > 2$$

The second statement tells how to calculate any Fibonacci number after the first two. With $N = 3$, the statement is

$$F(3) = F(2) + F(1)$$

In general, the statement tells us to calculate any number in the array as the sum of the two preceding numbers. Thus the first few Fibonacci numbers are

$$1 \quad 1 \quad 2 \quad 3 \quad 5 \quad 8 \quad 13 \quad 21 \quad 34 \ldots$$

These numbers arise in mathematical problems in a variety of ways. A classical setting is the mating of rabbits. It takes two months for a newborn pair of rabbits to mature, mate, and give birth to a new pair. From then on, the mature rabbits produce a new pair each month. Each newborn generation is assumed to have the same number of males and females, so that all rabbits become part of a mating pair. The Fibonacci numbers give the number of pairs of rabbits at the end of each month, starting with one newborn pair at the beginning of the first month.

Program 8.2 calculates the first forty Fibonacci numbers with subscripted variables. The program writes the array as a short list.

■
PROGRAM 8.2

```
      PROGRAM FIBONA
*----------------------------------------------------------*
*       Calculate the first 40 Fibonacci numbers.          *
*----------------------------------------------------------*
      INTEGER N, F(40)

      F(1) = 1
      F(2) = 1
      DO 11 N = 3, 40
         F(N) = F(N-1) + F(N-2)
11    CONTINUE

      PRINT 10, F
10    FORMAT (1X, 5I12)

      END
```

The output from this program is

1	1	2	3	5
8	13	21	34	55
89	144	233	377	610
987	1597	2584	4181	6765
10946	17711	28657	46368	75025
121393	196418	317811	514229	832040
1346269	2178309	3524578	5702887	9227465
14930352	24157817	39088169	63245986	102334155

Quite a few rabbits!

This program could be written without subscripted variables, but the logic is much simpler with them. Notice how the loop counter N automatically generated the subscripts.

Short-list statements read or write an entire array. In the previous problem, the array F had size 40, and the program printed all 40 values. Many times, we must specify a size without knowing exactly how many elements the program will use each time it runs. We choose a size that we think will be large enough to satisfy any user. Then most runs of the program will not use the entire array, so the program should not use short-list statements.

A DO or while loop can read or write all or part of an array. Suppose, for example, that a program opens a file on unit number 2. Then it can read values from the file with the following segment:

```
    INTEGER  TOTAL(100)
       .
       .
       .
    DO 11 I = 1, 12
       READ (2, *)  TOTAL(I)     { Reads one value per record }
11  CONTINUE
```

With this approach, each record in the file must contain one number. If some records have more than one number, the program reads only the first number in each such record.

Example 8.3 Finding Scores above the Mean

Program 8.3 reads values for a real array from a file. It counts the values, calculates the mean of the array, and prints out all values above the mean.

The statement of the problem gives the outline of the program:

1. Read and count values from the file into the array.

2. Calculate the mean of the array.

3. Print those array values that are above the mean.

We use X for the array, and declare it

```
REAL  X(100)
```

but, of course, we do not expect that the array will contain 100 elements each time the program runs.

We ask the user for the name FILNAM of the file. The variable COUNT counts the values in the file. The mean of a set of scores is the total of the scores divided by COUNT, so we use variables TOTAL and MEAN with the obvious meanings. An integer variable I acts as a DO loop index.

To read values for the array, we use a familiar structure, a loop beginning with a READ statement containing an END specifier. Just before the loop, we assign I the value 1. Inside the loop, I is the subscript for the array X. We read a value for X(I), and increase I by 1, each time through the loop. At the end of the loop, I is too large by 1, so we set COUNT = I - 1.

```
       I = 1
11     READ (9, *, END = 22) X(I)
          I = I + 1
       GO TO 11
22     COUNT = I - 1
```

The calculation of the mean is straightforward. The loop counter I is the subscript on X in the following segment:

```
       TOTAL = 0.0
       DO 33 I = 1, COUNT
          TOTAL = TOTAL + X(I)
33     CONTINUE
       MEAN = TOTAL / REAL(COUNT)
```

Printing the scores above the mean also requires a DO loop with I ranging from 1 to COUNT, as in

```
       DO 44 I = 1, COUNT
          IF (X(I) .GT. MEAN) PRINT *, X(I)
44     CONTINUE
```

The declarations, obtaining the file name, opening the file, and a few output statements finish the program. See Program 8.3.

■

PROGRAM 8.3
```
      PROGRAM ABOVEM
*------------------------------------------------------------*
*  Read values into a real array.  Calculate the mean of the *
*  values and print those values which are above the mean.   *
*------------------------------------------------------------*
      CHARACTER*20  FILNAM
      INTEGER       COUNT, I
      REAL          X(100), TOTAL, MEAN

      PRINT *, 'This program calculates the mean of a set'
      PRINT *, 'of scores, and prints those scores higher'
      PRINT *, 'than the mean.'
      PRINT *, 'What is the name of the file?'
      READ '(A)', FILNAM

      OPEN (9, FILE = FILNAM, STATUS = 'OLD')
*------------------------------------------------------------*
*           Read and count the values in the file.           *
*------------------------------------------------------------*
      I = 1
11    READ (9, *, END = 22) X(I)
         I = I + 1
      GO TO 11

22    CLOSE (9)
      COUNT = I - 1
*------------------------------------------------------------*
*                    Calculate the mean.                     *
*------------------------------------------------------------*
      TOTAL = 0.0
      DO 33 I = 1, COUNT
         TOTAL = TOTAL + X(I)
33    CONTINUE

      MEAN = TOTAL / REAL(COUNT)

      PRINT *
      PRINT *, COUNT, ' scores in the file.'
      PRINT *, 'The mean of the scores is', MEAN
      PRINT *
      PRINT *, 'The following scores are above the mean:'
```

```
*-----------------------------------------------------------*
*               Print the scores above the mean.            *
*-----------------------------------------------------------*
      DO 44 I = 1, COUNT
         IF (X(I) .GT. MEAN) PRINT *, X(I)
 44   CONTINUE

      END
```

When you use program variables to generate subscripts for an array, you must ensure that the subscript values stay within the bounds stated in the array declaration. The most common error in dealing with arrays is having a subscript out of bounds.

Example 8.4 Searching an Array of Names

Suppose a data file contains a list of last names of some privileged people. We will write a program that asks the user for a name and tells the user whether that name is on the list. To find the name, we perform a **sequential search** on an array. In Chapter 12 we will perform the same type of search on a file.

Here again, a subscripted variable is not strictly necessary, but the program will be simpler and faster if we read all the names into an array, and then search the array for the given name. Assuming you can code the reading and counting of names, we begin discussing the search process.

We will use an array NAME that holds up to fifty names. The name specified by the user will be called NEWNAM. In searching the array, we want to compare NEWNAM to NAME(1), NAME(2), and so on, until a match is found or the end of the array is reached. Thus, we want to continue comparing while a match has not been found and the subscript on NAME is less than or equal to the number of names on the list.

Let FOUND be a logical variable whose initial value is .FALSE., meaning simply that a matching name has not yet been found. Let COUNT be the number of names in the file. Then we set up a while loop to begin with

```
      FOUND = .FALSE.
      I = 1
      IF ( .NOT. FOUND .AND. I .LE. COUNT ) THEN
```

where I will be the subscript on NAME.

Inside the loop, the actual comparison is performed. If `NEWNAM` matches `NAME(I)`, then `FOUND` is set to `.TRUE.` and a message is printed. If the names do not match, I increases by 1. A block IF takes care of these possibilities:

```
IF (NEWNAM .EQ. NAME(I)) THEN
    PRINT *, 'That name is on the list in position', I
    FOUND = .TRUE.
ELSE
    I = I + 1
END IF
```

After the loop, if a match was never found, then the user is told that the name is not on the list. See Program 8.4

■
PROGRAM 8.4
───

```
      PROGRAM SEARCH
*------------------------------------------------------------*
* Read a list of names from a data file.  Ask the user for a  *
* name, and tell the user whether that name is on the list.   *
*------------------------------------------------------------*
      CHARACTER*20  NAME(50), NEWNAM
      INTEGER       I, COUNT
      LOGICAL       FOUND

      OPEN (1, FILE = 'NAMEFL.DAT', STATUS = 'OLD')
*------------------------------------------------------------*
*        Read the names into the array NAME and count them.   *
*        Assume one name per record.                          *
*------------------------------------------------------------*
      I = 1
11    READ (1, '(A)', END = 22) NAME(I)
         I = I + 1
      GO TO 11
22    CLOSE (1)
*------------------------------------------------------------*
*        The last value of I was not used, so COUNT is I - 1. *
*------------------------------------------------------------*
      COUNT = I - 1
*------------------------------------------------------------*
*                  Ask the user for a name.                   *
*------------------------------------------------------------*
      PRINT *, 'What name are you looking for?'
      PRINT *, 'Please use capital letters.'
      READ '(A)', NEWNAM
```

```
*-------------------------------------------------------------*
*                  Search the list for that name.            *
*-------------------------------------------------------------*
      FOUND = .FALSE.
      I = 1
33    IF ( .NOT. FOUND .AND. I .LE. COUNT ) THEN

          IF (NEWNAM .EQ. NAME(I)) THEN
          PRINT *, 'That name is on the list in position', I
              FOUND = .TRUE.
          ELSE
              I = I + 1
          END IF
          GO TO 33

      END IF

      IF (.NOT. FOUND) PRINT *, 'That name is not on the list.'

      END
```

When the array elements are sorted into ascending or descending order, a **binary search** is much more efficient. We will see an example later.

Example 8.5 Counting Digits

A file contains responses to a questionnaire. For concreteness, assume the questionnaire makes twenty statements and asks respondents if they

> (0) Strongly disagree
> (1) Disagree
> (2) Agree
> (3) Strongly agree

The first record in the file contains the number of questionnaires, and each record after the first contains twenty responses, or digits 0, 1, 2, and 3, written in 2012 format. The first few records in the file could be

```
42
1 2 0 1 2 0 1 2 3 2 1 3 2 1 0 1 2 1 0 2
2 3 2 2 1 3 2 1 2 3 1 2 0 2 3 2 3 1 3 2
0 1 2 2 1 0 1 2 2 1 0 2 1 0 1 2 2 1 1 2
```

The maker of the questionnaire might want to analyze these data in several different ways. We consider only the simple question of counting the number of times each response occurs.

The best way to handle the twenty values in a record is to use an array with subscripts from 1 to 20. If X is the array name, we can read each record with the statement

```
READ (2, '(20I2)') X
```

To count responses of each type, we need four counters, one for each digit from 0 to 3. We could use four counter variables N0, N1, N2, and N3. Then, for each record read, we would have to look at the twenty values in X and use a segment similar to the following:

```
DO 11 Q = 1, 20
    IF (X(Q) .EQ. 0) THEN
        N0 = N0 + 1
    ELSE IF (X(Q) .EQ. 1) THEN
        N1 = N1 + 1
    ELSE IF (X(Q) .EQ. 2) THEN
        N2 = N2 + 1
    ELSE IF (X(Q) .EQ. 3) THEN
        N3 = N3 + 1
    END IF
11  CONTINUE
```

The four variable names differ only in the numbers after N, which suggests using an array N with subscripts running from 0 to 3. N(0) counts the number of zeroes, N(1) counts the number of ones, and so on. The counting becomes much easier. For each digit read, the counter for that digit should increase by 1. For now, suppose the digit is in variable DIGIT. Then the corresponding counter is N(DIGIT). X(Q) holds the digit we are concerned with, so we can replace the entire block IF with

```
DIGIT = X(Q)
N(DIGIT) = N(DIGIT) + 1
```

Program 8.5 shows the entire program.

■
PROGRAM 8.5
_____

```
      PROGRAM COUNTD
*---------------------------------------------------------------*
*        Count number of digits 0, 1, 2, 3 in a file.           *
*---------------------------------------------------------------*
      INTEGER  Q, COUNT, DIGIT, RECNO, N(0:3), X(20)
      DATA     N /4 * 0/

      OPEN (2, FILE = 'QUEST', STATUS = 'OLD')

      READ (2, *) COUNT

      DO 22 RECNO = 1, COUNT
          READ (2, '(20I2)') X

          DO 11 Q = 1, 20
             DIGIT = X(Q)
             N(DIGIT) = N(DIGIT) + 1
11        CONTINUE

22    CONTINUE
      CLOSE (2)

      DO 33 DIGIT = 0, 3
         PRINT 20, DIGIT, N(DIGIT)
33    CONTINUE

20    FORMAT(1X, I2, ' occurred ', I4, ' times.')

      END
```

_____

Implied-DO Lists

When a program reads an array with a READ statement inside a DO or while loop, it can read either the whole array or only one element value from each record. Each time the READ executes, it begins a new record. We will often want to store several array values in each record, so we need a better way to read arrays.

The better way is a device called an **implied-DO list**. An example is

```
READ (12, 10) ( TOTAL(I), I = 1, 12 )
```

The implied-DO list in this case is

```
( TOTAL(I), I = 1, 12 )
```

The list requires opening and closing parentheses and has the general form

$$(<read\ list>,\ <DO\text{-}variable> = <initial>,\ <limit>,\ <step>)$$

The comma after the read list must be present, and what follows can be any valid DO statement with the word DO missing but implied.

This READ statement will read twelve values, for TOTAL(1) through TOTAL(12). The associated FORMAT statement will determine the number of values read from each record. Possible FORMAT specifications and their effects are:

FORMAT Specification	Effect
(12I5)	Read all twelve values from one record.
(6I5)	Read six values from one record, then six values from a second record.
(4I5)	Read four values from each of three records.
(5I5)	Read five values from the first two records, then two values from the third record.

In all but the first case, we rely on FORMAT reversion. Thus, assuming there are six integer values in each record, the implied-DO statement

```
READ (2, '(6I5)') ( TOTAL(I), I = 1, 12)
```

reads six values from one record for TOTAL(1) through TOTAL(6), then six values from the next record for TOTAL(7) through TOTAL(12).

We also can use an implied-DO list in a WRITE statement. Suppose the array PRICE has been declared with the statement

```
REAL  PRICE(200)
```

The segment

```
      WRITE (3, 10) ( PRICE(K), K = 1, 100 )
10    FORMAT (1X, 8F10.2)
```

will write twelve records with eight numbers per record, then one record with four values. The FORMAT specification 8F10.2 dictates eight values per record, but after twelve records are written, there are only four values left.

Several items can precede the implied-DO statement, as in

```
      WRITE (3, 10) ( '##', K, PRICE(K), K = 1, 80 )
10    FORMAT ( 4(1X, A2, I2, F8.2, 2X) )
```

This WRITE/FORMAT pair produces twenty lines of output. A typical line might look like

```
##21  345.20   ##22   89.98   ##23  215.98   ##24  423.95
```

More than one implied-DO list can appear in the same output statement

```
      PRINT *, (A(I), I = 1, 5), (B(I), I = 4, 7)
```

This statement writes five values of A, then four values of B. In contrast, the statement

```
      PRINT *, (A(I), B(I), I = 1, 5)
```

writes five pairs of values: A(1), B(1); A(2), B(2); and so on.

An implied-DO list, including the parentheses, acts as *one* item in a list, so other items can appear before or after it, as in

```
      READ *, NAME, (TEST(J), J = 1, 5), GRADE
```

This statement reads a name, five values of the array TEST, and a grade.

The next few programs read and write arrays with an implied-DO list.

■

8.2 SORTING AND SEARCHING

A major application of arrays is *sorting*; a list of numbers is given and sorted into increasing or decreasing order. Alternatively, a list of names may be sorted into alphabetical order. We first consider the problem of sorting numeric values. Entire books have been written on methods of sorting. The method we use here is the **selection sort**, because it is one of the simplest ways to sort items.

Example 8.6 Sorting a List of Numbers

Assume a numeric array X has elements X(1) through X(N). Here is an outline of the selection sort:

Step 1.　Find the smallest value in the array. Switch this value with the value of X(1).

Step 2.　Find the smallest value in X(2), X(3),..., X(N). Switch this value with the value of X(2).

.

.

.

Step K.　Find the smallest value in X(K), X(K+1),..., X(N). Switch this value with the value of X(K).

Step K is the most important; it is the general rule for any step. Exactly N-1 steps are required to sort an array with N elements; once the first N-1 values are in their proper places, the last value must be in its proper place. You should see that sorting can be performed with a DO loop beginning

```
DO 22 K = 1, N-1
```

Inside the loop, we must *do step K*, or find the smallest value in X(K), X(K+1),..., X(N). You already know how to find the smallest value in a list. The only extra complication here is the subscripts. The code for step K is

```
      SMALL = X(K)           This part of the
      POS = K                program duplicates
      DO 11 I = K + 1, N     part of the program
         IF (X(I) .LT. SMALL) THEN   in Example 5.3, with
            SMALL = X(I)     SMALL in place of LARGE,
            POS = I          LT in place of GT,
         END IF              and subscripts added.
11    CONTINUE

      X(POS) = X(K)          Put value of X(K) in X(POS)
      X(K)   = SMALL         Put value of SMALL in X(K)
```

We enclose this code for step K in a loop for values of K from 1 to N-1. The outer loop must initialize the value for SMALL and POS, so the loop begins

```
      DO 22 K = 1, N - 1
         SMALL = X(K)
         POS   = K
```

We will read the values for the array X from a data file SORDAT.DAT. The first record in SORDAT contains the number of values for the array. The second record contains the format specification for reading the rest of the values. The file might look like

```
32
(7F8.2)
    123.45  236.92   89.23  354.29  836.50  165.34  129.78
    435.31  319.23  524.36  287.62  983.12  654.19  429.44
    306.48  428.29  659.23  244.11  876.33  419.22  735.79
    408.23  619.35  799.42  963.21  138.55  310.23  579.22
    724.58  853.26  629.22  197.63
```

Here is an outline of the program:

1. Read the values from the file into the array X.
2. Print the values in the array.
3. Sort the array.
4. Print the sorted array.

The hardest part is the sort, and we have completed that. The layout of the file suggests how it should be read:

```
READ (9, *) N
READ (9, '(A)') FILEF
READ (9, FILEF) (X(I), I = 1, N)
```

We print the array twice, the first time to see if the program has read the data properly, the second time to see the result of the sort. See Program 8.6.

■
PROGRAM 8.6

```
      PROGRAM SORT
*-------------------------------------------------------*
*                Sort a list of numbers.                *
*-------------------------------------------------------*
      REAL          X(100), SMALL
      INTEGER       POS, I, K, N
      CHARACTER*40  FILEF
```

```
      OPEN (9, FILE = 'SORDAT', STATUS = 'OLD')
*---------------------------------------------------------------*
*               Read the file into the array X.                 *
*---------------------------------------------------------------*
      READ (9, *) N
      READ (9, '(A)') FILEF
      READ (9, FILEF) (X(I), I = 1, N)

      CLOSE (9)
*---------------------------------------------------------------*
*                      Write the array.                         *
*---------------------------------------------------------------*
      PRINT *
      PRINT *, 'Elements in array:'
      PRINT *
      WRITE (6, FILEF) (X(I), I = 1, N)
*---------------------------------------------------------------*
*   Outer loop; repeat for every position but the last.         *
*---------------------------------------------------------------*
      DO 22 K = 1, N-1

         SMALL = X(K)
         POS = K
*---------------------------------------------------------------*
*   Inner loop; find smallest value left and its position.      *
*---------------------------------------------------------------*
         DO 11 I = K+1, N
            IF (SMALL .GT. X(I) ) THEN
               SMALL = X(I)
               POS = I
            END IF
11       CONTINUE

         X(POS) = X(K)
         X(K)   = SMALL

22    CONTINUE
*---------------------------------------------------------------*
*                   Write the sorted array.                     *
*---------------------------------------------------------------*
      PRINT *
      PRINT *, 'Sorted Array:'
      PRINT *
      PRINT FILEF, (X(I), I = 1, N)

      END
```

This program prints the output

```
Elements in array:

    123.45  236.92   89.23  354.29  836.50  165.34  129.78
    435.31  319.23  524.36  287.62  983.12  654.19  429.44
    306.48  428.29  659.23  244.11  876.33  419.22  735.79
    408.23  619.35  799.42  963.21  138.55  310.23  579.22
    724.58  853.26  629.22  197.63

Sorted array:

     89.23  123.45  129.78  138.55  165.34  197.63  236.92
    244.11  287.62  306.48  310.23  319.23  354.29  408.23
    419.22  428.29  429.44  435.31  524.36  579.22  619.35
    629.22  654.19  659.23  724.58  735.79  799.42  836.50
    853.26  876.33  963.21  983.12
```

With very minor modifications, the sort routine can handle integer or character data, and can sort into decreasing order. To arrange a list of words in alphabetical order, for example, simply declare X and SMALL to be character variables instead of real. Of course, references should be made to words instead of to numbers in comments and output statements.

Example 8.7 Binary Searching

Example 8.4 involved searching an array with a sequential search scheme, which works fine for small arrays but can be very inefficient for large arrays. Here we introduce the **binary search** of an array, which is a very efficient method for searching *sorted* arrays.

We discussed the idea behind a binary search in Chapter 6. The main point is that the number of elements to be searched is cut in half at each step. If an array of 1,000 names is searched *sequentially*, the computer must examine 1,000 names whenever it is searching for a name that is not in the array. With a binary search, the computer would have to examine only ten names. To see this, begin with the number 1,000 and, at each step, cut the number in half. It takes ten steps to get the number down to 1.

Step	1	2	3	4	5	6	7	8	9	10
Number left	500	250	125	63	32	16	8	4	2	1

Another way to put this is: 10 is the power that must be applied to 2 to get 1,000 or more, or 10 is roughly the logarithm of 1,000 to the base 2.

Even if the search name is always in the array, the binary search is far more efficient than a sequential search. It is reasonable to assume that the item sought has the same likelihood of being at any position in the list. On the average then, sequential search would require 500 steps (averaged over all the names in the list), while the binary search cannot take more than ten steps.

This binary search process is much like a guessing game. At any step, we are considering a subset of the array from some point LOW to some other point HIGH. At the beginning, LOW is 1 and HIGH is the number of items in the array. At each step, we look at the middle value in this range. Call this value MID. Then

```
MID = (LOW + HIGH) / 2
```

The value of NAME(MID) may be just right, too high, or too low. If it is correct, print a message. If it is too high, set the new value of HIGH to the value of MID − 1. If it is too low, set the new value of LOW to MID + 1. The required IF block is

```
IF (NAME(MID) .EQ. SRCHNM) THEN
     PRINT *, 'That name is in position', MID
ELSE IF (NAME(MID) .GT. SRCHNM) THEN
     HIGH = MID − 1
ELSE
     LOW = MID + 1
END IF
```

This IF block will be inside a while loop. As in the sequential search program, we use a logical variable FOUND, initialized to .FALSE.. If the search name is found in the array, FOUND will be set to .TRUE.. We must also have a condition that indicates that the entire array has been searched without finding the search name. Since values of HIGH are getting smaller and/or values of LOW are getting larger, at some point LOW will become larger than HIGH if the search name is not in the array. Thus, the appropriate IF block begins

```
IF (.NOT. FOUND .AND. (LOW .LE. HIGH)) THEN
```

Program 8.7 gives the complete program.

■

PROGRAM 8.7

```
      PROGRAM BISRCH
*--------------------------------------------------------*
*         Illustrate binary search of an array of names.      *
*--------------------------------------------------------*
      CHARACTER * 20    NAME(1000), SRCHNM
      INTEGER           TOTAL, HIGH, LOW, MID
      LOGICAL           FOUND
*--------------------------------------------------------*
*  Names are in a file called NAMES.DAT.  Open the file.  *
*--------------------------------------------------------*
      OPEN (1, FILE = 'NAMES.DAT', STATUS = 'OLD')
*--------------------------------------------------------*
*   Read the file, counting number of names with TOTAL.   *
*--------------------------------------------------------*
      TOTAL = 1
11    READ (1, '(A20)', END = 22) NAME(TOTAL)
         TOTAL = TOTAL + 1
      GO TO 11

22    TOTAL = TOTAL - 1

      CLOSE (1)
*--------------------------------------------------------*
*                Ask for search name.                    *
*--------------------------------------------------------*
      PRINT *, 'What name are you looking for?'
      READ '(A)', SRCHNM
*--------------------------------------------------------*
*           Initialize FOUND, LOW, and HIGH.             *
*--------------------------------------------------------*
      FOUND = .FALSE.
      LOW = 1
      HIGH = TOTAL
*--------------------------------------------------------*
*                  Main search loop                      *
*--------------------------------------------------------*
33    IF (.NOT. FOUND .AND. (LOW .LE. HIGH)) THEN

          MID = (LOW + HIGH) / 2

          IF ( NAME(MID) .EQ. SRCHNM ) THEN
               PRINT *, 'That name is in position', MID
               FOUND = .TRUE.
```

```
      ELSE IF (NAME(MID) .GT. SRCHNM) THEN
        HIGH = MID - 1
      ELSE
        LOW = MID + 1
    END IF

    GO TO 33

  END IF

  IF (.NOT. FOUND) PRINT *, 'That name is not on the list.'

  END
```

This program is easily altered to search for a number in an array of numbers. Remember, the elements of the array must be in increasing order for this binary search method to work. The program requires only minor changes if the array is in decreasing order.

Two problems related to sorting and searching arrays are inserting and deleting values in an array. After sorting an array, we might have to insert a new value, or after searching an array for a name, we might want to delete that name from the array. We consider simple versions of these problems here.

First, consider the problem of inserting a value in an array that is already sorted. Let the array be

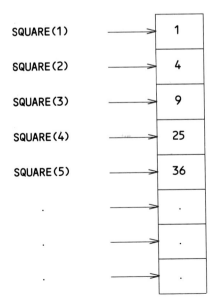

For obvious reasons, we want to insert the value 16 in SQUARE(4) and push the other values down.

Suppose the variable N is keeping track of the number of elements stored in SQUARE. Then, to make room for a new value in SQUARE(4), we want to push the value in each element of SQUARE up to the next storage location, starting with the element in SQUARE(N) and ending with SQUARE(4). This leaves a duplicate value (25) in SQUARE(4) and SQUARE(5), but our next step is to assign the proper value to SQUARE(4). Finally, N should now increase by 1 to count the inserted value. The code is

```
      DO 11 I = N, 4, -1
         SQUARE(I + 1) = SQUARE(I)
11    CONTINUE
      SQUARE(4) = 16
      N = N + 1
```

This method will fail if the value of N is already the declared size of the array.

Deleting an array value is a similar process. Consider, for instance, deleting the twentieth element of a real array X of N elements. Some of the elements of X might be:

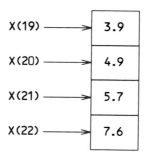

Here we can merely assign the twenty-first value to X(20), the twenty-second value to X(21), and so on, until we assign the Nth value to X(N-1). We code this in the loop

```
      DO 11 I = 21, N
         X(I-1) = X(I)
11    CONTINUE
```

Finally, we must decrease N with the statement

```
N = N - 1
```

to account for the deleted value.

■
8.3 CHARACTER ARRAYS

Fortran character variables have **fixed length**. No matter how many characters you enter for a character variable, the length remains as it was declared. Fortran drops characters if you enter too many, or adds trailing blanks if you do not enter enough characters to fill the variable.

Example 8.8 Finding the *Length* of a Character String

Sometimes it is handy to know how many characters, if any, a string has before the trailing blanks. That is really the effective length of the string in most cases. Suppose a line is to be entered, and we do not know in advance how long it will be, except that it will not be more than eighty characters, the width of most terminal screens. Our job is to find out how many characters appear before the trailing blanks, and to write those characters in reverse.

We can read the line as the value of one character variable eighty characters long, but let us read it as an array of eighty elements, each one character long. This array will allow us to look at each character of the string. We will call the array LINE and declare it as

```
CHARACTER  LINE(80)
```

We read the value of LINE with the short-list statement

```
READ '(80A1)', LINE
```

To find out how many trailing blanks are in LINE, we assign an integer variable ENDLIN the beginning value of 80, then look at LINE(ENDLIN). We let ENDLIN decrease as long as LINE(ENDLIN) is blank. The code is simple:

```
        ENDLIN = 80
  11    IF (LINE(ENDLIN) .EQ. ' ') THEN
            ENDLIN = ENDLIN - 1
            GO TO 11
        END IF
```

We shall actually use a parameter SPACE to represent ' '. After finding the end of the line, it is a simple matter to write it in reverse, using LINE in an implied-DO list with subscript ranging from ENDLIN down to 1. See Program 8.8.

■

PROGRAM 8.8

```
      PROGRAM READLN
*-----------------------------------------------------*
*  Read an input line as an 80-character array.       *
*  Count the characters before the trailing spaces.   *
*-----------------------------------------------------*
      CHARACTER  LINE(80), SPACE
      INTEGER    I, ENDLIN
      PARAMETER  (SPACE = ' ')

      PRINT *, 'Enter a line.'
      READ '(80A1)', LINE

      ENDLIN = 80
  11  IF (LINE(ENDLIN) .EQ. SPACE) THEN
          ENDLIN = ENDLIN - 1
          GO TO 11
      END IF

      PRINT *, 'Nonblank characters end at position', ENDLIN
      PRINT *, 80 - ENDLIN, ' trailing spaces'
      PRINT *
      PRINT *, 'Here is the reversed line.'
      PRINT *, (LINE(I), I = ENDLIN, 1, -1)

      END
```

You should try this program with several input lines. Extreme cases should always be checked. Find out what happens if you simply enter a carriage return in response to the READ statement, and what happens if you enter a nonblank character for LINE(80). The exercises at the end of this chapter suggest a few modifications of this program.

Example 8.9 Printing a Chessboard

The Eight Queens is a famous problem that asks the programmer to find a way to place eight queens on a chessboard so that no two queens are attacking each other. We consider a much simpler problem here, printing a chessboard with eight queens on it. What we have in mind is printing something fairly simple, such as:

```
Q _____
  _____
    Q _____
  Q _____
  _____
    Q _____
  Q _____
  _____
    Q _____
  Q _____
  _____
    Q
```

This layout is a bit too simple, but let us see how to print it, then look for something a little better.

Each row contains seven underscores (_) and a Q. We can use a character array ROW of size 8, with each element of length 1. Declare ROW as

```
CHARACTER  ROW(8)
```

First fill each element with an underscore. We call the underscore BLANK in this case, because it looks like the bottom edge of a square with nothing on it.

```
      DO 11 COL = 1, 8
         ROW(COL) = BLANK
11    CONTINUE
```

Where should the Qs come from? We will ask the user of the program to enter eight column numbers, and we will store them in an integer array COLUMN with size 8. Then the Q in a given row, say row I, goes into column COLUMN(I). The code is

```
      COL = COLUMN(I)
      ROW(COL) = 'Q'
```

We do this for eight rows, so we enclose these statements in a DO loop and print ROW inside the loop:

```
        DO 33 I = 1, 8

          DO 22 COL = 1, 8
            ROW(COL) = BLANK
22        CONTINUE

          COL = COLUMN(I)
          ROW(COL) = 'Q'

          PRINT *, ROW

33      CONTINUE
```

That will print the simple layout.

We would like to be able to see if any two queens are attacking each other, and this layout is not much help. A slightly more complicated board is

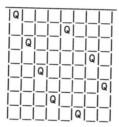

Definitely an improvement. The top line is the easiest; only 17 underscores (_). What about the other rows?

Each row is just like the rows in the simpler layout above, with a vertical bar (|) before and after each underscore or Q. We can print each ROW as an implied-DO list, with the | character appearing once before each element of ROW, and once after the entire implied-DO list:

```
    PRINT *, ('|', ROW(COL), COL = 1, 8), '|'
```

Program 8.9 shows the program, with a parameter QUEEN = 'Q'.

■
PROGRAM 8.9

```
      PROGRAM BOARD
*-------------------------------------------------------*
*          Print a chessboard with eight queens.        *
*    Ask the user for the column positions of the queens.   *
*-------------------------------------------------------*
      INTEGER    I, COL, COLUMN(8)
      CHARACTER  BLANK, ROW(8), QUEEN, TOP(17)
      PARAMETER  (QUEEN = 'Q', BLANK = '_')
      DATA       TOP /17 * '_'/

      PRINT *, 'Enter eight digits from 1 to 8'
      READ *, COLUMN

      PRINT *, TOP
      DO 22 I = 1, 8

         DO 11 COL = 1, 8
            ROW(COL) = BLANK
11       CONTINUE

         COL = COLUMN(I)
         ROW(COL) = QUEEN

         PRINT *, ('|', ROW(COL), COL = 1, 8), '|'

22    CONTINUE

      END
```

■
8.4 SUMMARY OF CHAPTER 8

■ *Terms Introduced in This Chapter*

Array
Array element
Array name
Binary search, of an array
Dimension
Implied-DO list

Sequential search
Short list
Size, of an array
Sort
Subscript
Subscript bound

■ *What You Should Know*

1. An array name is one name for several storage locations. The separate locations are specified by the array name and a subscript giving the position of the location in the array.

2. The array size must be declared at the beginning of the program, and remains constant while the program runs.

3. A program can read or write an entire array by giving only the array name, without subscripts, in a short-list statement.

4. Normally, the lower bound for subscripts of an array is 1, but the lower bound can be declared to be any integer.

5. Subscripts can be any integer expressions, but the value of a subscript must not go beyond the declared bounds.

6. A DO or while loop can assign values to elements of an array, one at a time.

7. A DO loop index often serves as the subscripts for array elements.

8. An input/output statement with an implied-DO list can process several elements of an array at once.

9. The format specification for the statement with an implied-DO list determines how many elements of the array are read or written from one record.

10. Both arrays and files are useful for storing many pieces of related information.

11. The information in an array disappears when the program that declares the array finishes running. Information in a file has an existence independent of any program that creates or uses the file.

12. Many files contain more information than a program can hold. A program can deal with such a file one record at a time, so the program never has to hold all the information at once.

13. An array has a data type, so it can hold information only of that type. A file can hold information of several types in one record.

14. Arrays make many tasks, such as sorting, much easier by allowing a program to hold all the array values at once.

■

8.5 EXERCISES

■ *Self-Test*

1. Which of the following are legal array declarations in a Fortran program?
   a.   REAL A(5)
   b.   INTEGER NUMBER(5 * 50)

    c.   REAL A(-5)
    d.   CHARACTER STATE('AA' : 'ZZ')
    e.   REAL A(-5:5)
    f.   LOGICAL TRUTH(10)

2. Write declarations for the following arrays:

    a.   A real array A with subscripts from 1 to 100.
    b.   An integer array X with subscripts from 0 to 50.
    c.   An array NAME of 4-character names with subscripts from -2 to 8.

3. Suppose an array A has been declared INTEGER A(6). Specify the values assigned to the array elements by the segments below.

    a.

```
        DO 11 I = 1, 6
           A(I) = I / 2
    11  CONTINUE
```

    b.

```
        DO 11 I = 1, 6
           A(I) = MOD(I, 3)
    11  CONTINUE
```

    c.

```
        DO 11 I = 2, 6, 2
           A(I) = I * I
           A(I / 2) = A(I) / 2
    11  CONTINUE
```

    d.

```
        A(1) = 3
        DO 11 I = 2, 6
           A(I) = 2 * A(I-1)
    11  CONTINUE
```

4. A program contains the declaration

```
INTEGER  A(4), B(4)
```

A sequential file contains the record

```
05101520253035404550
```

In the program the file is opened as unit 1. Show the values assigned to elements of the arrays A and B by the following READ statements.

    a.   READ (1, '(8I2)') (A(I), I = 1, 4), (B(I), I = 1, 4)

    b.   READ (1, '(8I2)') (A(I), B(I), I = 1, 4)

c. READ (1, '(6I3)') (A(I), B(I), I = 1, 3)

d. READ (1, '(2X, 8I2)') A, B

e. READ (1, '(4(2X, I2))') A

5. Array C is declared REAL C(12). How many records are read from the file associated with unit 1 by each of the following segments?

a. READ (1, '(2F6.4)') C

b. READ (1, '(3F8.2)') C

c. READ (1, '(3F10.2)') (C(I), I = 1, 8)

d. READ (1, '(6F10.3)') (C(I), I = 1, 12, 2)

■ Programming Exercises

1. Write a program to

    a. Read and count values of a real array X,
    b. Calculate the mean of the values,
    c. Subtract the mean from each array element,
    d. Print the revised array.

2. One-dimensional arrays are well suited to vector calculations. For example, if X is a vector with n components $x_1, x_2, \cdots, x_n$, then the *length* of X is

$$Len(X) = \sqrt{x_1^2 + x_2^2 + \cdots + x_n^2}$$

Write a program that reads the number of components in a vector X, then reads the component values and finds and prints the length of X.

3. If X and Y are vectors of the same length n, with components x_i and y_i, then the *dot product* of X and Y is

$$x_1 \times y_1 + x_2 \times y_2 + \cdots + x_n \times y_n$$

Write a program that reads the number of components in vectors X and Y and the component values, then calculates and prints their dot product.

4. Write a program that asks the user to enter digits (0 through 9), stops when a negative number is entered, and counts the number of times each digit occurs.

5. The program of Example 8.6 sorts real numbers into ascending order. Modify that program to sort integers into *descending* order.

6. The sort program of Example 8.6 is easily modified to do an *incomplete sort*. That is, the program might find only the largest five numbers in an array containing 100 numbers. Write a program that reads an array of real numbers, asks how many of the largest values the user wants, then finds and prints those numbers.

7. Write a program to sort real numbers into ascending order but discard *duplicate* values. If the original array has several identical values, only one of them should be kept in the sorted array.

8. Modify the binary search program to handle an array of integers in descending order.

9. Write a program to search an array for a given name, and delete that name from the array if it is found.

10. Write a program to read a sorted array of real numbers, ask the user for a new number, and insert that number in its proper place in the array. Print the new array.

11. Write a program that calculates the *median* of an array of real numbers. When there is an odd number of scores, the median is the middle value of the *ordered* scores. In an array of seven scores, the middle score is the fourth score. When there is an even number of scores, the median is the mean (or average) of the middle two scores in the ordered list. In an array of eight scores, the middle two scores are the fourth and fifth.

    For this problem, assume the array is already sorted, and test the program only with sorted data.

12. Two or more arrays with the same number of elements, and some relationship between corresponding elements, are called **parallel arrays**. For example, a store might keep three arrays for each item the store carries:

    ITEM   a character array that holds the names of the items.
    ONHAND   an integer array holding the number on hand for each item.
    PRICE   a real array containing the prices of the items.

    If ITEM(6) is 'HAMMER', ONHAND(6) is 4, and PRICE(6) is 8.95, then the store has four hammers, and the price of a hammer is $8.95.

    Write a program to read three such parallel arrays. The program should sort the ITEM array alphabetically, keeping the values of ONHAND and PRICE adjacent to the proper value of ITEM; that is, the subscripts on ONHAND and PRICE must change in exactly the same way the subscripts on ITEM change.

13. Write a program to perform an **insertion sort**. Assume that an array A of N real numbers is already sorted into ascending order, and a new number X is to be placed in the array. Compare X to A(1). If X ≤ A(1), then X belongs in the first position. If not, compare X to A(2), A(3), . . ., until a place is found for X. Call this place K. To make room for X at position K, all the elements from A(K) through A(N) must be moved up one position. The value of A(N) will become the value of A(N+1), and so on.

    Remember that N must increase as numbers are added to the array. Start with N = 0 and read some numbers. The first number becomes A(1) with no comparisons needed. This is a reasonable sorting method for small arrays.

14. Write a program that reads an input line up to 80 characters long, and prints that line with all spaces deleted.

15. A **palindrome** is a string of characters that looks the same when read backwards. The word RADAR is a palindrome, as is the statement ABLE WAS I ERE I SAW ELBA. Write a program that determines if an input line is a palindrome. The program should ignore trailing blanks.

16. Write a program to check an algebraic expression for the proper number and order of right and left parentheses. The expression must, of course, have the same number of each. Also, when the expression is read from left to right, the number of right parentheses must never exceed the number of left parentheses.

17. Write a program that reads two real arrays, A and B, both of size N, and determines the smallest positive ratio A(I)/B(I). The elements of B should all be positive, but the elements of A can be positive, negative, or zero.

18. Write a program that adds two integers of arbitrary length (say up to 60 digits). Store each integer as an array, with elements holding 4-digit integers. For example, the number 123,456,789 can be stored in an integer array A with A(1) = 6789, A(2) = 2345, and A(3) = 1. When two such arrays A and B are added to give a sum C, C(1) will be the sum of A(1) and B(1) if this sum is not more than 9999. When the sum is larger than 9999, a digit must be carried to C(2). (If the sum is 12035, then C(1) is 2035, and the 1 is carried to the next sum, which becomes A(2) + B(2) + 1, and so on.)

19. Write a program that multiplies two integers of arbitrary length. Store the integers as in the previous problem.

20. Write a program to **merge** two arrays A and B into a third array C. Read two arrays A and B of real numbers, each of which is already in ascending order. Make and print a third array C that contains all the values in A and B, arranged in ascending order. Do not use a sort procedure; let C(1) be the smaller of A(1) and B(1), and so on.

chapter 9

FUNCTION SUBPROGRAMS

In Chapter 3 we discussed statement functions, a type of user-defined function. This chapter deals with another kind of user-defined function, **function subprograms**.

We use the term **program unit** to refer to programs or subprograms. Subprograms are program units that can be invoked from another program unit. We have already encountered several subprograms, the Fortran intrinsic functions. Here the prefix *sub* emphasizes that a subprogram is meant to be used by another program; a subprogram cannot run by itself. A **program system** refers to a collection of program units that are linked together.

In addition to the intrinsic functions, Fortran recognizes two *external* types of user-supplied subprograms, function subprograms and subroutine subprograms. The term *external* signifies that the functions and subroutines exist *outside* the invoking program, in contrast to statement functions. External also distinguishes function subprograms from the intrinsic Fortran functions. This chapter deals with function subprograms, which we routinely call functions. The next chapter discusses subroutines.

Subprograms perform computations for the programs that invoke them. Several important reasons for writing an external subprogram are:

1. Many programs can use one subprogram.
2. Very complex programs can be constructed easily by using subprograms as building blocks.
3. A subprogram allows the programmer to avoid repetition of code in a main program.
4. Subprograms allow several programmers to work on the same program system simultaneously, with each programmer working on a separate program unit.

■

9.1 FUNCTION SUBPROGRAMS

A function subprogram is a subprogram that returns a single value each time it is invoked. You invoke it the same way you invoke a statement function, by using the function name followed by the actual arguments in parentheses. However, the definition of the function is not in a single line in the program, but is in a separate program unit.

The Function Name Statement

Names of external functions follow the same rules as names of statement functions or variables. A program must not use the same name for a function and any other entity (such as a variable, array, or another subprogram). Every function subprogram must begin with a **function name statement**, which can consist of the word FUNCTION followed by the name of the function with an argument list in parentheses. An example is

        FUNCTION MEDIAN(A, B, C)

   The data type of the result or value returned by a function is determined by the function name. Implicitly, the name MEDIAN specifies an integer value. If a real value is desired, the word REAL must be placed before FUNCTION, as in

        REAL FUNCTION MEDIAN(A, B, C)

Functions can have any of the Fortran data types. We will always specify the data type of the function, just as we always specify the data types of all variables.
   The letters A, B, and C in the argument list of the function denote the *dummy arguments* of the function, the same as with statement functions. In the function subprogram, they act as variable names or addresses. Dummy arguments must be variable names, not expressions or constants. In an external function, a dummy argument can be an array *name* but cannot be an array *element*. The invoking program may have variables A, B, and C, which designate storage entirely separate from the storage designated by A, B, and C in the subprogram.
   Since the letters A, B, and C are variables in the subprogram, we will declare them as we do for all programs. A suitable type declaration is

        REAL   A, B, C

This type declaration statement identifies MEDIAN as a function with three real arguments. If any other variables are used in the subprogram, they should be declared as well.

Example 9.1 A Function to Calculate a Median

The obvious purpose of the function MEDIAN is to find the median of the three values in A, B, and C. MEDIAN could be a statement function, which is simpler than a function subprogram. However, the main point here is to illustrate the use of function subprograms, so we start with a simple function.

Program 9.1a shows the entire function subprogram.

■

PROGRAM 9.1a

```
      REAL FUNCTION MEDIAN(A, B, C)
*-------------------------------------------------------------*
*       Calculate the median of three real values.        *
*-------------------------------------------------------------*
      REAL   A, B, C

      MEDIAN = A + B + C - MAX(A, B, C) - MIN(A, B, C)

      END
```

The form of the subprogram is similar to the form of a program. An END statement is required. A subprogram can contain any Fortran statement except another program unit name statement. A subprogram can invoke another subprogram, but it may not invoke itself.

Notice, too, that the function name MEDIAN is used in the subprogram without arguments; the function name is a variable in the subprogram. The function subprogram must assign a value to the function name, because the value calculated by the function is passed back to the invoking program through the function name.

As with statement functions, the invoking statement contains an expression involving the function name. If ONE, TWO, and THREE are real variables, the function MEDIAN can be invoked with a statement such as

```
      Y = 6.5 * MEDIAN(ONE, TWO, THREE)
```

The actual arguments ONE, TWO, and THREE in the invoking statement must correspond to the dummy arguments in the function name statement both in number and data type. Since the MEDIAN name statement has three real arguments (A, B, and C), an invoking statement must have three real arguments. The correspondence in this case should be obvious.

```
Y = 6.5 * MEDIAN(ONE, TWO, THREE)
```

```
REAL FUNCTION MEDIAN(A, B, C)
```

That is, ONE corresponds to A, TWO corresponds to B, and THREE corresponds to C.

The actual arguments can be any *real* expressions, including constants, in contrast to the dummy arguments, each of which must be a single variable name. If X, Y, and Z are real variables in the main program, then MEDIAN could be invoked with the statement

```
PRINT *, MEDIAN(X ** 2, Y + Z, -26.4)
```

Once again, the correspondence is obvious:

$$X ** 2 \text{ corresponds to } A$$
$$Y + Z \text{ corresponds to } B$$
$$-26.4 \text{ corresponds to } C$$

When the function subprogram runs, the computer treats each reference to a dummy argument as if the corresponding actual argument were copied in place of the dummy argument.

The short program in Program 9.1b invokes the function MEDIAN.

■
PROGRAM 9.1b
───

```
      PROGRAM CALMED
*-------------------------------------------------------------------*
* Call function MEDIAN to calculate the median of 3 real numbers.   *
*-------------------------------------------------------------------*
      REAL  X, Y, Z, MEDIAN, M
*-------------------------------------------------------------------*
*                    Ask for 3 numbers.                             *
*-------------------------------------------------------------------*
      PRINT *, 'Enter 3 real numbers for calculation of median.'
      READ  *, X, Y, Z
```

```
*------------------------------------------------------------------*
*                    Invoke the function MEDIAN.                   *
*------------------------------------------------------------------*
      M = MEDIAN(X, Y, Z)
      PRINT *, 'The median of these numbers is', M

      END
```

The function is invoked in the assignment statement. At this point, the program passes the addresses pointed to by X, Y, and Z to the function MEDIAN. The function names these three addresses as A, B, and C, and begins to execute.

The main statement in the function subprogram is the assignment statement, which calculates the median value and assigns this value to MEDIAN. When the END statement of the function subprogram is encountered, the value of MEDIAN is passed back to the invoking program, and execution continues with the invoking statement in the main program.

The invoking program does not have to know what variable names the subprogram uses. Similarly, the subprogram does not have to know the variable names used in the main program. The program refers to three storage locations as X, Y, and Z, while the function refers to these same locations as A, B, and C. The function name MEDIAN must, of course, be the same in the function and the main program.

The main program also contains a variable M which is not passed as an argument to MEDIAN. Therefore the address M is not available to MEDIAN. Figure 9.1 depicts the addressing scheme.

This method of passing values to a subprogram is called **passing by address**, **by location**, or **by reference**, because the invoking program gives the subprogram the *address* or *location* of a value, not the value itself. An important consequence is that, if one of the values of A, B, or C is changed when the function executes, then the corresponding X, Y, or Z value is changed in the main program. Most versions of Fortran pass *numeric* arguments by location.

Example 9.2 Using a Function Subprogram

A subprogram can be appended to a main program and compiled along with it, or it can be compiled separately and linked to the main program. In the first case, one simply writes the subprogram after the main program, as shown in Program 9.2. (The function could come before, instead of after, the main program.)

FIGURE 9.1
Addresses available to
the main program and
the function subpro-
gram MEDIAN

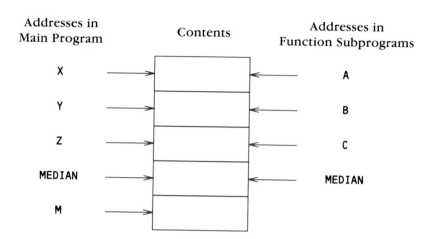

PROGRAM 9.2

```
      PROGRAM CALMED
*------------------------------------------------------------------*
*  Call function MEDIAN to calculate the median of 3 real numbers. *
*------------------------------------------------------------------*
      REAL  X, Y, Z, MEDIAN, M
*------------------------------------------------------------------*
*                      Ask for 3 numbers.                          *
*------------------------------------------------------------------*
      PRINT *, 'Enter 3 real numbers for calculation of median.'
      READ *, X, Y, Z
*------------------------------------------------------------------*
*                  Invoke the function MEDIAN.                     *
*------------------------------------------------------------------*
      M = MEDIAN(X, Y, Z)
      PRINT *, 'The median of these numbers is', M

      END
*******************************************************************
*      End of main program.  Beginning of function MEDIAN.       *
*******************************************************************
```

```
      REAL FUNCTION MEDIAN(A, B, C)
*-----------------------------------------------------------------*
*              Calculate the median of three real values.         *
*-----------------------------------------------------------------*
      REAL    A, B, C

      MEDIAN = A + B + C - MAX(A, B, C) - MIN(A, B, C)

      END
```

The program and function above are written in one source file, so the function is obviously tied to the main program. If a subprogram is to be used with several main programs, it is better to compile the program and subprogram separately. Check with your instructor for details.

When trying to decide whether to compile a subprogram separately from a main program, ask yourself if the subprogram can be used with other programs you may write. If it can, put it in a separate file and compile it separately. If not, put it in the same file as the main program.

Example 9.3 Finding a Root of an External Function

Any program that contains a statement function could use a function subprogram instead. If the program is relatively long and the function is likely to be changed often, the subprogram approach saves the programmer from having to recompile the main program.

In PROGRAM BISECT of Example 5.6, we used a statement function to provide the function whose root we wanted to find. Here we give essentially the same program, but with the statement function replaced by a function subprogram. See Program 9.3.

■
PROGRAM 9.3

```
      PROGRAM BISECT
*-----------------------------------------------------------------*
*  Find root of a function by repeatedly bisecting an interval.   *
*  The function F is in a function subprogram REAL FUNCTION F.     *
*-----------------------------------------------------------------*
      REAL    ROOT, FROOT, ERROR, F, A, B, LOW, HIGH, T
      INTEGER N, I
```

```
      PRINT *
      PRINT *, 'What interval?'
      READ  *, A, B
      PRINT *

      IF (F(A) * F(B) .GT. 0) THEN
          PRINT *, 'Function values have the same sign at'
          PRINT *, 'the endpoints of the given interval. '
          PRINT *, 'Cannot continue. '
      ELSE
          PRINT *, 'How close should the approximate root be?'
          READ  *, ERROR
          PRINT *

          LOW  = A
          HIGH = B

          T = (B - A) / ERROR
          N = LOG(T) / LOG(2.0)

          DO 11 I = 1, N

              ROOT = (HIGH + LOW) / 2.0
              FROOT = F(ROOT)

              IF (FROOT * F(HIGH) .GT. 0.0) THEN
                  HIGH = ROOT
              ELSE IF (FROOT * F(LOW) .GT. 0.0) THEN
                  LOW = ROOT
              END IF

11        CONTINUE
          PRINT *, 'Approximate root:', ROOT
          PRINT *, 'Function value: ', FROOT
          PRINT *, N, ' Iterations used.'

      END IF

      END
*----------------------------------------------------------------*
*         End of program BISECT.  Beginning of function F.       *
*----------------------------------------------------------------*
      REAL FUNCTION F(X)
      REAL X

      F = X - 2.0 * SIN(X)

      END
```

Incompatible Arguments

When actual and dummy arguments of an external function do not have the same types, the Fortran compiler may not issue a warning as it does for statement functions, but results can be quite strange. Consider the program and function below. The program is run on a VAX; similar, but not identical, results might occur with any computer.

```
      PROGRAM BADBIG
*--------------------------------------------------*
*  Incompatibility of actual and dummy arguments   *
*--------------------------------------------------*
      REAL X, Y, Z, LARGE

      READ *, X, Y
      Z = LARGE(X, Y)
      PRINT *, Z

      END
**************************************************
      REAL FUNCTION LARGE(A, B)
      INTEGER A, B

      LARGE = MAX(A, B)

      END
```

If you enter 12.5 and 30.2 in response to the READ statement, the computer will print

    16968.00

To see what is happening, place the statement

```
      PRINT *, 'A = ', A, ' B = ', B
```

in the function LARGE, right after the declarations. A run of the program then gives

```
 A =        16968  B =  -1717943567
    16968.00
```

The program has passed the *real* values of X and Y to the function LARGE, but LARGE reads the values in the variables A and B as *integers*. The computer's representation of the real number 12.5 is the same as its representation of the integer 16968.

A similar, but harder to detect, problem occurs in the following program and function.

```
PROGRAM BADBG2
REAL X, Y, Z

READ *, X, Y
Z = LARGE(X, Y)
PRINT *, Z

END
************************************
REAL FUNCTION LARGE(A, B)
REAL A, B

LARGE = MAX(A, B)

END
```

With the same input, the computer now prints

–1.7179436E+09

Try to see what the problem is before reading on.

This time, the incompatibility is in the function name LARGE. The function name statement declares LARGE to be REAL. The main program does not declare the name LARGE, so implicit typing makes LARGE an integer. The function calculates LARGE to be the real number 30.2, but the main program misinterprets the real representation of 30.2 as the integer representation of –1717943567. The assignment statement gives Z the real value –1.7179436E+09.

These examples should convince you to declare all variables and function names, and to make sure the declarations in the main program match the declarations in the function.

Output Statements in Functions

We put a PRINT statement in the first function LARGE above to help find the error. As a rule, do not put output statements in functions except for debugging purposes, because output from a function interrupts the normal flow of the program. Further, if an output statement such as

```
PRINT *, 'Large = ', LARGE(X, Y)
```

calls a function LARGE, and LARGE also contains a PRINT * statement, the program crashes with a *recursive I/O operation* message. The main program has directed the computer to write something to the default output device. While the computer is in the middle of this writing process, the function LARGE tells the computer to write something else to the same device. The computer cannot satisfy one of these commands without fouling up the other, so it quits. Therefore, avoid invoking external functions with output statements.

Example 9.4 Calculating a Greatest Common Divisor

The **greatest common divisor** of two positive integers m and n, not both zero, is the largest integer that divides both m and n. The greatest common divisor of m and n is often denoted by $\gcd(m, n)$. For example, $\gcd(16, 24)$ is 8 because 8 divides 16 and 24, and no larger integer divides both 16 and 24.

Euclid devised a famous algorithm for finding the greatest common divisor of two integers. With q's to represent quotients and r's for remainders, the algorithm is as follows.

1. Divide m by n, and write $m = q_0 \times n + r_1$, with $r_1 < n$
2. Divide n by r_1, and write $n = q_1 \times r_1 + r_2$, with $r_2 < r_1$
3. Divide r_1 by r_2, and write $r_1 = q_2 \times r_2 + r_3$, with $r_3 < r_2$

Continue dividing one remainder by the next until a remainder of zero occurs. This must happen because each remainder is less than the previous one. The last remainder before the zero remainder is the greatest common divisor of m and n.

As an example, consider finding $\gcd(126, 140)$. Using Euclid's algorithm, we obtain

$$126 = 0 \times 140 + 126 \qquad (n = 140, r_1 = 126)$$
$$140 = 1 \times 126 + 14 \qquad (r_2 = 14)$$
$$126 = 9 \times 14 + 0 \qquad (r_3 = 0)$$

Since the remainder r_3 is 0, $\gcd(126, 140)$ is r_2, or 14.

To program the algorithm, notice that each equation contains two numbers from the previous equation. The remainder in one equation becomes the number after $\times$ in the next equation, and the number after $\times$ in the first equation becomes the number on the left of $=$ in the next equation. Thus, at each step, we can let m assume the old value of n, and let n take the value of the previous remainder. The process is then repeated until the value of n is zero. Program 9.4a shows how the algorithm is coded.

■

PROGRAM 9.4a

```
      INTEGER FUNCTION GCD(M, N)
*------------------------------------------------------*
*  Calculate the greatest common divisor of two integers.  *
*  Calculation is correct, but bad side effects can occur. *
*------------------------------------------------------*
      INTEGER M, N, REMAIN
*------------------------------------------------------*
*                Euclid's algorithm                    *
*------------------------------------------------------*
      REMAIN = MOD(M, N)
11    IF (REMAIN .NE. 0) THEN
          M = N
          N = REMAIN
          REMAIN = MOD(M, N)
          GO TO 11
      END IF
*------------------------------------------------------*
*                Assign value to GCD.                  *
*------------------------------------------------------*
      GCD = N

      END
```

Program 9.4b shows a main program to call the function GCD.

■

PROGRAM 9.4b

```
      PROGRAM CALGCD
*------------------------------------------------------*
*          Calculate gcd of two positive integers.     *
*------------------------------------------------------*
      INTEGER   I, J, K, GCD
*------------------------------------------------------*
*                Ask for two integers.                 *
*------------------------------------------------------*
      PRINT *, 'Two positive integers? '
      READ  *, I, J
```

```
*-------------------------------------------------------------*
*                    Invoke the function GCD.                 *
*-------------------------------------------------------------*
      K = GCD(I,J)

      PRINT 20, I, J, K
20    FORMAT ( ' GCD(',I5, ',', I5, ') = ' ,I5, '.' )

      END
```

When this program runs, suppose the integers 6400 and 3232 are entered for I and J. Then the computer prints

```
GCD(   64,   32) =   32
```

The computer has calculated the correct gcd value, 32, but it says that the integers I and J have values 64 and 32! To see what has happened, recall the relation between addresses in the main program and the function. Variables M and N in the function GCD refer to the same addresses as variables I and J in the main program. When the function GCD is called, these addresses have the following values.

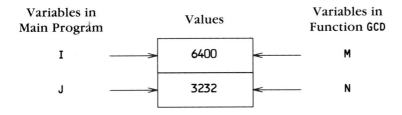

Tracing through the function GCD, we find that values of M, N, and REMAIN change as follows:

Statement	M	N	REMAIN
	6400	3232	
REMAIN = MOD(M, N)	6400	3232	3168
M = N	3232	3232	3168
N = REMAIN	3232	3168	3168
REMAIN = MOD(M, N)	3232	3168	64
M = N	3168	3168	64
N = REMAIN	3168	64	64
REMAIN = MOD(M, N)	3168	64	32
M = N	64	64	32
N = REMAIN	64	32	32
REMAIN = MOD(M, N)	64	32	0

Thus, when REMAIN becomes 0, M has value 64 and N has value 32, so the common addresses look like:

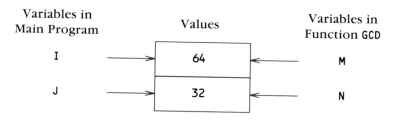

When control returns to the main program, the values of I and J are 64 and 32, respectively.

Side Effects

A function that changes values of addresses in the invoking program is said to have **side effects**. The task of function GCD is to pass back the value of GCD, period. It should not affect values of variables in the main program. Although this changing of values obviously did not violate the rules of the Fortran compiler because no error messages occurred, it is a bad practice.

To avoid side effects it is often necessary to *protect* addresses shared by a main program and a subprogram. A simple way to do this is to use auxiliary variables in the subprogram, which take the values of the dummy arguments that need to be protected. In our case, we can protect M and N by using two auxiliary variables M1 and N1 as in Program 9.4c.

■
PROGRAM 9.4c

```
      INTEGER FUNCTION GCD(M, N)
*----------------------------------------------------------*
*  Calculate the greatest common divisor of two integers.  *
*----------------------------------------------------------*
      INTEGER M, N, M1, N1, REMAIN
*----------------------------------------------------------*
*     M1 and N1 may change, but M and N will not.          *
*----------------------------------------------------------*
      M1 = M
      N1 = N
*----------------------------------------------------------*
*                 Euclid's algorithm                       *
*----------------------------------------------------------*
      REMAIN = MOD(M1, N1)
11    IF (REMAIN .NE. 0) THEN
         M1 = N1
         N1 = REMAIN
         REMAIN = MOD(M1, N1)
         GO TO 11
      END IF
*----------------------------------------------------------*
*               Assign value to GCD.                       *
*----------------------------------------------------------*
      GCD = N1

      END
```

Notice that M and N are used only to give values to M1 and N1. In particular, M and N never assume new values, so the function GCD cannot change values in the main program.

Local Variables

Recall that a variable name is really a symbolic name for an address or storage location in the computer. A symbolic address known only to the program unit that includes it is called a **local variable**, or is said to be **local** to that program unit. A variable used as a dummy argument or an actual argument is not local to any one program unit. The point of having local variables is protection. A local variable cannot affect values of variables in other program units, and conversely, other program units cannot affect their values.

The variables M1, N1, and REMAIN above are local to GCD. If the main program happened to contain a variable named M1, for example, the computer would have two entirely separate storage areas for the two variables named M1. One of these areas could be accessed only by the main program, the other only by the subprogram.

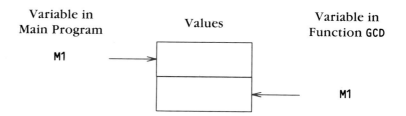

This fact is important, because it allows programmers to write subprograms without knowing anything about the variable names used in the invoking program. Only the number of arguments and their types must be known.

Example 9.5 A Function to Calculate Combinations

We can rewrite many of our previous programs as functions. Take, for instance, the program of Example 4.9, which calculates the number of ways *K* objects can be chosen from a set of *N* objects. That program began with the declaration

```
INTEGER  N, K, COMBIN, DEN, MAXI, MINI
```

where COMBIN is the calculated number. To turn the program into a function, let the function name be COMBIN. N and K are the dummy arguments, and DEN, MAXI, and MINI are local variables. Then the function name statement and declarations are

```
INTEGER  FUNCTION COMBIN(N, K)
INTEGER  DEN, MAXI, MINI
```

The body of the function could be the same as the body of the program, with PRINT statements removed:

```
MAXI = MAX(K, N-K)
MINI = MIN(K, N-K)
```

```
      COMBIN = 1
      DO 11 DEN = 1, MINI
         COMBIN = COMBIN * (DEN + MAXI) / DEN
11    CONTINUE

      END
```

However, most programmers avoid using the function name in expressions and prefer to assign the name a value only once. Therefore, an auxiliary variable C replaces COMBIN until the end of the program, when COMBIN is assigned the final value of C. The function subprogram appears as Program 9.5.

■
PROGRAM 9.5

```
      INTEGER  FUNCTION COMBIN(N, K)
*----------------------------------------------------------*
*       Calculate binomial coefficient C(N, K) of          *
*       two positive integers N and K with N >= K.         *
*----------------------------------------------------------*
      INTEGER  DEN, MAXI, MINI, C
*----------------------------------------------------------*
*  Cancel the larger of k! and (n-k)! from the numerator.  *
*----------------------------------------------------------*
      MAXI = MAX(K, N-K)
      MINI = MIN(K, N-K)

      C = 1
      DO 11 DEN = 1, MINI
         C = C * (DEN + MAXI) / DEN
11    CONTINUE

      COMBIN = C

      END
```

One of the exercises at the end of this chapter asks you to write a program that calls this function.

Adjustable and Assumed-Size Arrays

Often a program must pass an entire array to a subprogram. When this occurs, only the array *name* appears in the actual argument list in the main program, as in

```
REAL    A(100), SMALL, Y
INTEGER N
        .
        .
        .
Y = SMALL(A, N)
```

The function SMALL returns the smallest value in the list A(1), A(2), . . ., A(N). The function name statement must then include two arguments: a real array name and an integer variable name.

We have been saying that the actual arguments and dummy arguments must agree in number and type. In fact, they must agree in number, type, and *structure*. Suitable function name and type declaration statements in the function are

```
REAL FUNCTION SMALL(X, M)
REAL    X(100)
INTEGER M
```

Again, only the name of the array X is used in the dummy argument list for SMALL. However, X must be defined to be an array in a type declaration (or DIMENSION) statement.

Notice that array X contains 100 elements, exactly the same number as array A in the main program. Therefore, the function SMALL can be used only by programs that pass an array with 100 elements, severely restricting the programs that can use SMALL. However, Fortran contains two devices that allow array arguments of subprograms to take on a size compatible with the corresponding array in the main program.

The first such device is called an **assumed-size array**, whose size is given in the subprogram by an asterisk, as in

```
REAL FUNCTION SMALL(X, M)
REAL X(*)
```

Assumed-size arrays are allowed only in subprograms, never in main programs. When the function is called, the size of the array X will be the same size as the actual array argument corresponding to X. A program with any size array can now call SMALL.

The asterisk can stand for only the *upper* bound of the array size. For example, REAL X(0:*) is permitted, but REAL X(*:100) is not. Also, if the array has more than one dimension, the asterisk can be used for only the *last* dimension, as in REAL Y(100, *). It is not legal to have REAL Y(*, 100).

The second device is called an **adjustable array**, in which a dummy argument specifies the size of the array in the subprogram. Again with the function SMALL, an example of an adjustable array is

```
REAL FUNCTION SMALL(X, M)
INTEGER M
REAL    X(M)
```

In the invoking program, array A has 100 elements. However, in one run of the program, the number of elements actually used could be designated by N. (The user could be asked, "How many numbers in your list?" and the response stored in N.) If the value of N is 15 when the function SMALL is called, then the value of M in the subprogram is 15, so X will be an array with fifteen elements. The size of an adjustable array cannot be *larger* than the size of the corresponding actual array argument, but it can be *smaller*.

We shall use adjustable arrays rather than assumed-size arrays in functions, so the function will have a value for the array size.

Example 9.6 A Function to Find the Smallest Value in an Array

We have already written a program to find the smallest value in a list. Here the main concern is the use of an adjustable array in a subprogram. The main program contains an array A dimensioned by REAL A(100). The program asks the user for the number of elements in the array, assigns this value to the variable N, then reads the array elements. The program calls the function SMALL to calculate the smallest element of A, passing the actual arguments A and N. The function SMALL has dummy arguments X and M, with M declared INTEGER and X declared REAL X(M). Program 9.6 has the main program and function.

■
PROGRAM 9.6
_____

```
      PROGRAM CALLSM
*------------------------------------------------------------*
* Read a real array and call SMALL to find smallest value. *
*------------------------------------------------------------*
      REAL    A(100), SMALL, X
      INTEGER N, I
```

```
*-----------------------------------------------------*
*              Ask how many numbers will be given.     *
*-----------------------------------------------------*
      PRINT *, 'Program finds smallest number in a list.'
      PRINT *, 'How many numbers? '
      READ  *, N
*-----------------------------------------------------*
*                  Read the numbers.                   *
*-----------------------------------------------------*
      DO 11 I = 1, N
         PRINT *, 'Number?'
         READ *, A(I)
  11  CONTINUE
*-----------------------------------------------------*
*              Call SMALL to find smallest number.     *
*-----------------------------------------------------*
      X = SMALL(A, N)
      PRINT 10, X
  10  FORMAT ('0The smallest number is', F10.2)

      END
*****************************************************************
      REAL  FUNCTION SMALL(X, M)
*-----------------------------------------------------*
*   Calculate smallest in a list of M real numbers.    *
*-----------------------------------------------------*
      INTEGER  M, I
      REAL     X(M)

      SMALL = X(1)
      DO 11 I = 2, M
         SMALL = MIN(X(I), SMALL)
  11  CONTINUE

      END
```

Example 9.7 Counting the Number of Strings Following a Given String

Program 9.7 displays another function using an array. This time, the array contains character data, and the function counts the number of array items that follow a given value. We will assume that all array elements are words composed of uppercase letters, so here *follow* means *come after, in alphabetical order*. The problem is quite simple. The main point is the mechanics of passing character data.

Passing Character Data

Passing character data resembles passing arrays; the subprogram must know the length of character strings, just as it must know the number of items in an array. The strings could be declared with a constant length, 20 for example, in both the subprogram and the invoking program. Then, however, the subprogram could be used only with programs that pass strings of length 20. Fortran allows subprograms to use **passed-length** character declarations for dummy arguments, a method much like passing assumed-size arrays. If NAME is a dummy character argument, it can be declared as

```
CHARACTER NAME*(*)
```

or

```
CHARACTER*(*) NAME
```

The asterisk inside parentheses indicates that NAME will take the length of the corresponding actual argument. This device can be used only in subprograms, not in main programs.

Let the function COUNT receive a character array A with N items, and let GIVEN be the given string. Then A and GIVEN can both be given passed lengths with the declaration

```
CHARACTER A(N)*(*), GIVEN*(*)
```

Notice that array A has adjustable size N, and each element of A has a passed length. GIVEN also has passed length, which may be different from the passed length of the elements in A. The remaining function code is quite simple, as shown in Program 9.7.

■

PROGRAM 9.7

```
      INTEGER FUNCTION COUNT(A, N, GIVEN)
*-----------------------------------------------------*
*    Count number of strings following a given        *
*    string value in alphabetical order.              *
*-----------------------------------------------------*
      INTEGER   N, I, C
      CHARACTER A(N)*(*), GIVEN*(*)
```

```
      C = 0
      DO 11 I = 1, N
         IF (A(I) .GT. GIVEN) C = C + 1
11    CONTINUE

      COUNT = C

      END
```

We do not present an entire invoking program, but suppose the program has the declarations

```
      INTEGER   NAFTER, SIZE, COUNT
      CHARACTER WORD(100)*20,   STRING*10
```

where NAFTER is to be the number of array elements in WORD that follow the value of STRING in alphabetical order, and SIZE is the number of elements in WORD that are given values. The function COUNT can be invoked with the statement

```
      NAFTER = COUNT(WORD, SIZE, STRING)
```

The argument correspondence should be obvious, but it is a good idea to be very explicit about this correspondence when you use subprograms, since so many errors are caused by mismatched arguments.

Actual Argument	Dummy Argument	Type (and Structure)
WORD	A	Character array
SIZE	N	Integer
STRING	GIVEN	Character

Also worth stressing: COUNT must be declared INTEGER in the invoking program. If COUNT were REAL in the invoking program, a type mismatch would occur because the main program considers COUNT to be REAL while the function considers COUNT to be INTEGER. Depending on your version of Fortran, the type mismatch could cause an error message or an incorrect value for COUNT in the main program.

Example 9.8 A Logical External Function

A logical function is a function that returns one of the logical values, .TRUE. or .FALSE.. The following logical statement function ORDER takes the value .TRUE. if three real numbers X, Y, and Z are in either increasing or decreasing numerical order.

```
      ORDER(X, Y, Z) = (X .LE. Y) .AND. (Y .LE. Z)
     1                 .OR. (X .GE. Y) .AND. (Y .GE. Z)
```

We can use the function ORDER to build an external logical function SORTED that determines whether an array of real numbers is in numerical order, either increasing or decreasing.

The external function can use ORDER with actual arguments

```
        A(1), A(2), A(3)
```

then with

```
        A(2), A(3), A(4)
```

and

```
        A(3), A(4), A(5)
```

and so on, up to

```
        A(N-2), A(N-1), A(N)
```

If any set of actual arguments causes ORDER to return the value .FALSE., then the array is not sorted. We could use a DO loop with index I running from 2 to N − 1, and call ORDER with arguments A(I−1), A(I), and A(I+1). This method will work, but the DO loop would run to completion even if the first three elements were not in order.

It is preferable to use a loop that will stop when any three consecutive elements are out of order, or a while loop. We can let the logical variable SORT begin with value .TRUE. and, inside the loop, assign SORT the value of .FALSE. whenever ORDER returns a value of .FALSE.. Then the index variable I starts with value 2, and the while loop begins

```
11      IF (SORT .AND. I .LT. N) THEN
```

That is, continue the loop as long as SORT has not been assigned the value .FALSE. and there are elements remaining to be compared. The function subprogram is shown in Program 9.8.

■

PROGRAM 9.8

```
      LOGICAL FUNCTION SORTED(A, N)
*------------------------------------------------------------*
*  Return the value .TRUE. if an array A of N real           *
*  numbers is in either increasing or decreasing order.      *
*------------------------------------------------------------*
      INTEGER N
      REAL    A(N), X, Y, Z
      LOGICAL SORT, ORDER
      ORDER(X, Y, Z) = (X .LE. Y) .AND. (Y .LE. Z)
     1           .OR. (X .GE. Y) .AND. (Y .GE. Z)

      SORT = .TRUE.
      I = 2
11    IF (SORT .AND. I .LT. N) THEN
          IF (ORDER( A(I-1), A(I), A(I+1) ) )THEN
              I = I + 1
          ELSE
              SORT = .FALSE.
          END IF
          GO TO 11
      END IF

      SORTED = SORT

      END
```

■

9.2 SUMMARY OF CHAPTER 9

■ *Terms Introduced in This Chapter*

Actual argument
Adjustable array
Assumed-size array
Dummy argument
External function
Function name statement
Greatest common divisor

Local variables
Passing arguments
  by address
  by location
  by reference
Program system
Program unit
Side effects

■ *What You Should Know*

1. User-defined functions are either statement functions or function subprograms. Function subprograms are also known as external functions.

2. A user-defined function returns a value in its name, so the function name should be given a type in the invoking program.

3. An external function should be given a type in the function name statement. Be sure that type matches the type in the invoking program.

4. The generic intrinsic functions do not follow the implicit typing scheme, and so should not be declared in a program that uses them. For example, MAX returns a real value if its arguments are real, and ABS returns an integer value if its argument is an integer.

5. Actual arguments of functions must correspond to dummy arguments in number, type, and structure.

6. Dummy arguments must be variable names, but actual arguments can be variable names, constants, or expressions.

7. A function subprogram can have an array name for an argument, but a statement function cannot.

8. User-defined functions cannot have array elements as dummy arguments.

9. A program unit is either a program, a function subprogram, or a subroutine.

10. A local variable is an address whose contents can be changed only by the program unit in which it is defined.

11. Changes in a local variable in one program unit cannot cause changes in variables in other program units.

12. The purpose of a function is the calculation of one value. Avoid side effects.

13. You can protect variables used as actual arguments from side effects by avoiding the assignment of values to dummy arguments.

14. External functions can be compiled separately from, or together with, an invoking program.

15. An external function can contain a statement function.

16. A function cannot invoke itself, nor can it invoke another program unit that invokes it.

17. Declare all variables used in a program unit in that unit. Check carefully to see that actual and dummy arguments have matching types.

■

9.3 EXERCISES

■ *Self-Test*

1. True or false

   a.   A dummy argument in an external function can be an array name.
   b.   An actual argument for a function can be an array element.
   c.   A subprogram must be compiled with the program that calls it.
   d.   External functions always return real or integer values.
   e.   A dummy argument for a function can be an expression.
   f.   A function subprogram can have the same name as a variable in the invoking program.

2. Are the following statements valid or invalid in Fortran? If invalid, explain why.

   a.   REAL FUNCTION HALF(WHOLE/2)
   b.   REAL FUNCTION(X, N)
   c.   AVERAGE = MEAN(X, Y, X(1))
   d.   Y = REAL SQUARE(A, B)

3. The following problems show certain statements from a main program and others from a function invoked by the main program. Specify valid or invalid. If invalid, explain why.

	Main Program	Function
a.	REAL R, A	REAL FUNCTION AREA(RAD, A)
	CALL AREA(R, A)	REAL RAD, AREA
b.	REAL A, B, Z	REAL FUNCTION QUIRK(D, X, Y)
	CHARACTER * 12 NAME	REAL X, Y
	Z = QUIRK(A, B, NAME)	CHARACTER * 12 D
c.	REAL X(100), Y	REAL FUNCTION MEAN(A, SIZE)
	INTEGER N	INTEGER SIZE
	Y = MEAN(X, N)	REAL A(200)
d.	INTEGER N	REAL FUNCTION POWER(A, B)
	REAL X	REAL B
	CALL POWER(X, N)	INTEGER A
e.	INTEGER X, Y, RIT	INTEGER FUNCTION RIT(ON, TO)
	WRITE (12, 10) RIT(X, Y)	INTEGER ON, TO
	10 FORMAT (1X, 'XY = ', I5)	WRITE (12, *) 'Here we are.'

```
f.        REAL    X(100), Y       REAL FUNCTION MEAN(Y, X)
          INTEGER N               INTEGER X
          Y = MEAN(X, N)          REAL Y(100)
```

■ *Programming Exercises*

1. A main program is:

```
PROGRAM GETAVG
INTEGER N, I
REAL X(100), XBAR, MEAN

OPEN (15, FILE = 'DATA1', STATUS = 'OLD')
READ (15, *) N
READ (15, *) (X(I), I = 1, N)

XBAR = MEAN(X, N)
PRINT *, 'The mean of the list is', XBAR

END
```

   Write a subprogram that will calculate the mean of the array.

2. Write a program that reads two positive integers M and J with J < M and invokes the function COMBIN to calculate the number of ways to choose J items from a set of M items.

3. The **least common multiple** (lcm) of two positive integers M and N is the smallest integer L that has both M and N as factors. Write a program to calculate the lcm of two positive integers, using the GCD (greatest common divisor) function.

4. Write an external function to calculate the factorial of a positive integer, and a program to invoke the function.

5. Write an external function to calculate the median of a real array X with N elements. The median of a sorted array of N numbers is the middle number if N is odd, and is the mean of the two middle numbers if N is even. You may assume the array is sorted. Write a program to read an array and invoke this function.

6. At Piedmont College, a normal credit load is defined to be from 14 through 18 credits per semester. The tuition charge for a normal load is $2,000. For fewer than 14 credits, the charge is $150 per credit. For more than 18 credits, the charge is $2,000 plus $100 for each credit above 18. Write a function to calculate the tuition charge for a given number of credits, and a main program that reads the number of credits for several students and invokes the function to calculate each charge.

7. A teacher gives five tests in a year, and calculates the final numerical average for every student by dropping the student's lowest grade and taking the mean of the remaining four grades. Write a function FINAL that returns the final average, given the five test grades. Write a program that reads a file with each record containing the

name and five test grades, invokes the function FINAL to get the final average, and calls LETGRD to figure the course grade. Output should include each student's name, final average, and course grade.

8. Write a logical function PRIME that receives a positive integer and returns .TRUE. if that integer is prime, and otherwise returns .FALSE..

10 SUBROUTINES

Subroutines, like functions, can be building blocks in large program systems. Some subroutines, such as sort subroutines, will be useful to many programs. Once written and tested, these subroutines are available for use by any program. Other subroutines are useful to only one program, but these subroutines still serve the important purpose of breaking a large problem into smaller parts.

10.1 SUBROUTINES

Subroutines differ from functions in that subroutines do not return a single value, but usually modify more than one of the values in the actual argument list.

The Subroutine Name Statement

A subroutine begins with a **subroutine name statement** of the form

        SUBROUTINE *<name>*(*<dummy argument list>*)

The subroutine name is not used as a variable in the subroutine, so subroutines do not have data types.

The CALL Statement

Since a subroutine does not return a single value, programs do not invoke subroutines the same way thay invoke functions. The program unit that uses the subroutine contains a CALL **statement** of the form

$$CALL <name>(<actual\ argument\ list>)$$

All the rules concerning number, order, type, and structure of variables in the two argument lists are the same for subroutines as they are for functions.

When a program calls a subroutine, control passes to the subroutine. At the end of the subroutine, control passes back to the calling program at the first executable statement *after* the CALL statement. Recall that, with a function, control passes back to the invoking statement itself. The passing of control is simpler with subroutines because control comes back to the main program at the beginning of a new statement, not in the middle of the calling statement. In particular, it is safe to print in a subroutine without worrying about the calling program.

Example 10.1 Subroutine to Swap Integer Values

Program 10.1 is a simple example of a subroutine that swaps the values of two integer variables; actual arguments in the calling program.

■
PROGRAM 10.1

```
      PROGRAM CALLSW
*-----------------------------------------------------------*
*  Ask for two integers and call SWAP to interchange them.  *
*-----------------------------------------------------------*
      INTEGER   N1, N2

      PRINT *, 'Enter two integers.'
      READ  *, N1, N2

      CALL SWAP(N1, N2)

      PRINT *, 'Here are the numbers in reverse order.'
      PRINT *, N1, N2

      END
*-----------------------------------------------------------*
      SUBROUTINE  SWAP(ONE, TWO)
*-----------------------------------------------------------*
*            Swap values of two integer variables.          *
*-----------------------------------------------------------*
      INTEGER  ONE, TWO, TEMP
```

```
      TEMP = ONE
      ONE  = TWO
      TWO  = TEMP

      END
```

When the program calls the subroutine, the actual argument N1 is paired with the dummy argument ONE, and N2 is paired with TWO. Swapping values of ONE and TWO then swaps the values N1 and N2.

As with functions, subroutines can either follow the main program in the same file or occupy a separate file. Subroutines that apply to only one program should be stored with that program. Subroutines that may serve several programs should be kept in separate files. When you are developing programs, it is probably easier for you to keep the program and subroutine in the same file.

Example 10.2 An Instruction Subroutine

An instruction subroutine is an example of a subroutine with no arguments. If a program must give a lengthy set of instructions to the user, it makes sense to put these instructions in a subroutine and have the program call the subroutine. The program structure will then be clearer because only a single statement,

```
      CALL INSTR
```

appears in the main program, in place of the many lines of instructions. The subroutine INSTR consists entirely of output statements. An example appears in Program 10.2

■

PROGRAM 10.2

```
      SUBROUTINE INSTR
*-----------------------------------------------------------------*
*  This subroutine gives instructions for playing tic-tac-toe. *
*-----------------------------------------------------------------*
      PRINT *
      PRINT *, 'This program will play tic-tac-toe with you.'
      PRINT *, 'The board is arranged like this:'
      PRINT *
```

```
PRINT *, '     1 | 2 | 3 '
PRINT *, '    ----------- '
PRINT *, '     4 | 5 | 6 '
PRINT *, '    ----------- '
PRINT *, '     7 | 8 | 9 '
PRINT *
PRINT *, 'When you are asked for a move, choose a number'
PRINT *, 'from 1 through 9.'
PRINT *

END
```

This subroutine is obviously useful only to a program that plays tic-tac-toe. The idea, however, is useful in any program that requires a long list of instructions.

A subroutine cannot run by itself, so testing a subroutine requires a calling program. A simple program, written exclusively to test subprograms, is a **driver**. A driver for the instruction subroutine can be a very simple program:

```
PROGRAM DRIVER

CALL INSTR

END
```

Reading and Writing Arrays

Programs often must read data from a file into an array, and equally often must write arrays as output. This section presents two subroutines to perform these tasks. These subroutines, perhaps with modifications of your choosing, will be very useful in nearly every one of your programs that deals with arrays.

Example 10.3 A Subroutine to Read from a File

The simple subroutine presented here asks the user for the file name, opens the file, and reads the data into a real array A, counting the number of array elements and storing this value in the variable SIZE. The subroutine assumes the file has one real value per record.

The subroutine is named `READAR`, so the subroutine name statement is

```
SUBROUTINE READAR(A, SIZE)
```

It seems natural to use an adjustable array, as we have been doing, and write declarations such as

```
INTEGER  SIZE
REAL     A(SIZE)
```

However, we must think about the situation in the calling program when this subroutine is invoked. What values would be passed to the dummy arguments `A` and `SIZE`? The calling program would not have assigned any values to the actual arguments, because that is the point of the subprogram. `READAR` does not receive any data from the calling program, but it reads data (values for `A` and `SIZE`) and passes the data back to the calling program.

If the actual argument corresponding to `SIZE` was not initialized, `SIZE` could be zero or some negative integer when `READAR` is called. Then the declaration `REAL A(SIZE)` will be an error; an array cannot have zero or negative size. The way out of this problem is to use an assumed-size array, as in

```
REAL  A(*)
```

This illustrates our rule for deciding whether to use adjustable or assumed-size arrays in a subprogram:

1. Use an adjustable array when the calling program has a value for the actual size of the array, and passes it to the subprogram. The subprogram should not change the value.
2. Use an assumed-size array when the calling program does not have a value for the actual size of the array, and requires the subprogram to calculate this value.

The body of the subprogram reads the file, storing entries in the array `A`, until the end of the file is reached. An integer variable `I` serves as a counter and as the subscript on `A`. `I` takes the initial value 1, and `A(I)` is read. Each time a value `A(I)` is read, `I` increases by 1. When the end of the file is reached, `I` has been incremented in preparation for reading a new value. Since there is no new value, `I` now has value 1 more than the number of values in the file. Therefore, `SIZE` is assigned the final value of `I` minus 1. The code for this is

```
                      I = 1
             11     READ (9, *, END = 22)  A(I)
                        I = I + 1
                    GO TO 11

             22    SIZE = I - 1
```

Program 10.3 shows the entire subroutine.

■
PROGRAM 10.3

```
      SUBROUTINE READAR(A, SIZE)
*-----------------------------------------------------------------*
*          1. Ask for the name of a data file that holds a list of    *
*             real numbers, one number per record.                    *
*          2. Open the file and read to the end, storing the numbers  *
*             in the array A.                                          *
*          3. Calculate the number, SIZE, of the elements in the file. *
*-----------------------------------------------------------------*
      INTEGER    SIZE, I
      REAL       A(*)
      CHARACTER  FILNAM * 13
*-----------------------------------------------------------------*
*          Get the file name and open the file.                       *
*-----------------------------------------------------------------*
      PRINT *, 'What is the name of the data file? '
      READ '(A)', FILNAM

      OPEN (9, FILE = FILNAM, STATUS = 'OLD')
*-----------------------------------------------------------------*
*          Read and count the values in the file.                     *
*-----------------------------------------------------------------*
      I = 1
11    READ (9, *, END = 22)  A(I)
          I = I + 1
      GO TO 11

22    SIZE = I - 1

      CLOSE (9)

      END
```

This is certainly not the most general READ subroutine, but it is useful. Whenever you are developing a program that reads values into an array, put the array values into a file instead of having the program read them from the terminal. You can create the data file with an editor or a Fortran program. Then you will not have the tedious task of entering all the array values each time you run the program to test it. It is also a simple matter to modify the file to generate different data sets to test the program.

Ordinarily, for each subroutine we write, we show a short program that calls the subroutine. We postpone the program to call READAR until after the next example, which gives a subroutine to write an array.

Example 10.4 A Subroutine to Write an Array

You will write an array about as often as you read one, because you should echo input data to ensure that the program is reading them correctly. The problem in writing an array is formatting. It is permissible to write one array element per line, but then you cannot see the entire array on the terminal screen if the array is of moderate size. One value per line would also waste a lot of paper when the program prints a hardcopy.

In special cases, you can "custom fit" the format to the data. If all values have one or two digits before and two digits after the decimal point, then a 10F8.2 data descriptor will print ten values per line, with at least two spaces between values. For 80-column output, an 8F10.2 descriptor often works well too.

The E descriptor will fit all valid real data. While many scientists and engineers would use it, many other people do not find the exponential format pleasing. An alternative is the G data descriptor, which prints moderate values in decimal notation, but switches to E format for large or small values. In the subroutine in Program 10.4, we use a G12.4 descriptor and a space between values. Each value then takes 13 columns, so six values can be written in an 80-column line with a 6(1X, G12.4) format.

■

PROGRAM 10.4

```
      SUBROUTINE WRITAR(A, SIZE)
*---------------------------------------------------------------*
*  Receive a real array A, and the number SIZE of elements      *
*  in the array.  Write the array in G12.4 format.              *
*---------------------------------------------------------------*
      INTEGER   SIZE, I
      REAL      A(SIZE)
```

```
       PRINT *
       PRINT *, SIZE, ' elements in this array:'
       PRINT *
       PRINT 10, (A(I), I = 1, SIZE)
10     FORMAT ( 6(1X, G12.4) )

       END
```

The G descriptor does not always give beautiful output. Decimal points may not line up, and some numbers may be written in exponential notation. Nevertheless, the G descriptor is sturdy; it handles all real data without producing strings of asterisks and error messages. If all numbers are of comparable size, the output is quite neat. It is well suited to echoing real data.

Here is a driver program for READAR and WRITAR. The output from the program lines up nicely because all the numbers are between 10 and 20. We will see more output from WRITAR later.

```
       PROGRAM REDWRT
       REAL      X(200)
       INTEGER   N

       CALL READAR(X, N)
       CALL WRITAR(X, N)

       END
```

Output from this program is

```
What is the name of the data file? STATFL

        23 elements in this array:
    12.50         13.60         14.80         15.30         15.20         18.30
    12.40         19.30         16.30         17.20         18.40         19.20
    14.30         15.60         16.50         17.60         18.10         19.30
    12.10         13.50         14.60         15.20         16.30
```

Sorting Subroutines

Our previous programs can supply some useful subroutines as well as functions. A sort procedure is a particularly useful subroutine because the sorting problem arises in so many applications. Here we show how to turn our earlier sort program into a subroutine, and give an example of another sorting method called Shell sort.

Example 10.5 A Sort Subroutine

The sort subroutine SORTRL in Program 10.5 uses the sort code from Program 8.6. SORTRL has two dummy arguments, a real array X and an integer N. The array X is declared with adjustable size N.

■

PROGRAM 10.5

```
      SUBROUTINE SORTRL(X, N)
*------------------------------------------------------------*
*  Sort a list X of N real numbers into increasing order.  *
*------------------------------------------------------------*
      INTEGER   POS, I, K, N
      REAL      X(N), SMALL
*------------------------------------------------------------*
*  Main sort loop; repeat for every position but the last.*
*------------------------------------------------------------*
      DO 22 K = 1, N-1
*------------------------------------------------------------*
*          Initialize SMALL and its position.            *
*------------------------------------------------------------*
         SMALL = X(K)
         POS = K
*------------------------------------------------------------*
*  Interior loop; find smallest number and its position.  *
*------------------------------------------------------------*
         DO 11 I = K+1, N
            IF (SMALL .GT. X(I) ) THEN
               SMALL = X(I)
               POS = I
            END IF
11       CONTINUE
*------------------------------------------------------------*
*          Switch smallest number with X(K).            *
*------------------------------------------------------------*
         X(POS) = X(K)
         X(K)   = SMALL

22    CONTINUE

      END
```

The driver to use this subroutine also will use the subroutines READAR and WRITAR. The driver is very simple because we have already done most of the work by writing the subroutines READAR, WRITAR, and SORTRL.

```
PROGRAM CALLSO

REAL     X(200)
INTEGER  N

CALL READAR(X, N)
PRINT *, 'Original data'
CALL WRITAR(X, N)

CALL SORTRL(X, N)
PRINT *
PRINT *, 'Sorted data'
CALL WRITAR(X, N)

END
```

Example 10.6 The Shell Sort Subroutine

The subroutine SORTRL does a reasonable job of sorting small arrays of numbers. It should sort 100 numbers in less than a second, not enough time to make you impatient. But sorting 10,000 numbers would take SORTRL several minutes, which can seem like eternity to someone sitting and staring at a terminal screen.

We present here an advanced sorting method known as the **Shell sort** in honor of its originator, Donald Shell. The Shell sort typically can sort 10,000 numbers in less than two seconds (depending, as always, on the computer involved).

Instead of comparing adjacent numbers, such as A(I) and A(I+1), the Shell method compares numbers a certain gap apart: A(I) and A(I + gap). The gap begins with value equal to half the number of items to be sorted. Then the gap is successively cut in half until it becomes 1. We illustrate the method for a list of seven numbers to be sorted into ascending order. Suppose the numbers are:

A(1)	A(2)	A(3)	A(4)	A(5)	A(6)	A(7)
13.6	12.4	17.5	9.3	2.7	6.2	4.9

First the gap is 7 / 2 = 3. (Use integer division by 2 to cut a gap in half, or as close to half as possible.) Then compare array elements whose subscripts are three units apart. That is, compare A(1) to A(4), A(2) to A(5), A(3) to A(6), and finally A(4) to A(7). The comparisons proceed as follows.

		Resulting values of						
Comparison	Swap?	A(1)	A(2)	A(3)	A(4)	A(5)	A(6)	A(7)
< Beginning values >		**13.6**	12.4	17.5	**9.3**	2.7	6.2	4.9
A(1) to A(4)	Yes	9.3	**12.4**	17.5	13.6	**2.7**	6.2	4.9
A(2) to A(5)	Yes	9.3	2.7	**17.5**	13.6	12.4	**6.2**	4.9
A(3) to A(6)	Yes	9.3	2.7	6.2	**13.6**	12.4	17.5	**4.9**
A(4) to A(7)	Yes	9.3	2.7	6.2	4.9	12.4	17.5	13.6

We are not yet finished with gap 3. Notice, for example, that A(1) and A(4) are still not in their proper order. Therefore, repeat the same process with gap 3:

		Resulting values of						
Comparison	Swap?	A(1)	A(2)	A(3)	A(4)	A(5)	A(6)	A(7)
< Beginning values >		**9.3**	2.7	6.2	**4.9**	12.4	17.5	13.6
A(1) to A(4)	Yes	4.9	**2.7**	6.2	9.3	**12.4**	17.5	13.6
A(2) to A(5)	No	4.9	2.7	**6.2**	9.3	12.4	**17.5**	13.6
A(3) to A(6)	No	4.9	2.7	6.2	**9.3**	12.4	17.5	**13.6**
A(4) to A(7)	No	4.9	2.7	6.2	9.3	12.4	17.5	13.6

Comparing elements a gap 3 apart, we see that they are all in proper order, so we do not have to write anything new. We do have to do all the comparisons mentally, and a program also will have to do the actual comparisons one final time. We know we are finished with a particular gap when we do all the comparisons for that gap and find that no swaps have to be made.

Now cut the gap in half, and compare elements with subscripts one unit apart. That is, compare A(1) to A(2), A(2) to A(3), and so on. The results of the comparisons with gap 1 are as follows.

Comparison	Swap?	Resulting values of					
		A(1)	A(2)	A(3)	A(4)	A(5)	A(6)
<Beginning values>		**4.9**	**2.7**	6.2	9.3	12.4	17.5
A(1) to A(2)	Yes	2.7	**4.9**	**6.2**	9.3	12.4	17.5
A(2) to A(3)	No	2.7	4.9	**6.2**	**9.3**	12.4	17.5
A(3) to A(4)	No	2.7	4.9	6.2	**9.3**	**12.4**	17.5
A(4) to A(5)	No	2.7	4.9	6.2	9.3	**12.4**	**17.5**
A(5) to A(6)	No	2.7	4.9	6.2	9.3	12.4	**17.5**
A(6) to A(7)	Yes	2.7	4.9	6.2	9.3	12.4	13.6

A glance at the numbers shows they are now sorted, so we are finished. Remember that we actually have to make all comparisons with gap 1 again before we *know* we are finished.

The subroutine must receive an array (which we call A) and the size (N) of the array. An outline of the Shell subroutine is:

1. Set the gap to N.
2. Repeat until the gap is 1:

    a. Cut the gap in half.
    b. Sort elements one gap apart.

Part 2b is the most complicated. Using I as an array subscript and GAP for the gap value, we can refine it into the following outline:

2b. Repeat until the numbers one gap apart are sorted: For all pairs of subscripts I and I + GAP, compare A(I) and A(I + GAP) and, if necessary, swap them.

The code for the last sentence is a DO loop containing an IF block. Since we are comparing A(I) and A(I + GAP), the terminal value of I should be N − GAP. Inside the IF block, swap the values of A(I) and A(I + GAP), using a temporary storage variable TEMP:

```
      DO 33 I = 1, N - GAP
        IF ( A(I) .GE. A(I + GAP) ) THEN
          TEMP        = A(I)
          A(I)        = A(I + GAP)
          A(I + GAP) = TEMP
        END IF
33    CONTINUE
```

Notice that I + GAP occurs three times. We will replace I + GAP with the variable NEXT, to make the code both easier for us to read and faster for the computer to execute.

Part 2b tells us to repeat this loop until the elements one gap apart are sorted. We use a logical variable SORTED to indicate that this is the case. Then part 2b is a while loop beginning with

```
IF (.NOT. SORTED) THEN
```

Just before this IF block, we assign SORTED the value .FALSE. to force the loop body to execute at least one time. SORTED will indicate whether a swap was made when comparing values, so immediately after

```
IF (.NOT. SORTED)
```

we assign SORTED the value .TRUE. because no swaps have yet been made. Whenever a swap is made, SORTED should become .FALSE.; therefore, before the code to swap values, we assign SORTED the value .FALSE.. Part 2b now looks like this:

```
        SORTED = .FALSE.
22      IF (.NOT. SORTED) THEN
            SORTED = .TRUE.

            DO 33 I = 1, N - GAP

              NEXT = I + GAP
              IF ( A(I) .GE. A(NEXT) ) THEN
                    SORTED  = .FALSE.
                    TEMP    = A(I)
                    A(I)    = A(NEXT)
                    A(NEXT) = TEMP
              END IF

33          CONTINUE

            GO TO 22
        END IF
```

Part 2 is simply a while loop beginning

```
IF (GAP .GT. 1) THEN
```

The entire subroutine body is this IF block. One final minor change: we introduce the variable TOP to represent N - GAP. See Program 10.6 for the complete SHELL sort subroutine.

■

PROGRAM 10.6

```fortran
      SUBROUTINE   SHELL(A, N)
*------------------------------------------------------------*
*  Perform the Shell sort (ascending) on a list A of N       *
*  real numbers.  Start with GAP = N / 2 and compare         *
*  elements a GAP apart, and swap if necessary.  Repeat      *
*  with the same GAP value until all values a GAP apart      *
*  are in their proper order.  Then cut GAP in half and      *
*  repeat the process.  Continue until the GAP is 1.         *
*------------------------------------------------------------*
      INTEGER   N, GAP, TOP, I, NEXT
      LOGICAL   SORTED
      REAL      A(N), TEMP

      GAP = N
11    IF (GAP .GT. 1) THEN
         GAP    = GAP / 2
         TOP    = N - GAP
         SORTED = .FALSE.

22       IF (.NOT. SORTED) THEN
            SORTED = .TRUE.

            DO 33 I = 1, TOP

               NEXT = I + GAP
               IF ( A(I) .GE. A(NEXT) ) THEN
                  SORTED  = .FALSE.
                  TEMP    = A(I)
                  A(I)    = A(NEXT)
                  A(NEXT) = TEMP
               END IF

33          CONTINUE

            GO TO 22

         END IF

         GO TO 11

      END IF

      END
```

■

10.2 PROGRAM SYSTEMS

The last driver program could easily call SHELL instead of SORTRL. In either case, this driver program with the subroutines READAR, WRITAR, and a sort subroutine, is a useful program system. In this section we construct two larger systems, one to merge two arrays and one to perform statistical summaries for an array of data.

Merging Arrays

A standard programming problem is **merging** two arrays, which means using two sorted arrays to create a new sorted array that contains all values in the original arrays. We call the original arrays A and B and the merged array C. The number of elements in these arrays will be called NA, NB, and NC. The problem states that A and B are *sorted*, and we assume that means *sorted into ascending order*. Then we want C also to be sorted into ascending order. Is the statement of the problem clear?

Consider a small example with NA = 3 and NB = 4:

A(1)	A(2)	A(3)		B(1)	B(2)	B(3)	B(4)
2.1	3.5	8.7		4.2	5.8	8.7	9.3

What should the array C look like? The first five elements are no problem:

C(1)	C(2)	C(3)	C(4)	C(5)	C(6)
2.1	3.5	4.2	5.8	8.7	?

The problem is that there are two values of 8.7, one in A and one in B. Does the problem require two values of 8.7 in C or only one? Rereading the problem does not help, because the statement does not say what to do with duplicate values. A programmer writing this program for a client would ask the client to clarify the problem. We will simply assume that values duplicated in the two arrays are to be discarded, and we will note this in our problem statement.

There is another potential problem. Perhaps you can see what it is. In any case, we will bring it up later.

Example 10.7 Merging Two Arrays into One

A rough outline of the solution to the problem is:

1. Read array A.

2. Read array B.

3. Merge the two arrays to form array C.

4. Write array C.

Subroutine READAR will handle parts 1 and 2, and WRITAR will take care of part 4, so we turn our attention to writing a subroutine MERGAR to handle part 3.

MERGAR will receive the arrays A and B and their sizes NA and NB. It will calculate array C and its size NC, and send them back to the main program. The subroutine can use adjustable sizes for A and B, but not for C, since MERGAR is calculating the size NC of array C. Thus, MERGAR uses an assumed size for C. The subroutine name statement and declarations for the dummy arguments are

```
SUBROUTINE MERGAR(A, B, C, NA, NB, NC)
INTEGER  NA, NB, NC
REAL     A(NA), B(NB), C(*)
```

One obvious way to do the problem is to read all the elements of A into C(1), C(2), . . ., C(NA); then read all elements of B into C(NA+1), . . ., C(NA+NB); and finally, sort the array C. This method is not bad for small arrays, but it takes too much time on large arrays, because it does not take advantage of the fact that A and B are already sorted.

To merge the arrays A and B, first compare A(1) and B(1), and assign the smaller value of the two to C(1). If the smaller value was A(1), compare A(2) and B(1) and assign the smaller value to B(2), and so on.

It should be clear that the merge subroutine requires subscripts for the arrays A, B, and C. We will use subscripts IA, IB, and IC, all declared INTEGER and all assigned the value 1 at the start. Then a general step in the program involves comparing A(IA) to B(IB), assigning the smaller value to C(IC), and updating the subscripts. Continue doing this until no more comparisons are possible; that is, until one of the arrays, A or B, is exhausted. Then copy the remaining elements of the other array into C. The merge process is now two separate steps:

1. Repeat until one array is exhausted:

    a.   Compare values of A(IA) and B(IB), assigning the smaller value to C(IC).

    b.   Update the subscripts.

2. Repeat until the other array is exhausted:

    a.   Copy elements of the other array into C.

    b.   Update the subscripts.

The comparisons in part 1a are performed easily with a block IF statement of the form

```
IF ( A(IA) .LT. B(IB) ) THEN
    C(IC) = A(IA)
ELSE
    C(IC) = B(IB)
END IF
```

For part 1b, when the value of an element, A(IA) for example, is assigned to C(IC), then IA must be incremented by 1. Similarly, if the value of B(IB) is assigned to C(IC), then IB must be incremented. And in either case, IC must be incremented. The IF block then becomes

```
IF ( A(IA) .LT. B(IB) ) THEN
    C(IC) = A(IA)
    IA    = IA + 1
ELSE
    C(IC) = B(IB)
    IB = IB + 1
END IF

IC = IC + 1
```

Does anything seem wrong? We have not settled the case of duplicate values. If A(IA) = B(IB), then C(IC) can take either value, but *both* IA and IB must be incremented. The IF block needs another component:

```
IF ( A(IA) .LT. B(IB) ) THEN
    C(IC) = A(IA)
    IA    = IA + 1
ELSE IF ( A(IA) .GT. B(IB) ) THEN
    C(IC) = B(IB)
    IB    = IB + 1
ELSE
    C(IC) = A(IA)
    IA = IA + 1
    IB = IB + 1
END IF
IC = IC + 1
```

Repeat this block of code as long as comparisons can be made, or as long as the subscripts IA and IB are in their proper ranges. Since IA can be as large as NA and IB can be as large as NB, the loop control statement is

```
11      IF ( (IA .LE. NA) .AND. (IB .LE. NB) ) THEN
```

For step 2 in the merge process, we must copy elements of the other array into C. How can we know which is the *other* array? The while loop above will terminate when *one* of the subscripts, IA or IB, becomes too large. The other subscript will still be in range, because only one of the subscripts is incremented at each step. If IA is still in range, the remaining elements of A are copied into C, and subscripts are updated, with the loop

```
22      IF (IA .LE. NA) THEN
            C(IC) = A(IA)
            IA = IA + 1
            IC = IC + 1
            GO TO 22
        END IF
```

You can see that this loop will not be executed if IA initially is larger than NA, making it appropriate whether A or B is first to be exhausted. The loop handles only the case in which B is exhausted first, so the subroutine requires another loop of the same form to copy the remaining elements of B into C.

The only thing left to do is to calculate the value for NC. The subscript IC is keeping track of the elements of C, but in the last while loop, IC is incremented once after the last element of C is assigned a value. Therefore, NC is one less than the final value of IC. Program 10.7a shows the complete subroutine.

■

PROGRAM 10.7a

```
        SUBROUTINE MERGAR(A, B, C, NA, NB, NC)
*---------------------------------------------------------------*
*  Receive two real arrays A and B with NA and NB elements      *
*  respectively, both sorted into ascending order.  The arrays  *
*  are merged to form a third array C, also in ascending order. *
*  Duplicate values in the original arrays are discarded.       *
*  Calculate NC, the number of elements in the merged array.    *
*---------------------------------------------------------------*
        INTEGER  NA, NB, NC, IA, IB, IC
        REAL     A(NA), B(NB), C(*)

        IA = 1
        IB = 1
        IC = 1
```

```
*-----------------------------------------------------------*
*    Compare elements of A and B until one array is exhausted,   *
*    assign the smaller value to C, and update subscripts.       *
*-----------------------------------------------------------*
11     IF ( (IA .LE. NA) .AND. (IB .LE. NB) ) THEN

          IF ( A(IA) .LT. B(IB) ) THEN
             C(IC) = A(IA)
             IA   = IA + 1
          ELSE IF ( A(IA) .GT. B(IB) ) THEN
             C(IC) = B(IB)
             IB   = IB + 1
          ELSE
             C(IC) = A(IA)
             IA = IA + 1
             IB = IB + 1
          END IF

          IC = IC + 1

          GO TO 11


       END IF
*-----------------------------------------------------------*
*    Copy remaining elements of the unexhausted array into C.  *
*-----------------------------------------------------------*
22     IF (IA .LE. NA) THEN
          C(IC) = A(IA)
          IA = IA + 1
          IC = IC + 1
          GO TO 22
       END IF

33     IF (IB .LE. NB) THEN
          C(IC) = B(IB)
          IB = IB + 1
          IC = IC + 1
          GO TO 33
       END IF

*-----------------------------------------------------------*
*                 Calculate size of merged array.             *
*-----------------------------------------------------------*
       NC = IC - 1

       END
```

The body of a main program to use the MERGAR subroutine could have a skeletal form:

1. CALL READAR(A, NA)
2. CALL READAR(B, NB)
3. CALL MERGAR(A, B, C, NA, NB, NC)
4. CALL WRITAR(C, NC)

We would not leave it at that. The program should echo-print the arrays A and B with WRITAR, and a few PRINT statements will provide nicer-looking output. Program 10.7b gives the complete program.

■
PROGRAM 10.7b

```
      PROGRAM MERGE
*---------------------------------------------------------------*
*   Read two arrays A and B, and merge them into a third array C.  *
*   A and B are already sorted into ascending numerical order.     *
*   The output array C will also be in ascending numerical order.  *
*   Duplicate values in A and B are discarded.                     *
*                                                                 *
*   SUBROUTINES:  READAR reads the arrays A and B from data files. *
*                 WRITAR writes the arrays A, B, and C.            *
*                 MERGAR merges arrays A and B to form array C.     *
*---------------------------------------------------------------*
      REAL     X, A(100), B(100), C(200)
      INTEGER  I, NA, NB, NC
*---------------------------------------------------------------*
*            Read and write the values in the first array.         *
*---------------------------------------------------------------*
      PRINT *
      PRINT *, 'First Array'
      CALL READAR(A, NA)
      CALL WRITAR(A, NA)
      PRINT *
*---------------------------------------------------------------*
*               Do the same for the second array.                  *
*---------------------------------------------------------------*
      PRINT *
      PRINT *, 'Second Array'
      CALL READAR(B, NB)
      CALL WRITAR(B, NB)
      PRINT *
```

```
*-------------------------------------------------------------*
*            Merge the two arrays into a third array.         *
*-------------------------------------------------------------*
      CALL MERGAR(A, B, C, NA, NB, NC)
      PRINT *
      PRINT *, 'Merged Array'
      CALL WRITAR(C, NC)

      END
```

Suppose the data files that hold the arrays are named ONE.DAT and TWO.DAT, and contain the following data:

ONE.DAT	TWO.DAT	
12E-5	9.5	
.0013	10.2	Notice that 10.2
12.3	10.2	is duplicated in TWO.
13.4	12.3	
14.5	12.4	
15.6	13.4	Values of 12.3, 13.4,
16.7	13.5	and 119.0 are in both
17.8	14.8	files ONE and TWO.
18.9	19.0	
19.0	21.3	
123.4567	21.4	
12.2E6	21.7	
	21.9	

When the program runs, this is how the output looks

```
First Array

What is the name of the data file? ONE

        12 elements in this array:

0.1200E-03  0.1300E-02   12.30      13.40      14.50      15.60
 16.70       17.80       18.90      19.00      123.5      0.1220E+08


Second Array

What is the name of the data file? TWO
```

```
      13 elements in this array:

9.500      10.20      10.20      12.30      12.40      13.40
13.50      14.80      19.00      21.30      21.40      21.70
21.90
```

Merged Array

```
      22 elements in this array:

0.1200E-03  0.1300E-02  9.500     10.20      10.20      12.30
12.40       13.40       13.50     14.50      14.80      15.60
16.70       17.80       18.90     19.00      21.30      21.40
21.70       21.90       123.5     0.1220E+08
```

The program properly handled the values contained in both files, but left the duplicated value 10.2 in the merged file. The latter occurred because we did not even consider the possibility that one of the arrays might have duplicate values. This is the "possible problem" we mentioned earlier. There are several reasonable alternatives:

1. Change the problem statement to require that each original array be free of duplicate values, or change the problem to allow duplicates in one array to be kept in the merged array.
2. Write a subroutine DISCRD that takes duplicate values out of a sorted array, and rewrite MERGE to call DISCRD for A and B.
3. Rewrite MERGAR to handle the case in which one array contains duplicate values.

Alternative 1 is not meant to be frivolous. For some real-world problems, it will be reasonable to expect that each input array is free of duplicate values. This is a textbook problem, so it is hard for you to know what is a reasonable expectation. If you are taking a course in Fortran, you should ask the instructor if you need to consider this case. Most instructors would be impressed that you recognized there could be a problem.

Assuming that alternative 1 is not possible, which of the others seems easier? Two of the exercises at the end of this chapter ask you to incorporate these alternatives into the program.

Statistical Summaries

One way to summarize a large set of numerical scores is with a **frequency distribution**, a set of categories or classes, together with the number of scores in each class. In statistics, the word *frequency* means number of *scores*.

We specify classes by giving *lower* and *upper boundaries*, or *bounds*. A class might have lower boundary 35.75 and upper boundary 40.75. Then this class consists of all scores between those two numbers. The upper boundary for one class is the lower boundary for the next class, so no scores can be left out by falling between the classes.

The following frequency table is a standard way to present a frequency distribution. It shows six classes and the frequency, or number of scores, in each class.

Frequency Table

Boundaries	Frequency
30.75 – 35.75	12
35.75 – 40.75	22
40.75 – 45.75	35
45.75 – 50.75	28
50.75 – 55.75	20
55.75 – 60.75	8

These common boundaries solve one problem but present another. What about scores that fall on a boundary? The trick to making up a good set of boundaries is to choose boundaries that cannot equal scores. If the scores are given with two decimal places, for example, choose boundaries with three decimal places, and put a 5 in the third place. Our subroutine will warn the user about choosing boundaries, but will do nothing to check for scores falling on the boundaries. We assume the user is familiar with the data.

The width of a class is the upper bound of the class minus the lower bound. In our example frequency distribution, every class has width 5. Equal class widths are desirable, but not necessary, in frequency distributions. Our subroutine will use equal class widths.

Example 10.8 Calculating a Frequency Distribution

The subroutine, called FRQDST, will have dummy arguments A and N, with integer N, and A a real array of adjustable size N. The variable A will appear often with a subscript, and we will use the integer variable COUNT for this subscript.

Since FRQDST will calculate frequencies for several classes, it will have an integer array FRQNCY with size 15, a large enough number of classes for most situations, and an integer variable NCLASS for the number of classes. The integer CLASS will appear as a subscript for FRQNCY.

FRQDST also will have a real array BOUND for the bounds of the classes. Every bound except the first one is an upper bound for a class, so we will declare BOUND with

```
REAL  BOUND(0:15)
```

with the understanding that BOUND(0) is the lower bound of the first class. For any other subscript CLASS, BOUND(CLASS) is the upper bound of the class numbered CLASS.

Finally, we are using equal class widths, for which we use the real variable WIDTH. Thus, the declarations for subroutine FRQDST are

```
INTEGER  N, NCLASS, COUNT, CLASS, FRQNCY(15)
REAL     A(N), WIDTH, BOUND(0:15)
```

We assume that FRQDST receives the array A sorted into ascending order. FRQDST could call SHELL, but we let a main program take care of that.

Since we are using equal class widths, we ask the user only for BOUND(0) and WIDTH. The subroutine must perform the following steps:

1. Get values for BOUND(0) and WIDTH (and check them).
2. Calculate the number of classes needed.
3. Calculate the remaining bounds.
4. Initialize the frequencies to zero.
5. Calculate the frequencies.
6. Print the frequency distribution.

The subroutine should check the input values for BOUND(0) and WIDTH because an inexperienced user might enter inappropriate values. It might happen that the user enters a value for BOUND(0) that is higher than some of the scores. We can check for that case with the while loop

```
11    IF (BOUND(0) .GT. A(1)) THEN
         PRINT *, 'That lower bound is higher than the score', A(1)
         PRINT *, 'Please enter a lower bound.'
         READ *, BOUND(0)
         GO TO 11
      END IF
```

Even with a proper value of BOUND(0), a user might enter a value of WIDTH so small that the first class would not contain any scores, which will happen if BOUND(0) + WIDTH is less than A(1). Therefore, we check WIDTH with the while loop

```
22     IF ( BOUND(0) + WIDTH .LT. A(1) ) THEN
          PRINT *, 'Width is too small.  The first class will'
          PRINT *, 'not contain any scores.  Reenter width.'
          READ *, WIDTH
          GO TO 22
       END IF
```

We can see how to calculate the number of classes needed by considering how many WIDTHs it would take to stretch from BOUND(0) to A(N), the largest element in the array. That is, we need to know

$$(A(N) - BOUND(0)) / WIDTH$$

Suppose for concreteness that BOUND(0) is 35.75, A(N) is 69.2, and WIDTH is 5. Then

$$(A(N) - BOUND(0)) / WIDTH = (69.2 - 35.75) / 5 = 6.69$$

The number of classes must be an integer, so we would round 6.69 up to 7. In general, we use

$$NCLASS = 1 + INT((A(N) - BOUND(0)) / WIDTH)$$

Next, we need to get the rest of the boundaries. After BOUND(0), each bound is the previous bound plus the class width, so we calculate the boundaries with the code

```
       DO 33 CLASS = 1, NCLASS
          BOUND(CLASS) = BOUND(CLASS - 1) + WIDTH
33     CONTINUE
```

Similar code initializes the FRQNCY array to 0:

```
       DO 44 CLASS = 1, NCLASS
          FRQNCY(CLASS) = 0
44     CONTINUE
```

Yes, the two DO loops could be combined into one, but it is easier to see what the separate DO loops are doing.

Now for the main task of the subroutine: calculate the frequency distribution. We need two loops, one for the classes and one for the scores. A straightforward approach is

```
          DO 66 SCORE = 1, N
            DO 55 CLASS = 1, NCLASS

               IF ( A(SCORE) .GT. BOUND(CLASS - 1) .AND.
     1              A(SCORE) .LE. BOUND(CLASS) )
     2              FRQNCY(CLASS) = FRQNCY(CLASS) + 1

   55       CONTINUE
   66    CONTINUE
```

With 1,000 scores and 10 boundaries, this method requires 20,000 comparisons because every one of the 1,000 scores is matched with every CLASS value and compared to the upper and lower boundaries of that class.

However, we do not need to compare every score to two boundaries because the scores are already sorted. We look at a very small example to make things concrete.

Suppose the first ten scores are

```
A(1)   A(2)   A(3)   A(4)   A(5)   A(6)   A(7)   A(8)   A(9)   A(10)
12.5   13.6   13.8   14.2   14.7   15.8   16.3   17.2   18.6   21.5
```

and the bounds for the first two classes are

```
BOUND(0)   BOUND(1)   BOUND(2)
 10.75      14.75       18.75
```

Because of our checking of BOUND(0) and WIDTH, we know the first score, A(1), goes into the first class. Look at the upper bound of the first class, 14.75. Move along the scores A(COUNT), counting each score as being in the first class until a score A(COUNT) is bigger than 14.75. At that point, five scores have been counted in class 1.

The first score above 14.75 is 15.8, and we compare it and the following scores to the next bound, 18.75, until we reach a score higher than that bound. The first score above 18.75 is 21.5, and at that point, four scores have fallen into the second class.

We can start CLASS at 1 and use one loop for the scores beginning

```
   DO 10 COUNT = 1, N
```

Inside the loop, we want to increase the FRQNCY of the class if A(COUNT) is less than BOUND(CLASS). If A(COUNT) is bigger than BOUND(CLASS), we increase CLASS and count the score in the new class:

```
        CLASS = 1
        DO 55 COUNT = 1, N

            IF ( A(COUNT) .LE. BOUND(CLASS) ) THEN
                FRQNCY(CLASS) = FRQNCY(CLASS) + 1
            ELSE
                CLASS = CLASS + 1
                FRQNCY(CLASS) = FRQNCY(CLASS) + 1
            END IF

55      CONTINUE
```

That brings us back to 1,000 comparisons. `CLASS` cannot increase beyond `NCLASS` because all scores are less than or equal to `BOUND(NCLASS)`.

This counting process will work smoothly for frequency distributions with no empty classes. But suppose a class *is* empty. Our process counts at least one score in each class because, as soon as we increase `CLASS`, we add 1 to `FRQNCY(CLASS)`. We can overcome this problem with a while loop immediately after `ELSE`:

```
        IF ( A(COUNT) .LE. BOUND(CLASS) ) THEN
            FRQNCY(CLASS) = FRQNCY(CLASS) + 1
        ELSE
44          IF (A(COUNT) .GT. BOUND(CLASS) ) THEN
                CLASS = CLASS + 1
                GO TO 44
            END IF
            FRQNCY(CLASS) = FRQNCY(CLASS) + 1
        END IF
```

We continue increasing the class number until we find the proper class for the value in `A(COUNT)`.

The only thing left to do is print the frequency table. We will not discuss the printing, but it is contained in the subroutine in Program 10.8.

■
PROGRAM 10.8
_____

```
        SUBROUTINE FRQDST(A, N)
*-----------------------------------------------------------------*
*    Receive a real array A of N elements, in ascending order.    *
*    Ask the user for the class width and lower boundary of the   *
*    first class.  Calculate and print a frequency table.         *
*-----------------------------------------------------------------*
        INTEGER  N, NCLASS, COUNT, CLASS, FRQNCY(15)
        REAL     A(N), WIDTH, BOUND(0:15)
```

```
        PRINT *
        PRINT *, '          Frequency Distribution'
        PRINT *
        PRINT *, 'Choose class width and lower bound for first'
        PRINT *, 'class so that no scores fall on a boundary. '
        PRINT *, 'If a score falls on a boundary between two  '
        PRINT *, 'classes, it will count in the lower class.  '
        PRINT *
*-------------------------------------------------------------*
*   Ask user for lower bound of first class and compare to A(1).  *
*-------------------------------------------------------------*
        PRINT *
        PRINT *, 'What is the lower bound for the first class?'
        READ  *, BOUND(0)

11      IF ( BOUND(0) .GT. A(1) ) THEN
            PRINT *, 'That bound is higher than the score', A(1)
            PRINT *, 'Please enter a lower bound.'
            READ  *, BOUND(0)
            GO TO 11
        END IF
*-------------------------------------------------------------*
*    Ask user for class width; compare BOUND(0) + WIDTH to A(1).  *
*-------------------------------------------------------------*
        PRINT *
        PRINT *, 'What is the class width?'
        READ  *, WIDTH

22      IF ( BOUND(0) + WIDTH .LT. A(1) ) THEN
            PRINT *, 'Width is too small.  The first class will'
            PRINT *, 'not contain any scores.  Reenter width.'
            READ  *, WIDTH
            GO TO 22
        END IF
*-------------------------------------------------------------*
*    Calculate number of classes and boundaries of each class.  *
*    Initialize frequencies of classes to 0.                    *
*-------------------------------------------------------------*
        NCLASS = 1 + INT( ( A(N) - BOUND(0) ) / WIDTH )

        DO 33 CLASS = 1, NCLASS
            BOUND(CLASS) = BOUND(CLASS - 1) + WIDTH
            FRQNCY(CLASS) = 0
33      CONTINUE
```

```
*---------------------------------------------------------------*
*                Calculate frequencies for each class.          *
*---------------------------------------------------------------*
      CLASS = 1
      DO 55 COUNT = 1, N

         IF ( A(COUNT) .LE. BOUND(CLASS) ) THEN
               FRQNCY(CLASS) = FRQNCY(CLASS) + 1
         ELSE
44             IF (A(COUNT) .GT. BOUND(CLASS) ) THEN
                  CLASS = CLASS + 1
                  GO TO 44
               END IF

               FRQNCY(CLASS) = FRQNCY(CLASS) + 1
         END IF

55    CONTINUE
*---------------------------------------------------------------*
*                     Print frequency table.                    *
*---------------------------------------------------------------*
      PRINT *
      PRINT *
      PRINT 10
      PRINT 20, ('_', COUNT = 1, 38)

      DO 66 CLASS = 1, NCLASS
         PRINT 30, BOUND(CLASS-1), BOUND(CLASS), FRQNCY(CLASS)
66    CONTINUE

      PRINT 20, ('_', COUNT = 1, 38)

10    FORMAT (1X, 10X, 'CLASS BOUNDARIES',9X, 'FREQUENCY')
20    FORMAT (1X, 8X, 38A)
30    FORMAT (1X, F16.3, ' -', F8.3, I15)

      END
```

We show the output from this subroutine in the next section.

Example 10.9 A Statistical Summary Program

Here we develop a program to calculate several summary statistics for a real array X of N scores. The program will use the subroutines READAR, WRITAR, SHELL, and FRQDST.

The program will also calculate the following statistics: *median, minimum* and *maximum* values, *range, mean, variance,* and *standard deviation.* We explain these terms as we develop the code for them.

One reason for sorting is that it makes some of the remaining calculations almost trivial. The minimum value is just A(1) and the maximum is A(N), for example, after SHELL sorts the scores. The range of the scores is the largest value minus the smallest, or A(N) - A(1).

The *median* of a set of scores is the middle value of the ordered scores, so here, too, the sorting helps. Technically, there is *a* middle score only if the number of scores is odd. With seven scores, the fourth score in order is the middle score, because there are three scores below it and three above.

When the number of scores is even, it is customary to take the average, or mean, of the two middle scores as the median. With eight scores in order, the fourth and fifth scores are the middle scores, so the median of eight ordered scores is

$$(X(4) + X(5)) / 2.0$$

With N odd, (N + 1) / 2 gives the middle position. We let MID be this position. When N is even, X(MID) is still one of the middle scores, the other one being X(MID + 1). We use the MOD function to determine whether the number N of scores is even or odd. The following code calculates the median.

```
MID = (N + 1) / 2
IF ( MOD(N, 2) .EQ. 0 )THEN        | Even number
    MEDIAN = (X(MID) + X(MID + 1)) / 2.0   | of scores
ELSE
    MEDIAN = X(MID)                | Odd  number
END IF
```

The mean is easy enough to calculate; add up all the scores and divide by REAL(N). The variance can be calculated as

$$(X(1)-MEAN)**2 + (X(2)-MEAN)**2 + \cdots + (X(N)-MEAN)**2) / (N-1)$$

That is, add the squares of X(I) - MEAN, for each score I, and divide the sum by N - 1. The numerator is often called the *sum of squares* in statistics, so we name it SUMSQ. The calculation is straightforward.

```
       SUMSQ = 0.0
       DO 11 I = 1, N
          SUMSQ = SUMSQ + (X(I) - MEAN) ** 2
11     CONTINUE
       VARNCE  = SUMSQ / REAL(N-1)
```

The standard deviation, called STDDEV in the program, is the square root of the variance. Statistical calculations are certainly not the most difficult things to program.

The entire statistics program is in Program 10.9.

■

PROGRAM 10.9

```
       PROGRAM STATS
*-------------------------------------------------------------------*
*   Read a real array X of N scores from a file and calculate the   *
*   following summary statistics:                                   *
*                                                                   *
*                Median      Mean                                   *
*                Minimum     Variance                               *
*                Maximum     Standard deviation                     *
*                Range                                              *
*                                                                   *
*   The program uses the following subroutines:                     *
*                                                                   *
*                Subroutine  Task                                   *
*                                                                   *
*                ----------------------------------------------     *
*                READAR      Open a data file, read the array X,     *
*                            and count the scores.                  *
*                                                                   *
*                WRITAR      Write the original and sorted arrays.   *
*                                                                   *
*                SHELL       Sort the array into ascending order.   *
*                                                                   *
*                FRQDST      Print a frequency distribution.        *
*********************************************************************
       REAL    X(500), MEDIAN, MINIM, MAXIM, RANGE, MEAN
       REAL    TOTAL, SUMSQ, VARNCE, STDDEV
       INTEGER I, N, COUNT, NCLASS, MID

       PRINT *
       PRINT *, ' This program gives summary statistics for a set of'
       PRINT *, ' scores: median, minimum and maximum values, range,'
       PRINT *, ' mean, variance, and standard deviation.'
       PRINT *
       PRINT *
```

```
*-----------------------------------------------------------------*
*               Call subroutine READAR to open the data           *
*               file and read and count the scores.               *
*-----------------------------------------------------------------*
      CALL READAR(X, N)
*-----------------------------------------------------------------*
*               Call subroutine WRITAR to write the scores.        *
*-----------------------------------------------------------------*
      CALL WRITAR(X, N)
*-----------------------------------------------------------------*
*               Call subroutine SHELL to sort the array X.         *
*-----------------------------------------------------------------*
      CALL SHELL(X, N)
*-----------------------------------------------------------------*
*               Call subroutine WRITAR to write the sorted scores. *
*-----------------------------------------------------------------*
      PRINT 10
10    FORMAT ('0Here are the sorted data:' /)
      CALL WRITAR(X, N)
*-----------------------------------------------------------------*
*                    Calculate median.                            *
*-----------------------------------------------------------------*
      MID = (N + 1) / 2

      IF ( MOD(N, 2) .EQ. 0 )THEN
         MEDIAN = (X(MID) + X(MID + 1)) / 2.0
      ELSE
         MEDIAN = X(MID)
      END IF
*-----------------------------------------------------------------*
*                    Find minimum, maximum, and range.            *
*-----------------------------------------------------------------*
      MINIM = X(1)
      MAXIM = X(N)
      RANGE = MAXIM - MINIM
*-----------------------------------------------------------------*
*                    Calculate mean.                              *
*-----------------------------------------------------------------*
      TOTAL = 0.0
      DO 11 I = 1, N
         TOTAL = TOTAL + X(I)
11    CONTINUE

      MEAN = TOTAL / REAL(N)
```

```
*------------------------------------------------------------*
*           Calculate variance and standard deviation.       *
*------------------------------------------------------------*
      SUMSQ = 0.0
      DO 22 I = 1, N
         SUMSQ = SUMSQ + (X(I) - MEAN) ** 2
22    CONTINUE

      VARNCE = SUMSQ / REAL(N-1)
      STDDEV = SQRT(VARNCE)
*------------------------------------------------------------*
*                        Print results.                      *
*------------------------------------------------------------*
      PRINT 20
20    FORMAT ('0', '        SUMMARY  STATISTICS' /)
      PRINT *, 'Number of scores: ', N
      PRINT *
      PRINT *, 'Mean of scores:    ', MEAN
      PRINT *, 'Variance:          ', VARNCE
      PRINT *, 'Standard deviation:', STDDEV
      PRINT *
      PRINT *, 'Median of scores:  ', MEDIAN
      PRINT *, 'Minimum value:     ', MINIM
      PRINT *, 'Maximum value:     ', MAXIM
      PRINT *, 'Range of scores:   ', RANGE
      PRINT *
*------------------------------------------------------------*
*   Call subroutine FRQDST to calculate frequency distribution. *
*------------------------------------------------------------*
      CALL FRQDST(X, N)

      END
```

A run of the program using the file STFILE produces the output

```
This program gives summary statistics for a set of
scores: median, minimum and maximum values, range,
mean, variance, and standard deviation.

What is the name of the data file? STFILE

   23 elements in this array:

        12.50      13.60      14.80      15.30      15.20      18.30
        12.40      19.30      16.30      17.20      18.40      19.20
        14.30      15.60      16.50      17.60      18.10      19.30
        12.10      13.50      14.60      15.20      16.30
```

Here are the sorted data:

23 elements in this array:

12.10	12.40	12.50	13.50	13.60	14.30
14.60	14.80	15.20	15.20	15.30	15.60
16.30	16.30	16.50	17.20	17.60	18.10
18.30	18.40	19.20	19.30	19.30	

SUMMARY STATISTICS

Number of scores:	23
Mean of scores:	15.89565
Variance:	5.104980
Standard deviation:	2.259420
Median of scores:	15.60000
Minimum value:	12.10000
Maximum value:	19.30000
Range of scores:	7.199999

Frequency Distribution

Choose class width and lower bound for first class so that no scores fall on a boundary. If a score falls on a boundary between two classes, it will count in the lower class.

What is the lower bound for the first class?
<u>11.75</u>

What is the class width?
<u>2.0</u>

CLASS BOUNDARIES	FREQUENCY
11.750 – 13.750	5
13.750 – 15.750	7
15.750 – 17.750	5
17.750 – 19.750	6

■

10.3 ADDITIONAL TOPICS
CONCERNING SUBPROGRAMS

Many more aspects of subprograms could be included here. We mention a few which are included in most Fortran texts.

The RETURN **Statement**

At one time, Fortran required every subprogram to contain one or more RETURN **statements** to return control to the calling program. The normal placement of the RETURN statement was immediately before the subprogram END statement. This statement is still part of Fortran, but is not needed because the subprogram END statement automatically returns control to the calling program.

A RETURN statement anywhere in a subprogram immediately returns control to the calling program. The following segment of a subprogram to calculate a factorial shows a typical use of RETURN.

```
IF (N .EQ. 0 .OR. N .EQ. 1) THEN
    FACTORIAL = 1
    RETURN
END IF

(Code to calculate the
factorial when N > 1)
```

Nowadays, the preferred way to handle this calculation is

```
IF (N .EQ. 0 .OR. N .EQ. 1) THEN
    FACTORIAL = 1
ELSE

(Code to calculate the
factorial when N > 1)

END IF
```

This construction does away with the need for most RETURN statements, but you might find situations where the RETURN statement comes in handy.

Other Subroutine Topics

Many Fortran texts discuss **alternate entry and return points** in subroutines as well as COMMON **blocks**, which provide a means for programs and subprograms to share data without passing arguments. We advise against the use of these devices. However, you might see them in Fortran programs, so a brief discussion is given in Appendix A.

■
10.4   SUMMARY OF CHAPTER 10

■ *Terms Introduced in This Chapter*

CALL statement
COMMON statement
Frequency distribution
Median
Merge

Range
RETURN statement
Standard deviation
Subroutine name statement
Variance

■ *What You Should Know*

1. A subroutine name can be any legal Fortran symbolic name.
2. A subroutine name does not store a value and has no type.
3. The first statement in a subroutine is the subroutine name statement, and the last statement is END.
4. All the rules for passing arguments to subroutines are the same as the rules for function subprograms.
5. Subroutines often change values of one or more actual arguments.
6. A program unit invokes a subroutine with a CALL statement.
7. After a subroutine executes, it returns control to the first executable statement after CALL in the calling program.
8. When trying to decide whether to use a function subprogram or a subroutine to perform a task, use a function if only one value must be calculated.
9. Use a subroutine when the task involves computing or changing several values.
10. Use a subroutine when the task involves output operations.
11. A subroutine cannot call itself or call another subprogram that calls it.
12. An adjustable array dimension cannot be used in a subroutine if the calling program has no value for the dimension.
13. A program system can have many subroutines and functions, but only one main program.

■

10.5 EXERCISES

■ *Self-Test*

1. Are the following statements valid or invalid in Fortran? If invalid, explain why.

    a.   `SUBROUTINE SORT(SCORE, 100)`
    b.   `CALL S = SMALL(X, N)`
    c.   `REAL SUBROUTINE SORT(X, N)`
    d.   `CALL SORT(SCORE, 100)`
    e.   `SUBROUTINE (X, Y, N)`
    f.   `CALL FINAL(A, A(1), B)`
    g.   `SUBROUTINE TOT(X(1), X(5) )`
    h.   `CALL FIX(12.5, FIX)`

2. The following problems contain statements from a main program and from a subprogram that is being called by the main program. Specify valid or invalid. If invalid, tell why.

	Main Program	Subprogram
a.	`INTEGER N, NFAC` `CALL FACTOR(N, NFAC)`	`SUBROUTINE FACTOR(M, FAC)` `INTEGER M, FAC`
b.	`CALL ADD(X, Y)`	`SUBROUTINE ADD(A, B, SUM)`
c.	`Y = ADD(X, Y)`	`SUBROUTINE ADD(A, B)`

d.	`INTEGER A, B`
	`CALL TWIST(A, B, 5)`
		`SUBROUTINE TWIST(X, Y, Z)`
		`INTEGER X, Y, Z`
		`Z = X + Y`

e.	`REAL R, A` `CALL AREA(R, A)`	`SUBROUTINE AREA(RADIUS, A)` `REAL RADIUS, A, AREA`

■ *Programming Exercises*

1. Write a subroutine `HERE` and a program to call it. The subroutine should print

```
Here we are.
The number passed is xxx
```

where xxx is the number passed by the calling program.

2. Write a program to read four real numbers and call a subroutine EXTREM that calculates the largest and smallest of the numbers. The program should print the largest and smallest numbers.

3. Write a subroutine that receives two real arrays A and B, each with N elements, and calculates a third array C with N elements. For each I, C(I) is the larger of the two elements A(I) and B(I). The subroutine should pass the array C back to the main program.

4. Write a subroutine that receives an integer array SCORE with N elements. SCORE and N are dummy arguments. The subroutine calculates a character array GRADE, whose elements will be letter grades A, B, C, D, or F, and passes the GRADE array back to the calling program. If SCORE(I) is above 90, GRADE(I) is an A, and so on. If a score is above 100 or below 0, place an X in the GRADE array. Write a program to read the integer array and call the subroutine.

5. The sort subroutine SHELL sorts real numbers into ascending order. You might need a subroutine that sorts real numbers into descending order, or one that sorts character data or integers. Modify the sort subroutine in the text to handle each of the five possibilities:

   a. Sort a real array into descending order.
   b. Sort a character array into ascending order.
   c. Sort a character array into descending order.
   d. Sort an integer array into ascending order.
   e. Sort an integer array into descending order.

6. Here are several problems that involve variations of the program system MERGE. In each case, rewrite one or more of the program units, possibly inserting new units.

   a. Deal with the case of duplicate values in one of the input arrays by writing a subroutine DISCRD that keeps only one copy of any value in an array. Rewrite the main MERGE program to call DISCRD for each of the input arrays.

   b. Deal with the case of duplicate values in one array by rewriting the MERGAR subroutine.

   c. Rewrite MERGAR so that duplicate values appear in the merged array as often as they appear in either of the input arrays.

   d. Rewrite the merge program system to handle the case in which the input arrays are not sorted.

   e. Rewrite the MERGAR subprogram so that it merges three arrays of real numbers to create a fourth array. Assume the input arrays are sorted into ascending order and that each one contains no duplicates.

   f. Rewrite the entire MERGE system to handle the problem of merging two files of real numbers into a third file arranged in ascending order. Assume the input files are sorted into ascending order, and that neither file contains duplicate values, but there may be values that appear in both files. Do not read the contents of the files into arrays, but merge the files directly. That is, read the first value in each file, and write the smaller value into the output file. At each step, read the next value from the appropriate file, compare to the current value from the other file, and put the smaller value in the output file.

7. Write a program to play *tic-tac-toe* with the user. Use subprograms to:

   a.   Give instructions.
   b.   Print the tic-tac-toe board with characters X and 0 showing the moves of the computer and user.
   c.   Choose the computer's move.
   d.   Test to see if either player won.

   Board positions are numbered from 1 to 9 as in the INSTR subroutine. Use a character array with nine elements to store the characters X and 0.

   For the first try at the program, always let the user go first and use X. Later, you might want to let the user choose whether to go first or second and which letter to use.

   Choosing good moves for the computer is difficult. At first, let the computer look at positions 1 to 9, and select the first available position. When the program is working, you can experiment with more complicated strategies.

8. Write a subroutine that calculates all the factors of a positive integer passed to it, stores these factors in an array, and passes the array and its size back to the calling program. Include the factors 1 and the integer itself.

9. Write a subroutine that calculates the prime factors of a positive integer passed to it, stores these prime factors in an array, and passes the array and its size back to the calling program.

10. A standard problem in electrical engineering is determining the **equivalent resistance** (or *ER* for short) of a circuit or part of a circuit. *ER* calculations are based on two rules:

   a.   If R_1 and R_2 are the resistances (ohms) of two resistors in *parallel*, the *ER* of R_1 and R_2 is

$$R = \frac{1}{\dfrac{1}{R_1} + \dfrac{1}{R_2}}$$

   b.   If R_1 and R_2 are the resistances of two resistors in *series*, the *ER* of R_1 and R_2 is

$$R = R_1 + R_2$$

Here is an electrical circuit diagram of part of a circuit.

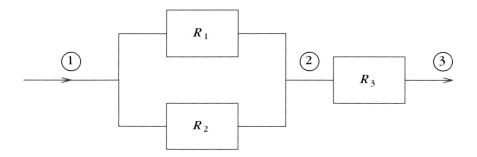

R_1, R_2, and R_3 represent *resistances* (ohms) and the circled 1, 2, and 3 represent *nodes* of the circuit, or points of the circuit that are separated by resistors.

R_1 and R_2 are in parallel, so their *ER* is R_4, for example, where

$$R_4 = \frac{1}{\dfrac{1}{R_1} + \dfrac{1}{R_2}}$$

Then the circuit is equivalent to

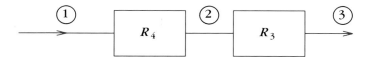

Now the circuit has only R_4 and R_3 in series, so its *ER* is $R_4 + R_3$. Note that it is important to deal with resistors in parallel before dealing with those in series.

In general, of course, we might have to resolve many series and parallel configurations to get the final value for *ER*.

The *parameters* of a circuit are:

a. The *number* of *resistors* in the circuit
b. The *number* of *nodes* in the circuit
c. The *resistance value* for each resistor
d. The *beginning* and *ending node* for each resistor

For the circuit above, the value for number of resistors and number of nodes is 3. The remaining values are given in the following table.

Resistor number	Beginning node	Ending node	Resistance value
1	1	2	R_1
2	1	2	R_2
3	2	3	R_3

We illustrate the use of a table such as this in the calculation of *ER*. To deal with resistors in parallel, using this table, first find two resistors with the same beginning and ending node. In the table, resistors 1 and 2 both begin at node 1 and end at node 2, so we know they are in parallel. Then combine the resistors into R_4 according to the formula

$$R_4 = \frac{1}{\dfrac{1}{R_1} + \dfrac{1}{R_2}}$$

In the table, replace R_1 with R_4, and set all the parameters for resistor 2 to zero. Then the table becomes

Resistor number	Beginning node	Ending node	Resistance value
1	1	2	R_4
2	0	0	0
3	2	3	R_3

To find resistors in series, find a node which is the beginning node for exactly one resistor and the ending node for exactly one other resistor. Node 2 is obviously such a node, being the beginning node for resistor 3 and the ending node for resistor 1. Calculate the *ER* as $R_4 + R_3$ and make this value the resistance value for resistor 1. As before, place zeroes in the parameter values for resistor 3. The table is now:

Resistor number	Beginning node	Ending node	Resistance value
1	1	2	$R_4 + R_3$
2	0	0	0
3	0	0	0

Since only one row in the table has nonzero entries, the solution is complete and the *ER* is the resistance value in that row, $R_4 + R_3$.

Write a program that asks for the parameters of a circuit and calculates the ER of the circuit. Use one subroutine to deal with parallel configurations and one to deal with series configurations. *Hint:* Use a variable NEFF to represent the *effective number* of resistors at any given point in the program. The initial value of NEFF is the number of resistors at the start of the program. Whenever the program performs a parallel or series calculation, decrease the value of NEFF by one. The problem is solved when NEFF becomes one. The program should use a while loop that repeatedly calls the two subroutines, first the parallel subroutine, then the series subroutine.

11. If a polynomial $a_n x^n + a_{n-1} x^{n-1} + \cdots + a_1 x + a_0$ has integer coefficients, then any real roots of the polynomial are rational. Further, any rational root has the form $\pm$NUM/DEN, where NUM is a factor of a_0 and DEN is a factor of a_n. For example, if the polynomial is $4x^4 - 12x^3 + 5x^2 + 7x - 9$, the factors of $a_0 = 9$ are 1, 3, and 9, and the factors of $a_n = 4$ are 1, 2, and 4. Then the possible rational roots of the polynomial are:

1/1	1/2	1/4	3/1	3/2	3/4	9/1	9/2	9/4
–1/1	–1/2	–1/4	–3/1	–3/2	–3/4	–9/1	–9/2	–9/4

You could plug each of these values into the polynomial to see if any of them are roots. But this is a programming text, so . . .

Write a program that reads coefficients of a polynomial, and calculates and prints the rational roots, if any exist. Do all calculations in integer arithmetic. Use subprograms to:

a. Calculate all the factors of a_0 and a_n.
b. Calculate the value of the polynomial for given input values of NUM and DEN. You only need to know whether the value is zero, not the actual value of the polynomial. Therefore, clear powers of DEN from the denominators of all terms so the value can be calculated with integer arithmetic. (To give a little protection against integer overflow, notice that each term has a factor of NUM in the numerator.)

If you solve this problem, the computer will print some roots twice. For example, you might get both 1 / 2 and 2 / 4 as roots. Write a logical function NOTCOM that returns .TRUE. when two passed integers have no factors in common other than 1. Use this function to prevent the computer from printing numerators and denominators with a common factor.

11 TWO-DIMENSIONAL ARRAYS

One-dimensional arrays allow us to refer to an entire set of related numbers with one variable name. That name, followed by a position, can specify any element in the array. We often work with tables, or sets of numbers laid out in a two-dimensional pattern. A **two-dimensional array** allows us to specify an element in the table by a variable name followed by two subscripts giving the row and column position of the element in the table. Fortran allows arrays with up to seven dimensions, but we will discuss only the two-dimensional case.

11.1 MATRICES

We use the following example to illustrate some standard techniques for dealing with two-dimensional arrays. A small college has schools of Liberal Arts, Business, and Engineering. The table in Figure 11.1 gives numbers of full-time students at the college, arranged according to class and school.

School	Class			
	Freshman	Sophomore	Junior	Senior
Liberal Arts	420	385	379	370
Business	225	218	206	198
Engineering	186	172	165	162

FIGURE 11.1
A two-dimensional table

A **matrix** is a rectangular array, or table, of elements, all of the same type. The numbers in the table (Figure 11.1) are integers laid out in a rectangular pattern; thus, they form a matrix. A matrix is also called a *two-dimensional array*, but we generally use the term *matrix* because it is less cumbersome. The numbers can be abstracted from the table and written as the matrix

$$\text{STUDNT} = \begin{bmatrix} 420 & 385 & 379 & 370 \\ 225 & 218 & 206 & 198 \\ 186 & 172 & 165 & 162 \end{bmatrix}$$

The name STUDNT refers to the entire matrix. The name followed by two subscripts specifies one element of the matrix. By convention, the first subscript designates the row, and the second subscript the column. For example, STUDNT(2, 4) names the element at the intersection of the second row and the fourth column, or 198. You can identify any number in the matrix by specifying the row and column in which it appears. In terms of element names, the matrix looks like

$$\text{STUDNT} = \begin{bmatrix} \text{STUDNT(1, 1)} & \text{STUDNT(1, 2)} & \text{STUDNT(1, 3)} & \text{STUDNT(1, 4)} \\ \text{STUDNT(2, 1)} & \text{STUDNT(2, 2)} & \text{STUDNT(2, 3)} & \text{STUDNT(2, 4)} \\ \text{STUDNT(3, 1)} & \text{STUDNT(3, 2)} & \text{STUDNT(3, 3)} & \text{STUDNT(3, 4)} \end{bmatrix}$$

Notice the patterns of the subscripts. Elements in the same row have the same first subscript, and elements in the same column have the same second subscript.

Fortran represents a matrix as a two-dimensional array, an array variable with individual elements specified by the variable name followed by two subscripts in parentheses. However, the storage locations in the computer are arranged in one dimension, so we need a rule for assigning these locations to the array elements.

The natural way to order the elements in a matrix is **row-major order**; take the first row from left to right, then the second row from left to right, and so on. This order also corresponds to the way most people read a table. Unfortunately, Fortran does not store a two-dimensional array in this way, but uses **column-major order**, starting with the first column top to bottom, then the second column top to bottom, and so on. Thus, Fortran stores the STUDNT array as in Figure 11.2.

As far as Fortran is concerned, either subscript could designate the row number. In fact, the computer knows nothing about rows and columns. It merely requires two subscripts, and the user is free to interpret these subscripts in any fashion. We could, for instance, call the first subscript the column number and the second subscript the row number. This convention would make reading and writing arrays in Fortran more natural, but it would put our notation at odds with virtually every text that discusses matrices, so we will continue calling the first subscript the row number and the second subscript the column number.

Storage Location	Array Element Name	Value	
1	STUDNT(1, 1)	→ 420	
2	STUDNT(2, 1)	→ 225	Column 1
3	STUDNT(3, 1)	→ 186	
4	STUDNT(1, 2)	→ 385	
5	STUDNT(2, 2)	→ 218	Column 2
6	STUDNT(3, 2)	→ 172	
7	STUDNT(1, 3)	→ 379	
8	STUDNT(2, 3)	→ 206	Column 3
9	STUDNT(3, 3)	→ 165	
10	STUDNT(1, 4)	→ 370	
11	STUDNT(2, 4)	→ 198	Column 4
12	STUDNT(3, 4)	→ 162	

FIGURE 11.2
Column-major order for the STUDNT matrix

Declaring Matrices

The STUDNT matrix has three rows and four columns, so it is a "3 by 4" matrix. As with one-dimensional arrays, the dimension bounds for matrices must be declared. An appropriate declaration statement for the STUDNT matrix is

```
INTEGER  STUDNT(3, 4)
```

which tells the computer to set aside storage space for a matrix variable STUDNT whose first subscript can assume values in the range from 1 to 3, and whose second subscript can range from 1 to 4. The subsequent use of a subscript outside these ranges will cause an error.

By default, Fortran assumes the lower dimension bounds are 1, so the computer will set aside twelve storage locations, for three rows numbered 1 to 3 and four columns numbered 1 to 4. We can specify a lower dimension bound other than 1 by writing the lower and upper bounds separated by a colon (:), as in

```
INTEGER  MATRIX(3:5, -1:2)
```

This statement identifies MATRIX as a two-dimensional array whose first subscript can be 3, 4, or 5, and whose second subscript can be −1, 0, 1, or 2. The lower bound must be less than or equal to the upper bound.

Dimension bounds for matrices in a main program must be integer expressions with constant operands.

Initializing Matrices

A DATA statement can give a matrix initial values. For example, the statements

```
INTEGER  X(2, 2)
DATA     X /1, 2, 3, 4/
```

give the elements of X the initial values 1, 2, 3, and 4. Since the values are stored according to the internal storage order, the particular element values are

```
X(1, 1) → 1
X(2, 1) → 2
X(1, 2) → 3
X(2, 1) → 4
```

or the matrix X is

$$\begin{bmatrix} 1 & 3 \\ 2 & 4 \end{bmatrix}$$

As with one-dimensional arrays, repeat counts can appear between the slashes. The statements

```
REAL   X(10, 10)
DATA   X /100 * 1.0/
```

fill the array X with 100 values of 1.0.

Executable statements, such as assignment and READ statements, can also give initial values to array elements. The following segment assigns the values from 1 to 5 to a 5 by 10 matrix.

```
      INTEGER  A(5, 10), ROW, COL
         .
         .
         .
      DO 11 ROW = 1, 5
         DO 11 COL = 1, 10
            A(ROW, COL) = ROW
11    CONTINUE
```

Each element in the first row gets value 1, each element in the second row gets value 2, and so on.

Reading and Writing Matrices

Fortran offers several ways to read values for a matrix. Most ways involve nested loops, with one loop for the row number and one for the column number, as in:

```
      INTEGER  ROW, COL, STUDNT(3, 4)
      DO 11 ROW = 1, 3
         DO 11 COLUMN = 1, 4
            READ *, STUDNT(ROW, COL)
 11   CONTINUE
```

The outer `DO` starts the row number at 1; then the inner `DO` causes the column number to range from 1 to 4. Next the row number increases to 2, and the column number again goes from 1 to 4. Finally, the row number increases to 3, and the column number goes from 1 to 4. The `READ` statement reads one value per record or input line. Thus, the values for the matrix elements must be given in *row-major* order:

420	
385	*Row*
379	*1*
370	
225	
218	*Row*
206	*2*
198	
186	
172	*Row*
165	*3*
162	

Often a program will read the values for a matrix from a file. To simplify checking the input data, the values should be placed in the file as they would appear in the matrix. For the `STUDNT` matrix, the values in the file should look something like

```
420  385  379  370
225  218  206  198
186  172  165  162
```

We can read these values into the matrix with the following segment:

```
      DO 11 ROW = 1, 3
         READ (9, *) (STUDNT(ROW, COL), COL = 1, 4)
 11   CONTINUE
```

Notice that we still have two loops, an explicit DO loop for ROW and an implied DO loop for COL. The READ statement reads four elements per record because there are four elements in the implied-DO list:

```
STUDNT(ROW, 1), STUDNT(ROW, 2), STUDNT(ROW, 3), STUDNT(ROW, 4)
```

We can get the same effect with two implied-DO lists in one READ statement:

```
      READ (9, 10) ( (STUDNT(ROW, COL), COL = 1, 4), ROW = 1, 3 )
10    FORMAT (4I5)
```

Notice that the entire implied-DO list

```
(STUDNT(ROW, COL), COL = 1, 4)
```

is nested inside the implied-DO for ROW, just as the DO loop for COL was nested inside the DO loop for ROW in our first example. In this case, the read list contains twelve elements, so a format specification (4I5) is necessary to tell the computer how many values (four) to read from each record.

Finally, an entire matrix can be read with a short-list statement such as

```
      READ *, STUDNT
```

Because of the storage order for matrices, the input values must appear in *column-major* form.

A formatted short-list statement is often used to read one column of a matrix per record. For instance, the statements

```
      READ (9, 10) STUDNT
10    FORMAT (3I5)
```

cause the computer to read three values per record, with the first three values stored as the first column, the second three as the second column, and so on. Then the values must appear in the file as

```
420 225 186   (Column 1)
385 218 172   (Column 2)
379 206 165   (Column 3)
370 198 162   (Column 4)
```

We now have seen four ways to read matrix values:

1. Nested DO loops, with the column loop nested inside the row loop

2. A DO loop for rows, with an implied-DO for columns
3. Implied-DO lists for both rows and columns, with the column list inside the row list
4. A short-list READ statement

Method 1 is useful only for reading one value per record, so we shall seldom use it. Method 3 is slightly shorter than 2, but method 2 seems clearer and less likely to lead to syntax errors, so we prefer method 2.

Many programmers use the short-list statement to read values for a matrix because it is so concise. The short-list method also has a speed advantage over the other methods because it reads the element values in their storage order. Remember that this method reads the entire matrix as it is dimensioned, so it does not apply to reading parts of matrices. Also keep in mind that the rows in the data file are actually the columns of the matrix.

Exactly the same options exist for *writing* matrix values. Method 1 writes only one value per record or line, so we do not often use it. We will generally prefer method 2 to method 3. Method 4, the short-list method, is not useful for writing matrices because it writes in column-major form.

Example 11.1 Summing the Rows of a Matrix

Now that we know how to read values for a matrix, let us write a small program to do something with the values. Considering the student example again, suppose we want to know how many students are enrolled in each school, and we do not care about the numbers of students in individual classes. To find the number of students in a particular school, we must sum the numbers in the appropriate row. Therefore, we will use a loop DO 33 ROW = 1, 3. Inside this ROW loop, we add the values in the row numbered ROW with the following segment.

```
      SUM = 0
      DO 22 COLUMN = 1, 4
         SUM = SUM + STUDNT(ROW, COLUMN)
22    CONTINUE
```

We have done exactly this sort of thing before with a statement like

```
      SUM = SUM + X
```

All we have done here is to change X to STUDNT(ROW, COLUMN).

We assume the data are in a file named STUDNT.DAT in (A12, 4I5) form:

```
Liberal Arts  420  385  379  370
Business      225  218  206  198
Engineering   186  172  165  162
```

The school names will be placed in a character array SCHOOL. The segment to read the data is

```
      DO 11 ROW = 1, 3
          READ (9, 10) SCHOOL(ROW), (STUDNT(ROW, COL), COL = 1, 4)
10        FORMAT (A12, 4I5)
11    CONTINUE
```

With matrices, echoing data read from files is quite important, so we include in the loop a PRINT statement:

```
      PRINT '(1X, 4I5)', ( STUDNT(ROW, COL), COL = 1, 4 )
```

Program 11.1 shows the entire program.

■
PROGRAM 11.1

```
      PROGRAM SUMROW
*----------------------------------------------------------------------*
*        Find total number of students in each of three schools.       *
*        Schools are in rows; classes are in columns.                  *
*        Data are in STUDNT.DAT; each record contains a school name    *
*        followed by four integers for the enrollments in the classes. *
*----------------------------------------------------------------------*
      INTEGER    ROW, COL, SUM, STUDNT(3, 4)
      CHARACTER  SCHOOL(3)*12
*----------------------------------------------------------------------*
*          Open the data file; read and write the matrix.              *
*----------------------------------------------------------------------*
      OPEN (9, FILE = 'STUDNT.DAT', STATUS = 'OLD')

      PRINT *, 'This is the enrollment matrix.  Schools'
      PRINT *, 'are rows and columns are classes.'
      PRINT *
```

```
      DO 11 ROW = 1, 3
         READ (9, 10) SCHOOL(ROW), (STUDNT(ROW, COL), COL = 1, 4)
         PRINT '(1X, 4I5)', ( STUDNT(ROW, COL), COL = 1, 4 )
11    CONTINUE

      CLOSE (9)
*------------------------------------------------------------*
*                     Print header.                          *
*------------------------------------------------------------*
      PRINT 20, 'School', 'Enrollment'
      PRINT 30
*------------------------------------------------------------*
*              Find and print the sums of the rows.          *
*------------------------------------------------------------*
      DO 33 ROW = 1, 3

         SUM = 0
         DO 22 COL = 1, 4
            SUM = SUM + STUDNT(ROW, COL)
22       CONTINUE

         PRINT 40, SCHOOL(ROW), SUM

33    CONTINUE

10    FORMAT (A12, 4I5)
20    FORMAT ('0', A, 7X, A)
30    FORMAT (1X, 23('-') )
40    FORMAT (1X, A, I6)

      END
```

The program produces the output

```
This is the enrollment matrix.  Schools
are rows and columns are classes.

   420   385   379   370
   225   218   206   198
   186   172   165   162

School        Enrollment
-----------------------
Liberal Arts  1554
Business       847
Engineering    685
```

Example 11.2 Printing a Table

Program 11.1 is a first step toward a more realistic problem. We often want to sum both the rows and columns of a matrix or table, and display the results in a form such as that in Figure 11.1. We now write a program to construct such a table.

An outline of the program is

1. Read data.
2. Accumulate totals.
3. Print the table.

As before, we use a 3 by 4 STUDNT matrix, and an array SCHOOL with three elements to hold the school names. We also shall use an array CLASS with four elements to hold the class names. We assume the data file, COLLEG.DAT, is in the form

```
Freshman
Sophomore
Junior
Senior
Liberal Arts  420  385  379  370
Business      225  218  206  198
Engineering   186  172  165  162
```

The reading of the file poses no new problems, so we turn our attention to accumulating the sums.

We will use integer arrays SUMSCH and SUMCLS to hold the obvious sums. For example, SUMSCH(2) will hold the number of business students, and SUMCLS(3) will accumulate the juniors. A variable SUM will accumulate the total number of students in the college. We set all the accumulator variables to zero.

All the summing takes place inside nested DO loops with indices ROW and COL. Once inside these loops, we are dealing with a specific element STUDNT(ROW, COL). This element must be added to the total for the class specified by COL, to the total for the school specified by ROW, and to the grand total SUM. The following segment accomplishes the summing.

```
      DO 22 ROW = 1, 3
         DO 11 COL = 1, 4

            TEMP = STUDNT(ROW, COL)
            SUMCLS(COL) = SUMCLS(COL) + TEMP
            SUMSCH(ROW) = SUMSCH(ROW) + TEMP
            SUM = SUM + TEMP

11          CONTINUE
22    CONTINUE
```

Notice the variable TEMP, whose main function is to save us from writing STUDNT(ROW, COL) three times. TEMP also saves the computer from having to retrieve the value for STUDNT(ROW, COL) three times, but this is a minor consideration.

The hardest part of the program is printing the table, and the tough part of printing the table is knowing where to start. The layout of each line depends on the layout of other lines. Some of the lines can easily adjust to others, and some cannot. The lines containing only dashes can easily be adjusted, so we leave them until last.

The header line, beginning with 'School', is a critical line. Without knowing exactly what format specification to use, we can write it with

```
    PRINT 30, 'School', (CLASS(COL), COL = 1, 4), 'Total'
```

At this point, we need to know the length of the character elements in CLASS. 'Sophomore' is the longest class name, with nine characters, so let us declare

```
    CHARACTER   CLASS(4)*9
```

The three lines in the body of the table will be written with

```
    DO 55 ROW = 1, 3
        PRINT 50, SCHOOL(ROW), (STUDNT(ROW, COL), COL = 1, 4),
   1            SUMSCH(ROW)
55  CONTINUE
```

These lines must line up properly under the header line. The SCHOOL names have length 12, and 'Liberal Arts' is exactly that long. This length is longer than the word 'School', so this line is the appropriate one to start with. We want at least one space before the vertical bar (|), so the format statement begins with

```
50     FORMAT (1X, A12, X, '|',
```

Then, for the header line, the format statement begins

```
30     FORMAT (1X, A6, 7X, '|',
```

We could use the A specifications without widths, but it is easier to match up two specifications if the widths are present.

After the vertical bar, the numbers must line up under the appropriate class names. The names take up more columns than the numbers, so it will be easier to adjust the numbers. Therefore, we finish the header format first.

There should be a space after the vertical bar and at least one space between names, so we will write the names under a 4(X, A9) specification. The end of the line should look like

| Total |

so the remaining format specification is

'|', 1X, A5, 1X, '|')

The entire specification for the header line is

```
30    FORMAT (1X, A6, 7X, '|', 4(1X, A9), '|', 1X, A5, 1X, '|')
```

To line up the numbers under the names, we can use the specification 4(I6, 4X). The complete format statement is

```
50    FORMAT (1X, A12, 1X, '|', 4(I6, 4X), '|', I5, 2X, '|')
```

Notice how the pieces of the two format specifications fit together.

```
(1X, A6, 7X, '|', 4(1X, A9), '|', 1X, A5, 1X, '|')
(1X, A12, 1X, '|', 4(I6, 4X), '|', I5, 2X,  '|')
```

Up to the first vertical bar, there are 13 columns, given by A6, 7X in the first specification, and by A12, 1X in the second. After the bar, 4(1X, A9) and 4(I6, 4X) specify 40 columns. After the second bar, 1X, A5, X and I5, 2X each take 7 columns.

These two format specifications determine all the others. You should try to write the others before reviewing this program in Program 11.2.

■

PROGRAM 11.2

```
      PROGRAM TABLE
*-------------------------------------------------------------*
*     Sum rows and columns of a matrix and print a table.     *
*     Data are in COLLEG.DAT; the first four records          *
*     contain class names, the next three contain school      *
*     names, and the last three contain the matrix data.      *
*-------------------------------------------------------------*
      INTEGER    ROW, COL, SUM, TEMP
      INTEGER    STUDNT(3, 4), SUMSCH(3), SUMCLS(4)
      CHARACTER  SCHOOL(3)*12, CLASS(4)*9
```

```
*-------------------------------------------------------*
*        Open file and read CLASS, SCHOOL, and STUDNT.   *
*-------------------------------------------------------*
      OPEN (9, FILE = 'COLLEG', STATUS = 'OLD')

      READ (9, '(4A)') (CLASS(COL), COL = 1, 4)

      DO 11 ROW = 1, 3
         READ (9, '(A12, 4I5)') SCHOOL(ROW),
     1        ( STUDNT(ROW, COL), COL = 1, 4 )

11    CONTINUE

      CLOSE (9)
*-------------------------------------------------------*
*              Initialize all counters to zero.          *
*-------------------------------------------------------*
      DO 22 COL = 1, 4
         SUMCLS(COL) = 0
22    CONTINUE

      DO 33 ROW = 1, 3
         SUMSCH(ROW) = 0
33    CONTINUE

      SUM = 0
*-------------------------------------------------------*
*                   Accumulate totals.                   *
*-------------------------------------------------------*
      DO 55 ROW = 1, 3
         DO 44 COL = 1, 4

            TEMP = STUDNT(ROW, COL)
            SUMCLS(COL) = SUMCLS(COL) + TEMP
            SUMSCH(ROW) = SUMSCH(ROW) + TEMP
            SUM = SUM + TEMP

44       CONTINUE
55    CONTINUE
*-------------------------------------------------------*
*                     Print table.                       *
*-------------------------------------------------------*
      PRINT 10, 'Class'
      PRINT 20
      PRINT 30, 'School', (CLASS(COL), COL = 1, 4), 'Total'
      PRINT 40
```

```
      DO 66 ROW = 1, 3
         PRINT 50, SCHOOL(ROW), (STUDNT(ROW, COL), COL = 1, 4),
     1              SUMSCH(ROW)
 66   CONTINUE

      PRINT 40
      PRINT 60, 'Total', (SUMCLS(COL), COL = 1, 4), SUM
      PRINT 40

 10   FORMAT ('1', 32X, A)
 20   FORMAT (1X, 13X, 50('-'))
 30   FORMAT (1X, A6, 7X, '|', 4(X, A9), '|', 1X, A5, 1X, '|')
 40   FORMAT (1X, 63('-'))
 50   FORMAT (1X, A12, 1X, '|', 4(I6, 4X), '|', I5, 2X, '|')
 60   FORMAT (1X, A5, 8X, '|', 4(I6, 4X), '|', I5, 2X, '|')

      END
```

The program produces the following output

		Class			
School	Freshman	Sophomore	Junior	Senior	Total
Liberal Arts	420	385	379	370	1554
Business	225	218	206	198	847
Engineering	186	172	165	162	685
Total	831	775	750	730	3086

Example 11.3 Finding the Largest Value in Each Column

Consider the problem of finding the largest value in each column of a matrix. We have already written programs to find the largest value in a set of numbers, but the matrix notation and the fact that there are several largest numbers (one for each column) make this problem a little more complicated.

We will again use ROW and COL to represent row and column numbers. This time we let A be the matrix variable. We could decide now to use four rows and six columns, for instance, but let us try to write a more general program, and let NRCOL represent the number of columns and NRROW the number of rows. We will place values for NRROW and NRCOL in the first record of the data file, so now our data file might look like this:

```
4  5
 -42.03  38.53  37.91  -37.08  -55.23
  22.45  12.18  20.56   19.88  -42.18
  18.16  17.92  26.35   16.72  -63.25
 -65.34  41.29  18.52   17.76  -55.22
```

When we do not know in advance what the actual size of the matrix might be, we will often place size data in a file in this manner. List-directed read statements can read the file.

For the largest numbers we have a choice. We can use one variable, LARGE, to represent all the largest numbers (one at a time), or we can use a subscripted variable LARGE so all the largest values can be stored at the same time. We will choose the latter course, not because it is necessary here, but because the method is more general.

We need a loop beginning

```
DO 22 COL = 1, NRCOL
```

the calculation of the largest number in each column will occur inside this loop. We will begin writing the part of the program inside the COL loop. For whatever value COL has, the largest number in the column will be designated LARGE(COL), and we begin by letting LARGE(COL) have the value of the first number in the column. That is,

```
LARGE(COL) = A(1, COL)
```

because A(1, COL) is the first element in the column numbered COL. We then compare the values in rows 2, 3, ..., NRROW to LARGE(COL), with the code:

```
      LARGE(COL) = A(1, COL)
      DO 11 ROW = 2, NRROW
         LARGE(COL) = MAX( LARGE(COL), A(ROW,COL) )
11    CONTINUE
      PRINT 10, COL, LARGE(COL)
10    FORMAT (1X, 'Largest in column', I3, ' is', G12.4)
```

We finish the program by putting the COL loop around this segment and reading values into the matrix A. See Program 11.3 for the full program.

■

PROGRAM 11.3

```fortran
      PROGRAM LARGEC
*----------------------------------------------------------------*
*     Find largest number in each column of a matrix.            *
*     Data are in MATRIX.DAT; the first record contains          *
*     the numbers of rows and columns in the matrix.             *
*----------------------------------------------------------------*
      INTEGER   ROW, COL, NRROW, NRCOL
      REAL      A(20, 20), LARGE(20)
*----------------------------------------------------------------*
*           Open file and read dimensions.                       *
*----------------------------------------------------------------*
      OPEN (9, FILE = 'MATRIX', STATUS = 'OLD')

      READ (9, *) NRROW, NRCOL
*----------------------------------------------------------------*
*              Read and write matrix.                            *
*----------------------------------------------------------------*
      PRINT *, ' Matrix:'
      PRINT *

      DO 11 ROW = 1, NRROW
         READ (9, *) ( A(ROW, COL), COL = 1, NRCOL )
         PRINT *, ( A(ROW, COL), COL = 1, NRCOL )
11    CONTINUE

      PRINT *

      CLOSE (9)
*----------------------------------------------------------------*
*     Find and print largest number in each column.              *
*----------------------------------------------------------------*
      DO 22 COL = 1, NRCOL

         LARGE(COL) = A(1, COL)
         DO 33 ROW = 2, NRROW
            LARGE(COL) = MAX( LARGE(COL), A(ROW,COL) )
33       CONTINUE

         PRINT 10, COL, LARGE(COL)

22    CONTINUE
```

```
10      FORMAT (1X, 'Largest in column', I3, ' is', G12.4)

        END
```

The output from the program is

```
Matrix:

    -42.0300      38.5300      37.9100     -37.0800     -55.2300
     22.4500      12.1800      20.5600      19.8800     -42.1800
     18.1600      17.9200      26.3500      16.7200     -63.2500
    -65.3400      41.2900      18.5200      17.7600     -55.2200

Largest in column 1 is    22.45
Largest in column 2 is    41.29
Largest in column 3 is    37.91
Largest in column 4 is    19.88
Largest in column 5 is   -42.18
```

Notice that A is dimensioned 20 by 20. However, the program reads only as many rows and columns as are specified by the first two numbers in the file. We assumed that users would not have matrices with more than twenty rows or more than twenty columns. You can, of course, use larger dimension bounds if you need them.

List-directed output of matrices looks reasonable on a terminal screen if there are not more than five columns in the matrix. With six or more columns, the sixth column prints underneath the first column, so the output does not look like a matrix. Line printers typically use 132-column lines, enough to handle an 8-column matrix in list-directed format. The ninth and succeeding columns will wrap around to the next line. If the purpose of writing the matrix is simply to check that the computer has read the data properly, this wrapping is not a serious problem. If, however, good-looking output is important, you should know what kinds of values to expect, and then you can use formatted output statements.

Passing Matrices to Subprograms

Fortran allows subprograms to use assumed-size arrays, but only the *last upper* dimension bound can have an assumed size. A subprogram can contain the dimensioning statement

```
    REAL  X(10, *)
```

but REAL X(*, *) and REAL X(5:10, *:*) are illegal.

Fortran allows adjustable array sizes for both dimension bounds, but because of the storage order for two-dimensional arrays, such dimension bounds can be hazardous. The following example shows why. The program does nothing but read a matrix and call a subroutine BADWRT to write the matrix. The data are in a file MAT.DAT with the number of rows and columns in the first record, and each succeeding record containing a row of the matrix.

```
      PROGRAM ADJUST

      REAL     A(3, 3)
      INTEGER  NROW, NCOL, ROW, COL

      OPEN (9, FILE = 'MAT', STATUS = 'OLD')

      READ (9, *) NROW, NCOL

      DO 11 ROW = 1, NROW
         READ (9, *) (A(ROW, COL), COL = 1, NCOL)
11    CONTINUE

      CALL BADWRT (A, NROW, NCOL)

      END
*****************************************************************
      SUBROUTINE BADWRT (A, NROW, NCOL)

      INTEGER  NROW, NCOL, ROW, COL
      REAL     A(NROW, NCOL)

      DO 11 ROW = 1, NROW
         PRINT *, (A(ROW, COL), COL = 1, NCOL)
11    CONTINUE

      END
*****************************************************************
```

If the data file MAT.DAT is

```
2 2
 1  2
 3  4
```

the output will be

```
      1.000000      0.0000000E+00
      3.000000       2.000000
```

The 4 got lost, and the 2 and 3 are not where we expected them to be! To see why this happened, consider the storage order for A in the main program, and the order assumed by the subprogram:

Main Program			Subprogram
A(1, 1)	→ 1.0	←	A(1, 1)
A(2, 1)	→ 3.0	←	A(2, 1)
A(3, 1)	→ ?	←	A(1, 2)
A(1, 2)	→ 2.0	←	A(2, 1)
A(2, 2)	→ 4.0		
A(3, 2)	→ ?		
A(1, 3)	→ ?		
A(2, 3)	→ ?		
A(3, 3)	→ ?		

If we change the declaration for A in the subprogram to

```
REAL  A(3, NCOL)
```

then everything will turn out all right because the storage orders are now

Main Program			Subprogram
A(1, 1)	→ 1.0	←	A(1, 1)
A(2, 1)	→ 3.0	←	A(2, 1)
A(3, 1)	→ ?	←	A(3, 1)
A(1, 2)	→ 2.0	←	A(1, 2)
A(2, 2)	→ 4.0	←	A(2, 2)
A(3, 2)	→ ?	←	A(3, 2)
A(1, 3)	→ ?		
A(2, 3)	→ ?		
A(3, 3)	→ ?		

It is the *first* dimension bound that causes problems. The first bound in the subprogram must be exactly the same as the first bound in the main program. The second dimension bound in the subprogram can be assumed or adjustable. It even can be a constant, as long as that constant does not exceed the second dimension bound in the calling program.

One way out of this problem is to use a constant first dimension bound in the calling program, and be sure to use the same constant for the first dimension bound in all subprograms. We could, for example, always use 50 as a first dimension bound in our programs and subprograms. This solution is not entirely satisfactory because a program might require a bound larger than 50, or a bound much smaller.

An alternative is to pass the first dimension bound to the subprogram. This is the alternative we generally shall use. We will call the first dimension bound a parameter **MAXROW** and pass this value to subprograms. The programs in the next section illustrate this procedure.

■

11.2 MATRIX CALCULATIONS

Many operations used for numbers also can be used with matrices: addition, subtraction, and multiplication, for instance. However, when two matrices A and B are to be added or multiplied, there are restrictions on the sizes of A and B.

Matrix Addition

In order for the sum $A + B$ to be defined, A and B must have exactly the same size. Then the sum of A and B is a matrix C of the same size with

$$C_{ij} = A_{ij} + B_{ij}$$

That is, the element of C in a particular place is the sum of the elements of A and B in that same place. Subtraction of matrices is defined in the same way, with a minus sign in place of a plus sign. For example:

$$\begin{pmatrix} 2 & 4 & -2 \\ 7 & 5 & 2 \\ 4 & 7 & 4 \end{pmatrix} + \begin{pmatrix} 4 & -2 & 4 \\ 2 & -4 & 7 \\ 4 & -7 & 3 \end{pmatrix} = \begin{pmatrix} 2+4 & 4+(-2) & -2+4 \\ 7+2 & 5+(-4) & 2+7 \\ 4+4 & 7+(-7) & 6+3 \end{pmatrix}$$

$$= \begin{pmatrix} 6 & 2 & 2 \\ 9 & 1 & 9 \\ 8 & 0 & 9 \end{pmatrix}$$

and

$$\begin{pmatrix} 2 & 4 & -2 \\ 7 & 5 & 2 \\ 4 & 7 & 6 \end{pmatrix} - \begin{pmatrix} 4 & -2 & 4 \\ 2 & -4 & 7 \\ 4 & -7 & 4 \end{pmatrix} = \begin{pmatrix} 2-4 & 4-(-2) & -2-4 \\ 7-2 & 5-(-4) & 2-7 \\ 4-4 & 7-(-7) & 6-4 \end{pmatrix}$$

$$= \begin{pmatrix} -2 & 6 & -6 \\ 5 & 9 & -5 \\ 0 & 14 & 2 \end{pmatrix}$$

We will write a program to add two matrices. Matrix data will be in the file `MATADD.DAT`. Even with two matrices, only one pair of dimension bounds must be supplied, because the two matrices must be the same size. We will put a format specification in the second record in the file. This specification will be read into a format variable used to write the matrices and their sum. The data file `MATADD.DAT` could be

```
3  5
(X, 5F10.2)
 23.45 -13.62  15.88  35.43 -45.01
 32.54  31.26 -19.77  12.34 -15.02     Matrix  A
-18.18 -12.34  18.55  40.10 -12.03
 18.42  32.14  15.58  14.01  20.31
 24.31 -11.34  19.58  32.11 -45.20     Matrix  B
 55.81 -22.21 -57.85  28.62  24.50
```

Example 11.4 Matrix Addition

A program to add matrices is not complicated but is rather long because of the double loops required. We use subroutines to read and print the matrices. Here is an outline of the program.

1. Open the file and read the first two records, which contain the sizes of the matrices and the format for writing the matrix data.
2. Call subroutines REDMAT and WRIMAT for each of the input matrices A and B.
3. Calculate the sum matrix D.
4. Call WRIMAT to write the sum matrix D.

The subroutine REDMAT is:

```
      SUBROUTINE REDMAT(X, MAXROW, NROW, NCOL, UNITNO)

      INTEGER   MAXROW, NROW, NCOL, ROW, COL, UNITNO
      REAL      X(MAXROW, NCOL)

      DO 11 ROW = 1, NROW
         READ (UNITNO, *) ( X(ROW, COL), COL = 1, NCOL)
11    CONTINUE

      END
```

The dummy argument MAXROW receives a value that gives the first dimension bound for the matrix in the calling program. The dummy arguments NROW and NCOL are the numbers of rows and columns actually used in the matrix. The array X uses adjustable dimension bounds MAXROW and NCOL.

Notice that subroutine REDMAT has a dummy argument UNITNO, an integer specifying the unit number of the file opened in the program.

Subroutine WRIMAT is almost identical, but contains a dummy argument OUTF for the output format. The subroutine name statement is

```
SUBROUTINE WRIMAT(X, MAXROW, NROW, NCOL, OUTF)
```

and the PRINT statement is

```
PRINT OUTF, (X(ROW, COL), COL = 1, NCOL)
```

See Program 11.4 for the full program.

■
PROGRAM 11.4

```
      PROGRAM ADDMAT
*------------------------------------------------------------------*
*                    Add two matrices.                             *
*                                                                  *
*     Data are in MATADD.DAT.  The first record has the sizes      *
*     of the two matrices.  The second record has the format       *
*     specification for writing the matrices and their sum.        *
*------------------------------------------------------------------*
      INTEGER    NROW, NCOL, ROW, COL, MAXROW, UNITNO
      PARAMETER  (MAXROW = 10)
      REAL       A(MAXROW, MAXROW), B(MAXROW, MAXROW)
      REAL       SUM(MAXROW, MAXROW)
      CHARACTER  OUTF*30
      PARAMETER  (UNITNO = 9)
*------------------------------------------------------------------*
*          Open the file.  Read the size and format.               *
*------------------------------------------------------------------*
      OPEN (UNITNO, FILE = 'MATADD', STATUS = 'OLD')

      READ (UNITNO, *) NROW, NCOL
      READ (UNITNO, '(A)') OUTF
*------------------------------------------------------------------*
*               Read and print first matrix, A.                    *
*------------------------------------------------------------------*
      PRINT 10, 'Matrix A'
```

```
      CALL REDMAT(A, MAXROW, NROW, NCOL, UNITNO)
      CALL WRIMAT(A, MAXROW, NROW, NCOL, OUTF)
*------------------------------------------------------------*
*   Read and print second matrix, B, and close the file.   *
*------------------------------------------------------------*
      PRINT 10, 'Matrix B'

      CALL REDMAT(B, MAXROW, NROW, NCOL, UNITNO)
      CLOSE (9)
      CALL WRIMAT(B, MAXROW, NROW, NCOL, OUTF)
*------------------------------------------------------------*
*              Calculate elements of SUM = A + B.            *
*------------------------------------------------------------*
      DO 22 ROW = 1, NROW
         DO 11 COL = 1, NCOL
            SUM(ROW, COL) = A(ROW, COL) + B(ROW, COL)
11       CONTINUE
22    CONTINUE
*------------------------------------------------------------*
*              Print elements of the sum matrix.             *
*------------------------------------------------------------*
      PRINT 10, 'The sum of matrices A and B'

      CALL WRIMAT(SUM, MAXROW, NROW, NCOL, OUTF)

10    FORMAT ('0', A)

      END
*************************************************************
      SUBROUTINE REDMAT(X, MAXROW, NROW, NCOL, UNITNO)
      INTEGER    MAXROW, NROW, NCOL, ROW, COL, UNITNO
      REAL       X(MAXROW, NCOL)

      DO 11 ROW = 1, NROW
         READ (UNITNO, *) ( X(ROW, COL), COL = 1, NCOL)
11    CONTINUE

      END
*************************************************************
      SUBROUTINE WRIMAT(X, MAXROW, NROW, NCOL, OUTF)
      INTEGER    MAXROW, NROW, NCOL, ROW, COL
      REAL       X(MAXROW, NCOL)
      CHARACTER  OUTF*30

      PRINT *
      DO 11 ROW = 1, NROW
         PRINT OUTF, ( X(ROW, COL), COL = 1, NCOL)
11    CONTINUE
```

```
PRINT *

END
```

The output from the program is

```
Matrix A

    23.45    -13.62     15.88     35.43    -45.01
    32.54     31.26    -19.77     12.34    -15.02
   -18.18    -12.34     18.55     40.10    -12.03


Matrix B

    18.42     32.14     15.58     14.01     20.31
    24.31    -11.34     19.58     32.11    -45.20
    55.81    -22.21    -57.85     28.62     24.50


The sum of matrices A and B

    41.87     18.52     31.46     49.44    -24.70
    56.85     19.92     -0.19     44.45    -60.22
    37.63    -34.55    -39.30     68.72     12.47
```

Matrix Multiplication

Matrices A and B can be multiplied in the order AB if the number of *columns* in A is the same as the number of *rows* in B. That is, if A is a 3 by 5 matrix, then B must be 5 by something. When A is m by n and B is n by p, the product AB is an m by p matrix. If A is 3 by 5 and B is 5 by 4, then AB is 3 by 4. The element of AB in the i row and j column is

$$A_{i1}B_{1j} + A_{i2}B_{2j} + \cdots + A_{in}B_{nj}$$

where n is the common number of columns in A and rows in B. Look at just the elements of A in that expression:

$$A_{i1}, A_{i2}, \ldots, A_{in}$$

They are simply the elements from the ith row of A. Similarly, the elements of B are

$$B_{1j}, B_{2j}, \ldots, B_{nj}$$

or the *j*th column of *B*. Thus, the rule for matrix multiplication can be stated as: The *i, j* element of the product *AB* is the *i*th row of *A* *times* the *j*th column of *B*.

Example 11.5 Matrix Multiplication

We will write a program to calculate the product of two matrices *A* and *B*. Data will be in the file MATPRO.DAT. The first record contains three integers giving the number of rows in *A*, the common number of columns in *A* and rows in *B*, and the number of columns in *B*. We call these three values NROWA, NAB, and NCOLB.

The next three records contain output formats for writing matrices *A*, *B*, and their product, in that order. A sample data file MATPRO.DAT might look like

```
5  2  7
(2F5.1)
(7F5.1)
(7F8.2)
   5.0  1.0
   1.5  3.5
  -1.0  2.5      Matrix A
   2.0  1.5
   3.0 -2.0
   1.0  2.5  3.0  4.5  5.0  6.5  7.0  Matrix B
   1.5  2.5 -1.0  3.5  1.5  4.5 -5.0
```

We will call the product matrix *P*. The calculation of *P* requires triply nested loops. The two outer loops determine the row and column numbers, ROW and COL, as before. The innermost loop calculates P(ROW, COL) by accumulating the products of an element of *A* times an element of *B*. The segment to calculate *P* is

```
      DO 33 ROW = 1, NROWA
         DO 22 COL = 1, NCOLB

            P(ROW, COL) = 0.0
            DO 11 K = 1, NAB
               P(ROW, COL) = P(ROW, COL) + A(ROW, K) * B(K, COL)
11          CONTINUE

22       CONTINUE
33    CONTINUE
```

Program 11.5 contains the entire program.

■
PROGRAM 11.5

```
      PROGRAM MATMUL
*-------------------------------------------------------------*
*                  Multiply two matrices.                     *
*                                                             *
*  Data are in MATPRO.DAT.  The first record has three dimension *
*  bounds for matrices A and B.  The next three records contain *
*  formats for writing A, B, and their product.  The rest of the *
*  records contain the rows of matrices A and B.              *
*-------------------------------------------------------------*
      INTEGER       MAXROW, ROW, COL, NROWA, NAB, NCOLB, K, U
      PARAMETER     (MAXROW = 10)
      REAL          A(MAXROW, MAXROW), B(MAXROW, MAXROW)
      REAL          P(MAXROW, MAXROW)
      CHARACTER*30  OUTAF, OUTBF, OUTPF
      PARAMETER     (U = 7)
*-------------------------------------------------------------*
*    Open file and read dimension bounds for the two matrices. *
*-------------------------------------------------------------*
      OPEN (U, FILE = 'MATPRO', STATUS = 'OLD')

      READ (U, *) NROWA, NAB, NCOLB
      READ (U, '(A)') OUTAF
      READ (U, '(A)') OUTBF
      READ (U, '(A)') OUTPF
*-------------------------------------------------------------*
*                  Read and write matrix A.                   *
*-------------------------------------------------------------*
      PRINT 10, 'Matrix A'
      CALL REDMAT(A, MAXROW, NROWA, NAB, U)
      CALL WRIMAT(A, MAXROW, NROWA, NAB, OUTAF)
*-------------------------------------------------------------*
*         Read matrix B, close the file, and write B.         *
*-------------------------------------------------------------*
      PRINT 10, 'Matrix B'
      CALL REDMAT(B, MAXROW, NAB, NCOLB, U)
      CLOSE (9)
      CALL WRIMAT(B, MAXROW, NAB, NCOLB, OUTBF)
```

```
*--------------------------------------------------------*
*               Calculate product matrix P.              *
*--------------------------------------------------------*
      DO 33 ROW = 1, NROWA
         DO 22 COL = 1, NCOLB
            P(ROW, COL) = 0.0
            DO 11 K = 1, NAB
               P(ROW, COL) = P(ROW, COL) + A(ROW, K) * B(K, COL)
11          CONTINUE

22       CONTINUE
33    CONTINUE
*--------------------------------------------------------*
*               Write the product matrix P.              *
*--------------------------------------------------------*
      PRINT 10, 'Product Matrix AB'

      CALL WRIMAT(P, MAXROW, NROWA, NCOLB, OUTPF)

10    FORMAT ('0', A)

      END
```

The program produces the output

```
Matrix A

  5.0  1.0
  1.5  3.5
 -1.0  2.5
  2.0  1.5
  3.0 -2.0

Matrix B

  1.0  2.5  3.0  4.5  5.0  6.5  7.0
  1.5  2.5 -1.0  3.5  1.5  4.5 -5.0

Product Matrix AB

    6.50   15.00   14.00   26.00   26.50   37.00   30.00
    6.75   12.50    1.00   19.00   12.75   25.50   -7.00
    2.75    3.75   -5.50    4.25   -1.25    4.75  -19.50
    4.25    8.75    4.50   14.25   12.25   19.75    6.50
    0.00    2.50   11.00    6.50   12.00   10.50   31.00
```

The next two programs illustrate two useful matrix applications, the calculation of a *determinant* and solving a system of *linear equations*. These programs are considerably more complex than the previous two, and will be difficult for readers who are not already familiar with the computational aspects of these problems.

Determinants

Associated with every square matrix is a number called the **determinant** of the matrix. The determinant can be calculated in many ways. Here is one of the simplest ways, involving three rules. First we give two definitions.

Definition: The **main diagonal** of a square matrix is the set of elements with equal subscripts. In a 3 by 3 matrix A, the diagonal elements are A_{11}, A_{22}, and A_{33}.

Definition: An **upper triangular matrix** is a square matrix with only zeroes below the diagonal, as in

$$\begin{bmatrix} 2 & 1 & 3 \\ 0 & 3 & 7 \\ 0 & 0 & -4 \end{bmatrix}$$

Rule 1:   The determinant of an upper triangular matrix is the product of the diagonal elements. For the matrix above, the determinant is $2 \times 3 \times (-4) = -24$.

Rule 2:   If a multiple of one row of a square matrix is added to another row, the determinant of the matrix is not changed.

For example, the determinant of the matrix $\begin{bmatrix} 2 & 3 & 4 \\ 0 & 5 & 7 \\ 4 & 6 & 12 \end{bmatrix}$ is

the determinant of $\begin{bmatrix} 2 & 3 & 4 \\ 0 & 5 & 7 \\ 0 & 6 & 4 \end{bmatrix}$, since the second matrix is

the result of adding (-2) times the first row to the third row of the first matrix. It is easy to see that the determinant of the second matrix is $2 \times 5 \times 4 = 40$.

Rule 3:   If two rows of a matrix are *switched*, the determinant of the new matrix is (-1) times the determinant of the original matrix.

Consider the matrix

$$A = \begin{bmatrix} 2 & 1 & 3 \\ 4 & 4 & 9 \\ 6 & 9 & 8 \end{bmatrix}$$

To reduce A to upper-triangular form, start with the first column. Use the 2 in the first row to "wipe out" the 4 below it by adding -2 times row 1 to row 2 to obtain

$$\begin{bmatrix} 2 & 1 & 3 \\ 0 & 2 & 3 \\ 6 & 9 & 8 \end{bmatrix}$$

Then add -3 times row 1 to row 3 to get

$$\begin{bmatrix} 2 & 1 & 3 \\ 0 & 2 & 3 \\ 0 & 4 & -1 \end{bmatrix}$$

That takes care of the first column. Add -2 times row 2 to row 3 to obtain

$$\begin{bmatrix} 2 & 1 & 3 \\ 0 & 2 & 3 \\ 0 & 0 & -7 \end{bmatrix}$$

The matrix is now in upper-triangular form, and the determinant is

$$2 \times 2 \times (-7) = -28$$

Example 11.6 Calculating a Determinant

The basic idea is to use the diagonal elements to turn the numbers below the diagonal into zeroes. We started with the element A_{11} and turned the numbers below it into zeroes by adding appropriate multiples of row 1 to row 2 and row 3. Then we used A_{22} to turn the element below it into zero. Elements used to turn other elements into zero are called **pivot elements**.

Using N as the common number of rows and columns in the matrix A, we can turn this idea into the following program segment.

```
DO 33 ROW = 1, N

        PIVOT = A(ROW, ROW)
        DO 22 KROW = ROW + 1, N
*-------------------------------------------------------------------*
*        Subtract the proper multiple of row ROW from row KROW.     *
*-------------------------------------------------------------------*
            P = A(KROW, ROW)
            DO 11 COL = ROW, N
                A(KROW, COL) = A(KROW, COL) - P * A(ROW, COL) / PIVOT
11          CONTINUE
22      CONTINUE
33  CONTINUE
```

This method will work for some matrices, but it will fail in some cases. Consider the matrix

$$B = \begin{pmatrix} 1 & 1 & 3 \\ 2 & 2 & 4 \\ 3 & 4 & 8 \end{pmatrix}$$

After using B_{11} as a pivot, the matrix becomes

$$\begin{pmatrix} 1 & 1 & 2 \\ 0 & 0 & 1 \\ 0 & 1 & 2 \end{pmatrix}$$

Our program segment would use the zero in the 2, 2 position as the next pivot. But the segment then divides by the pivot value, causing a fatal error.

Rule 3 states that interchanging rows changes the sign of the determinant. We can interchange rows 2 and 3 to obtain

$$\begin{pmatrix} 1 & 1 & 2 \\ 0 & 1 & 2 \\ 0 & 0 & 1 \end{pmatrix}$$

This matrix has determinant 1, so the original matrix has determinant -1.

To fix our program segment, we use a subroutine called GETPIV that will interchange rows when such interchanges are necessary or desirable.

An interchange was necessary in our example because the proposed pivot was zero, but it is often desirable to change rows even when the pivot is not zero. A small pivot can lead to great round-off error in the calculation of a determinant, so a good strategy is to choose the pivot with the largest possible absolute value.

In place of the statement

```
PIVOT = A(ROW, ROW)
```

we put the statements

```
CALL GETPIV(A, MAXROW, N, N, ROW, PIVOT)
IF (PIVOT .EQ. 0.0) THEN
    DETER = 0.0
    GO TO 55
ELSE
    DO 22 KROW = ROW + 1, N
      .
      .
      .
```

GETPIV has dummy arguments A, MAXROW, NROW, NCOL, ROW, and PIVOT. The first N in the actual argument list is the number of rows in the matrix A, corresponding to the dummy argument NROW. The second N corresponds to NCOL, the number of columns in A. The determinant of A exists only when the number of rows is equal to the number of columns, but the pivot operation is useful in other problems involving nonsquare matrices.

The subroutine looks at A(ROW, ROW) and each element below A(ROW, ROW) to find the one with largest absolute value. If the largest absolute value is zero, then all the elements in the column, from A(ROW, ROW) down, must be zero. In this case the determinant is zero, so the program could simply stop here and notify the user that the determinant is zero. However, we merely bypass the segment that subtracts multiples of the pivot row from other rows.

Otherwise, the row in which the element with largest absolute value appears is called PIVROW. The subroutine interchanges the elements in the rows numbered ROW and PIVROW. Since interchanging rows multiplies the determinant by −1, GETPIV compensates for the interchange by multiplying the old row PIVROW by −1, an operation that also multiplies the determinant by −1. Changing pivots in this manner is called **partial pivoting**.

The full program is given in Program 11.6.

■

PROGRAM 11.6

```
      PROGRAM DETERM
*-------------------------------------------------------------------*
*              Calculate the determinant of a square matrix.        *
*                                                                   *
*  Data are in file DETER.DAT.  First record contains the order of  *
*  the matrix.  Second record has the format for writing the matrix.*
*  Remaining records contain rows of the matrix.                    *
*-------------------------------------------------------------------*
      INTEGER    MAXROW, ROW, COL, N, R, U
      PARAMETER  (MAXROW = 10)
      REAL       A(MAXROW, MAXROW), DETER, P, PIVOT
      CHARACTER  OUTF*30
      PARAMETER  (U = 3)
*-------------------------------------------------------------------*
*      Open file.  Read order of matrix and output format.          *
*-------------------------------------------------------------------*
      OPEN (U, FILE = 'DETER', STATUS = 'OLD')

      READ (U, *) N
      READ (U, '(A)') OUTF
*-------------------------------------------------------------------*
*         Call REDMAT and WRIMAT to read and write the matrix.      *
*-------------------------------------------------------------------*
      CALL REDMAT(A, MAXROW, N, N, U)
      CLOSE (9)
      PRINT 10, 'Matrix'
      CALL WRIMAT(A, MAXROW, N, N, OUTF)
*-------------------------------------------------------------------*
*               Reduce A to an upper-triangular matrix.             *
*-------------------------------------------------------------------*
      DO 33 ROW = 1, N

         CALL GETPIV(A, MAXROW, N, N, ROW, PIVOT)
         IF (PIVOT .EQ. 0.0) THEN

            DETER = 0.0
            GO TO 55

         ELSE
```

```
              DO 22 R = ROW + 1, N

                 P = A(R, ROW)
                 DO 11 COL = ROW, N
                    A(R, COL) = A(R, COL) - P * A(ROW, COL) / PIVOT
11                  CONTINUE

22            CONTINUE

           END IF

33     CONTINUE
*-----------------------------------------------------------------*
*   Calculate determinant as the product of diagonal elements of A.   *
*-----------------------------------------------------------------*
       DETER = 1.0
       DO 44 ROW = 1, N
          DETER = DETER * A(ROW, ROW)
44     CONTINUE

55     PRINT 20, DETER

10     FORMAT ('0', A /)
20     FORMAT ('0', 'The determinant is', G13.4)

       END
*******************************************************************
*                   SUBROUTINE GETPIV                            *
*                                                               *
*   Find element with largest absolute value at or below A(ROW, ROW).   *
*   Interchange rows ROW and PIVROW if necessary, changing sign in      *
*   the old pivot row.                                          *
*******************************************************************
       SUBROUTINE GETPIV(A, MAXROW, NROW, NCOL, ROW, PIVOT)
       INTEGER  MAXROW, NROW, NCOL, ROW, PIVROW, REMROW, COL
       REAL     PIVOT, TEMP, A(MAXROW, NCOL)
*-----------------------------------------------------------------*
*      Pivot on largest element in column ROW at or below row ROW.    *
*-----------------------------------------------------------------*
       PIVOT = A(ROW, ROW)
       PIVROW = ROW

       DO 11 REMROW = ROW + 1, NROW

          IF ( ABS(A(REMROW, ROW)) .GT. ABS(PIVOT) ) THEN
             PIVOT  = A(REMROW, ROW)
             PIVROW = REMROW
          END IF
11     CONTINUE
```

```
*-------------------------------------------------------------------*
*          If new pivot row, swap PIVROW and ROW and change sign in  *
*          old PIVROW to compensate for changing the determinant.    *
*-------------------------------------------------------------------*
      IF (PIVROW .NE. ROW) THEN

         DO 22 COL = ROW, NCOL
            TEMP             = A(PIVROW, COL)
            A(PIVROW, COL) = -A(ROW, COL)
            A(ROW, COL)     = TEMP
22       CONTINUE

      END IF


      END
*********************************************************************
      SUBROUTINE REDMAT(X, MAXROW, NROW, NCOL, U)
      INTEGER    MAXROW, NROW, NCOL, ROW, COL, U
      REAL       X(MAXROW, NCOL)

      DO 11 ROW = 1, NROW
         READ (U, *) ( X(ROW, COL), COL = 1, NCOL)
11    CONTINUE


      END
*********************************************************************
      SUBROUTINE WRIMAT(X, MAXROW, NROW, NCOL, OUTF)
      INTEGER    MAXROW, NROW, NCOL, ROW, COL
      REAL       X(MAXROW, NCOL)
      CHARACTER  OUTF*30

      DO 11 ROW = 1, NROW
         PRINT OUTF, ( X(ROW, COL), COL = 1, NCOL)
11    CONTINUE

      PRINT *

      END
```

If the data file contains

```
4
(4F6.2)
 1 2 3 4
 2 3 4 1
 3 4 1 2
 4 1 2 3
```

then the program produces the output

```
Matrix
```

```
1.00  2.00  3.00  4.00
2.00  3.00  4.00  1.00
3.00  4.00  1.00  2.00
4.00  1.00  2.00  3.00
```

```
The determinant is    160.0
```

Simultaneous Equations

A set of equations such as:

$$2x + 3y - 4z = 9$$
$$5x - 2y - 3z = 8$$
$$x + 4y - 4z = 8$$

is called a system of **simultaneous linear equations**. A **solution** for such a system is a set of values for x, y, and z such that this one set of values simultaneously satisfies the three equations. The **augmented matrix** for this system is

$$(A\ B) = \begin{pmatrix} 2 & 3 & -4 & 9 \\ 5 & -2 & -3 & 8 \\ 1 & 4 & -4 & 8 \end{pmatrix}$$

where A is the 3 by 3 matrix of coefficients, and B is the 3 by 1 matrix, or **vector**, of constants on the right side of the equations.

To solve the system of equations, we operate on the matrix $(A\ B)$ until it is in the form

$$\begin{pmatrix} 1 & 0 & 0 & X \\ 0 & 1 & 0 & Y \\ 0 & 0 & 1 & Z \end{pmatrix}$$

Then the solution is $x = X$, $y = Y$, $z = Z$. The allowable operations are to:

1. Add a multiple of one row to another row.
2. Interchange two rows.
3. Multiply a row by a nonzero constant.

These three operations are called **elementary row operations** on a matrix. We have used the first two operations in finding the determinant of a matrix.

Example 11.7 Solving a Simultaneous System of Linear Equations

The program is very similar to the program for calculating a determinant. The differences are that:

1. The matrix is not square now, but has one more column than the number of rows.
2. Each diagonal element must become 1.0, so each row is divided by its pivot element.
3. The pivot element is now used to make *all* other elements in its column zero, not just those elements below the pivot. This method is called **Gaussian elimination**. It is not the most efficient way to solve a system of equations, but it is one of the simplest.

Systems of equations can have a unique solution, many solutions, or no solution. The following program can find a unique solution or let the user know that it cannot find a unique solution. It cannot differentiate between no solution and many solutions. Also, even with the pivoting operation, round-off error can cause the program to find a *solution* for a system of equations that has no solution.

See Program 11.7 for the complete program to solve simultaneous linear equations.

■

PROGRAM 11.7

```
      PROGRAM SIMULT
*-------------------------------------------------------------------*
*   Solve, if possible, a system of N linear equations in N unknowns. *
*                                                                   *
*   Data are in SYSTEM.DAT.  The first record contains the number of  *
*   equations, which must be equal to the number of unknowns.  The    *
*   second record has the format for writing the matrix.  The rest of *
*   the records contain rows of the augmented matrix.                 *
*-------------------------------------------------------------------*
      INTEGER    MAXROW, ROW, COL, N, KROW, U
      PARAMETER  (MAXROW = 10)
      REAL       A(MAXROW, MAXROW + 1), P, PIVOT
      CHARACTER  OUTF*30
```

```
      PARAMETER  (U = 9)
*-----------------------------------------------------------------*
*       Open file.  Read number of equations and output format.   *
*-----------------------------------------------------------------*
      OPEN (U, FILE = 'SYSTEM', STATUS = 'OLD')

      READ (U, *) N
      READ (U, '(A)') OUTF
*-----------------------------------------------------------------*
*                   Read and write the matrix.                    *
*-----------------------------------------------------------------*
      CALL REDMAT(A, MAXROW, N, N + 1, U)

      CLOSE (U)

      PRINT 10, 'Matrix'
      CALL WRIMAT(A, MAXROW, N, N + 1, OUTF)
*-----------------------------------------------------------------*
*   Reduce the coefficient matrix to 1s on the diagonal, 0s off.  *
*-----------------------------------------------------------------*
      DO 44 ROW = 1, N

         CALL GETPIV(A, MAXROW, N, N + 1, ROW, PIVOT)
         IF (PIVOT .EQ. 0.0) STOP  'No unique solution.'
*-----------------------------------------------------------------*
*                   Divide pivot row by pivot.                    *
*-----------------------------------------------------------------*
         DO 11 COL = ROW, N + 1
            A(ROW, COL) = A(ROW, COL) / PIVOT
11       CONTINUE
*-----------------------------------------------------------------*
*   Subtract proper multiples of the pivot row from each other row. *
*-----------------------------------------------------------------*
         DO 33 KROW = 1, N

            IF (KROW .NE. ROW) THEN
               P = A(KROW, ROW)
               DO 22 COL = ROW, N + 1
                  A(KROW, COL) = A(KROW, COL) - P * A(ROW, COL)
22             CONTINUE
            END IF

33       CONTINUE

44    CONTINUE
*-----------------------------------------------------------------*
*                        Print solution.                          *
*-----------------------------------------------------------------*
```

```
       PRINT 20
       PRINT 30, (A(ROW, N + 1), ROW = 1, N)

10     FORMAT ('0', A)
20     FORMAT ('0The solution is:' /)
30     FORMAT (1X, G12.4)

       END
```

With the data file

```
4
(5F7.1)
 2.5  3.0  2.5  1.0  25.0
 3.5 -2.0 -1.5  2.0   7.0
 4.0  5.0  3.5  3.0  41.0
 5.5 -1.0  4.5 -5.0  23.0
```

the program produces the following output.

```
Matrix

     2.5    3.0    2.5    1.0   25.0
     3.5   -2.0   -1.5    2.0    7.0
     4.0    5.0    3.5    3.0   41.0
     5.5   -1.0    4.5   -5.0   23.0

The solution is:

     4.000
     3.000
     2.000
     1.000
```

You should check to see that these values do satisfy all four of the equations. Also, remember that this method works only when the coefficient matrix is *square* and the system *does* have a unique solution, and even then, round-off error can cause it to fail.

■

11.3 SUMMARY OF CHAPTER 11

■ *Terms Introduced in This Chapter*

Column-major order	Matrix	Row-major order
Column subscript	Nested implied-DO lists	Row subscript
Determinant	Partial pivoting	Simultaneous linear equations
Gaussian elimination	Pivot	Two-dimensional array

■ *What You Should Know*

1. A matrix, or two-dimensional array, is useful for storing data that appear in rows and columns.
2. An array declaration must appear at the top of the program.
3. The array declaration can contain both lower and upper bounds for the dimensions of the array.
4. If lower bounds are given, each lower bound must not exceed the corresponding upper bound.
5. If only the upper bounds are specified, Fortran assumes the lower bounds to be one.
6. In a main program, a dimension bound must be an integer expression in which each operand is a constant.
7. A single matrix element is specified by the array name followed by two subscripts in parentheses.
8. The array name refers to the entire array.
9. The only times the array name can appear without subscripts in the body of a program unit are in short-list statements and actual argument lists for subprograms.
10. Fortran stores matrices by columns.
11. Short-list statements read and write matrices by columns.
12. Aside from short-list statements, reading and writing a matrix requires two DO loops or two implied-DO lists or one of each.
13. When a matrix is passed to a subprogram, it is crucial that the first dimension bounds in the program and the subprogram be exactly the same.
14. The second upper dimension bound for a dummy argument matrix can have an assumed size.
15. In a subprogram, a dimension bound must be an integer expression in which each operand is either a constant or a dummy argument.
16. In Fortran 77, array subscripts must be integer expressions.

■

11.4 EXERCISES

■ Self-Test

1. Give the number of elements in each of the following arrays.

    a.   `REAL  X(3, 4)`

    b.   `INTEGER  A(2:5, -2:2)`

2. What is wrong with each of the following segments? You may assume each array is properly declared.

    a.   `READ *, (A(ROW, COL), COL = 1, 3), ROW = 1, 4)`

    b.   `READ *, ((A(ROW, COL), COL = 1, 3, ROW = 1, 4)`

    c.
```
      REAL  A(5, 10)
         .
         .
         .
      DO 11 I = 1, 10
         READ *, (A(I, J), J = 1, 5)
   11 CONTINUE
```

    d.
```
      INTEGER  A(4, 5), B(4, 5)
         .
         .
         .
      READ *, A
      B = A
```

3. Specify the values assigned to the matrix elements by the following segments.

    a.
```
      INTEGER  X(2, 3)
      DATA     X /1, 2, 3, 4, 5, 6/
```

    b.
```
      REAL  A(2, 50)
      DATA  A /50 * 1.0, 50 * 2.0/
```

    c.
```
      INTEGER  HIGH(2, 3), ROW, COL
         .
         .
         .
```

```
          DO 22 ROW = 1, 2
            DO 11 COL = 1, 3
              HIGH(ROW, COL) = COL + 3 * (ROW - 1)
      11      CONTINUE
      22   CONTINUE
```

d.
```
          REAL  X(3, 3)
          DATA  X /9 * 1.0/
            .
            .
            .
          DO 11 I = 1, 3
            X(I, I) = 0.0
      11   CONTINUE
```

4. How many values does each of the following READ statements read from each record?

a.
```
          DO 11 ROW = 1, 5
            READ (12, *), (X(ROW, COL), COL = 1, 6)
      11   CONTINUE
```

b.
```
          DO 22 ROW = 1, 8
            DO 11 COL = 1, 3
              READ (9, 10) A(ROW, COL)
      10      FORMAT (3F8.2)
      11      CONTINUE
      22   CONTINUE
```

c.
```
          INTEGER  LOW(5, 10)
            .
            .
            .
          READ 10, LOW
      10  FORMAT (10I5)
```

d.
```
          DO 11 ROW = 1, 4
            READ (9, 10)  (B(ROW, COL), COL = 1, 8)
      10      FORMAT (F12.4)
      11   CONTINUE
```

■ Programming Exercises

1. Write a program for the STUDNT example that finds and prints the number of students in each class.
2. Write a program to read the size of a matrix and the element values, and find the largest number in the matrix.

3. Write a program to read an integer matrix and ask for an integer value for a variable SPEC. The program should then search the matrix and print the row and column numbers of any matrix elements with values equal to SPEC.

4. In the student example, suppose student activity costs vary by class. A freshman pays $10.00, a sophomore pays $14.50, a junior pays $17.50, and a senior pays $20.00. Write a program to calculate the total student activity costs for each class and the total for the entire college.

5. Write a program to read a real matrix and find the largest number in the matrix and its position in the matrix.

6. Many of the matrix calculation programs would make useful subprograms. Change the matrix multiplication program into a subroutine. Write a program to read a square matrix B and call this subroutine to calculate the square of B, or $B \times B$.

7. Several students in a class each took five tests. Read a matrix corresponding to the scores on the tests. Calculate the mean grade for each student and the mean grade for each test. Also, for each test score, calculate how far above or below the mean for the test that score is. Display these last results as a matrix.

8. Answers on a questionnaire are often *cross-tabulated*; that is, a matrix display is given showing the number of people who responded with each possible pair of answers to two questions. For example, suppose question 1 has two possible answers, 1 or 2, which could stand for *male* or *female*. Question 2 might give a statement such as *Apartheid should be abolished*, and ask if the respondent agrees strongly (1), agrees (2), is neutral (3), disagrees (4), or strongly disagrees (5). Then the results of asking fifty people these questions might result in the following cross-tabulation:

		Question 1	
		1	2
	1	3	2
	2	10	13
Question 2	3	5	7
	4	2	3
	5	4	1

Suppose a questionnaire has 10 questions and all answers are coded from 1 to the possible number of responses. Data are placed in a file in 10I2 format, with the first record indicating the number of possible responses for each question. The first few records might look like:

```
2 2 5 5 3 3 5 5 5 5
1 2 4 4 2 2 3 4 2 1
2 2 3 4 3 3 4 2 4 3
```

The first record shows that questions 1 and 2 have two responses, questions 5 and 6 have three responses, and all other questions have five responses. Write a program that asks the user for two question numbers, then produces the proper cross-tabulation.

9. In a **matrix game**, a matrix is written down, player R chooses a row, player C chooses a column, and the players simultaneously announce their choices. Then player R pays player C the amount in dollars found in the chosen row and column.

For example, suppose the matrix is

$$\begin{pmatrix} 2 & -3 & 4 & -3 \\ 5 & -2 & -4 & 1 \\ -4 & 2 & -1 & 1 \end{pmatrix}$$

If player R chooses row 1 and player C chooses column 3, then player R pays player C \$4.00, the amount in row 1, column 3. A negative amount in the position indicated means player R receives this (positive) amount from player C. So if R chooses row 3 and C chooses column 1, R receives \$4.00 from C.

a. A conservative strategy for player R is to look at the largest number in each row, then choose the row that has the smallest of these largest numbers. This strategy is called the **minimax strategy** for R because it minimizes his maximum loss. In the matrix above, the largest numbers in the rows are:

Row	Largest number
1	4
2	5
3	2

Therefore, the minimax strategy for player R is to choose row 3, which guarantees that he cannot lose more than \$2.00.

Write a program that finds the largest number in each row, then finds the smallest of these numbers, and tells which row has this smallest number.

b. A similar conservative strategy for player C is to look at the smallest number in each column, then choose the column that has the largest of these numbers. Modify the program from part a. so that it also finds the smallest number in each column, then finds the largest of these numbers, and tells which column contains this smallest number.

10. The game of **Life** was invented by J. H. Conway. Life takes place on a rectangular grid of cells, each of which may or may not contain an organism. In theory, the grid can be infinite, but we restrict the problem to a finite grid with twelve rows and twenty-four columns. One way to draw the grid is as follows, with asterisks denoting organisms.

```
                      1 1 1 1 1 1 1 1 1 1 2 2 2 2 2
      1 2 3 4 5 6 7 8 9 0 1 2 3 4 5 6 7 8 9 0 1 2 3 4
     --------------------------------------------------
  1| | | | | | | | | |*| | | | | |*| | | | | | | | |
  2| | | | | | | | |*| | | |*| | | | | | |*|*| | | |
  3| | |*| | | |*| | | | |*| |*| | | | | |*| | |*| |
  4| | | |*| |*| | | | | | |*| | | | | | | |*|*| | |
  5| | | |*| | | | | | | | | | | | | | | | | | | | |
  6| | | |*| |*| | | | | | | | | | | | | | | | | | |
  7| | |*| | |*| | | | | | | | | | | | | | | | | | |
  8| | | | | | | | | | | |*|*|*|*| | | | | | | | | |
  9| | | | | | | | | | | |*| | |*| | | | | | | | | |
 10| | | | | | | | | | | |*| | |*| | | | | | | | | |
 11| | | | | | | | | | | |*|*|*|*| | | | | | | | | |
 12| | | | | | | | | | | | | | | | | | | | | | | | |
     --------------------------------------------------
```

Each interior cell in the grid has eight neighbors:

1	2	3
4		5
6	7	8

Cells on the edge of the grid have fewer neighbors.

The game begins with the user giving the row and column numbers of some cells that contain organisms. This is the *zero generation*. The next generation is generated according to the following rules:

a. An organism in a cell *survives* to the next generation if there are two or three organisms in neighboring cells; otherwise it *dies*.

b. An empty cell gives birth to a new organism if there are exactly three organisms in neighboring cells; otherwise the cell remains empty.

Write a program to do the following:

a. Ask the user for an initial configuration of occupied cells, and print the zero generation. Print a 12 by 24 grid with asterisks designating organisms.

b. Ask how many new generations the user wants to see.

c. Calculate and print that many generations, with each one numbered, and give the total number of organisms in each generation.

d. When two succeeding generations are identical, the configuration is called *stable*. If a stable configuration occurs, the program should inform the user and stop without printing future generations.

e. Tell the user if the population dies out (no organisms), and do not print the empty grid.

Some examples:

a.   The configuration

   leads, in the next generation, to the configuration

b.   This pattern is stable.

```
| |*|*| |
|*| | |*|
| |*|*| |
```

c.   The following pattern will die out at the third generation, because two organisms, one at each end, will die in each generation.

```
| | | | |*|
| | | |*| |
| | |*| | |
| |*| | | |
|*| | | | |
```

Here are some hints on this problem. The program must contain two grids, an *old* grid and a *new* grid; the old grid is used to calculate the new one. Also, the two grids must be compared to check for stability.

The calculation of neighbors will be simpler if the grids contain a border of cells that stays empty. The border consists of rows 0 and 13 and columns 0 and 25.

This problem definitely calls for subprograms. Use at least the following subprograms, if not more.

a.   A subroutine to write the grid
b.   A subroutine to initialize the grids
c.   A subroutine to copy the new grid into the old grid
d.   A function to calculate the number of neighbors for a particular cell
e.   A subprogram to check for stability

11. **The Eight Queens**. Write a program to find a way to place eight queens on a chessboard so that no two queens *attack* each other. This is not a long program, but the logic is difficult. The program does not require two-dimensional arrays, but the problem requires some familiarity with the layout of a chessboard. For readers unfamiliar with chess, two queens attack each other if they are in the same row, in the same column, or on the same diagonal. Two queens are on the same diagonal if the signed difference between their row numbers equals the signed difference between their column numbers.

12 SEQUENTIAL AND DIRECT-ACCESS FILES

We have been using data files in the simplest possible ways, and have relied on a system of defaults built into Fortran. In this chapter, we discuss files more formally and introduce several options that give us explicit control over the files we use.

A **record** is a set of logically related data items. In this chapter we will discuss **files**, which are collections of related records arranged in a certain order. Files normally reside on a disk; the computer stores them in the same way Fortran programs are stored. However, magnetic tape and punched cards also can hold files. Sets of records read from a terminal, or written to a terminal or printer, also are files.

Application files often contain large numbers of records. Utility companies, department stores, and magazines maintain files which hold information regarding each customer account. An airline must keep files with information on each flight during a period of several months. Obviously, some of these files could include millions of records. Our files will be much more modest. The main point of having files, though, is to have a place, other than the program itself, to store data. There are several reasons for putting data in a file:

1. The amount of information in the file is more than any program can hold. A program can read one record at a time, and thus needs storage for only one record.

2. Several different programs can read the same data file.

3. Often a program reads a large amount of data from a user at a terminal, and then does some calculations and prints results. It is convenient to put the data into a file when it is read, both so the program can be written in small modules (read data, do calculations, print results), and to keep the input of data from being mixed with output printed at the terminal.

■

12.1 SEQUENTIAL FILES

File Access

Fortran 77 deals with two kinds of files, **sequential-access files** and **direct-access files**. Usually we say just *sequential file* instead of sequential-access file. Also, direct-access files are sometimes called *random-access files*.

The word *access* is used here as a noun, but we also use it as a verb when we say "The program will *access* the records sequentially." The most important ways to access records are to write them and to read them, so think of access as including both input and output operations.

A computer always *stores* records in a file sequentially; one record follows another. Sequential access is the access of one record after another, in the order in which the records are stored in the file. To read the fiftieth record, for example, you must first read the first forty-nine records. Direct access allows you to have access to the fiftieth record immediately, without accessing the previous records. With direct access, you can always read the records in a file in sequence, if you wish.

For examples removed from the computer field, consider cassette tapes and phonograph records. Both contain musical selections in a given order. To get to the fourth selection on a cassette tape, you must first pass over the first three selections. Therefore, you have only sequential access to the selections on the tape. With a phonograph record, however, you can pick up the stylus and place it at the beginning of the fourth selection; you have direct access to any part of the record. If you wish, you also have sequential access to the selections on the record.

The OPEN Statement

We have already used OPEN statements with three specifiers. Fortran provides many more, but we will not use all of them. Here we review the OPEN statement specifiers for *unit number*, *file name*, and *status*.

The simplest form of the OPEN statement is

OPEN (*<unit number>*, FILE = *<filename>*)

The unit number acts as a *connection* between the file and the program containing the OPEN statement. Later, the program will refer to the file by the unit number, not the file name. If a program requires several files to be connected at the same time, the files must have different unit numbers.

We can think of the unit number as a line physically connecting the program and file. The three OPEN statements

```
OPEN (7, FILE = 'FILE1')
OPEN (8, FILE = 'FILE2')
OPEN (9, FILE = 'FILE3')
```

establish the three connections shown in Figure 12.1. Data will be transmitted to FILE1 across line 7, FILE2 across line 8, and FILE3 across line 9.

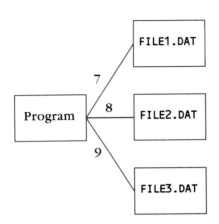

FIGURE 12.1
A program connected
to three files

We have used 'NEW' and 'OLD' as status values. There are two other possible values in Fortran 77, 'UNKNOWN' and 'SCRATCH'. The table in Figure 12.2 lists the four status values and their effects.

Character variables can appear in place of the given character constants, both for the status value and for the file name. A program can ask the user to specify the name of the file and its status, as in the following program segment.

```
      PRINT *, 'What is the name of the file?'
      READ 10, FILENM
10    FORMAT (A)

      PRINT *, 'What is the status of the file?'
      READ 10, STAT

      OPEN (3, FILE = FILENM, STATUS = STAT)
```

These three specifiers are enough to create a sequential file. Notice that the OPEN statements discussed so far do not mention the word SEQUENTIAL. By default, Fortran assumes the access mode of a file is SEQUENTIAL if no other access type is specified in the OPEN statement.

The WRITE statement that writes formatted data to a sequential file is called the **formatted sequential WRITE statement**. One example we have already used is

FIGURE 12.2
The four STATUS values
and their effects

Status	Effect
NEW	Create a new file. In Fortran 77, if a file with the given name already exists, this file is erased by the creation of a new file with the same name. In some versions of Fortran, the old file remains and the new file recives the same name and type, but perhaps a higher version number than the existing file.
OLD	Connect the program to a file that already exists. If no such file exists, an error occurs.
UNKNOWN	First, try to find an old file with the given name and connect it to the program. If no such file exists, create a new file. This is the default status value.
SCRATCH	Create a new file and delete the file when the program completes execution or the file is closed.

```
      WRITE (3, 10) NAME, AGE, SALARY
10    FORMAT (A20, I3, F8.2)
```

We can use the run-time format specification, in apostrophes, in place of the label, as in

```
      WRITE (3, '(A20, I3, F8.2)')  NAME, AGE, SALARY
```

At times we will use a run-time format in this way to avoid FORMAT statements.

Certain unit numbers have predefined meanings in Fortran. Unit number 6 is the *standard output device* for the system (usually your terminal screen). Thus, in the absence of an OPEN statement with unit number 6, a WRITE statement beginning

```
      WRITE (6,
```

tells the computer to write the output to this standard device. Therefore,

```
      WRITE (6, 10) list
```

means exactly the same as

```
      PRINT 10, list
```

Similarly, unit number 5 is the *standard input device* (probably your terminal keyboard). Your system might have predefined meanings for some other unit numbers, to refer to devices such as tape drives and printers. However, an OPEN statement with one of these special unit numbers will override the default values. If an OPEN statement is

```
      OPEN (6, FILE = 'DATA12')
```

then a later statement

```
      WRITE (6, 10) list
```

causes the computer to write data to the file DATA12.DAT, not the standard output device.

The purpose of the CLOSE statement is to break the connection between a program and a file. The CLOSE statement is not, in the strictest sense, necessary. When a program ends normally (at a STOP or END statement), the computer closes all open files. We will always include a CLOSE statement because programs do not always end normally. When a program is aborted because of an error, open files can be left in an unreadable state.

The following two programs create and read a sequential file POWERS.DAT. Neither program contains any new statements or specifiers. Later, though, we use this small data file to illustrate some new concepts.

Example 12.1 Creating a Sequential File

The short program in Program 12.1 creates a file named POWERS.DAT with five records. Each record contains one of the integers from 1 to 5, followed by that integer's second, third, and fourth powers.

■
PROGRAM 12.1

```
      PROGRAM FILE1
*------------------------------------------------------------*
*  Create a data file with four powers of the first five integers. *
*------------------------------------------------------------*
      INTEGER  X

      OPEN (4, FILE = 'POWERS', STATUS = 'NEW')
```

```
      DO 11 X = 1, 5
         WRITE (4, 10) X, X**2, X**3, X**4
10       FORMAT (1X, 2I3, I4, I5)
11    CONTINUE

      CLOSE (4)

      END
```

After the program runs, the file POWERS.DAT contains

```
Column: 1234567890123456
            1  1   1    1
            2  4   8   16
            3  9  27   81
            4 16  64  256
            5 25 125  625
```

Ordinarily, one WRITE statement writes one record, but the slash descriptor in the middle of a FORMAT specification will cause the computer to start a new record. If the FORMAT specification in the program above were

(2I4 / 2I4)

then the file would contain ten records with two numbers in each record:

```
      1   1
      1   1
      2   4
      8  16
      3   9
     27  81
      4  16
     64 256
      5  25
    125 625
```

■

12.2 READING FROM A SEQUENTIAL FILE

To read data from a file, open the file, giving the file name and STATUS = 'OLD'. To open the file POWERS.DAT created by Program 12.1, use the statement

```
OPEN (7, FILE = 'POWERS', STATUS = 'OLD')
```

Notice that this statement uses logical unit 7, while the program that created POWERS.DAT used logical unit 4. Each unit number has meaning only while the program that contains it is running, so any unit number will do. The file name must, of course, be the same. STATUS is now 'OLD' because the file must exist before it can be read.

The Formatted Sequential READ Statement

The simplest **formatted sequential READ statement** has the same form as the corresponding WRITE statement. In fact, an identical FORMAT specification should be used. That is, a record written with the FORMAT specification

$$(1X, 2I3, I4, I5)$$

should be read with the same specification or an equivalent one, such as

$$(1X, I3, I3, I4, I5)$$

One of the most common errors in reading from files comes from mismatched format specifications. The slightest deviation can cause havoc, so keep track of the format specification you use to write the file, and use that same specification to read the file.

With records that contain only numbers, you will have far fewer errors if you use the list-directed READ and WRITE statements. Most of our records will be more complicated and will require formats, so consider this example as just an introduction to reading and writing formatted records.

An appropriate READ statement for the records in POWERS is

```
      READ (7, 10) FIRST, SECOND, THIRD, FOURTH
10    FORMAT (1X, 2I3, I4, I5)
```

Program 12.2 reads and prints the values in each record of the file POWERS.DAT created by Program 12.1.

■
PROGRAM 12.2

```
      PROGRAM READFL
*-------------------------------------------------------------*
*        Read the file POWERS.DAT and print its contents.     *
*-------------------------------------------------------------*
      INTEGER  FIRST, SECOND, THIRD, FOURTH, I

      OPEN (7, FILE = 'POWERS', STATUS = 'OLD')

      PRINT 10, 'CONTENTS OF FILE POWERS'

11    READ (7, 20, END=22) FIRST, SECOND, THIRD, FOURTH
         PRINT 20, FIRST, SECOND, THIRD, FOURTH
         GO TO 11

22    CLOSE (7)

10    FORMAT ('0', A //)
20    FORMAT (1X, 2I3, I4, I5)

      END
```

This program will print the records of **POWERS.DAT** exactly as they appear in the file, except for the initial blank in each record, because the PRINT statement uses the same **FORMAT** specification that reads the records, and uses the initial blank as a carriage control character. The output is

```
CONTENTS OF FILE POWERS

      1   1    1    1
      2   4    8   16
      3   9   27   81
      4  16   64  256
      5  25  125  625
```

The REWIND **Statement**

When a sequential file is opened, Fortran sets a **current record pointer** that points to the first record. After a record is read or written, the pointer automatically advances to the next record. This is the reason for the name *sequential*; one record simply follows another in sequence. When one program writes a file, and then reads from the file, the record pointer must be reset to the first record before reading begins. This is the function of the REWIND **statement**. Its form is

REWIND (<*unit*>)

where unit is the logical unit number to which the file is attached.

When the file resides on a magnetic tape, the REWIND statement actually does rewind the tape to its beginning. For such files, it is wise to include a REWIND statement after all records in the file are written or read, so the file will be in position to be read the next time it is used. Example 12.3 illustrates the REWIND statement.

Example 12.3 Writing a Table from Input Data

This is a very simplified version of a payroll problem, so we can concentrate on the file aspects of the problem. Suppose the user of a program enters payroll data: name, hours worked, and hourly rate of pay for each employee. The program calculates gross pay as hours worked times hourly rate and prints the employee name, hours, rate, and gross pay.

It is easy to write a program that prints results for each employee immediately after the employee's data are entered, but then the output from the program is interspersed with the input. To separate the output from the input, we need to enter all data first, then write all output, which we can accomplish by putting the input data into a file. Since the program will print all the input data, the file can be a temporary file, deleted when the program is finished. A file used in this way is commonly called a **scratch file**.

To create a scratch file, specify

STATUS = 'SCRATCH'

in the OPEN statement that creates the file. A later CLOSE statement will then automatically delete the file.

An outline of the program is:

1. Open a scratch file.
2. Describe data entry.
3. Read NAME, HOURS, and RATE, and put them in the file.
4. Rewind the file.
5. Print headers.
6. Read the file. After reading a record, do calculations and print results.

The OPEN statement for a scratch file does not require a FILE clause, so Step 1 takes the single statement

```
OPEN (9, STATUS = 'SCRATCH')
```

Step 2 involves several PRINT statements, which we ignore for now. Step 3 calls for a loop; we will use a while loop, ending when the name entered is 'STOP'. Inside the loop, the computer will read the input data and write them to the scratch file.

Step 4 is the REWIND statement

```
REWIND (9)
```

Step 5 requires additional PRINT statements. Step 6 will use a while loop beginning with

```
22     READ (9, 20, END = 33) NAME, HOURS, RATE
```

as in the previous program. This statement will cause an exit from the loop when the computer tries to read past the last record in the file. See Program 12.3.

■

PROGRAM 12.3

```
      PROGRAM PAYFIL
*------------------------------------------------------*
*      Print a payroll table for several employees.    *
*      Use a scratch file for temporary storage.       *
*------------------------------------------------------*
      CHARACTER*20  NAME
      REAL          HOURS, RATE, GROSS
*------------------------------------------------------*
*      Open a scratch file for temporary data storage. *
*------------------------------------------------------*
      OPEN (9, STATUS = 'SCRATCH')
*------------------------------------------------------*
*                Describe data entry.                  *
*------------------------------------------------------*
      PRINT *, 'For each employee, enter name on one line.'
      PRINT *, 'On next line, enter hours and rate.'
      PRINT *, 'Hours can be given to one decimal place.'
      PRINT *, 'Rate can be given to two decimal places.'
      PRINT *, 'To stop, enter STOP for the employee name.'
```

```
*-----------------------------------------------------------------*
*    Main input loop.  Stop when STOP is entered for name.        *
*-----------------------------------------------------------------*
11      PRINT *, 'Employee name?'
        READ  10, NAME
        IF (NAME .NE. 'STOP') THEN

            PRINT *, 'Hours and rate?'
            READ  *, HOURS, RATE
*-----------------------------------------------------------------*
*           Put name, hours, and rate in scratch file.            *
*-----------------------------------------------------------------*
            WRITE (9, 20) NAME, HOURS, RATE
            GO TO 11

        END IF
*-----------------------------------------------------------------*
*        Rewind so reading can begin with first record.           *
*-----------------------------------------------------------------*
        REWIND (9)
*-----------------------------------------------------------------*
*             Write headers for payroll report.                   *
*-----------------------------------------------------------------*
        PRINT 30, 'PAYROLL REPORT'
        PRINT 40, 'NAME', 'HOURS', 'RATE', 'GROSS PAY'
*-----------------------------------------------------------------*
*   Read file, perform calculations and write payroll table.      *
*-----------------------------------------------------------------*
22      READ (9, 20, END = 33) NAME, HOURS, RATE
            GROSS = HOURS * RATE
            PRINT 50, NAME, HOURS, RATE, GROSS
        GO TO 22
*-----------------------------------------------------------------*
* Close the file and, because it is a scratch file, delete it.  *
*-----------------------------------------------------------------*
33      CLOSE (9)

10      FORMAT (A)
20      FORMAT (A, F6.1, F7.2)
30      FORMAT ('0', 15X, A /)
40      FORMAT (1X, 8X, A, 10X, A, 5X, A, 3X, A )
50      FORMAT (1X, A, 3X, F4.1, 4X, F5.2, 3X, F8.2)

        END
```

With three names input before STOP, the output might look like

PAYROLL REPORT

NAME	HOURS	RATE	GROSS PAY
Ralph T. Arbuthnot	36.0	3.65	131.40
Harold Hartkewitz	42.5	6.30	267.75
Harmon Killebrew	28.0	16.90	473.20

Adding Records to a Sequential File

Records can be added only at the *end* of an existing sequential file. First the record pointer must be pointing to the end of the file, or the position immediately after the last record in the file. We can set the record pointer to the end of the file by reading the entire file. For example, if POWERS.DAT is opened as unit 6, we can set the record pointer to the end of the file with the following loop.

```
11      READ (6, 20, END = 22) Y, Y, Y, Y
        GO TO 11
22      <Remainder of program>
```

Program 12.4 opens and reads the file POWERS.DAT, then asks if the user wishes to add a record. If so, the computer asks for an integer and writes to the file a record containing the first four powers of that integer.

■

PROGRAM 12.4

```
      PROGRAM ADDREC
*-----------------------------------------------------------------*
*                 Add records to the file POWERS.DAT.             *
*-----------------------------------------------------------------*
      CHARACTER   ANS*3
      INTEGER     Y

      PRINT *, 'Opening the file POWERS.DAT.'
      OPEN (6, FILE = 'POWERS', STATUS = 'OLD')
*-----------------------------------------------------------------*
*                     Read to end of file.                       *
*-----------------------------------------------------------------*
11    READ (6, 20, END = 22) Y, Y, Y, Y
      GO TO 11
*-----------------------------------------------------------------*
*   Loop: If response is YES, get an integer and write a record. *
*-----------------------------------------------------------------*
```

```
22      PRINT *, 'Do you wish to add a record (YES or NO)? '
        READ 10, ANS
        IF (ANS .EQ. 'YES') THEN

            PRINT *, 'An integer?  '
            READ *, Y
            WRITE (6, 20) Y, Y*Y, Y ** 3, Y ** 4
            GO TO 22

        END IF

        PRINT *, 'Closing file.'
        CLOSE (6)

10      FORMAT (A)
20      FORMAT (1X, 2I3, I4, I5)

        END
```

When the program runs, suppose the responses are as follows:

```
Do you wish to add a record (YES or NO)?
YES
An integer?
6
Do you wish to add a record (YES or NO)?
YES
An integer?
7
Do you wish to add a record (YES or NO)?
NO
```

Then the file POWERS.DAT contains

```
1  1   1    1
2  4   8   16
3  9  27   81
4 16  64  256
5 25 125  625
6 36 216 1296
7 49 343 2401
```

Fortran *allows* the writing of a record at *any* point in an existing sequential file. However, with sequential access, the computer places an end-of-file mark immediately after the record just written. You can push this end-of-file mark down by writing another record. However, if a program is reading a file of several hundred records, and writes one record where the tenth record was, then the end-of-file mark comes after that tenth record, and all the other records in the file are no longer accessible! With sequential access, be sure to write records *only* at the end of the file.

Searching a Sequential File

Consider the following small file containing phone numbers and names.

```
342-5859 ARABELLA GORGE
563-2418 CASSANDRA CASE
235-9428 ARTURO ANDERSON
123-4567 DUDLEY TOWNSEND
362-8881 THOMAS WALKER
989-0102 LESLIE HORNBY
362-1600 ALEXANDER PICKLE
848-2105 TERRENCE LEE
```

Each record in the file is written with the format specification

$$(1X, A8, 1X, A20)$$

We will write a program to ask the user for a name, then search the file for that name. If the name is in the file, the program will print the corresponding phone number. If the name is not in the file, the program will so inform the user.

The search method we use is the *sequential search*, which is really the only way to search a sequential file. We use a logical variable FOUND, set to .FALSE. originally. The program asks for a name, ASKNAM, then reads records containing values for PHONE and NAME, trying to find a value of NAME that matches ASKNAM. The reading takes place inside a while loop beginning

```
IF (.NOT. FOUND) THEN
```

The READ statement

```
READ (1, 20, END = 22) PHONE, NAME
```

contains an END specifier, so the loop actually has two stopping conditions: the end of the file; and a .TRUE. value in the variable FOUND. Immediately after the READ statement in the loop, a logical IF statement

```
IF (ASKNAM .EQ. NAME) FOUND = .TRUE.
```

compares ASKNAM to NAME and sets FOUND to .TRUE. if the two names are identical.

When the loop ends, a block IF statement determines which stopping condition occurred and prints an appropriate message in either case. Program 12.5 shows the entire program.

■

PROGRAM 12.5

```
      PROGRAM SEARCH
*----------------------------------------------------------*
*                 Search a file sequentially.              *
*----------------------------------------------------------*
      CHARACTER*20  NAME, ASKNAM, PHONE*8
      LOGICAL    FOUND

      OPEN (1, FILE = 'PHONE' , STATUS = 'OLD')

      PRINT *, 'Whose phone number would you like to see?'
      READ 10, ASKNAM

      FOUND = .FALSE.
*----------------------------------------------------------*
*   Main search loop continues until it finds a match      *
*   or until it reaches the end of the file.               *
*----------------------------------------------------------*
11    IF (.NOT. FOUND) THEN
          READ (1, 20, END = 22) PHONE, NAME
          IF (ASKNAM .EQ. NAME) FOUND = .TRUE.
          GO TO 11
      END IF

22    IF (FOUND) THEN
          PRINT *, PHONE
      ELSE
          PRINT *, 'There is no one by that name.'
      END IF

      CLOSE (1)

10    FORMAT (A)
20    FORMAT (1X, A8, 1X, A20)

      END
```

Example 12.6 Updating a Sequential File

An inventory file contains records for all items of a certain type belonging to a company or individual. Most stores keep an inventory file of items they stock for sale. A record in such an inventory file would hold at least the name of the item and the number of items on hand, and probably many more pieces of information, such as a part number, price, reorder quantity, and so on.

An inventory file for even a small store can include thousands of records. We consider here a very small inventory file for a blood bank. The file, BLOOD.DAT, contains eight records, one for each of the blood types: A+, A−, AB+, AB−, B+, B−, O+, and O−. Each record contains the blood type and the number of pints of that type on hand. We assume each record is written with the format specification

$$(1X, A3, 1X, I5)$$

On a given day, the file might contain:

```
A+      227
A-       85
AB+     130
AB-      79
B+      124
B-       78
O+      294
O-      130
```

The blood bank must update the quantities on hand each working day, adding the number of pints of each type donated that day and subtracting the number used. We will write a program to update the file. The program is as simple as can be, ignoring such fine points as error checking, so we can concentrate on the update process.

The program has sequential access to the file, which does not permit the program actually to change anything in the file BLOOD.DAT. The standard Fortran technique for updating a sequential file is to create a new file incorporating the updated data. The new file would, of course, have a name different from the old file name. In some versions of Fortran, opening a new file with a given name erases any existing file with that same name. We will name the data files OBLOOD.DAT and NBLOOD.DAT (for old blood and new blood).

We use the character variable BLTYPE for the blood types, and the integer variable ONHAND for the number of pints on hand. The integer variables DONATD and USED represent the number of pints donated and the number used on a given day.

After the declarations and OPEN statements, the program consists mainly of a while loop beginning

```
11    READ (7, 10, END = 22) BLTYPE, ONHAND
```

Inside the loop, the program:

1. Reads a record from the old file OBLOOD.DAT, using the END specifier to exit from the loop.
2. Prints the blood type and number of units on hand.
3. Asks the user for the number of pints donated and the number used that day.
4. Calculates the new quantity on hand with the statement

```
      ONHAND = ONHAND + DONATD - USED
```

5. Writes the updated information to the new file NBLOOD.DAT.

See Program 12.6 for the complete program.

■
PROGRAM 12.6
_____

```
      PROGRAM UPDATE
*---------------------------------------------------------------*
*    Update a sequential file OBLOOD.DAT by creating a new      *
*    file with the name NBLOOD.DAT.  Each record contains       *
*    a blood type and number of pints of that type on hand,     *
*    written under the FORMAT specification (1X, A3, 1X, I5).    *
*---------------------------------------------------------------*
      CHARACTER  BLTYPE*3
      INTEGER    ONHAND, USED, DONATD

      OPEN (7, FILE = 'OBLOOD', STATUS = 'OLD')
      OPEN (8, FILE = 'NBLOOD', STATUS = 'NEW')

      PRINT *, 'Blood Inventory Update'

11    READ (7, 10, END = 22) BLTYPE, ONHAND

         PRINT *
         PRINT 20, BLTYPE, ONHAND
         PRINT *
         PRINT *, 'Number of pints donated today?'
         READ  *, DONATD
```

```
        PRINT *
        PRINT *, 'Number of pints used today'
        READ  *, USED

        ONHAND = ONHAND + DONATD - USED

        WRITE (8, 10) BLTYPE, ONHAND

     GO TO 11

22   PRINT *
     PRINT *, 'Closing old and new files.'
     CLOSE (7)
     CLOSE (8)

10   FORMAT (1X, A3, X, I5)
20   FORMAT (1X, 'Blood type: ', A, 3X, I5, ' pints on hand')

     END
```

Unformatted Sequential Files

A formatted file stores information according to a standard coding scheme such as ASCII or EBCDIC code. When formatted files are listed on a terminal screen or printer, the computer automatically converts these codes to the proper characters. Thus, you can usually read formatted disk files with a single command such as TYPE or LIST, without going to the bother of writing a complete Fortran program to read and print the file.

In contrast, you cannot list an **unformatted file** in readable form, because information is stored in such a file according to the internal representation scheme of the particular computer on which it is created. Also, because different computers use different internal representation schemes, unformatted files usually cannot be transported from one type of machine to another.

The big advantage to unformatted files, however, is speed. It takes time for the computer to convert data from its internal form to the external form required by a formatted file, so writing records to an unformatted file is faster than writing them to a formatted file. The same is true for reading records. Formatted files require the computer to convert data from the external (formatted) form to the internal representation form. Unformatted files allow the computer to skip this step.

The internal representation of numerical data usually requires less storage than the formatted form, so unformatted files also have the advantage of requiring less space than formatted files.

Creating an unformatted file with sequential access requires the specifier

FORM = 'UNFORMATTED'

in the OPEN statement because the default value of FORM is 'FORMATTED' for sequential access. (With direct access, 'UNFORMATTED' is the default value for FORM.)

Unformatted READ and WRITE statements are rather simple. They look like any other READ and WRITE statements except that the format specification is omitted. For example, to write an unformatted record consisting of a name, an age, and a social security number, we could have

WRITE (9) NAME, AGE, SSN

where 9 is the unit number on which the file was opened. The corresponding READ statement could be

READ (9, END = 33) NAME, AGE, SSN

Programs 12.7 and 12.8 are revisions of Programs 12.1 and 12.2, illustrating the changes required for using unformatted files.

■

PROGRAM 12.7

```
      PROGRAM UNFORM
*----------------------------------------------------------------*
*     Create a small data file with four powers of the first five  *
*     integers.  The file is to be an unformatted sequential file. *
*----------------------------------------------------------------*
      INTEGER  X

      OPEN (4, FILE = 'POWER', STATUS = 'NEW', FORM = 'UNFORMATTED')

      DO 11 X = 1, 5
         WRITE (4) X, X**2, X**3, X**4
11    CONTINUE

      CLOSE (4)

      END
```

PROGRAM 12.8

```
        PROGRAM READUN
*-------------------------------------------------------------*
*                Read an unformatted sequential file.         *
*-------------------------------------------------------------*
        INTEGER  FIRST, SECOND, THIRD, FOURTH, I

        OPEN (7, FILE = 'POWER', STATUS = 'OLD', FORM = 'UNFORMATTED')

        PRINT 10, 'Contents of file POWERS.DAT'

        DO 11 I = 1, 5
            READ (7) FIRST, SECOND, THIRD, FOURTH
            PRINT 20, FIRST, SECOND, THIRD, FOURTH
11      CONTINUE

        CLOSE (7)

10      FORMAT ('0', A //)
20      FORMAT (1X, 2I3, I4, I5)

        END
```

Sequential files are fine for applications that require processing every record in a file. However, it is not easy to make changes in a sequential file, except for adding records at the end of the file. The remaining section in this chapter deals with direct-access files, a useful topic, but one that involves some new details. This section can be skipped without loss of continuity.

12.3 DIRECT-ACCESS FILES

To create a direct-access file, we must consider some new specifiers for the OPEN statement.

The ACCESS **Specifier**

The ACCESS **specifier** has the form

$$ACCESS \ = \ <Access \ mode>$$

The two possible access modes are 'SEQUENTIAL' and 'DIRECT'. The default mode is 'SEQUENTIAL', so up to now we have not had to specify the access mode. You have probably guessed that, for a direct-access file, the ACCESS specifier is

$$ACCESS = 'DIRECT'$$

Do not forget the quotes.

The RECL **Specifier**

All records in a direct-access file must have the same length, so direct access requires the record length to be given, with the specifier

$$RECL = \ <Length>$$

For formatted records, the length is the number of columns, or characters, in the record. You can calculate the number of characters just as you counted columns for FORMAT specifications. For example, if a record is written with the FORMAT specification

$$(1X, \ A20, \ I5, \ 3X, \ F8.2)$$

$$1 \quad 20 \quad 5 \quad 3 \quad 8$$

then the number of columns required is $1 + 20 + 5 + 3 + 8 = 37$, so the length of the record is 37.

If you specify RECL = 37, then all records in the file have length 37. An attempt to write a record with more than 37 characters will cause a fatal error. A record with fewer than 37 characters causes no problem. The computer simply adds blanks to the record to make its length 37.

Direct access requires *fixed-length* records so that Fortran can calculate the position of a record in a file. Consider the following small file in which each record was written with the FORMAT specification (A2, I2).

```
A 12
A-23
B+42
B 55
B-36
C+22
```

Fortran stores this file as if it were

```
A 12A-23B+42B 55B-36C+22$
```

and keeps track only of the starting position of the file, position 0. The $ signifies the end-of-file mark that Fortran places at the end of a sequential file. We can write all the file positions:

```
Position in file: 01234567890123456789_0123
Elements in file: A 12A-23B+42B 55B-36C+22
```

Since each record has length 4, the records start at positions 0, 4, 8, and so on. The sixth record starts at position

$$4 \times (6 - 1) = 20$$

In general, with record length L, the nth record starts at position

$$L \times (n - 1)$$

The FORM Specifier for Direct Access

We have already mentioned the FORM specifier in connection with unformatted sequential files. For direct access, the default value of FORM is 'UNFORMATTED'; therefore to create a formatted direct-access file, we must specify

$$FORM = 'FORMATTED'$$

The REC Specifier in the Direct-Access WRITE Statement

The WRITE statement to write a record into a direct-access file uses a REC specifier designating the record number, as in

```
WRITE (4, 10, REC = RECNO) NAME, G1, G2, G3, G4
```

The integer variable RECNO must have a positive integer value. In Program 12.9, we start RECNO with value 1 and increment the value by 1 every time a record is written.

Example 12.9 Creating a Direct-Access File

We will create a file called GRADES.DAT in which each record has a 20-character student name and four test grades. Each record is written with FORMAT specification (1X, A20, 4I5), so the record length is

$$1 + 20 + 4(5) = 41$$

The required OPEN statement is

```
OPEN (4, FILE = 'GRADES', STATUS = 'NEW', RECL = 41,
1           FORM = 'FORMATTED', ACCESS = 'DIRECT')
```

See Program 12.9.

■

PROGRAM 12.9

```
      PROGRAM CREDIR
*-------------------------------------------------------*
*          Create a direct-access file GRADES.DAT.      *
*-------------------------------------------------------*
      CHARACTER*20  NAME
      INTEGER       G1, G2, G3, G4, RECNO

      OPEN (4, FILE = 'GRADES', STATUS = 'NEW', RECL = 41,
1           FORM = 'FORMATTED', ACCESS = 'DIRECT')

      PRINT *, 'Creating a file named GRADES.DAT.'
      PRINT *, 'Program asks for each student''s name'
      PRINT *, 'and four grades.  Enter STOP for the'
      PRINT *, 'name when you are finished.'

      RECNO = 0
11    PRINT *, 'Name?'
      READ '(A)', NAME

      IF (NAME .NE. 'STOP') THEN
          PRINT *, 'Four grades?'
          READ *, G1, G2, G3, G4
```

```
      RECNO = RECNO + 1
      WRITE (4, 10, REC = RECNO) NAME, G1, G2, G3, G4
      GO TO 11
   END IF

   PRINT *
   PRINT *, 'File has', RECNO, ' records.'
   PRINT *, 'Closing file'
   CLOSE (4)

10 FORMAT (1X, A20, 4I5)

   END
```

Example 12.10 Reading a Direct-Access File

To read the file GRADES.DAT with direct access, we must use essentially the same OPEN statement as in the previous program, but of course with STATUS = 'OLD'.

```
    OPEN (4, FILE = 'GRADES', STATUS = 'OLD', RECL = 41,
   1      ACCESS = 'DIRECT', FORM = 'FORMATTED')
```

The Direct-Access READ Statement

The **direct-access READ statement** also contains some new specifiers. First, the *record number* must be specified. The form for this specifier is the same as for the direct-access WRITE statement:

$$REC = \ <Integer\ expression>$$

The IOSTAT Specifier

Second, the END specifier can be used only with sequential access. A more versatile specifier is IOSTAT (for input/output status), whose form is

$$IOSTAT = \ <Integer\ variable>$$

We will use IOS as the integer variable, which makes the direct access READ statement

```
    READ (4, 10, REC = RECNO, IOSTAT = IOS) NAME, G1, G2, G3, G4
```

The `IOSTAT` specifier causes an integer value to be deposited in `IOS` each time the `READ` is attempted. A value of zero indicates a successful read, and any other value indicates that an error occurred on the attempt. Without the `IOSTAT` specifier, an error would cause the program to crash. With it, Fortran gives the programmer a chance to do something about the error.

What we do is to put a block `IF` immediately after the `READ` statement.

```
IF (IOS .EQ. 0) THEN
    PRINT 10, NAME, G1, G2, G3, G4
ELSE
    PRINT *, 'Error trying to read record'
END IF
```

If the value of IOS is 0, simply print the record. For any other value of IOS, print the message *Error trying to read record*. An attempt to read a record with a number larger than any record in the file will cause an error. So will many other things, unfortunately. The error number for the error, *Attempt to access nonexistent record*, is 36, so it would be wise to make the IF block handle this condition separately:

```
IF (IOS .EQ. 0) THEN
    PRINT 10, NAME, G1, G2, G3, G4
ELSE IF (IOS .EQ. 36) THEN
    PRINT *, 'There is no such record.'
ELSE
    PRINT *, 'Error trying to read record.'
END IF
```

Now we will know if the error was indeed caused by the value of `RECNO` or by something else. See the program in Program 12.10.

■

PROGRAM 12.10
_____

```
      PROGRAM READIR
*-----------------------------------------------------------*
*     Read the direct-access file GRADES.DAT.        *
*-----------------------------------------------------------*
      CHARACTER*20  NAME
      INTEGER       G1, G2, G3, G4, RECNO, IOS

      OPEN (4, FILE = 'GRADES', STATUS = 'OLD', RECL = 41,
     1      ACCESS = 'DIRECT', FORM = 'FORMATTED')
```

```
        PRINT *, 'Give the number of the record you want.'
        PRINT *, 'Enter 0 to stop.'

11      PRINT *, 'Record number?'
        READ *, RECNO

        IF (RECNO .NE. 0) THEN

            READ (4, 10, REC = RECNO, IOSTAT = IOS)
1               NAME, G1, G2, G3, G4

            IF (IOS .EQ. 0) THEN
                PRINT 10, NAME, G1, G2, G3, G4
            ELSE IF (IOS .EQ. 36) THEN
                PRINT *, 'There is no such record.'
            ELSE
                PRINT *, 'Error trying to read record.'
            END IF

            PRINT *
            GO TO 11

        END IF

        CLOSE (4)
        PRINT *, 'File is closed.'

10      FORMAT (1X, A20, 4I5)

        END
```

Example 12.11 Editing a Direct-Access File

A major benefit of direct access is that records can be updated or changed without creating a new version of the file, which is impossible with sequential access. The following program is similar to the previous one in its OPEN and READ statements. The difference is that this program allows the user to change the grades. If any changes are desired, the program asks for a new set of grades and writes the new record. The direct-access formatted WRITE statement is, as before,

```
        WRITE (4, 10, REC = RECNO) NAME, G1, G2, G3, G4
```

This statement places the values of NAME, G1, G2, G3, and G4 into record number RECNO. If that record already exists, the values in the write list replace it. If it does not exist, the WRITE statement creates it.

We will build on the previous program. In fact, we place all the new statements into the block immediately following

```
IF (IOS .EQ. 0) THEN
```

That block in the previous program has only a WRITE statement. Now, after that WRITE statement, the program will ask if the user wishes to change the grades. If so, the program will ask for new data and WRITE the new record. The required new statements are

```
PRINT *, 'Do you wish to change the grades(YES/NO)?
READ '(A)', ANS
IF (ANS .EQ. 'YES' ) THEN
    PRINT *, 'Enter 4 integer values.'
    READ  *, G1, G2, G3, G4
    WRITE (4, 10, REC = RECNO) NAME, G1, G2, G3, G4
END IF
```

Program 12.11 shows the complete program.

■
PROGRAM 12.11
_____

```
    PROGRAM EDITDI
*-----------------------------------------------------------*
*              Read from the file GRADES.DAT.               *
*              Allow the user to change grades.             *
*-----------------------------------------------------------*
    CHARACTER*20 ANS*3, NAME
    INTEGER      G1, G2, G3, G4, RECNO, IOS

    OPEN (4, FILE = 'GRADES', STATUS = 'OLD', RECL = 41,
   1      ACCESS = 'DIRECT', FORM = 'FORMATTED')

    PRINT *, 'Give the number of the record you want.'
    PRINT *, 'Enter 0 to stop.'

11  PRINT *, 'Record number?'
    READ  *, RECNO

    IF (RECNO .NE. 0) THEN
        READ (4, 10, REC = RECNO, IOSTAT = IOS)
   1             NAME, G1, G2, G3, G4
```

```
        IF (IOS .EQ. 0) THEN

            PRINT 10, NAME, G1, G2, G3, G4
            PRINT *, 'Do you wish to change the grades(YES/NO)?'
            READ 20, ANS
            IF (ANS .EQ. 'YES' ) THEN
                PRINT *, 'Enter 4 integer values.'
                READ  *, G1, G2, G3, G4
                WRITE (4, 10, REC = RECNO) NAME, G1, G2, G3, G4
            END IF

        ELSE IF (IOS .EQ. 36) THEN
            PRINT *, 'There is no such record.'
        ELSE
            PRINT *, 'Error trying to read record.'
        END IF

        GO TO 11

    END IF

    CLOSE (4)
    PRINT *, 'File is closed.'

10  FORMAT (1X, A20, 4I5)
20  FORMAT (A)

    END
```

The record numbers in a direct-access file determine the order of the records in a file. If two records are numbered 7 and 12, record 7 comes before record 12 in the file. If you write only two records, numbered 7 and 12, in a direct-access file, the file has space for 12 records numbered 1 through 12. Therefore, try to number records sequentially, starting with record number 1, or the file will contain a lot of empty space.

Unformatted Direct-Access Files

Direct-access files, as well as sequential files, can be unformatted as well as formatted. In fact, 'UNFORMATTED' is the default for direct-access files, so the OPEN statement to create GRADES.DAT as an unformatted direct-access file would be

```
    OPEN (4, FILE = 'GRADES', STATUS = 'NEW',
  1       ACCESS = 'DIRECT', RECL = 41)
```

The OPEN statement for a program that reads the file would be identical, except for a STATUS = 'OLD' specifier.

The READ and WRITE statements for an unformatted direct-access file are just like their counterparts for a formatted direct-access file, except that no format specifier is present. Thus, READ and WRITE statements for the unformatted direct-access file GRADES.DAT could be

```
READ (4, REC = RECNO, IOSTAT = IOS) NAME, G1, G2, G3, G4
WRITE (4, REC = RECNO) NAME, G1, G2, G3, G4
```

■
12.4 SUMMARY OF CHAPTER 12

■ *Terms Introduced in This Chapter*

ACCESS specifier	IOSTAT specifier	STATUS specifier
'DIRECT'	READ statement	'NEW'
'SEQUENTIAL'	direct-access formatted	'OLD'
CLOSE statement	direct-access unformatted	'SCRATCH'
Direct access	sequential formatted	'UNKNOWN'
END specifier	sequential unformatted	WRITE statement
File access	RECL specifier	direct-access formatted
direct	REWIND statement	direct-access unformatted
sequential	Sequential access	sequential formatted
FORM specifier		sequential unformatted
'FORMATTED'		
'UNFORMATTED'		

■ *What You Should Know*

1. An OPEN statement that creates a file, without specifying the file access, creates a sequential file by default.
2. An OPEN statement that opens a sequential file, without specifying the file access, opens the file for sequential access by default.
3. In standard Fortran 77, it is not possible to create a sequential file that can later be accessed directly.
4. Sequential files are most useful for situations in which the entire file is processed, in order.
5. Files on certain devices, such as magnetic tapes, can have only sequential access.
6. Records can be added only at the end of sequential files.
7. You cannot delete records in a sequential file, except by placing an end-of-file mark somewhere in the file, which effectively deletes all records after that mark.

8. A program that has sequential access to a file cannot change records already in that file.

9. Disk files can have sequential or direct access.

10. The END specifier in the sequential READ statement checks for the end of a file.

11. The sequential READ and WRITE statements access the record pointed to by the current-record pointer.

12. The direct-access READ and WRITE statements access the record whose number is given by the REC specifier.

13. A direct access READ cannot use the END specifier.

14. The IOSTAT specifier in a READ statement deposits zero in the specifier variable if the READ was successful, and deposits an error number otherwise.

15. IOSTAT also prevents a program from crashing after an unsuccessful READ.

16. You cannot read the information in an unformatted file, except by writing a program that reads the file with an unformatted READ statement and writes output you can read.

17. Computers can process unformatted files more quickly than formatted files.

18. Unformatted files take up less memory than formatted files.

19. When reading from a formatted file, be sure the format specification for the READ statement matches the format specification of the WRITE statement that wrote the data.

20. For strictly numerical data, the list-directed READ and WRITE statements can save you some headaches.

■

12.5 EXERCISES

■ Self-Test

1. Write an OPEN statement for each of the following requirements.
   a. Create a sequential file called PAYROL.DAT.
   b. Connect the program to an existing sequential file named ADDRES.DAT.
   c. Connect the program to an existing sequential file named GRADES.DAT, or create such a file if one does not already exist.
   d. Create a file named CALC.DAT that will be deleted by the statement that closes it.

2. What is wrong with the following OPEN statements?
   a. `OPEN (355, FILE = 'A', STATUS = 'OLD')`

b.   OPEN (22, FILE = PERSNL, STATUS = NEW

c.   OPEN (14, FILE = "DATA", STATUS = 'OLD')

d.   OPEN (12, FILE = 'BLOOD', STATUS = 'DIRECT')

e.   OPEN (15, 'DATA6', STATUS = 'SCRATCH')

f.   OPEN (9, FILE = 'BOOKS', STATUS = 'NEW'

3. Are the following statements valid or invalid in Fortran? All files are open for sequential access. Assume variable names and format specifications will not cause errors.

a.   READ (9, FILE = 'BLOOD') B, T

b.   REWIND (9)

c.   WRITE (9, 10, END = 33) NAME, AGE

d.   WRITE (*, 1) AGE

e.   READ (12, 20, REC = 6) X, Y, Z

f.   CLOSE (9, END)

4. A data file named DATA1.DAT was created with sequential access. All records in the file were written with the format specification

$$(1X, A20, A10, 3X, I2, F12.2)$$

a.   Write an OPEN statement that connects this file to your program.
b.   Write type declarations, a READ statement, and a FORMAT statement to read one record in this file. Make up your own variable names.

■ Programming Exercises

1. Each record in a sequential data file named DATA2.DAT was written with the format specification

$$(1X, A20, I2, F12.2)$$

Write a program that will read the file and print its contents.

2.   a.   Write a program to create a sequential file named GRADES.DAT, in which each record is to contain the name of a student and four grades (from 0 to 100 inclusive). The program should ask for the names and grades, and write records to GRADES.DAT. Let the user decide when to stop entering data.

b. Write a program to read the file GRADES.DAT, calculate the mean grade for each student, and print each name, followed by the four grades and the mean grade, in a nicely-formatted table. This program should not contain, as a constant, the number of records in GRADES.DAT.

3. Write one program that accomplishes the same objective as the two programs in the previous exercise by putting the data in a scratch file.

4. Write a program that reads a sequential file with each record containing one real number, and finds the two largest values in the file and their positions.

5. A direct-access data file named DATA3.DAT has each record written with the format specification

(1X, A20, I2, F12.2)

Write a program that asks the user for a record number and prints that record, if it can.

6. a. Write a program to create a personnel file named PERSNL.DAT that can be accessed directly by other programs. Each record consists of:

> Employee name
> Social security number
> Hourly rate of pay
> Blue Cross status (SINGLE, MARRIED, or NONE)

Run the program and put at least a dozen records in the file.

b. Write a program that directly accesses the file created in part a. Allow the following options to the user:

> Display the entire file.
> Display a particular record.
> Update a record. Allow changes only to the pay rate.

7. Write a program to read real numbers from a sequential file and print the numbers in increasing order. The first number in the file is an integer giving the number of real numbers in the file. There should be no duplicate real numbers.

Do not read the numbers in the file into an array. The program must make several passes through the data file, finding and printing one number on each pass.

8. Write a program that sorts a direct-access file. You could, for example, sort the GRADES.DAT file on the names, assuming the names are given in the form 'Smith, John'. Either the Shell sort or our earlier selection sort can be used.

9. Write a program that performs a binary search on a direct-access file. Assume that each record in the file contains a name and four real numbers, as in GRADES.DAT, and that the records are in alphabetical order by name.

13 OPERATIONS WITH CHARACTER DATA

We shall generally refer to character data as **strings**. We have already introduced several examples of strings, including CHARACTER constants, variables, and arrays. We have also discussed the meaning of the logical relations applied to strings. We shall deal with several additional string operations in this chapter.

13.1 CHARACTER OPERATIONS AND FUNCTIONS

Concatenation

To **concatenate** two strings simply means to make one string by placing the second string after the first. The symbol for concatenation is a pair of slashes (//). If the first string is 'MARY' and the second string is 'LAND', then the concatenation of the two produces the string 'MARYLAND'. To perform this concatenation, suppose the variable STRING is declared

```
CHARACTER*8  STRING
```

Then we can use the statement

```
STRING = 'MARY' // 'LAND'
```

to assign the value 'MARYLAND' to STRING.

All the character variables we have been dealing with have **fixed length**; that is, the length of a character variable cannot change within a program. These fixed-length variables often contain trailing blanks that can cause problems. For example, suppose three variables are declared in the statement

```
CHARACTER*8  STRING, FIRST, SECOND
```

Further, suppose three assignment statements give values to these variables as follows.

```
FIRST  = 'MARY'
SECOND = 'LAND'
STRING = FIRST // SECOND
```

The value of STRING is not 'MARYLAND' but 'MARY□□□□' because the action of the assignment statements is:

Statement	Action
FIRST = 'MARY'	Assigns the value 'MARY□□□□' to FIRST.
SECOND = 'LAND'	Assigns the value 'LAND□□□□' to SECOND.
STRING = FIRST // SECOND	Calculates the value of FIRST // SECOND as 'MARY□□□□LAND□□□□'; then assigns this value to STRING. Since the value has 16 characters and STRING has declared length 8, STRING holds only the first 8 characters: 'MARY□□□□'.

Substrings

Problems like the previous one motivate us to find ways to strip blanks from string variables. In Example 8.8, we showed how to do this by reading a string of length 80 into an array variable holding eighty elements of length 1. We present here a similar method that allows some more powerful extensions.

A **substring** of a string is a set of one or more contiguous characters in the string. The string 'MARYLAND' has many substrings, including 'MARY', 'A', 'RYL', 'ND', and 'MARYLAND' itself. Although 'MARYLAND' contains the letters 'M', 'A', and 'N', in that order, the string 'MAN' is not a substring of 'MARYLAND' because the letters in 'MAN' are not contiguous (adjacent to each other) in 'MARYLAND'.

In Fortran, we refer to a substring of a character variable by the variable name followed by the starting and ending character positions of the substring. These starting and ending positions are separated by a colon (:) and enclosed in parentheses. For example,

STRING(4:6)

refers to the three-element substring of STRING beginning in position 4 and ending in position 6. If the value of STRING is 'VIRGINIA', then STRING(4:6) is 'GIN'.

The starting and ending positions can be any integer expressions. Obviously, the starting value should be less than or equal to the starting value.

Either the starting position or ending position, but not both, can be absent. With the starting position absent, as in

STRING(:6)

the substring starts in position 1 of STRING. With 'VIRGINIA' as the value of STRING, STRING(:6) is 'VIRGIN'.

With the ending position absent, as in

STRING(4:)

the substring consists of all characters from the starting position to the length of STRING, so STRING(4:) would be 'GINIA'.

Referring to a 1-character substring of a character variable is much like referring to one element of an array. We can refer to the Ith character of STRING as

STRING(I:I)

I must be an integer variable with value from 1 through the length of STRING.

Substrings can occur on either side of the equal sign in an assignment statement. For example, we can have

NAME = STRING(8:12)

or

STRING(5:) = 'NAME'

If STRING has length 8 and value 'ABCDEFGH', the assignment STRING(5) = 'NAME' gives STRING the value 'ABCDNAME'.

Substrings of the same string can occur on both sides of the equal sign. For example, if STRING has length 15 and value 'INCOMPATIBILITY', the assignment

        STRING(5:8) = STRING(12:15)

gives STRING the value 'INCOLITYIBILITY'. The two substrings of the same string must not overlap. That is,

        STRING(5:8) = STRING(6:9)

is illegal in Fortran 77.

Example 13.1 Concatenating Character Variables

The following program asks for a first name and a last name, and assigns the input strings to character variables FIRNAM and LASNAM. The program then assigns to variable NAME a string value containing the last name, a comma and space, and the first name. If the user enters the first and last names as 'George' and 'Smith', the program should store 'Smith, George' in NAME.

Both FIRNAM and LASNAM will have declared length 15. The problem is that the comma must come right after the last letter in the last name. The program will find the position of that last letter, and will assign the position value to a variable POSITN. Then NAME is formed with the statement

        NAME = LASNAM(:POSITN) // ', ' // FIRNAM

The segment to calculate POSITN is similar to a segment in the program of Example 8.8, but it uses a substring instead of a character array. See Program 13.1.

◼

PROGRAM 13.1

```
      PROGRAM MAKNAM
*------------------------------------------------------------*
*  Read a first name and a last name.  Concatenate them to make *
*  one name in the form: Last name-comma-space-first name.      *
*------------------------------------------------------------*
      INTEGER      LAST, POSITN
      CHARACTER*15 FIRNAM, LASNAM, NAME*30
```

```
*-----------------------------------------------------------*
*                  Read first and last names.               *
*-----------------------------------------------------------*
      PRINT *, 'First name?'
      READ '(A)', FIRNAM

      PRINT *, 'Last name?'
      READ '(A)', LASNAM
*-----------------------------------------------------------*
*      Get position of last nonblank character in LASNAM.   *
*-----------------------------------------------------------*
      POSITN = 15
11    IF (LASNAM(POSITN:POSITN) .EQ. ' ') THEN
         POSITN = POSITN - 1
         GO TO 11
      END IF
*-----------------------------------------------------------*
*                  Calculate and print NAME.                *
*-----------------------------------------------------------*
      NAME = LASNAM(:POSITN) // ', ' // FIRNAM
      PRINT 10, NAME
10    FORMAT ('0', 'Name: ', A)

      END
```

Example 13.2 A Function to Find the Last Nonblank Character in a String

The operation of trimming trailing blanks is important enough for us to make a subprogram of it. We will write a function subprogram LAST that takes a dummy character argument STRING and returns the value of the last nonblank position in STRING. STRING can take a passed length in the function, so we declare it

```
      CHARACTER*(*)  STRING
```

The LEN Function

To find the length of STRING, function LAST uses the intrinsic **function** LEN, which takes a string argument and returns the (integer) length of that string. LEN counts all characters in the string, including trailing blanks. Function LAST contains the statement

```
         LENGTH = LEN(STRING)
```

The function LENis usually used in subprograms, because the length of a character variable in a main program is always the declared length of that variable. Program 13.2 shows the function LAST.

■
PROGRAM 13.2

```
      INTEGER FUNCTION LAST(STRING)
*----------------------------------------------------------------*
*    Calculate last nonblank position in dummy argument STRING.  *
*----------------------------------------------------------------*
      INTEGER        LENGTH, I
      CHARACTER*(*)  STRING

      LENGTH = LEN(STRING)
      I = LENGTH

11    IF (STRING(I:I) .EQ. ' ') THEN
         I = I - 1
         GO TO 11
      END IF

      LAST = I

      END
```

Example 13.3 Printing a Centered String

We present here a program to print a string centered on the terminal screen. The program reads values for a string variable LINE and an integer variable WIDTH and prints the string centered in a field of width WIDTH. The program invokes LAST to find a value for POSITN, then prints LINE(:POSITN) centered in the field.

To center this substring, we determine a number of blanks to print before printing the substring. Since the substring has POSITN characters and the width of a line is WIDTH, the total number of blanks before and after the substring must be (WIDTH - POSITN). Half these blanks, or

```
      (WIDTH - POSITN) / 2
```

should come before the substring. Let `BLANK` be a string variable of length 40 containing forty blanks. Then we can print the appropriate number of blanks by printing `BLANK(:NBLANK)` before printing `LINE(:POSITN)`, where

```
NBLANK = (WIDTH - POSITN) / 2
```

That is, we use the following `PRINT/FORMAT` pair

```
      PRINT 10, BLANK(:NBLANK), LINE(:POSITN)
10    FORMAT (1X, 2A)
```

The complete program appears in Program 13.3.

■

PROGRAM 13.3
_____

```
      PROGRAM CENTER
*------------------------------------------------------*
*  Read a string LINE and an integer WIDTH.  Print *
*  the line centered in a field of width WIDTH.     *
*------------------------------------------------------*
      CHARACTER  LINE*80, BLANK*40
      INTEGER    WIDTH, POSITN, LAST, NBLANK
      DATA       BLANK /' '/

      PRINT *, 'This program will center a line'
      PRINT *, 'on the terminal screen.  How wide'
      PRINT *, 'is your terminal screen?'
      READ  *, WIDTH

      PRINT *
      PRINT *, 'Please enter a line.'
      READ '(A)', LINE

      POSITN = LAST(LINE)
      NBLANK = (WIDTH - POSITN) / 2

      PRINT 10, BLANK(:NBLANK), LINE(:POSITN)
10    FORMAT (1X, 2A)

      END
```

_____

The INDEX **Function**

The intrinsic function INDEX gives the starting position of a substring inside a (usually larger) string. The INDEX function takes two arguments separated by commas: first, the string to be searched, and then the substring to be searched for.

For example, if A = 'WASHINGTON' and B = 'IN', then INDEX(A, B) returns 5 because the substring 'IN' begins at the fifth character position in 'WASH-INGTON'. INDEX('WASHINGTON', 'N') is 6 because INDEX gives the position of the *first* occurrence of the substring. Notice that both arguments in INDEX must be string expressions. When the given string does not contain the specified substring, then INDEX returns the value 0. Thus INDEX('ABC', 'D') is 0.

Example 13.4 Finding a Character with the INDEX **Function**

Program 13.4 indicates where the letter E first occurs in an input string.

■
PROGRAM 13.4

```
      PROGRAM FINDE
*------------------------------------------------------*
*           Find E with the INDEX function.            *
*------------------------------------------------------*
      CHARACTER*80   LINE
      INTEGER        POSITN

      PRINT *, 'Enter a string:'
      READ '(A)', LINE
      POSITN = INDEX(LINE, 'E')

      IF (POSITN .EQ. 0) THEN
          PRINT 10, 'That string has no E.'
      ELSE
          PRINT 10, 'E first occurs at position' , POSITN
      END IF

10    FORMAT ('0', A, I3)

      END
```

A run of the program might be

```
Enter a string: THERE WE WERE
E first occurs at position  3
```

Example 13.5 Counting Characters in Lines of Text

Program 13.5 reads several lines of text from a data file TEXT.DAT. The program counts the numbers of characters in the text, uppercase and lowercase letters, vowels, and spaces. The program assumes the lines have 80 or fewer characters, and it invokes the function LAST to find the last nonblank character in each line.

The program uses an integer variable NVOWEL to count vowels. A character constant VOWEL is initialized to 'AEIOUaeiou'. The program checks to see if each character C is a vowel with the statement

```
IF (INDEX(VOWEL, C) .NE. 0)  NVOWEL = NVOWEL + 1
```

Similarly, UPPER and LOWER will be character constants holding the uppercase and lowercase letters, respectively.

■

PROGRAM 13.5
_____

```
      PROGRAM COUNTC
*-------------------------------------------------------------------*
*  Read lines of text from the file TEXT.DAT.  Count the numbers of *
*  characters, uppercase and lowercase letters, vowels, and spaces. *
*-------------------------------------------------------------------*
      INTEGER    J, POSIT, LAST, NUPPER, NLOWER, NSPACE, NCHAR, NVOWEL
      CHARACTER  C*1, LINE*80, VOWEL*10, UPPER*26, LOWER*26
      DATA       NUPPER, NLOWER, NSPACE, NCHAR, NVOWEL /5*0/
      PARAMETER  (VOWEL = 'AEIOUaeiou')
      PARAMETER  (UPPER = 'ABCDEFGHIJKLMNOPQRSTUVWXYZ')
      PARAMETER  (LOWER = 'abcdefghijklmnopqrstuvwxyz')

      OPEN (UNIT = 8, FILE='TEXT', STATUS = 'OLD')

11    READ (8, '(A)', END = 33) LINE

      PRINT *, LINE

      POSIT = LAST(LINE)
      NCHAR = NCHAR + POSIT
```

```
        DO 22 J = 1, POSIT

          C = LINE(J:J)

          IF (INDEX(LOWER, C) .NE. 0) THEN
              NLOWER = NLOWER + 1
          ELSE IF (INDEX(UPPER, C) .NE. 0) THEN
              NUPPER = NUPPER + 1
          ELSE IF (C .EQ. ' ') THEN
              NSPACE = NSPACE + 1
          END IF

          IF (INDEX(VOWEL, C) .NE. 0)  NVOWEL = NVOWEL + 1

22        CONTINUE

      GO TO 11

33    CLOSE (8)

      PRINT 10, 'UPPERCASE', 'LOWERCASE', 'SPACE', 'VOWELS',
     1          'CHARACTERS'
10    FORMAT ('0', 5A12)

      PRINT 20, NUPPER, NLOWER, NSPACE, NVOWEL, NCHAR
20    FORMAT (1X, I8, I13, I14, I11, I10)

      END
```

A run of the program might yield

```
The Owl and the Pussy Cat went to sea
in a beautiful pea-green boat.
They took some honey and plenty of money,
wrapped up in a five-pound note.
```

UPPERCASE	LOWERCASE	SPACE	VOWELS	CHARACTERS
5	106	24	46	140

Example 13.6 Simple Editing

Suppose you have made a typographical error in a string value and want to make a correction. The string functions we have been discussing will allow you to use the computer to make corrections.

Suppose the string variable you are dealing with is called LINE, and that you want to replace the substring DELETE in LINE with the string ADD. To be specific, imagine that

```
LINE   is 'Give the tickets to she and me.'
DELETE is 'she'
ADD    is 'her'
```

Call the corrected line NEWLIN. Then the problem is to use LINE, DELETE, and ADD to calculate the value of NEWLIN.

Since, in this case, we know the values of all the variables, we can write

```
NEWLIN = LINE(:20) // ADD // LINE(24:)
```

which means the same as

```
NEWLIN = 'Give the tickets to ' // 'her' // ' and me.'
```

That is, we take NEWLIN to be an initial segment of LINE, plus the string to be inserted, plus the remainder of LINE. What we need to do, in general, is to express the integers 20 and 24 in terms of the variables LINE, DELETE, and ADD.

Our program will invoke the function LAST to find the last nonblank characters in LINE, DELETE, and ADD. The effective lengths of these strings will be LLIN, LDEL, and LADD, so the appropriate assignment statements are

```
LLIN = LAST(LINE)
LDEL = LAST(DELETE)
LADD = LAST(ADD)
```

A problem arises if more characters are to be added than deleted. Then NEWLIN might be longer than 80 characters. We will simply declare the lengths of LINE, ADD, and DELETE to be 80, and the length of NEWLIN to be 100, allowing for LADD to have up to 20 more characters than LDEL.

Let

```
POS = INDEX(LINE, DELETE)
```

In our problem,

```
POS = INDEX('Give the tickets to she and me.', 'she')
```

so POS = 21. The first part of NEWLIN is to be the first part of LINE, from position 1 to position 20. In general, we want the part of LINE from position 1 to position POS − 1, or LINE(:POS − 1).

Since we took out the string DELETE = 'she', there are three positions removed from LINE: positions POS, POS + 1, and POS + 2. Thus, the third segment of LINE begins at position POS + 3, or POS + LDEL. The assignment statement to calculate NEWLIN is then

$$\text{NEWLIN} = \text{LINE}(:\text{POS} - 1) \; // \; \text{ADD}(:\text{LADD}) \; // \; \text{LINE}(\text{POS} + \text{LDEL:})$$

This line is the heart of a program to change characters in a line of text. The complete program is detailed in Program 13.6 and now should be easy to follow.

■

PROGRAM 13.6
_____

```
      PROGRAM EDIT
*-----------------------------------------------------------------*
*       Use string functions to change characters in text.        *
*-----------------------------------------------------------------*
      CHARACTER*80  LINE, ADD, DELETE, NEWLIN*100, ANSWER*3
      INTEGER       POS, LAST, LDEL, LADD, LLIN
*-----------------------------------------------------------------*
*                        Read the line.                           *
*-----------------------------------------------------------------*
      PRINT *
      PRINT *, 'Type a line'
      READ 10, LINE

      PRINT *, 'Any mistakes (YES/NO)?'
      READ 10, ANSWER

      IF (ANSWER .EQ. 'YES') THEN
*-----------------------------------------------------------------*
*                   Find what must be deleted.                    *
*-----------------------------------------------------------------*
         PRINT *, 'What needs to be deleted? '
         READ 10, DELETE
         LDEL = LAST(DELETE)
*-----------------------------------------------------------------*
* Check to see if the string to be deleted is part of the line. *
*-----------------------------------------------------------------*
```

```
            POS = INDEX( LINE, DELETE(:LDEL) )
11          IF (POS .EQ. 0) THEN
               PRINT *, 'Cannot find error.'
               PRINT *, 'What needs to be deleted? '
               READ 10, DELETE
               LDEL = LAST(DELETE)
               POS = INDEX( LINE, DELETE(:LDEL) )
               GO TO 11
            END IF
*---------------------------------------------------------------*
*              Find out what string is to be added.             *
*---------------------------------------------------------------*
            PRINT *, 'What replaces it? '
            READ 10,  ADD
*---------------------------------------------------------------*
*              Calculate and print the corrected line.          *
*---------------------------------------------------------------*
            LLIN = LAST(LINE)
            LADD = LAST(ADD)

            NEWLIN = LINE(:POS - 1) // ADD(:LADD) // LINE(POS + LDEL:)

            PRINT 20, NEWLIN

         END IF

10       FORMAT ( A )
20       FORMAT ('0', 'The corrected line is:' // 1X, A)

         END
```

Fortran has two built-in functions that convert strings to integers and integers to strings. In ANSI Fortran, the basis for translating between numeric and string data is the ASCII code (see Appendix B), which assigns to each character an integer value from 0 to 127. In particular, the ASCII code for a space is 32, and the ASCII codes for uppercase letters from *A* to *Z* are the numbers 65 to 90.

However, IBM and some other computers use the EBCDIC Code, which is also listed in Appendix B. The uppercase letters have EBCDIC codes from 193 for *A* through 233 for *Z*, with several gaps in the numbers.

The CHAR and ICHAR **Functions**

The CHAR **function** operates on an integer expression and gives the character that has this value in the computer's collating sequence. We call the characters that you can type on the keyboard **printable characters**. To see the character with a particular code, such as 78, use the statement

```
PRINT *, CHAR(78)
```

If your computer uses ASCII code, it will print an uppercase N. With EBCDIC code, the computer will print a plus sign (+), the character with EBCDIC code 78.

The `ICHAR` **function** operates on single-character expressions and gives the code for the character in the computer's collating sequence. For example, `ICHAR('H')` is 72 in ASCII and is 200 in EBCDIC. You can find your computer's code for any printable character by printing `ICHAR` followed by that character in parentheses.

Example 13.7 Counting All the Characters in a File

Program 13.7 counts all the characters in the file `CHARFL.DAT`. Like many of our programs, this one invokes the function `LAST` to find the position of the last nonblank character on each line.

If the computer code is ASCII, the printable characters have codes from 32 to 126. In EBCDIC code, however, the codes for printable characters run from 64 to 249. The program can handle either code with an array `COUNT` declared

```
INTEGER   COUNT(32:249)
```

The character variable `LINE` stores each line in the file, and the program determines the code (ASCII or EBCDIC) for each character with

```
CHARNO = ICHAR( LINE(J:J) )
COUNT(CHARNO) = COUNT(CHARNO) + 1
```

See Program 13.7

■

PROGRAM 13.7

```
     PROGRAM CCOUNT
*----------------------------------------------------------------------*
*          Count all the characters in the file CHARFL.DAT.            *
*----------------------------------------------------------------------*
     CHARACTER*80  LINE
     INTEGER       COUNT(32:249), END, J, CHARNO, LAST
     DATA          COUNT /218 * 0/
```

```
        OPEN (9, FILE = 'CHARFL', STATUS = 'OLD')

11      READ (9, '(A)', END = 33) LINE
          END = LAST(LINE)
*------------------------------------------------------------------*
*                 Count each character in LINE.                    *
*------------------------------------------------------------------*
          DO 22 J = 1, END

              CHARNO = ICHAR( LINE(J:J) )
              COUNT(CHARNO) = COUNT(CHARNO) + 1

22        CONTINUE

        GO TO 11

33      CLOSE (9)
*------------------------------------------------------------------*
*          Print all the characters that occurred at least         *
*          once, together with their frequencies.                  *
*------------------------------------------------------------------*
        PRINT 10
        DO 44 J = 32, 249
            IF (COUNT(J) .NE. 0) PRINT 20, CHAR(J), COUNT(J)
44      CONTINUE

10      FORMAT ('0', 'Character', 2X, 'Frequency')
20      FORMAT(1X, A6, I11)

        END
```

If the file `CHARFL.DAT` contains the four lines

```
F(X, Y, Z) = 729Y * 834Z + 2X - 563478SIN(XYZ) / 12345
/\/\/\/\/\/\/\/\/\/\/\/\/\/\/\/\/\/\
|*| |*| |*| |*| |*| |*| |*| |*| |*| |
| |*| |*| |*| |*| |*| |*| |*| |*| |*|
```

the program will print the following output

```
Character  Frequency
                  30
      (            2
      )            2
      *           19
      +            1
```

,	2
–	1
.	2
/	19
1	1
2	3
3	3
4	3
5	2
6	1
7	2
8	2
9	1
=	1
F	1
I	1
N	2
S	1
X	3
Y	3
Z	3
\	18
|	38

■

13.2   INTERNAL FILES

An **internal file** is not really a file, but is storage space within a program. Data items in an internal file have type CHARACTER. An internal file can be:

> A single character variable
> A character array
> A character array element
> A character substring

When the file is a character array, there is one record in the file for each array element. In all other cases, the file contains exactly one record.

Suppose a character variable DOLLAR contains a string representing a real number. For concreteness, let DOLLAR = '215.98'. How can we get a real variable AMOUNT equal to 215.98? It is possible to put the value of DOL-LAR into an external file with an A6 FORMAT then read that value with an F6.2 FORMAT. However, we can achieve the same effect by using DOLLAR as an internal file. The **internal** READ **statement**

```
     READ (UNIT = DOLLAR, FMT = '(F6.2)') AMOUNT
```

reads the value of AMOUNT from the string DOLLAR using an F6.2 data descriptor. The variable DOLLAR is used as the *logical unit* from which information is read. Since DOLLAR contains the string '215.98', the effect is the same as

```
     AMOUNT = 215.98
```

Conversely, suppose a real variable NUMBER has a value, and we want to convert that value to a string and store it in a character variable WORD. We can do this with an **internal WRITE statement** in the following way:

```
     CHARACTER*5   WORD
     REAL          NUMBER

     NUMBER = 1.0 / 8.0
     WRITE (UNIT = WORD, FMT = '(F5.3)') NUMBER
```

After the WRITE statement, WORD contains the value '0.125'.

To write several records into an internal file, the file must be a character array. If C is a character array defined by

```
     CHARACTER*2   C(10)
```

then each element of C can be given a value by

```
     WRITE(UNIT = C, 10) (I, I = 1, 10)
10   FORMAT ( 10(I2 /) )
```

Then C(1) will be ' 1', C(2) will be ' 2', . . ., and C(10) will be '10'.

It is possible to get more than one number stored in a single record. For example:

```
     INTEGER     M, N
     CHARACTER*10  CHAR

     M = 1234
     N = -245
     WRITE (CHAR, '(2I5)') M, N
```

This code segment causes CHAR to be ' 1234 -245'.

Example 13.8 Reading Records with One of Two Possible Formats

Each record in a data file contains a name, a gender (*M* or *F* for male or female), and an integer job code (0, 1, or 2). Unfortunately, two different people wrote the file. Both put the name first, but one of them put the job code second and one of them put the gender second.

Suppose the name is in columns 1 through 20 in every record. Some records have the gender in column 21 and the job code in column 23, while some records have the job code in column 21 and the gender in column 23. The file might look like

```
Abrahams, Mary        2 F
Blalock, Helen        F 0
Carbuncle, Todd       M 2
Davidson, Arthur      0 M
Edwards, Catherine    1 F
Featherstone, Will    M 1
```

Our assignment is to read the file and print each name, gender, and job code. We will use variables NAME, GENDER, and JOBCAT to hold these values. If the *gender* is in column 21, an appropriate READ/FORMAT pair is

```
      READ (9, 20) NAME, GENDER, JOBCAT
20    FORMAT (A20, A1, 1X, I1)
```

but if the *job code* is in column 21, we should use

```
      READ (9, 30) NAME, JOBCAT, GENDER
30    FORMAT (A20, I1, 1X, A1)
```

The problem is that we do not know beforehand which records are in which form. If the program tries to read an integer job code from a field containing M or F, a fatal error results.

The solution is to read the entire record into a character variable RECORD, look at RECORD(21:21) to find out what kind of data column 21 holds, and then use RECORD as an internal file to read values for NAME, GEN-DER, and JOBCAT.

Reading RECORD is no problem. We will use a single-character variable C to store RECORD(21:21). If C holds 'M' or 'F', then we use the first PRINT/FORMAT pair above; if C holds something else, we use the second. Now, however, instead of reading from unit 9, we read from RECORD. The following code is the heart of the program.

```
        IF (C .EQ. 'M' .OR. C .EQ. 'F') THEN
            READ (RECORD, 20) NAME, GENDER, JOBCAT
20          FORMAT (A20, A1, 1X, I1)
        ELSE
            READ (RECORD, 30) NAME, JOBCAT, GENDER
30          FORMAT (A20, I1, 1X, A1)
        END IF
```

The entire program is shown in Program 13.8.

■
PROGRAM 13.8

```
      PROGRAM TWOFMT
*-----------------------------------------------------------------*
* A file FORM2.DAT has records written in one of two formats:     *
*                                                                 *
*         (A20, I1, 1X, A1)   or   (A20, A1, 1X, I1)              *
*                                                                 *
* This program reads each record into a character variable        *
* RECORD with an A23 format, then uses RECORD as an internal       *
* file to determine which format to use.                          *
*-----------------------------------------------------------------*
      CHARACTER  RECORD*23, NAME*20, GENDER, C
      INTEGER    JOBCAT

      OPEN (9, FILE = 'FORM2', STATUS = 'OLD')

      PRINT 10

11    READ (9, '(A)', END = 22) RECORD

          C = RECORD(21:21)
          IF (C .EQ. 'M' .OR. C .EQ. 'F') THEN
              READ (RECORD, 20) NAME, GENDER, JOBCAT
          ELSE
              READ (RECORD, 30) NAME, JOBCAT, GENDER
          END IF

          PRINT 40, NAME, GENDER, JOBCAT

      GO TO 11

22    CLOSE (9)
```

```
10     FORMAT ('0', 6X, 'NAME', 12X, 'GENDER', 3X, 'JOB CATEGORY')
20     FORMAT (A20, A1, 1X, I1)
30     FORMAT (A20, I1, 1X, A1)
40     FORMAT (1X, A, 5X, A, 10X, I1)

       END
```

Example 13.9 Printing Only the Positive Numbers in a Table

A data file contains the following data:

```
123.45    -24.42    324.56    425.28
-103.22    216.78    365.88    409.23
148.21    229.47    -53.54    477.31
102.81    236.75    349.02    465.97
110.65    240.26    315.29    -85.34
115.85    213.89    357.24    424.66
```

Suppose that we must print each positive value in the row and column in which it appears in the file, but negative values are to be suppressed, or replaced with blanks.

We will read the four values in each record into a real array VALUE of size 4 with the list-directed READ statement

```
READ (9, *, END = 22) (VALUE(I), I = 1, 4)
```

Next, we write the four values to one character variable RECORD with

```
       WRITE (RECORD, 20) (VALUE(I), I = 1, 4)
20     FORMAT (4F9.2)
```

Now, we look at each VALUE(I) for I = 1 to 4. If VALUE(I) is negative, we replace that part of RECORD with blanks. The representation of VALUE(I) in RECORD ends in position $9 * I$, so it must start in position $9 * I - 8$. To blank out the appropriate part of RECORD, we use the statement

```
IF (VALUE(I) .LE. 0.0) RECORD(9 * I - 8 : 9 * I) = ' '
```

See Program 13.9 for the complete program.

■
PROGRAM 13.9

```
      PROGRAM PRNPOS
*-------------------------------------------------------------------*
*  Use an internal file to print only positive values in a table.  *
*-------------------------------------------------------------------*
      CHARACTER  RECORD*80
      REAL       VALUE(4)
      INTEGER    I

      OPEN (9, FILE = 'POSITV', STATUS = 'OLD')

      PRINT 10, ('Day', I, I = 1, 4)

11    READ (9, *, END = 33) (VALUE(I), I = 1, 4)
         WRITE (RECORD, 20) (VALUE(I), I = 1, 4)

         DO 22 I = 1, 4
            IF (VALUE(I) .LE. 0.0) RECORD(9 * I - 8 : 9 * I) = ' '
22       CONTINUE

         PRINT '(A)', RECORD

      GO TO 11

33    CLOSE (9)

10    FORMAT ('0', 4(2X, A, I2, 2X) / 1X, 36('-') )
20    FORMAT (4F9.2)

      END
```

The program produces the following output

Day 1	Day 2	Day 3	Day 4
123.45		324.56	425.28
	216.78	365.88	409.23
148.21	229.47		477.31
102.81	236.75	349.02	465.97
110.65	240.26	315.29	
115.85	213.89	357.24	424.66

Example 13.10 Printing a Histogram

In Chapter 11 we wrote a program to calculate various statistics and a frequency distribution for a set of data. One graphical way to present a frequency distribution is with a **histogram**, as shown in Figure 13.1. The height of each bar indicates the frequency in that class. The boundaries of the classes are given at the bottom of the graph. We present here a subroutine HISTOG to draw a histogram like this one.

FIGURE 13.1
A histogram

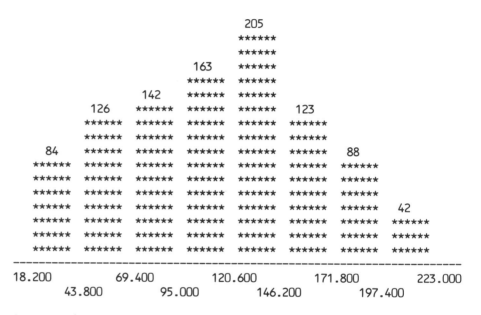

```
One row of stars represents 12.81 units.
```

HISTOG has three dummy arguments: BOUND, FREQNC, and NCLASS. NCLASS is an integer designating the number of classes. BOUND is a real array with subscripts from 0 to NCLASS. BOUND(0) is the lower boundary of the first class, and for J = 1 to NCLASS, BOUND(J) is the upper boundary of class J. FREQNC is an integer array with FREQNC(J) denoting the frequency in class J.

We should limit the number of rows of stars in the histogram because no one wants to see several hundred rows. We will set the limit at 16, so the entire histogram will fit on a terminal screen. The program calculates the *graphing frequencies* F(J), which will generally be smaller than the corresponding FREQNC(J). If the largest frequency LARGE is 16 or less, the program simply assigns the values of FREQNC to F.

If `LARGE` is greater than 16, the program will use exactly 16 rows of stars for the frequency `LARGE`. Then each row of stars represents a frequency of `REAL(LARGE) / 16.0`. The subprogram assigns values to F with

```
HEIGHT = REAL(LARGE) / 16.0

DO 11 J = 1, NCLASS
    F(J) = NINT(REAL(FREQNC(J)) / HEIGHT)
11  CONTINUE
    LARGE = 16
```

A row in the histogram will be stored in `LINE`, a character variable with length 80. (We use 80 because many terminals have 80 columns.) The rows will contain stars and blanks and possibly some frequencies at the top of a bar. There will be `LARGE + 1` rows because of the frequency at the top of the longest bar. Since we must draw the histogram from top to bottom, the `DO` loop for the rows begins

```
DO 44 ROW = LARGE + 1, 1, -1
```

Inside this `DO` loop, the program must assign values to the positions of `LINE`. Somewhat arbitrarily, we choose 8 columns per class and let the first 8 positions of `LINE` be blank for a left margin. Then positions 9 through 16 belong to the first class, positions 17 through 24 to the second class, and so on. In general, class J has positions $8 * J + 1$ through $8 * (J + 1)$, so for each class J we must assign values to

```
LINE(8 * J + 1 : 8 * (J + 1))
```

The values to be assigned fall into three categories: a row of stars, a row of 8 blanks, or the frequency at the top of the bar. Which of these to use depends on the relation between `ROW` and `F(J)`.

1. If `F(J) = ROW - 1`, `LINE(8 * J + 1 : 8 * (J + 1))` should hold a representation of the frequency `F(J)`.
2. If `F(J)` is greater than or equal to `ROW`, `LINE(8 * J + 1 : 8 * (J + 1))` should be a row of stars.
3. In any other case, `LINE(8 * J + 1 : 8 * (J + 1))` should be a row of blanks.

Cases 2 and 3 are easy to deal with. For case 1, we use an internal `WRITE` statement:

```
    WRITE (LINE(8 * J + 1 : 8 * (J + 1)), 20) FREQNC(J)
20  FORMAT (I5, 3X)
```

The complete subprogram is given in Program 13.10.

■
PROGRAM 13.10

```
      SUBROUTINE HISTOG(BOUND, FREQNC, NCLASS)
*-----------------------------------------------------------------------*
* Draw a histogram of a frequency distribution.  The BOUND array       *
* contains the boundaries of the classes.  The frequency array has     *
* frequencies for each class.  NCLASS is the number of classes.        *
*-----------------------------------------------------------------------*
      INTEGER     ROW, J, LARGE, NCLASS, F(20), FREQNC(NCLASS)
      REAL        BOUND(0:NCLASS), HEIGHT
      CHARACTER*8 BLANKS, STARS, LINE*80
      PARAMETER   (BLANKS = ' ', STARS = ' ****** ')
*-----------------------------------------------------------------------*
*                   Find largest frequency.                            *
*-----------------------------------------------------------------------*
      LARGE = FREQNC(1)
      DO 11 J = 2, NCLASS
         IF (LARGE .LT. FREQNC(J) ) LARGE = FREQNC(J)
11    CONTINUE
*-----------------------------------------------------------------------*
* Calculate the "graphing frequencies" F(J).  If LARGE is more than    *
* 16, use a maximum of 16 rows, because 16 rows plus a line on top     *
* and 5 rows on the bottom will almost fill up the screen.             *
*-----------------------------------------------------------------------*
      HEIGHT = REAL(LARGE) / 16.0

      IF (LARGE .GT. 16) THEN

         DO 22 J = 1, NCLASS
           F(J) = NINT(REAL(FREQNC(J)) / HEIGHT)
22       CONTINUE
         LARGE = 16

      ELSE

         DO 33 J = 1, NCLASS
           F(J) = FREQNC(J)
33       CONTINUE

      END IF
*-----------------------------------------------------------------------*
*                   Draw the histogram.                                *
*-----------------------------------------------------------------------*
      PRINT 10, 'Here is a histogram of the data:'
```

```
      LINE(1:8) = BLANKS
      DO 44 ROW = LARGE + 1, 1, -1

        DO 55 J = 1, NCLASS

          IF (F(J) .EQ. ROW - 1) THEN
*-----------------------------------------------------------------------*
*   Use substring of LINE as internal file to write FREQNC(J).          *
*-----------------------------------------------------------------------*
            WRITE (LINE(8 * J + 1 : 8 * (J + 1)), 20) FREQNC(J)
          ELSE IF (F(J) .GE. ROW) THEN
            LINE(8 * J + 1 : 8 * (J + 1) ) = STARS
          ELSE
            LINE(8 * J + 1 : 8 * (J + 1) ) = BLANKS
          END IF

55        CONTINUE

        PRINT '(A)', LINE

44      CONTINUE

      PRINT 30, ('-', J = 1, 8 * NCLASS)
*-----------------------------------------------------------------------*
*                   Write endpoints of intervals.                       *
*-----------------------------------------------------------------------*
      PRINT 40, ( BOUND(J), J = 0, NCLASS, 2 )
      PRINT 50, ( BOUND(J), J = 1, NCLASS, 2 )
      IF (HEIGHT .GT. 1) PRINT 60, HEIGHT

10    FORMAT ('0', 10X, A //)
20    FORMAT (I5, 3X)
30    FORMAT (1X, 8X, 80A )
40    FORMAT (1X, 10(F11.3, 5X))
50    FORMAT (1X, 8X, 10(F11.3, 5X))
60    FORMAT ('0', 'One row of stars equals', G12.4, ' units.')

      END
```

■

13.3 SUMMARY OF CHAPTER 13

■ *Terms Introduced in This Chapter*

CHAR function	ICHAR function	Internal WRITE statement
Concatenation	INDEX function	LEN function
Fixed-length character variable	Internal file	Substring
Histogram	Internal READ statement	

■ *What You Should Know*

1. A string is one of the following:

   A character constant
   A character variable
   An element of a character array
   A substring of any of the above

2. A substring is a sequence of adjacent characters in a string.

3. Substrings are more versatile than character arrays because substrings can have any length from 1 to the length of the string, while every element in a character array must have the same length.

4. The only string *operator* is the concatenation operator (//), which combines two strings into one.

5. INDEX(STRING, SUB) returns the starting position of SUB within STRING, or returns zero if STRING does not contain the substring SUB.

6. The LEN function returns the length of a string, and is most often used in subprograms to find the length of a passed-length character argument.

7. The ICHAR function takes a character argument and returns the integer ASCII or EBCDIC code for that character.

8. The CHAR function takes an integer argument and returns the character whose ASCII or EBCDIC code is that argument.

9. The fixed lengths of character variables and array elements often force us to use a substring extending from the beginning of a string to the position of the last nonblank character in the string.

10. An internal file can be any of the following strings:

    A character variable
    An element of a character array
    A substring of a character variable or array element
    A character array

11. When an array is used as an internal file, the file has as many records as the array has elements.

12. An internal file that is not an array consists of exactly one record.

13. An internal file is a file only for the duration of the internal READ or WRITE statement that uses the file. Storage for a string used as an internal file disappears when the program finishes execution, as is the case for any program variable.

14. An internal READ statement reads a string and assigns a value to each element in the read list.

15. An internal WRITE statement places a character representation of the write list into an internal file.

■

13.4 EXERCISES

■ *Self-Test*

1. What will the following programs print? Use □ to indicate a blank.

　　a.
```
       CHARACTER  A*2, B*3, C*4

       A = 'DW'
       B = A // A
       C = A // B
       PRINT 10, A, B, C
   10  FORMAT (1X, 3(A, X) )

       END
```

　　b.
```
       CHARACTER*4  A, B, C

       A = 'XX'
       B = A // A
       C = B // B
       PRINT 10, A, B, C
   10  FORMAT (1X, 3(A, X) )

       END
```

　　c.
```
       CHARACTER  A*2, B*3, C*4

       A = '12'
       B = A(1:1) // A
       C = B(1:1) // B
       PRINT 10, A, B, C
   10  FORMAT (1X, 3(A, X) )

       END
```

2. Assume the following declarations:

```
CHARACTER  NAME*10, A*2
DATA       NAME /'SINGING'/, A /'IN'/
```

Each of the following problems has a single number or single character for an answer.

    a.   `LEN(NAME)`

    b.   `INDEX(A, NAME)`

    c.   `INDEX(NAME, A)`

    d.   `NAME(4:4)`

    e.   `LEN(NAME(2:5))`

    f.   `INDEX(NAME(3:), A)`

3. Find values for the following expressions, using ASCII code. If you know that `ICHAR('A')` is 65, you do not even have to refer to the ASCII codes.

    a.   `ICHAR('D')`

    b.   `ICHAR('R') - ICHAR('N')`

    c.   `CHAR(72)`

    d.   `CHAR( ICHAR('D') + 5 )`

4. Assume the following declarations:

```
CHARACTER*6  A
INTEGER      I
REAL         X
```

    a.   What values are given to X and I by the following statements?

```
        A = '357.18'
        READ (A, 10) X
10      FORMAT (F6.2)
        READ (A(:3), 20) I
20      FORMAT (I3)
```

b.   What is the value of A after the following statements execute?

```
        X = 12.348
        I = 7
        WRITE (A, 10) I, X
   10   FORMAT (I1, F5.2)
```

■ *Programming Exercises*

1. Write a program to count the number of Es in several input lines.

2. Write a program to count the number of occurrences of the string 'ing' in a file of text. Look only for the lowercase letters, and assume the records in the file have a maximum length of 80.

3. Write a program to count the number of occurrences of the word 'and' in a file of text. Assume that all letters in the file are lowercase, and that all records have length 80 or less.

    Use the INDEX function and search for ' and ', to avoid counting 'and' imbedded in another word such as 'sand'. There is a problem if the word 'and' is at the beginning or end of a line. To avoid the problem, let LINE have length 82, and define LINE(1:1) and LINE(82:82) to be spaces. Read lines of text into LINE(2:81).

4. Write a program to find the number of words and the number of letters in a file of text. Assume that the file contains only uppercase letters and blanks. *Hint:* Every time a blank follows a letter, a word ends.

5. Write a program to find the number of words, the number of letters, and the number of other nonblank characters in a file of text. The file can contain lowercase and uppercase letters as well as punctuation marks and other special characters. You may assume there are no hyphenated words.

    This problem is a bit harder than the previous one. Still, a word ends when a letter is followed by a nonletter.

6. Modify the program of the previous problem to find the longest word and the average word length in several lines of text.

7. In a six-letter transposition code, each letter of the alphabet is simply replaced by the letter six places after it. For letters after *Z*, simply begin the alphabet over at *A*, as in the following table.

Original letter   *ABCDEFGHIJKLMNOPQRSTUVWXYZ*
Replacement letter   *GHIJKLMNOPQRSTUVWXYZABCDEF*

Write a program to read a message and an integer value *N*, then code the message with an *N*-letter transposition key, and print out the coded message.

8. Write a program to decode a message that was coded by the program in the previous exercise.

9. Blanks are often a nuisance in string comparisons. For instance, the names

'Carbuncle, Aristophanes'
'Carbuncle , Aristophanes'

almost certainly refer to the same person, but the computer does not consider them equal because of the space before the comma in the second string.

Suppose a file is meant to hold names, with up to 25 characters, in the form

Last name-comma-space-first name

but some names were carelessly entered with extra spaces, which can occur before the last name, or before or after the comma. Also, some names have no space after the comma. Write a program that reads the names and prints each one with the first character nonblank, the comma immediately after the last name, and exactly one space after the comma. Use the following data file or a similar one.

```
Arbuthnot,    Henry
  Butler, Jason
  Caldwell,   Taylor
Dennison , Michael
  Edwards,   Jonathan
Fotheringill,Mark
```

10. When reading a real number, a program will crash if the input field contains certain nonnumeric characters, such as a dollar sign or comma. Write a program that asks the user for a dollar amount, then reads the input into a character variable DOLLAR. If the value of DOLLAR includes dollar signs or commas, remove them. Assign a value to a real variable SALARY by reading DOLLAR as an internal file. Print the value of SALARY.

chapter 14 DOUBLE PRECISION AND COMPLEX NUMBERS

This chapter introduces two new data types, DOUBLE PRECISION and COMPLEX. These are the last of the six Fortran data types.

The DOUBLE PRECISION type is useful when a problem requires more than six or seven significant digits. Typically, DOUBLE PRECISION data have about sixteen significant digits; the specific number of digits depends on the computer involved.

COMPLEX numbers arise in situations that apparently involve only real quantities. In real arithmetic, we sometimes say the square root of a negative number is meaningless, but it is often useful to consider the square root of a real number as a complex number. Also, calculations for electric circuits frequently require complex numbers.

■

14.1 THE DOUBLE PRECISION DATA TYPE

The DOUBLE PRECISION data type is used, as its name implies, to give numbers with greater precision than numbers of type REAL. *Double* precision is a slight misnomer, because on most systems the precision is a little more than doubled. If your computer gives seven significant digits for real numbers, then double precision numbers will typically have sixteen significant digits. When discussing double precision, we often refer to real values as **single precision** values.

It is important to realize from the start that double precision does not solve all problems of round-off error. We noted earlier that for a real variable A, the expression

$$A * (1.0 / A)$$

is often not equal to 1.0, and this can still happen if A is a double precision variable.

The DOUBLE PRECISION data type is most useful in situations involving repeated calculations which cause round-off error to invade several significant digits. If a set of calculations causes loss of four significant digits, it is obviously less serious to lose four significant digits out of sixteen than to lose four of seven.

There is a price to pay for double precision. First, double precision variables and constants occupy twice as much storage space as real variables and constants. Second, double precision arithmetic is much slower than real arithmetic.

DOUBLE PRECISION **Variables and Constants**

The type declaration statement for double precision variables has the form

    DOUBLE PRECISION   <variable list>

To declare X, Y, and SQUARE to be double precision variables, use

    DOUBLE PRECISION X, Y, SQUARE

Double precision constants *must* be written in exponential form with D replacing E, as in the following examples.

    -1.23456789D16   3D-20   1.0D0

The last example shows how to write the real number 1.0 in double precision. (Many computers interpret any real number with more than seven digits as a double precision constant.)

DOUBLE PRECISION **Expressions**

Earlier we discussed mixed-mode numeric expressions with real and integer operands. Now we have the possibility of mixed-mode expressions involving double precision, real, and integer operands. Of these three numeric data types, double precision is the highest level, with real next, and integer the lowest type. The rule for mixed-mode expressions is:

> When an arithmetic operation involves two data types of different levels, the operand at the lower level type is converted to the higher level type, and arithmetic is carried out at the higher level type. The resulting type is the higher level type.

We saw in Chapter 3 that an arithmetic operation involving one real and one integer requires converting the integer to a real quantity. Here we have two further possibilities. If an arithmetic operation involves a real and a double precision quantity, the real quantity is converted to double precision. In an operation involving an integer and a double precision quantity, the integer is converted to double precision. In either of these last two cases, the result is a double precision number.

Thus, in the expression

$$6.25 * 1.987654321D0$$

the computer first converts the real number 6.25 to double precision, then performs a double precision multiplication.

Similarly, with

$$1234567.765432 1D0 / 7$$

the computer first converts the 7 to double precision, then performs a double precision division.

Be sure to include the D in double precision constants. If the last expression above were

$$1234567.7654321 / 7$$

most compilers would read 1234567.7654321 as a REAL constant, and several digits of precision would be lost.

Assignment statements offer further opportunities to lose precision. If DX is a double precision variable, the assignment statement

$$DX = 123456789.987654321$$

is mixed-mode. Some computers read the constant as a real number, losing several significant digits in the process. The resulting real number is converted to double precision before being stored in DX, but this amounts only to padding with zeroes at the right end of the number.

Example 14.1 Double Precision Output

A program can write double precision values with list-directed formatting or with the F, E, and G format descriptors. In addition, the D format descriptor is used to output double precision values. It acts exactly like the E descriptor, except that D replaces E in the exponential part of the number. The descriptor D12.4 causes the number 62.358 to be printed as

☐☐0.6236D+02

Program 14.1 illustrates the writing of a double precision value in four different ways: list-directed, and formatted with F, E, and D data descriptors.

■
PROGRAM 14.1

```
     PROGRAM PRINTD
*-----------------------------------------------------*
*  Illustrate printing double precision values.  *
*-----------------------------------------------------*
     DOUBLE PRECISION X

     X  = 123456789.987654321D0
     PRINT *
     PRINT *,  'List-directed:   ', X
     PRINT 10, 'Formatted F25.12:', X
     PRINT 20, 'Formatted E25.18:', X
     PRINT 30, 'Formatted D25.18:', X

10   FORMAT (1X, A, F25.12)
20   FORMAT (1X, A, E25.18)
30   FORMAT (1X, A, D25.18)

     END
```

The program produces the following output

```
List-directed:     123456789.9876543
Formatted F25.12:   123456789.987654320896
Formatted E25.18: 0.123456789987654321E+09
Formatted D25.18: 0.123456789987654321D+09
```

Example 14.2 Illustrating Double Precision Arithmetic

The outputs of the program segments in this section are typical for a machine that stores real values in 32 bits and double precision values in 64 bits. Results on your machine may differ.

Consider Program 14.2, which assigns the same double precision value to a real variable X and a double precision variable DX.

■

PROGRAM 14.2

```
      PROGRAM DBLSNG
*------------------------------------------------------*
*     Compare double and single precision values.      *
*------------------------------------------------------*
      REAL             X, Y
      DOUBLE PRECISION DX, DY, BIG
      PARAMETER        (BIG = 123456789.123456789D0)

      X = BIG
      PRINT 10, X
      DX = BIG
      PRINT 20, DX
10    FORMAT (1X, 'Single:', F50.35)
20    FORMAT (1X, 'Double:', F50.35)

      END
```

The output from the program is

```
Single:     123456792.00000000000000000000000000000000000
Double:     123456789.12345678918063640594482421875000000
```

Notice that the single precision X has the correct value for the first seven digits of BIG. The double precision DX has all eighteen digits correct, but contains some additional nonzero digits.

The statements below, placed in Program 14.2, produce the output following them.

```
      Y = BIG - 0.0001
      IF (Y .EQ. X) PRINT *, 'Single: Exactly equal!'
      PRINT 10, Y
      DY = BIG - 0.0001D0
      IF (DY .EQ. DX) PRINT *, 'Double: Exactly equal!'
      PRINT 20, DY
```

Output:

```
Single: Exactly equal!
Single:     123456792.00000000000000000000000000000000000
Double:     123456789.12335678935050964355468750000000000
```

With single precision subtraction, the values of X and

```
Y = X - 0.0001
```

are exactly the same. In double precision, the values of DX and

```
DY = DX - 0.0001D0
```

differ by one in the fourth decimal place.

Consider placing in Program 14.2 the following statements which cause the computer to execute two loops. Each loop has initial value zero, limit value one, and step size one-sixth. The first loop uses single precision arithmetic and the second uses double precision arithmetic.

```
      PRINT *, 'Single precision loop:'
      DO 11 X = 0.0, 1.0, 1.0 / 6.0
         PRINT 10, X
11    CONTINUE
      PRINT *
      PRINT *, 'Double precision loop:'
      DO 22 DX = 0.0D0, 1.0D0, 1.0D0 / 6.0D0
         PRINT 20, DX
22    CONTINUE
```

Here are the results printed by these loops.

```
Single precision loop:
Single:          0.00000000000000000000000000000000000000
Single:          0.16666667163372039794921875000000000
Single:          0.33333334326744079589843750000000000
Single:          0.50000000000000000000000000000000000000
Single:          0.66666668653488159179687500000000000
Single:          0.83333337306976318359375000000000000
Double precision loop:
Double:          0.00000000000000000000000000000000000000
Double:          0.16666666666666667823148983984538806
Double:          0.33333333333333335646297967969076613
Double:          0.50000000000000000000000000000000000000
Double:          0.66666666666666667129259593593815225
Double:          0.83333333333333334258519187187630450
```

You can see that the value stored for one-sixth is slightly larger than the exact value, both with real storage and double precision storage. Thus, both loops do not repeat with loop index 1, but stop one step short, with loop index approximately equal to 5/6.

Double Precision Functions

Most built-in numeric functions will give double precision results if the arguments of these functions are double precision expressions. These functions include ABS, SQRT, LOG, EXP, and the trigonometric functions. You can also use specific double precision function names, which are the generic names preceded by D. Thus, DABS, DSQRT, DLOG, DEXP, DSIN, and so on, are specific names for functions that return double precision values. We will generally stay with the generic names.

Example 14.3 Double Precision Functions

Program 14.3 applies each of the functions SIN, EXP, and SQRT to a real variable X and a double precision variable DX. Each function returns a real value when its argument is real, and a double precision value when its argument is double precision.

■
PROGRAM 14.3

```
      PROGRAM DUBFUN
*-----------------------------------------*
*  Illustrate double precision functions.  *
*-----------------------------------------*
      DOUBLE PRECISION DX
      REAL            X

      X  = 12.3456789987654321D0
      DX = 12.3456789987654321D0
      PRINT 10, 'Single', 'Double'
      PRINT 20, 'Value:', X, DX
      PRINT 20, 'Sin: ', SIN(X), SIN(DX)
      PRINT 20, 'Exp: ', EXP(X), EXP(DX)
      PRINT 20, 'Sqrt: ', SQRT(X), SQRT(DX)

10    FORMAT ('0', 21X, A6, 22X, A6 /)
20    FORMAT (1X, A6, 2F30.20)

      END
```

Output from the program is

	Single	Double
Value:	12.34567928314208984375	12.34567899876543206616
Sin:	-0.21890424191951751709	-0.21890451672779219147
Exp:	229964.28125000000000000	229964.21728159629128640518
Sqrt:	3.51364183425903320313	3.51364184269902957158

User-defined functions also can be double precision. We can, for example, write a double precision function subprogram as:

```
DOUBLE PRECISION FUNCTION F(X)
DOUBLE PRECISION X

F = EXP(-X * X) - 2.0D0 * SIN(X)

END
```

We will use this function in the following program.

Example 14.4 Bisection with Double Precision Arithmetic

Many programs will have difficulty with round-off error in real arithmetic. The difficulty can often be overcome by double precision arithmetic. Consider Example 9.3, the program BISECT which finds roots of a function by bisection of an interval. We can find more precise roots by declaring all the real variables in that program to be double precision instead, with

```
DOUBLE PRECISION ROOT, FROOT, ERROR, F, A, B, LOW, HIGH, T
```

It is not necessary to declare *all* these variables double precision, however. We want LOW, HIGH, and ROOT to be double precision because they are intermediate values of the approximate root. F and FROOT also should be double precision because they give function values of the intermediate approximate roots for the function F. We will keep the endpoints of the original interval (A, B) and the temporary variable T real. ERROR can also remain real because it is used only in the calculation of N, the number of iterations used.

Inside the program BISECT we change several constants to double precision form. See program 14.4.

■

PROGRAM 14.4

```
      PROGRAM BISECT
*-----------------------------------------------------------*
*  Find root of a function by repeatedly bisecting an interval. *
*  The function F is in a function subprogram REAL FUNCTION F.  *
*  All calculations done in double precision.                  *
*-----------------------------------------------------------*
      DOUBLE PRECISION  ROOT, FROOT, F, LOW, HIGH
      REAL              A, B, ERROR, T
      INTEGER           N, I

      PRINT *
      PRINT *, 'What interval?'
      READ  *, A, B
      PRINT *

      IF (F(A) * F(B) .GT. 0) THEN
          PRINT *, 'Function values have the same sign at'
          PRINT *, 'the endpoints of the given interval. '
          PRINT *, 'Cannot continue. '
      ELSE
          PRINT *, 'How close should the approximate root be?'
          READ  *, ERROR
          PRINT *

          LOW  = A
          HIGH = B

          T = (B - A) / ERROR
          N = 1 + INT(LOG(T) / LOG(2.0))

          DO 11 I = 1, N

              ROOT = (HIGH + LOW) / 2.0D0
              FROOT = F(ROOT)
              IF (FROOT * F(HIGH) .GT. 0.0D0) THEN
                  HIGH = ROOT
              ELSE IF (FROOT * F(LOW) .GT. 0.0D0) THEN
                  LOW = ROOT
              ELSE
                  PRINT *, 'Exact root:', ROOT
                  STOP
              END IF

11        CONTINUE
```

```
      PRINT *, 'Approximate root:', ROOT
      PRINT *, 'Function value:  ', FROOT
      PRINT *, N, ' Iterations used.'

   END IF

   END
*------------------------------------------------------------*
*        End of program BISECT.  Beginning of function F.    *
*------------------------------------------------------------*
   DOUBLE PRECISION FUNCTION F(X)
   DOUBLE PRECISION X

   F = EXP(-X*X) - 2.0D0 * DSIN(X)

   END
```

Other programs that can often benefit from double precision are those dealing with matrix calculations: finding determinants and inverses, and solving systems of linear equations.

The DPROD Function

The DPROD **function** takes two real arguments and returns their double precision product. DPROD is most useful in programs that accumulate sums of products of real numbers. Consider the following five pairs of x and y values.

x	y
1000000.0	2000000.0
10000.0	20000.0
100.0	200.0
10.0	20.0
1.0	2.0

It is easy enough to add the five products xy by hand. However, a Fortran program that simply uses real arithmetic to add the products in order will almost certainly get the wrong result. The first product is 2.0E12, while the third is 2.0E4, so addition of the third product will not change the (real) value of the sum. The fourth and fifth products will not change the sum either.

Here is a program to accumulate the same five products in both real and double precision arithmetic.

```
      PROGRAM DOPROD
      REAL            X, Y, SUM
      DOUBLE PRECISION  DSUM

      OPEN(9, FILE = 'DP', STATUS = 'OLD')

      SUM  = 0.0
      DSUM = 0.0D0

      DO 11 I = 1, 5
         READ (9, *) X, Y
         SUM  = SUM + X * Y
         DSUM = DSUM + DPROD(X, Y)
11    CONTINUE

      CLOSE (9)
      PRINT 10, 'Single precision sum:', SUM
      PRINT 10, 'Double precision sum:', DSUM

10    FORMAT (1X, A, F20.2)

      END
```

Output from the program is

```
Single precision sum:    2000200007680.00
Double precision sum:    2000200020202.00
```

The double precision result is correct, while the real result is too high by 7478. Once again, your output may not be exactly the same because of the different ways various computers store real and double precision values.

The SNGL and DBLE Functions

The SNGL **function** takes a double precision argument and converts it to single precision. The DBLE function performs the reverse conversion; it takes a single precision argument and converts it to double precision. DBLE also can take an *integer* argument. These functions are used mainly to avoid mixed modes.

Any process valid for real variables is also valid for double precision variables. For example, an array variable can have type DOUBLE PRECISION, and a DATA statement can initialize double precision data.

■

14.2 THE COMPLEX DATA TYPE

The sixth and last data type in Fortran is COMPLEX. Generally, complex numbers arise from operations involving square roots of negative numbers. The solutions to a quadratic equation of the form

$$ax^2 + bx + c = 0$$

are often given as

$$x_1 = \frac{-b + \sqrt{d}}{2a} \text{ and } x_2 = \frac{-b - \sqrt{d}}{2a}$$

where $d = b^2 - 4ac$.

In beginning algebra courses, you might simply have said that the equation has no solutions if d is negative. In fact, there are no *real* solutions if d is negative, but there are complex solutions. Suppose, for example, $a = 1$, $b = 2$, and $c = 2$. Then

$$d = 2^2 - 4 \times 1 \times 2 = 4 - 8 = -4$$

The solutions are

$$x_1 = \frac{-2 + \sqrt{-4}}{2} \text{ and } x_2 = \frac{-2 - \sqrt{-4}}{2}$$

Cancelling the factor 2 from each solution, we have

$$x_1 = -1 + \sqrt{-1} \text{ and } x_2 = -1 - \sqrt{-1}$$

When dealing with complex numbers, it is customary to use the symbol i to denote the square root of -1, so the solutions become

$$x_1 = -1 + 1i \text{ and } x_2 = -1 - 1i$$

Each complex number is a sum of two parts, the **real** part and the **imaginary** part, or coefficient of i. When one part is zero, we usually write just the other part. For example, we write $2 + 0i$ as 2, and $0 + 4i$ as $4i$. A complex number with real part 0 is a **pure imaginary** number. A complex number with imaginary part 0 can be considered a real number. In this sense, the complex numbers include all the real numbers.

Complex Input and Output

Fortran considers a complex number to be a pair of real numbers. The first real number is the real part of the complex number, and the second is the imaginary part. With list-directed output, the computer will print a complex number as a pair of reals, enclosed in parentheses and separated by a comma. Thus, list-directed formatting causes the complex number $12 + 5i$ to appear as

$$(12.0000,5.00000)$$

For list-directed input, you must supply a complex number in the same form.

When writing formatted I/O for complex values, just remember that a complex number is a *pair* of real numbers, and supply two real data descriptors for each complex value. For example, if z is a complex variable with value $3 + 4i$, the PRINT/FORMAT pair

```
      PRINT 10, Z
10    FORMAT (1X, 2F5.2)
```

creates the output

```
 3.00 4.00
```

You can get fancier and write z in the form $a + bi$ with the PRINT/FORMAT pair

```
      PRINT 20, Z
20    FORMAT (1X, F5.2, " + ", F5.2, "i")
```

In place of the F descriptor, you can use an E or G descriptor.

Example 14.5 Complex Input and Output

Program 14.5 illustrates complex Input/Output.

■

PROGRAM 14.5

```
      PROGRAM COMPIO
*---------------------------------------------*
*    Illustrate complex input and output.     *
*---------------------------------------------*
      COMPLEX  X
```

```
11    PRINT *, 'Enter a complex number.'
      READ (6, *, ERR = 22) X
      PRINT *, 'List-directed:', X
      PRINT 20, X
      GO TO 33

22    PRINT *, 'Remember to supply two real numbers, enclosed'
      PRINT *, 'in parentheses and separated by a comma.'
      GO TO 11

20    FORMAT (1X, 'Formatted:', F5.1, ' + ', F5.1, 'i')

33    END
```

If you run the program and enter (3.0, 4.0), the output is

```
List-directed: (3.000000,4.000000)
Formatted:  3.0 +   4.0i
```

The CMPLX **Function**

The CMPLX **function** can take one or two real arguments. With two arguments, CMPLX(a, b) is the complex number $a + bi$. With one argument, CMPLX(a) is $a + 0i$. In a standard use of the CMPLX function, A and B are real program variables and C is a complex variable. Then the statement

```
      Z = CMPLX(A, B)
```

assigns the value of A to the real part of Z, and the value of B to the imaginary part of Z.

Complex Arithmetic

Addition of complex numbers is quite simple; the real part of the sum is the sum of the real parts and the imaginary part of the sum is the sum of the imaginary parts. Thus, for example,

$$(2 + 5i) + (3 + 4i) = (2 + 3) + (4 + 5)i = 5 + 9i$$

Multiplication of complex numbers is a bit more complicated, but the important point is that

$$i \times i = -1$$

Thus,

$$(3 + 4i) \times (5 + 2i) = 3 \times 5 + 3 \times 2i + 4i \times 5 + 4i \times 2i$$

$$= 15 + 6i + 20i + 8 \times (-1)$$

$$= 7 + 26i$$

In general, the product of $a + bi$ and $c + di$ is

$$ac - bd + (ad + bc)i$$

Graphically, complex numbers are usually represented in the plane with a horizontal real axis and vertical imaginary axis. The complex number $2 + 4i$ can be considered the point (2, 4) or the vector from the origin to (2, 4). See Figures 14.1a and 14.1b.

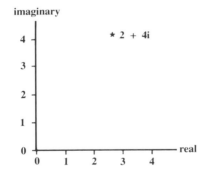

FIGURE 14.1a
Representation of 2 + 4i as a point

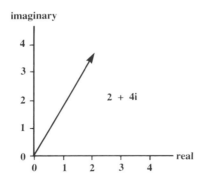

FIGURE 14.1b
Representation of 2 + 4i as a vector

Addition of complex numbers corresponds to vector addition. Figure 14.2 represents the familiar parallelogram rule for addition of vectors. The summands are $2 + 4i$ and $4 + i$, with sum, or resultant, $6 + 5i$.

FIGURE 14.2
Addition of complex numbers

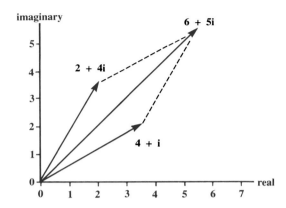

The **complex conjugate**, or simply **conjugate** of a complex number $z = a + bi$ is a complex number $\bar{z} = a - bi$. Notice that $z + \bar{z} = 2a$ is a real number, while $z - \bar{z} = 2bi$ is a pure imaginary number. Further,

$$z \times \bar{z} = (a + bi) \times (a - bi) = a^2 - abi + abi - (bi)(bi)$$

$$= a^2 + b^2$$

which is a real number. The square root of $z \times \bar{z}$ is called the **absolute value** or **modulus** of the complex number z. The modulus is the *length* of the vector z or the *distance* from the origin to the point z.

It is often desirable to express a complex number z in **polar form** by giving its modulus M and the angle A measured from the positive real axis to the vector z. See Figure 14.3. The angle is usually called the **argument** of the complex number, but we will use the word *angle* because we use *argument* so frequently when referring to functions. From the figure it is easy to see that the complex number

$$z = a + bi$$

can also be expressed as

$$z = M \cos(A) + M \sin(A)i$$

and this latter form is the polar form of z. The polar form is often written as

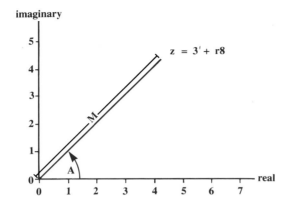

FIGURE 14.3.
Modulus M and Angle A of a Complex Number z.

$$z = Me^{iA}$$

using the convention that

$$e^{iA} = \cos(A) + i\sin(A)$$

It should be clear that the angle of a complex number is not unique. If A is an angle for a complex number, then so is $A \pm 2n\pi$ for any integer n.

Using the polar forms of two complex numbers, Me^{iA} and Ne^{iB}, it is easy to see that

$$(Me^{iA}) \times (Ne^{iB}) = MNe^{i(A + B)}$$

That is, the modulus of the product of two complex numbers is the *product* of their moduli, and the angle of the product is the *sum* of their angles.

Two complex numbers can be added, subtracted, multiplied, and divided, just as two real numbers can, with the proviso that a complex number cannot be divided by the zero complex number, $(0.0, 0.0)$. The symbols for the arithmetic operations are the same for complex arithmetic as they are for real arithmetic.

To divide one complex number by another, multiply the numerator and denominator by the conjugate of the denominator. For example,

$$\frac{5 + 8i}{3 + 4i} = \frac{(5 + 8i)(3 - 4i)}{(3 + 4i)(3 - 4i)} = \frac{47 + 4i}{25} = 1.68 + 0.16i$$

Complex numbers can have exponents, just as real numbers can. An integer exponent signifies repeated multiplication of the number by itself. For instance, if $z = 1 + 2i$, then z^3 means

$$(1 + 2i)(1 + 2i)(1 + 2i) = (-3 + 4i)(1 + 2i) = -11 - 2i$$

A complex quantity can be raised to any real power. For example, if a complex variable C has the value (3.0, 4.0), then the statement

```
PRINT *, 'Cube root', C ** (1.0/3.0)
```

produces the output

```
Cube root (1.628937,0.5201746)
```

The only restriction on exponentiating complex numbers is that zero cannot be raised to a negative power.

Taking the nth root of a complex number is quite simple if the number is expressed in polar form. If $z = Me^{iA}$, then an nth root of z has modulus equal to the nth root of M and angle equal to A/n. Every complex number has n nth roots. The modulus of each is the nth root of the modulus of M. The n different angles can be found by adding multiples of 2π to A, then dividing by n.

Complex numbers also can *be* exponents. If Z and W are complex variables, then Z ** W is a complex quantity.

Complex numbers can appear in relations, but only relations involving the operators .EQ. and .NE.. It does not make sense to ask if one complex number is greater or less than another.

Functions Involving the Complex Data Type

Fortran has several intrinsic functions that return quantities related to complex variables. The ABS function, with a complex argument, returns the modulus (a nonnegative real number) of the argument. The REAL function returns the real part of its complex argument. The AIMAG function returns the imaginary part (a real number) of a complex argument. The CONJG function returns the conjugate of its complex argument.

Example 14.6 Some Functions with Complex Arguments

Program 14.6 illustrates the use of the ABS, CONJG, REAL, and AIMAG functions.

■

PROGRAM 14.6

```
      PROGRAM COMPLX
*-----------------------------------------*
*      Illustrate complex functions.      *
*-----------------------------------------*
      COMPLEX  X, Y, Z

      X = (12, 5)
      Y = (3, 4)
      PRINT *, 'X =      ', X
      PRINT *, 'Y =      ', Y

      Z = X + Y
      PRINT *, 'X + Y = ', Z
      Z = X - Y
      PRINT *, 'X - Y = ', Z
      Z = X*Y
      PRINT *, 'X*Y =    ', Z
      Z = X/Y
      PRINT *, 'X/Y =    ', Z

      PRINT *, 'Modulus of X:         ', ABS(X)
      PRINT *, 'Conjugate of X:       ', CONJG(X)
      PRINT *, 'Real part of Y:       ', REAL(Y)
      PRINT *, 'Imaginary part of Y: ', AIMAG(Y)

      END
```

The program produces the following output

```
X =      (12.00000,5.000000)
Y =      (3.000000,4.000000)
X + Y = (15.00000,9.000000)
X - Y = (9.000000,1.000000)
X*Y =    (16.00000,63.00000)
X/Y =    (0.640000,1.320000)
Modulus of X:         13.00000
Conjugate of X:       (12.00000,-5.000000)
Real part of Y:       3.000000
Imaginary part of Y: 4.000000
```

Note that ABS with a *complex* argument behaves very differently from
ABS with a *real* argument. REAL behaves differently with a complex

argument too, but there is a similarity. Earlier we used REAL to convert an integer argument to a real quantity. Now we are using REAL to convert a complex argument to a real number.

Several other functions that we have used already with real arguments can take complex arguments. Some of these and their actions appear in Figure 14.4. The functions **sinh** and **cosh** in the figure are the **hyperbolic sine** and **cosine** respectively. For real x, they are:

$$\sinh(x) = \frac{e^x - e^{-x}}{2} \quad \cosh(x) = \frac{e^x + e^{-x}}{2}$$

FIGURE 14.4
Some generic functions with complex arguments

Function	Value of Function with Argument $z = a + bi$
LOG	$\log(a^2 + b^2)/2 + i\tan^{-1}(b/a)$
EXP	$e^a(\cos(b) + i\sin(b))$
SQRT	$\sqrt{(|z| + a)/2)} + i\sqrt{(|z| - a)/2)}$
SIN	$\sin(a\cosh(b)) + i\cos(a\sinh(b))$
COS	$\cos(a\cosh(b)) + i\sin(a\sinh(b))$

The generic names ABS, COS, SIN, LOG, EXP, and SQRT can be replaced by the specific names CABS, CCOS, CSIN, CLOG, CEXP, and CSQRT, respectively, to stress that the function involved takes a complex argument. We usually use the generic names.

Program 14.7 uses the CMPLX function as well as the EXP, LOG, and SQRT functions.

■
PROGRAM 14.7

```
      PROGRAM CMPFUN
*----------------------------------------------------------------*
*  Demonstrate the complex functions CMPLX, EXP, LOG, and SQRT.  *
*----------------------------------------------------------------*
      REAL    A, B
      COMPLEX C

      PRINT *, 'Enter the real and imaginary parts.'
      READ  *, A, B
      C = CMPLX(A, B)
```

```
PRINT *, C
PRINT *, 'Exp ', EXP(C)
PRINT *, 'Log ', LOG(C)
PRINT *, 'Sqrt', SQRT(C)

END
```

A run of the program produces the output below.

```
Enter the real and imaginary parts.
3.0 4.0
(3.000000,4.000000)
Exp  (-13.12878,-15.20078)
Log  (1.609438,0.9272952)
Sqrt (2.000000,1.000000)
```

Almost all Fortran statements that are valid for real variables are valid also for complex variables. An array variable can have type COMPLEX, and a DATA statement can initialize complex data.

■
14.3 SUMMARY OF CHAPTER 14

■ *Terms Introduced in This Chapter*

ABS function, with complex argument (or CABS)
ABS function, with double precision argument (or DABS)
AIMAG function
Argument, of a complex number
CMPLX function
COMPLEX data type
Complex number
Complex type declaration
CONJG function
COS function, with complex argument (or CCOS)
COS function, with double precision argument (or DCOS)
DOUBLE PRECISION data type
EXP function, with complex argument (or CEXP)
EXP function, with double precision argument (or DEXP)
LOG function, with complex argument (or CLOG)
LOG function, with double precision argument (or DLOG)
Modulus, of a complex value

Polar form
REAL function, with complex argument
SIN function, with complex argument (or CSIN)
SIN function, with double precision argument (or DSIN)
Single precision
SQRT function, with complex argument (or CSQRT)
SQRT function, with double precision argument (or DSQRT)

■ *What You Should Know*

1. A double precision constant must end with D and an exponent value.
2. Most computers store a double precision quantity with more than twice the precision of a real quantity.
3. On many computers, the exponent of a double precision value has the same range as the exponent of a real value.
4. The precision of a double precision number varies from one computer to another.
5. A complex constant contains two real constants, separated by a comma and enclosed in parentheses.
6. A complex value given in response to a list-directed READ statement must be a complex constant.
7. A formatted READ statement can read a pair of real constants and store them as the real and imaginary parts of a complex variable.
8. Complex arithmetic and real arithmetic have the same operators for addition, subtraction, multiplication, and exponentiation.
9. Complex numbers can be considered as vectors, with a special multiplication defined on them.
10. Many intrinsic Fortran functions that can take a real argument can also take a complex argument.
11. Intrinsic functions that can take real or complex arguments usually return the same value for the real argument x and the complex argument $x + 0i$.
12. A complex number z has, in general, n nth roots. If n is real, the expression $z^{1/n}$ gives one of these roots.

■

14.4 EXERCISES

■ *Self-Test*

1. Find out how many bits a double precision number has on your computer. How many decimal digits of precision is this? Find the range of values for a double precision number.

2. Let $z = 3 + 4i$, $w = 2 - i$, and $v = -3 + 2i$. Calculate by hand the values of the following expressions.

    a. $z + w$

    b. $w - v$

    c. $z \times v$

    d. $\dfrac{z}{w}$

    e. v^2

3. What output do the following programs produce?

    a.

```
PROGRAM COMPA
COMPLEX X, Y, Z

X = CMPLX(2.0)
Y = (2.0, 1.0)
Z = X*CONJG(Y)

PRINT *, 'Result is', Z

END
```

    b.

```
PROGRAM COMPB
REAL    A, B, M
COMPLEX C

A = 3.0
B = 4.0
C = COMPLX(A, B)
PRINT *, C*CONJG(C)

END
```

4. What is wrong with the following statements? A and B are real variables, while Z is complex.

    a.   `Z = COMPLEX(2.0, 4.0)`

    b.   `Z = REAL(A)`

    c.   `Z = CONJG(A, B)`

    d.   `Z = A + Bi`

    e.   `Z = 3.0, 5.0`

5. Find the two square roots of $4e^{i\pi/2}$ and the three cube roots of $8e^{i\pi}$.

■ *Programming Exercises*

1. Write a program to ask for an integer n and find the sum

$$1 + \frac{1}{4} + \frac{1}{9} + \frac{1}{16} + \cdots + \frac{1}{n^2}$$

   both in single precision and double precision. Input some fairly large values for n (10,000 or so).

2. The natural log (*ln*) of 2 is equal to the sum of the series

$$1 - \frac{1}{2} + \frac{1}{3} - \frac{1}{4} + \cdots + \frac{(-1)^{n-1}}{n} + \cdots$$

   Write a program that asks the user for a number n and then approximates *ln*(2) with the sum of the first n terms of the series, using double precision arithmetic. How many terms must be added to get the correct ten-place value of *ln*(2) (0.6931471806)?

   The series has alternating signs and terms that decrease, so if we stop at an odd-numbered term the approximate sum is too high, and if we stop at an even-numbered term, the sum is too low. (For instance, the first term, 1, is too large, but the sum of the first two terms, 0.50, is too low.) Thus we can get a better approximation by taking the average of two consecutive sums. Revise your program to calculate the average of the sum of the first n terms and the sum of the first $n+1$ terms. Now how many terms does it take to get *ln*(2) to the first ten places?

3. The Scottish mathematician James Gregory showed that

$$\frac{\pi}{4} = 1 - \frac{1}{3} + \frac{1}{5} - \cdots + \frac{(-1)^{n-1}}{2n-1} + \cdots$$

   Use the revised method of the previous exercise to find an approximation for π, correct to ten digits (3.141592654). (This is not a very efficient way to calculate π. See the next exercise.)

4. Another Scotsman, John Machin showed that

$$\frac{\pi}{4} = 4\,\mathrm{Arctan}\left(\frac{1}{5}\right) - \mathrm{Arctan}\left(\frac{1}{239}\right)$$

   For x between -1 and 1 inclusive, the Arctan has the power series

$$\mathrm{Arctan}(x) = x - \frac{x^3}{3} + \frac{x^5}{5} - \cdots + \frac{(-1)^{n-1}x^{2n-1}}{2n-1} + \cdots$$

Write a program to approximate π to ten digits, using two power series for Arctan(1/5) and Arctan(1/239). (This approximation has been used to calculate π to a great many digits.)

As a bonus question, can you figure out beforehand how many terms to add from the Arctan(1/5) series? The Arctan(1/239) series obviously can get the same accuracy with fewer terms.

5. Write a program that uses Simpson's rule to approximate the area under a curve. For Simpson's rule, see Programming Exercise 17 in Chapter 4. Calculate the area in double precision.

6. Write a program that asks for a complex number and finds the modulus and angle for the input number.

7. In an AC circuit, the (complex) **impedance** Z is

$$Z = R + i \left[\omega L - \frac{1}{\omega}C \right]$$

where:

R is the *resistance* in ohms
L is the *inductance* in henries
C is the *capacitance* in henries
ω is the *angular frequency* in radians per second

The angular frequency is 2π times f, the frequency in cycles per second.

If I is the *measured current* in amperes and V is the *effective voltage* in volts, then

$$I = \frac{V \times REAL(1/Z)}{\sqrt{2}}$$

Write a program that asks for V, R, L, C, and f, and then solves for the impedance and the measured current I.

8. Write a program to solve a quadratic equation. Use complex arithmetic when the discriminant, $b^2 - 4ac$, is negative.

9. Rewrite the program of Example 11.7 to solve a simultaneous system of linear equations with complex coefficients.

10. A cubic equation has the form, $px^3 + qx^2 + rx + s = 0$, with $p \neq 0$. With no loss of generality, assume $p = 1$. Substituting $y - q/3$ for x puts the equation in the form

$$y^3 + ay + b = 0$$

with

$$a = \frac{3r - q^2}{3}$$

and

$$b = \frac{2q^3 - 9qr + 27s}{27}$$

The three solutions of the equation for y are

$$A^{1/3} + B^{1/3}$$

$$(-A^{1/3} - B^{1/3} + (A^{1/3} - B^{1/3})\sqrt{-3})/2$$

$$(-A^{1/3} - B1/3 - (A^{1/3} - B^{1/3})\sqrt{-3})/2$$

where

$$A = -b/2 + D \text{ and } B = -b/2 - D, \text{ with } D = \sqrt{\frac{b^2}{4} + \frac{a^3}{27}}$$

Write a program that asks for the coefficients of a cubic equation and prints the three solutions.

Hint: Notice that A and B must be complex variables because each contains a square root whose argument can be negative. There is some ambiguity in the solution above because each complex number has two square roots and three cube roots. In Fortran, of course, a square root or cube root operation gives just one result. The only time a problem arises here is when A or B has value $c + 0i$ with c negative. In that case, $A^{1/3}$ and/or $B^{1/3}$ should have imaginary part zero. That is, if $A = (-8.0, 0.0)$, $A^{1/3}$ should be $(-2.0, 0.0)$. Deal with this case separately.

A

FORTRAN 77 TOPICS NOT COVERED IN THE TEXT

This appendix discusses several Fortran 77 statements that were not mentioned in the body of the text. We recommend that you do not use any of these constructs, because your programs will have better structure without them. They are shown here because you may have occasion to read Fortran programs which include one or more of them.

The Computed GO TO Statement

Fortran contains a **computed** GO TO **statement** that behaves like a block IF in which each statement block is simply a GO TO statement. We do not recommend any use of the computed GO TO statement. An example is

```
GO TO (10, 20, 30, 40) INDEX
```

The effect of this statement is the same as the following IF block:

```
IF (INDEX .EQ. 1) THEN
    GO TO 10
ELSE IF (INDEX .EQ. 2) THEN
    GO TO 20
ELSE IF (INDEX .EQ. 3) THEN
    GO TO 30
ELSE IF (INDEX .EQ. 4) THEN
    GO TO 40
END IF
```

The general form of the computed GO TO statement is:

GO TO (*list of line numbers*) *numeric expression*

The computer converts the value of the numeric expression to an integer if necessary. If this integer value specifies the position of a line number in the list, then control is transferred to that line. If the integer value is less than 1 or larger than the number of line numbers in the list, the computer ignores the computed GO TO statement.

The computed GO TO is obviously much shorter than the corresponding IF block. However, the computed GO TO often requires many other GO TO (or STOP) statements. Consider the following simple program with a computed GO TO statement.

```
      PROGRAM COMPGO
*---------------------------------------------------------*
*        Illustrate the computed GO TO statement.         *
*---------------------------------------------------------*
      INTEGER  A

      PRINT *, 'Please enter an integer: 1, 2, or 3.'
      READ *, A
      GO TO (10, 20, 30) A

      PRINT *, 'You can''t follow instructions.'
      STOP

11    PRINT *, 'To get here, you must have entered 1.'
      STOP

22    PRINT *, 'Do you always take the middle course?'
      STOP

33    PRINT *, 'Right, think big!'

      END
```

The computed GO TO statement is simple enough, but it forces three later STOP statements. In contrast, consider the program with an IF block:

```
      PROGRAM IFBLCK
*---------------------------------------------------------*
*  Show an IF BLOCK replacing a computed GO TO statement. *
*---------------------------------------------------------*
      INTEGER  A

      PRINT *, 'Please enter an integer: 1, 2, or 3.'
      READ  *, A
```

```
IF (A .EQ. 1) THEN
   PRINT *, 'To get here, you must have entered 1.'
ELSE IF (A .EQ. 2) THEN
   PRINT *, 'Do you always take the middle course?'
ELSE IF (A .EQ. 3) THEN
   PRINT *, 'Right, think big!'
ELSE
   PRINT *, 'You can''t follow instructions.'
END IF

END
```

This program has better structure than the program with the computed GO TO statement. Good programmers today do not use the computed GO TO statement.

The Arithmetic IF Statement

The form of the arithmetic IF statement is

$$IF \ (numeric \ expression) \ Ln_1, Ln_2, Ln_3$$

where Ln_1, Ln_3, and Ln_3 represent three line numbers in the program. The computer evaluates the numeric expression, and control passes to:

> Ln_1 if the value of the expression is less than zero
> Ln_2 if the value of the expression is zero
> Ln_3 if the value of the expression is greater than zero

An example of the arithmetic IF statement is:

```
IF (X - Y) 30, 40, 50
```

If the value of X − Y is	Control passes to line
Negative	30
Zero	40
Positive	50

Alternate Entries and Returns in Subprograms

Subprograms can have **alternate entry points**, which means a subprogram can start execution at some point other than its physical beginning. In addition, a subroutine (but not a function) can have **alternate returns**, which means the subroutine can send control back to one of several places in the calling program.

A subroutine can contain an ENTRY **statement** of the form

ENTRY <*name*> (*dummy argument list*)

The ENTRY name must be different from the subroutine name. A CALL statement can invoke the ENTRY name, causing the computer to begin executing the subroutine at the first statement after the ENTRY statement.

As an example, consider a subroutine SORT which sorts numbers into increasing order:

```
SUBROUTINE SORT(A, N)
INTEGER N, M(N)
REAL    A(N)
    .       | (Code  to
    .       |  sort  real
    .       |  numbers)
RETURN
ENTRY SORTIN(M, N)
    .       | (Code  to
    .       |  sort
    .       |  integers)
RETURN
END
```

A calling program can use subroutine SORT to sort 100 integers by using the entry SORTIN, as follows:

```
CALL SORTIN(B, 100)
```

where B is an integer array in the calling program.

Function subprograms can have alternate entry points that behave in much the same way. Consider, for example, the following function subprogram MEDIAN which can calculate the median of either three or four numbers.

```
REAL FUNCTION MEDIAN(A, B, C)
REAL  A, B, C, D, MEDIA4
MEDIAN = A + B + C - MAX(A, B, C) - MIN(A, B, C)
RETURN
ENTRY MEDIA4(A, B, C, D)
MEDIA4 = (A + B + C + D - MAX(A, B, C, D) - MIN(A, B, C, D)) / 2.0
RETURN
END
```

Notice that the subprogram declares `MEDIA4` to be real.

A main program can use the statement

```
Y = MEDIAN(U, V, W)
```

to calculate the median of three numbers or a statement such as

```
Y = MEDIA4(T, U, V, W)
```

to find the median of four numbers.

Only *subroutines* can utilize alternate returns. The calling program might have a `CALL` statement such as

```
CALL SUB(X, Y, *20, *10)
```

where X and Y are the usual actual arguments and 10 and 20 are statement labels in the calling program. The asterisks identify 20 and 10 as labels for alternate returns. The `SUBROUTINE` statement then takes the form

```
SUBROUTINE SUB(A, B, *, *)
```

where the first asterisk corresponds to the label 20 and the second asterisk corresponds to the label 10. The statement

```
RETURN 1
```

in the subroutine causes a return to the statement labeled 20 in the calling program, while

```
RETURN 2
```

causes a return to the statement labeled 10.

The COMMON Statement

The `COMMON` **statement** is an alternative to argument lists. We do not recommend use of the `COMMON` statement, because it is easier to ensure the independence of program units with argument lists.

The word *common* refers to a common storage area, shared by two or more program units. One `COMMON` statement is placed in each such program unit, listing the variables that are to share the common storage.

For example, suppose a main program has the following declarations:

```
REAL      X(100), SALARY
INTEGER   NCLASS, AGE
```

Further, suppose the program passes all these variables to a subprogram, a subroutine CALCUL for instance, with the statement

```
CALL CALCUL(X, NCLASS, SALARY, AGE)
```

Then the subroutine CALCUL must have a name statement of the form

```
SUBROUTINE CALCUL(A, B, C, D)
```

where A is a real array, B and D are integers, and C is a real variable.

The COMMON alternative is to place in the main program the statement

```
COMMON X, NCLASS, SALARY, AGE
```

and a corresponding statement

```
COMMON A, .B, C, D
```

in the subprogram CALCUL. The two COMMON lists set up exactly the same correspondence as the actual and dummy argument lists. Then the CALL statement can be simply

```
CALL CALCUL
```

and the subroutine statement

```
SUBROUTINE CALCUL
```

Arrays can be dimensioned in the COMMON statement, a type declaration statement, or a DIMENSION statement, but each array must be given a size exactly *once*. A variable can be passed to a subprogram either in a COMMON statement or in an actual argument list, but not both. Some variables can be passed through the argument list and others passed in COMMON. Variables in COMMON must not be initialized in DATA statements, either in a main program or a subprogram.

The COMMON statement we have been discussing is called **blank common** or **unlabeled common**. A program system can have only one blank common block, but can have several **named common blocks**. A common block is named by placing the block name in slashes after the word COMMON. The statement

```
COMMON /BLOCK1/ A, B
```

sets aside a common block named BLOCK1 which holds the values of A and B.

B

THE ASCII AND EBCDIC COLLATING SEQUENCES

The ASCII Codes

The ASCII collating sequence associates an integer from 0 to 127 with the set of characters. The first thirty-two characters, coded from 0 to 31, and the last character are special control characters. Printable characters have ASCII codes from 32 to 126.

American code
Standard code
for Information
interchange

ASCII Codes for the Printable Characters

Code	Character	Code	Character	Code	Character
32	Space	64	@ Commercial at	96	` Accent grave
33	! Exclamation point	65	A	97	a
34	" Quote mark	66	B	98	b
35	# Number sign	67	C	99	c
36	$ Dollar sign	68	D	100	d
37	% Percent sign	69	E	101	e
38	& Ampersand	70	F	102	f
39	' Apostrophe	71	G	103	g
40	(Left parenthesis	72	H	104	h
41	) Right parenthesis	73	I	105	i
42	* Asterisk	74	J	106	j
43	+ Plus sign	75	K	107	k
44	, Comma	76	L	108	l
45	− Minus sign or hyphen	77	M	109	m
46	. Period	78	N	110	n
47	/ Slash	79	O	111	o
48	0	80	P	112	p
49	1	81	Q	113	q
50	2	82	R	114	r
51	3	83	S	115	s
52	4	84	T	116	t
53	5	85	U	117	u
54	6	86	V	118	v
55	7	87	W	119	w
56	8	88	X	120	x
57	9	89	Y	121	y
58	: Colon	90	Z	122	z
59	; Semicolon	91	[Left bracket	123	{ Left brace
60	< Less than	92	\ Backslash	124	| Vertical line
61	= Equal sign	93	] Right bracket	125	} Right brace
62	> Greater than	94	^ Caret	126	~ Tilde
63	? Question mark	95	_ Underscore	127	DEL Delete

The EBCDIC Codes

EBCDIC codes for the printable characters run from 64 to 249, with a few gaps. That is, some numbers between 64 and 249 are not used as EBCDIC codes.

EBCDIC Codes for the Printable Characters

Nonalphabetic Characters		Alphabetic Characters			
Code	Character	Code	Character	Code	Character
64	Space	129	a	193	A
75	. Period	130	b	194	B
77	(Left parenthesis	131	c	195	C
78	+ Plus sign	132	d	196	D
79	| Vertical line	133	e	197	E
80	& Ampersand	134	f	198	F
90	! Exclamation point	135	g	199	G
91	$ Dollar sign	136	h	200	H
92	* Asterisk	137	i	201	I
93	) Right parenthesis	145	j	209	J
107	, Comma	146	k	210	K
108	% Percent sign	147	l	211	L
109	_ Underscore	148	m	212	M
110	> Greater than	149	n	213	N
111	? Question mark	150	o	214	O
123	# Number sign	151	p	215	P
124	@ Commercial at	152	q	216	Q
125	' Apostrophe	153	r	217	R
126	= Equal sign	162	s	226	S
127	" Quote mark	163	t	227	T
161	~ Tilde	164	u	228	U
240	0	165	v	229	V
241	1	166	w	230	W
242	2	167	x	231	X
243	3	168	y	232	Y
244	4	169	z	233	Z
245	5				
246	6				
247	7				
248	8				
249	9				

GLOSSARY

abort — The abnormal termination of a program caused by an error or by user intervention.

absolute value — The size of a quantity, ignoring its sign. For example, the numeric quantities +17.2 and –17.2 each have absolute value 17.2.

actual argument — A value passed to a function or subroutine.

address — A location in a computer's memory.

algorithm — A complete set of instructions to solve a problem.

alphabetic — Pertaining to the letters of the alphabet.

alphanumeric — Pertaining to letters, numbers, and other special characters.

.AND. — A logical operator in Fortran. If p and q are statements, then p .AND. q is true if, and only if, both p and q are true.

ANSI — Acronym for American National Standards Institute.

argument — In general, an item used in a calculation. *See also* actual argument; dummy argument.

arithmetic expression — A single numeric constant, variable, or function value, or a combination of these, joined by arithmetic operators so that the entire expression can be evaluated to produce a single numeric value.

arithmetic operation — Any of the operations addition, subtraction, multiplication, division, and exponentiation.

arithmetic operator — A symbol used to designate an arithmetic operation. In Fortran, the symbols +, -, *, /, and ** are used to designate addition, subtraction, multiplication, division, and exponentiation, respectively.

array — Generally, a set of related items. In Fortran, an array is a set of elements of the same data type with the property that each element is specified by the array name followed by one or more subscripts.

array declaration — A program statement specifying an array, its dimensions, and its dimension bounds.

array element — An item in an array, specified by the array name followed by one or more subscripts in parentheses.

ASCII — Acronym for American Standard Code for Information Interchange, a coding scheme that associates an integer from 0 through 127 with 128 characters.

assembly language — A low-level programming language that uses mnemonics to represent operations.

assignment statement — A program statement that assigns the value of an expression to a storage location.

base — The number of digits in a number system. For example, the decimal system uses ten digits and the binary system uses two digits.

binary — The property of having two possible states.

binary digit — One of the digits 0 or 1.

binary search — A search method that reduces the area to be searched by one-half at each step. The method is applicable only to ordered data.

bit — A contraction of binary digit. The smallest unit of information a computer can store.

blank — A space; the character produced by one press of the space bar on a keyboard.

block — Generally, a group of related items treated as a physical unit. Specifically, a block could be a sequence of program statements that perform a specific function, or a set of records accessed as a single unit, among other things.

branch — To jump, or transfer control, to a statement other than the next statement in sequential order.

buffer — A temporary storage area or storage device.

bug — An error in a program.

built-in function — A function supplied with a compiler. Also called an *intrinsic* or *library* function.

byte — A contiguous sequence of bits.

CALL — A program statement that transfers control to a subroutine and supplies any necessary actual arguments.

calling program — A program unit that calls or invokes a subprogram.

carriage control character — A character in the first position of a printed record, used to determine the vertical spacing of the output line.

central processing unit (CPU) — That part of a computer's hardware that directs other units and performs arithmetic and logical operations.

character — Fundamental part of a data item; a letter, digit, or special character. CHARACTER is one of the Fortran data types.

character data — Data considered as a string of characters.

character string — A sequence of characters treated as a single unit by the computer.

code — Some or all of the statements in a computer program.

coding — Writing program statements.

collating sequence — The order of characters in a particular coding scheme.

column — The horizontal position of a character on a printed line or punched card.

column-major order — The storage of a two-dimensional array so that all elements of column 1 come first, then all elements of column 2, and so on. This is the order used by Fortran.

comment — A remark within a program that is not a program statement but is included to explain all or part of the program.

common block — An area in memory shared by one or more program units.

compile — Translate a high-level source program into machine language.

compiler — A program that translates other programs, written in a specific language, into machine language.

computer — An electronic device that stores both data and instructions, and uses the instructions to manipulate the data.

concatenate — Combine two items into one by placing one of the items after the other.

condition — A logical expression; an expression that can be true or false.

conditional branch — A transfer of program control that takes place when a specified condition is satisfied.

constant — In general, a value that never changes. In Fortran, the address of a storage location whose value does not change for the duration of a program.

continuation — The writing of one logical program line across two or more physical lines.

control statement — A statement used to control the order in which the computer executes the statements of a program. The major Fortran control statements are DO, IF, CALL, and function references.

control structure — A block of statements with one of the following structures:

Sequential Each statement follows the previous one.

Repeat A block of statements is repeated either a specific number of times (DO loop), or while a given condition is true (while loop).

Selection One of several blocks of statements is executed, depending on which of several conditions is true.

counter — A variable used to count the number of times a certain condition occurs.

CPU — Acronym for central processing unit.

CRT — Acronym for cathode ray tube, a type of video screen.

cursor — A symbol, usually either a rectangle or an underline (_), shown on a CRT screen to indicate the current typing position in a line.

data — Elements of information that can be processed by a computer.

debug — Locate and correct errors in a computer program.

default value — A value used by the compiler or computer when the programmer or user does not supply a specific choice.

diagnostic message — A message from the computer concerning an error in a program.

dimension — The number of subscripts used to designate the position of an element in an array.

direct access — Access to a record in a file by specifying the record number, or the position of the record in the file. Also called random access.

disk — An auxiliary storage medium; usually a rotating magnetic disk.

DOUBLE PRECISION — A Fortran data type, utilizing twice as much storage space as the REAL data type.

dummy argument — A variable name used in a function or subroutine to reserve a place for an actual argument.

EBCDIC — An acronym for Extended Binary-Coded Decimal Interchange Code, a collating sequence used by many computers.

echo check — The printing of input data to verify that they are being read properly.

editor — An interactive utility program that allows the user to create and modify text files.

element — One of the items in an array.

end-of-file — The condition that exists when all records in a file open for sequential access have been read.

.EQV. — A logical operator in Fortran. If p and q are statements, then p .EQV. q is true if, and only if, p and q have the same truth value.

executable statement — A statement in a Fortran program that is translated into machine language by the Fortran compiler.

execute — Carry out an instruction. We often say the computer executes a Fortran statement when, in fact, the computer executes statements in the machine language version of a program.

exponent — A power to which a number is raised.

expression — A constant, a variable, a function, or any combination of these, joined by operators so that the expression can be reduced to a single value. An expression can have any one of the Fortran data types.

external file — A permanently stored file separate from any programs that access it.

external function — A user-defined function subprogram.

external storage — Storage outside the computer itself, generally on disks or magnetic tape.

field — One or more adjacent positions, considered as a single item, in a record or line.

flag — A constant value or values used to denote some special status, such as the end of a file.

floating point — A form of numeric representation in which a number is expressed as a fractional part times a power of the number base. For example, 864.5 can be expressed as 0.8645×10^3.

floating-point number — A real number; a number with a decimal point.

format — A specific layout, or arrangement, of data. A FORMAT statement specifies how data are to be read or written.

format specification — The part of a FORMAT statement, within parentheses, that specifies the data layout.

Fortran — An acronym for *for*mula *tran*slator; a high-level computer programming language.

function subprogram — A subprogram that returns a single value through its name.

function value — The value returned by a function.

hardcopy — A printout on paper.

hardware — The physical components of a computer system.

IF block — A Fortran control structure that selects for execution one block of statements from several blocks.

index — A loop counter; the variable named in a DO statement. The INDEX *function* is a built-in function specifying the starting position of a substring inside a string.

infinite loop — A loop with no terminating condition, or a loop whose terminating condition cannot be satisfied.

initialize — Assign an initial value to a variable.

input — Data that a program causes the computer to read.

input/output (I/O) — Data read or written by a program. Also, devices to read and write data.

integer — A whole number, or number without a fractional part. INTEGER is one of the Fortran data types.

internal storage — Main memory, or the primary storage area inside the computer.

intrinsic function — *See* built-in function.

invoke — Call upon; used especially with reference to functions. To invoke a function is to cause the computer to execute the function.

iteration — Repetition.

keyed access — Access to records in a file by specifying the information in a certain field, called a key field, of the records.

keyword — A word with special meaning in Fortran.

label — An integer, from one to five digits long, used as an identifier on a line in a Fortran program.

library function — *See* built-in function.

listing — A printed copy of a program.

literal — A constant data item. Often used in literal string to mean a character constant.

logical constant — A constant having the value .TRUE. or the value .FALSE..

LOGICAL data type — One of the Fortran data types, whose only possible values are .TRUE. and .FALSE..

logical expression — A logical constant, a variable, a function value, or any combination formed by joining these with logical operators so that the expression can be reduced to a single logical value.

logical operator — One of the operators .AND., .OR., .NOT., .XOR., and .EQV.. An operator whose operands are logical expressions.

logical variable — A variable that can be assigned the values .TRUE. and .FALSE..

loop — A block of statements executed repeatedly; the action of repeated execution.

loop body — Those statements repeated in a loop, exclusive of the statements that define the beginning and end of the loop.

loop counter — A variable used to count the iterations of a loop. Also called the loop *index*.

machine language — Binary code that is directly readable by the computer.

magnetic tape — A storage medium consisting of a ribbon of magnetized tape.

mainframe — A large, fast computer.

main program — The program unit in a program system that contains a PROGRAM statement. Used in contrast to subprogram.

master file — A relatively permanent file of records. Used in contrast to transaction file.

matrix — A two-dimensional array.

mean — The sum of a set of numbers divided by the number of numbers in the set.

memory — Storage, either internal or external. Some writers use memory to refer only to internal storage.

microcomputer — A small computer.

minicomputer — A medium-sized computer.

natural logarithm — A logarithm with e as a base (where $e = 2.7182818 \ldots$).

nesting — The placing of one construct inside another of the same kind (for example, nesting parentheses or nesting loops).

nonexecutable statement — A Fortran statement that provides information to the compiler, but that the compiler does not translate into machine language.

.NOT. — A logical operator in Fortran. If p is a statement, then .NOT. p is true if p is false, and is false if p is true.

null — The character with ASCII Code 0; an absence of information.

null string — An empty string.

numeric variable — A location in memory that holds a numeric value.

object program — A machine language program; the output produced by compiling a source program.

one-dimensional array — An array with one dimension, or an array in which each element can be specified by one subscript.

operand — In general, something that is acted upon. A component of an expression. Every expression must have at least one operand.

operator — A symbol denoting an operation; a component of an expression. An expression may have zero or more operators. Roughly, operands are the nouns, or passive elements, in expressions, and operators are the verbs, or active elements.

.OR. — A logical operator in Fortran. If p and q are statements, then p .OR. q is true when p is true, or q is true, or both are true.

output — Data a program causes the computer to write.

overflow — A condition caused by a mathematic operation whose result would exceed the capacity of the computer.

parameter — In general, any quantity of interest in a given situation. Programmers often use the term *parameter* in place of *argument*.

peripheral equipment — Input, output, and external storage devices for a computer.

precision — Usually refers to the number of significant digits in a real number.

program — A set of instructions for a computer.

program unit — A main program or subprogram.

prompt — A message from the computer indicating that it is ready to accept user input; an output statement in a program telling the user what kind(s) of data to enter.

radian — An angular measurement; π radians is equivalent to 180 degrees.

random access — *See* direct access.

real number — A number with a fractional part. REAL is one of the Fortran data types.

record — A component of a file; a set of logically related data.

relational expression — An expression containing one relational operator and two operands of numeric or character type.

relational operator — One of the operators .EQ., .NE., .LT., .GT., .LE., and .GE..

reserved words — Words in a programming language that cannot be used as symbolic names. Fortran has no reserved words.

row-major order — The storage of a two-dimensional array so that all elements of row 1 come first, then all elements of row 2, and so on. *See also* column-major order, the order used by Fortran.

row subscript — The first subscript (usually) for an element of a two-dimensional array.

run — To cause the computer to execute a program (verb). An execution of a program (noun).

run time — The time during which a computer executes the statements of a program.

scalar variable — A variable name specifying one storage location, in contrast to an array name.

semantics — The set of language rules governing the meaning of statements.

sequential access — Access to records in the order in which the records are stored.

sequential file — A file created with sequential organization.

sequential organization — File organization in which one record simply follows another.

sequential search — Search method in which each item is examined in whatever order the items have. Also called *linear* search.

single-precision number — A number with type REAL.

software — Programs, including system programs such as compilers and editors, as well as application programs to solve specific problems.

sort — To arrange items in order according to some characteristics.

source program — Program written by a programmer, contrasted with the *object* program produced by the compiler and the *executable* program produced by the linker.

statement — An instruction in a programming language.

statement function — A function defined by one statement of a program.

storage location — An addressable portion of main memory.

storage unit — Any device capable of retaining data.

string — A sequence of characters; a character constant.

string variable — A location in memory that holds character data.

subprogram — An external function or subroutine; a separate set of instructions to solve part of a problem.

subroutine — A program unit activated by a CALL statement in another program unit.

subscript — An integer value that specifies the position of an array element.

symbol — A character or group of characters used to represent an entity.

symbolic address — A variable name or symbol used to specify a storage location.

syntax — The rules governing the construction of statements in a language.

syntax error — An error in the construction of a program statement.

system — A combination of computer hardware and software that can perform specific operations.

terminal — A device used for both input and output in a time-sharing environment.

time-sharing — The sharing of a computer's time by several users simultaneously.

two-dimensional array — An array whose elements are identified by two subscripts.

type specification statement — A nonexecutable statement specifying the data type of one or more variables.

unary operator — An operator that operates on one operand. Examples are the minus sign in -X and the .NOT. operator in .NOT.(X .LT. Y).

variable — A symbolic name assigned to a storage location whose contents can change during the execution of a program.

warning message — A message from a compiler concerning a nonstandard or dangerous programming practice, or an error not severe enough to prevent compilation.

word — A unit of storage consisting of several contiguous bits.

■ ■ ■ ■ ■ ■ # ANSWERS TO THE SELF-TEST EXERCISES

CHAPTER 1

True/False

Statements 3 and 6 are true. The rest are false.

Fill in the Blanks

1. program
2. input
3. peripheral equipment
4. hardware
5. integer
6. bits
7. one byte or eight bits

Binary Exercises

1.   a.   1100
        b.   1000 1001
        c.   100 1101 0010
        d.   0.11
        e.   0.1000 11
        f.   111 1011.0111 01

2.   a.   21
        b.   75

    c.   0.625

    d.   10.3125

3.   a.   0001 0010

    b.   1010 1011

    c.   1011 1101

    d.   Too large

4.   a.   15

    b.   −38

    c.   −52

    d.   61

5.   a.   −0.875

    b.   0.1875

    c.   0.0625

    d.   −5.0

6.   a.   0010 0101

    b.   0010 1110

    c.   0111 0110

    d.   1010 0111

CHAPTER 2

True/False

Statements 1 and 3 are true. The rest are false.

Short Answer

1. Columns 7 through 72
2.   a.   Valid.

    b.   Invalid; contains period.

    c.   Valid.

    d.   Invalid; contains ★.

    e.   Invalid; starts with digit.

    f.   Invalid; too long.

3. END
4. Assignment, READ, and DATA statement

5. INTEGER NUMBER, AGE

CHAPTER 3

1.   a.   264.5
      b.   0.00612423
      c.   654.0

2.   a.   0.123456E+3
      b.   123456.0E–3
      c.   0.00123456E+5
         (The plus signs are not necessary)

3.   a.   REAL
      b.   CHARACTER
      c.   Not valid
      d.   REAL
      e.   Not valid
      f.   CHARACTER
      g.   INTEGER
      h.   CHARACTER
      i.   CHARACTER
      j.   Not valid (comma)
      k.   INTEGER

4. c, f, g, and h are mixed-mode expressions.

5.   a.   7
      b.   7.5
      c.   18.33333
      d.   55
      e.   4
      f.   –3.0
      g.   1500.0
      h.   –4.8

6. a, b, c, and f are mixed mode assignments.

7.   a.   1
      b.   1.0
      c.   2
      d.   Isn't that

      e.   150

      f.   1.0

      g.   Orthodox□□

      h.   6.666667

      i.   4

      j.   16

8.   a.   Valid.

      b.   Valid.

      c.   Invalid; argument is an integer.

      d.   Invalid; not a statement.

      e.   Invalid; too many arguments.

      f.   Invalid; 6.4 is not a possible sin value.

      g.   Invalid; only one argument.

      h.   Valid.

9.   a.   32.4

      b.   8.0

      c.   8.0

      d.   5

      e.   19

      f.   −7

      g.   8.0

      h.   0.0

10. All are false.

11.   a.   Valid.

      b.   Invalid; constant dummy argument.

      c.   Invalid; DIST on left of equal sign is a function name, but DIST on right is a program variable name.

      d.   Valid, but it is bad practice to include a dummy argument which is not used in the defining expression.

12.   a.   The function definition has two dummy arguments, but the calling statement has three actual arguments.

      b.   The integer actual argument N corresponds to the real dummy argument X, and the real actual argument Y to the integer dummy argument M.

CHAPTER 4

1. a. 5 times. 2
              3
              4
              5
              6

    b. 5 times. 12
               9
               6
               3
               0

    c. 0 times. (The loop body will not be executed.)

    d. 4 times. 0.25
                  0.75
                  1.25
                  1.75

2. a. 12
    b. 105
    c. 1
    d. 5

3. a. `DO 11 ITEM = 5, 100, 4`

    b. `DO 22 NUMBER = 100, 0, -7`

4. a. 4 times. 1   1
                  1   2
                  2   1
                  2   2

    b. 6 times. 0
                  1
                  2
                  0
                  1
                  0

CHAPTER 5

1. a. The word THEN does not appear in a logical IF statement.
    b. Only one statement can follow the condition.

       c.   The condition must be enclosed in parentheses.

       d.   Relational operator must be `.GT.`, not >.

       e.   The statement following the condition cannot begin with IF.

       f.   Assignment statement requires =, not the `.EQ.` operator.

2.   a.   Any value of I satisfies the condition.

       b.   No value of I satisfies the condition.

3.   a.   `.FALSE.`

       b.   `.FALSE.`

       c.   `.TRUE.`

       d.   `.FALSE.`

       e.   `.TRUE.`

       f.   `.TRUE.`

4.   a.   `.TRUE.`

       b.   `.TRUE.`

       c.   `.TRUE.`

       d.   `.FALSE.`

       e.   `.TRUE.`

5.   a.   `X .LT. 0.0 .OR. Y .GT. 100.0 .OR. NAME .EQ. 'ZZZZ'`

       b.   `X .LT. 0.0 .AND. Y .GT. 100.0 .AND. NAME .EQ. 'ZZZZ'`

       c.   `X .GE. 0.0 .AND. Y .LE. 100.0 .AND. NAME .NE. 'ZZZZ'`

       d.   `X .GE. 0.0 .AND. Y .LE. 100.0 .AND. NAME .EQ. 'ZZZZ'`

       e.   `X .LT. 0.0 .EQV. Y .GT. 100.0`

CHAPTER 6

1.   a.   `0`
               `2`
               `4`

```
              6
              8
              10

b.            3
              6
              9
              12

c.            64     27
              48     27
              36     27
              27     27

d.            0.25   3.50
              0.50   3.00
              0.75   2.50
              1.00   2.00
              1.25   1.50
              1.50   1.00
```

2. a. Infinite loop; all values of I are negative.

    b. Infinite loop; the value of I never changes.

    c. The condition I .LT. 10 must be enclosed in parentheses.

    d. Fortran does not use < as an operator.

3. a.
```
              I = 1
        11    IF (I .LE. 10) THEN
                 PRINT *, I
                 I = I + 1
                 GO TO 11
              END IF
```

    b.
```
        22    IF (I .GE. 0) THEN
                 PRINT *, I
                 I = I - 3
                 GO TO 22
              END IF
```

    c.
```
              I = 9
        33    IF (I .LT. 10000) THEN
                 PRINT *, I
                 I = I * 3
                 GO TO 33
              END IF
```

d.
```
        X = 20.25
    44  IF (X .LE. 99.99) THEN
            PRINT *, X
            X = X + SQRT(X)
            GO TO 44
        END IF
```

e.
```
        X = 1000.0
        Y = 1.5
    55  IF (X .GE. Y) THEN
            PRINT *, X, Y
            X = X / 2.0
            Y = 2.0 * Y
            GO TO 55
        END IF
        PRINT *, X, Y
```

4. a. 12.6

b.
```
    IF (A .LE. B / 4.0) THEN
        C = D
    ELSE IF (A .LE. B / 3.0) THEN
        C = 1.1 * D
    ELSE IF (A .LE. B / 2.0) THEN
        C = 2.1 * D
    ELSE IF (A .LE. B) THEN
        C = 4.2 * D
    ELSE
        C = 8.4 * D
    END IF
```

An alternative answer for b. is:

```
    IF (A .GT. B) THEN
        C = 8.4 * D
    ELSE IF (A .GT. B / 2.0) THEN
        C = 4.2 * D
    ELSE IF (A .GT. B / 3.0) THEN
        C = 2.1 * D
    ELSE IF (A .GT. B / 4.0) THEN
        C = 1.1 * D
    ELSE
        C = D
    END IF
```

CHAPTER 7

1. a. There is no data descriptor for 'Hello'.

   b. The I and F data descriptors should be exchanged.

   c. The output line will begin with 35 instead of 435, because the computer will use the 4 for carriage control.

2. a.
```
          1         2         3         4
 12345678901234567890123456789012345678901234567890
 12 is integer but25.600 is real.
```

   b.
```
          1         2         3         4
 12345678901234567890123456789012345678901234567890
 George Washington was the 1st president.
```

   c.
```
          1         2
 1234567890123456789001234567890
 Name Jack
 ge   23
 eight  67.500
```

   d.
```
          1         2         3
 123456789012345678901234567890
  18.65 1234   123.46   23
```

3. Many different answers can be correct in each part.

   a.
```
      PRINT 10, COUNT
 10   FORMAT (1X, 3X, 'Count is', 2X, I3)
```

   b.
```
      PRINT 20, NAME, AGE
 20   FORMAT (1X, 'Name is', 1X, A8, 2X, 'Age is', 1X, I2)
```

   c.
```
      PRINT 30, LENGTH, WIDTH, AREA
 30   FORMAT (1X, 'Length :', 2X, F6.2 /
     1        1X, 'Width  :', 2X, F6.2 /
     2        1X, 'Area   :', 1X, F7.2 )
```

   d.
```
      PRINT 40
 40   FORMAT(1X, 4X, 'Name', 8X, 'Age', 3X, 'Salary')
      PRINT 50, NAME, AGE, SALARY
 50   FORMAT (1X, 3X, A11, 2X, I3, 3X, F6.2)
```

4. a.
```
               1         2
      12345678901234567890123456789012345
       CORIOLANUS  WILLOW RUN
       12.63  17
        8.28   8
       -4.03 123
```

   b.
```
                 1         2         3         4
      12345678901234567890123456789012345678901234567890
           12.6     8.3    -4.0  17CORIOLAN
       8WILLOW R
      123
```

5. a.
```
      TITLE : 'ORTHODOXY□□□'
```

   b.
```
      X : 18.49
      Y : 9.42
```

   c.
```
      NAME : 'SAM SMITH□□3□□□□□□□□□'
      AGE  : 5
```

   d.
```
      X : 12.76
      N : 234
```

6. a.
```
      (1X, F8.2, I5, A10, F8.2, I5, A10, F8.2, I5, A10)
```

   b.
```
      (1X, 2(I6, 3X), 3(4X, F10.2) )
```

CHAPTER 8

1. a. Legal.
    b. Illegal; size cannot be an expression.
    c. Illegal; size cannot be negative.
    d. Illegal; subscript bounds must be integers.
    e. Legal.
    f. Legal.

2. a.
```
      REAL  A(100)
```

   b.
```
      INTEGER  X(0:50)
```

   c.
```
      CHARACTER*4  NAME(-2:8)
```

3. a.
```
      A(1)  A(2)  A(3)  A(4)  A(5)  A(6)
        0     1     1     2     2     3
```

b.

A(1)	A(2)	A(3)	A(4)	A(5)	A(6)
1	2	0	1	2	0

c.

A(1)	A(2)	A(3)	A(4)	A(5)	A(6)
2	8	18	16	not assigned	36

d.

A(1)	A(2)	A(3)	A(4)	A(5)	A(6)
3	6	12	24	48	96

4. a.

A(1)	A(2)	A(3)	A(4)	B(1)	B(2)	B(3)	B(4)
5	10	15	20	25	30	35	40

b.

A(1)	A(2)	A(3)	A(4)	B(1)	B(2)	B(3)	B(4)
5	15	25	35	10	20	30	40

c.

A(1)	A(2)	A(3)	B(1)	B(2)	B(3)
51	202	354	15	530	45

d.

A(1)	A(2)	A(3)	A(4)	B(1)	B(2)	B(3)	B(4)
10	15	20	25	30	35	40	45

e.

A(1)	A(2)	A(3)	A(4)	No values assigned
10	20	30	40	to elements of B.

5. a. 6
    b. 4
    c. 3
    d. 1

CHAPTER 9

1. Statements a. and b. are true, the rest are false.
2. a. Invalid; dummy argument cannot be an expression.
    b. Invalid; no function name.
    c. Valid.
    d. Invalid, most likely. The statement does not invoke a real function named SQUARE because the word REAL would not be used in that case. The computer considers the statement to be

    ```
    Y = REALSQUARE(A, B)
    ```

so the statement could be valid if REALSQ is a function name and the computer truncates names to six characters.

3.   a.   Invalid; AREA is used as the subroutine name and a variable name.

b.   Invalid; the real actual argument A corresponds to the character dummy argument D. (Similarly for NAME and Y.)

c.   Invalid; dummy array size is larger than actual array size.

d.   Invalid; types of actual and dummy arguments are reversed.

e.   Invalid; the invoking statement is an output statement and the function contains an output statement to the same file.

f.   Invalid; MEAN has type integer (implicitly) in the main program, but type REAL in the function.

CHAPTER 10

1.   a.   Invalid; dummy argument cannot be a constant.

b.   Invalid; CALL statement must not have = sign.

c.   Invalid; subroutine name statement must not have REAL.

d.   Valid.

e.   Invalid; subroutine name is missing.

f.   Valid, if A is an array.

g.   Invalid; dummy arguments cannot be array elements.

h.   Invalid; subroutine name cannot be the same as a variable name.

2.   a.   Valid.

b.   Invalid; the subprogram has three dummy arguments, but the CALL statement has two actual arguments.

c.   Invalid; the invoking statement must be a CALL.

d.   Invalid; the subroutine modifies the value of a dummy argument that corresponds to a constant actual argument.

e.   Invalid; AREA is both the subroutine name and the name of a variable in the subroutine.

1.   a.   12
        b.   20

2.   a.   There must be two left parentheses just before A.
        b.   There must be a right parenthesis just after 3.
        c.   The subscript I becomes larger than the first dimension bound of 5.
        d.   An assignment statement can assign only one value, not an entire array of values.

3.   a.

```
X(1, 1) = 1   X(1, 2) = 3   X(1, 3) = 5
X(2, 1) = 2   X(2, 2) = 4   X(2, 3) = 6
```

        b.   Elements in the first 25 columns receive the value 1.0, and elements in the last 25 columns get 2.0.

        c.

```
HIGH(1, 1) = 1   HIGH(1, 2) = 2   HIGH(1, 3) = 3
HIGH(2, 1) = 4   HIGH(2, 2) = 5   HIGH(2, 3) = 6
```

        d.

```
X(1, 1) = 0.0   X(1, 2) = 1.0   X(1, 3) = 1.0
X(2, 1) = 1.0   X(2, 2) = 0.0   X(2, 3) = 1.0
X(3, 1) = 1.0   X(3, 2) = 1.0   X(3, 3) = 0.0
```

4.   a.   6
        b.   1
        c.   10
        d.   1

CHAPTER 12

1.   a.   `OPEN (9, FILE = 'PAYROL', STATUS = 'NEW')`

        b.   `OPEN (8, FILE = 'ADDRES', STATUS = 'OLD')`

        c.   `OPEN (8, FILE = 'GRADES', STATUS = 'UNKNOWN')`

        d.   `OPEN (9, FILE = 'CALC', STATUS = 'SCRATCH')`

2.   a.   Unit number 355 is too large.
        b.   The final right parenthesis is missing. (PERSNL and NEW do not need apostrophes if they are variable names.)
        c.   Cannot have double quote marks around DATA.
        d.   DIRECT is not a possible status value.

e.   FILE = must be present.

f.   Final right parenthesis is missing.

3.   a.   Invalid; READ statement cannot contain a FILE specifier.

b.   Valid.

c.   Invalid; WRITE statement cannot contain an END specifier.

d.   Invalid; unit number cannot be an asterisk.

e.   Invalid; the sequential READ must not contain a REC specifier.

f.   Invalid; the CLOSE statement cannot contain an END specifier.

4.   a.
```
OPEN (9, FILE = 'DATA1', STATUS = 'OLD')
```

b.
```
      CHARACTER   LASTN*20, FIRSTN*10
      INTEGER     AGE
      REAL        SALARY
      READ (9, 10) LASTN, FIRSTN, AGE, SALARY
   10 FORMAT (1X, A20, A10, 3X, I2, F12.2)
```

CHAPTER 13

1.   a.   DW␣DWD␣DWDW

b.   XX␣␣␣XX␣␣␣XX␣␣

c.   12␣112␣1112

2.   a.   10

b.   0

c.   2

d.   'G'

e.   4

f.   3

3.   a.   68

b.   4

c.   'H'

d.   'I'

4.   a.   X is 357.18, I is 357

b.   '712.35'

CHAPTER 14

1. Answers depend on the specific computer.

2. a. $5 + 3i$
    b. $5 - 3i$
    c. $-17 - 6i$
    d. $0.4 + 2.2i$
    e. $5 - 12i$

3. a. $(4.00, -2.00)$
    b. $(25.0, 0.0)$

4. a. The *complex* function is spelled CMPLX.
    b. Z is complex but REAL(A) is real.
    c. Argument of CONJG must be a complex value. (A, B) is not.
    d. Fortran does not use the i to signify an imaginary part. The compiler considers A + Bi to be the sum of two real variables, A and BI.
    e. Need parentheses around 3.0, 5.0.

5. a. Square roots: $2e^{i\pi/4}$ and $2e^{i5\pi/4}$
    b. Cube roots: $2e^{i\pi/3}$, $2e^{i\pi}$, and $2e^{i5\pi/3}$

Index